OUR DIVINE DOUBLE

Our Divine Double

CHARLES M. STANG

Cambridge, Massachusetts
London, England   2016

Copyright © 2016 by the President and Fellows of Harvard College
All rights reserved
Printed in the United States of America

First printing

Library of Congress Cataloging-in-Publication Data

Names: Stang, Charles M., 1974- author.
Title: Our divine double / Charles M. Stang.
Description: Cambridge, Massachusetts : Harvard University Press, 2016. |
   Includes bibliographical references and index.
Identifiers: LCCN 2015030865 | ISBN 9780674287198 (alk. paper)
Subjects: LCSH: Self (Philosophy)—Middle East. | Twins—Mythology—
   Middle East. | Twins—Religious aspects. | Mysticism—History—
   Early church, ca. 30–600. | Philosophy, Ancient.
Classification: LCC B526 .S73 2016 | DDC 126—dc23
   LC record available at http://lccn.loc.gov/2015030865

For Sarabinh, my *syzygos*,

in whom I see myself reflected, not as I am,

but as I should be

Contents

Introduction: Narcissus and His Double 1

1   Reading Plato's Many Doubles 20

2   Thomas, Who Is Called "Twin" 64

3   Syzygies, Twins, and Mirrors 107

4   Mani and His Twin-Companion 145

5   Plotinus and the Doubled Intellect 185

6   Whither the Divine Double? 231

Conclusion 249

Notes 259

Acknowledgments 299

Index 303

OUR DIVINE DOUBLE

Everything exists in pairs, one set over against the other.
—Ben Sirach 42:24

I am a mirror to you who know me.
—Jesus, in the *Acts of John*

Plus d'un seul seul. C'est là que nous en sommes.
—Jacques Derrida

Introduction:
Narcissus and His Double

That friendly face holds out a certain promise to me,
And when I stretch out my arms to you, you do the same;
When I smile, you smile back, and I've often seen your tears
When I was crying; you tell me something with your nods,
And based on the movement of your beautiful mouth,
You're saying something—it's not coming to my ears!
He's me! I've realized it, and my reflection doesn't deceive me.

—(Ovid, *Metamorphoses* 3.457–463)

OVID WAS NEITHER THE first nor the last to tell the story of Narcissus, only the most famous. A contemporary of Ovid's by the name of Conon says that a handsome Narcissus spurned a lover who in grief took his own life, but not before appealing to the goddess Nemesis to avenge him. She did: when Narcissus saw his own face in the water of a spring, he fell in love with himself and, realizing how he had cruelly snubbed that lover, took his own life. From his blood sprang the flower that bears his name.[1] In the second century, the

Greek geographer Pausanias relays two stories.[2] The more popular one has it that Narcissus simply fell in love with his own image in the water, except that he did not realize that the image was his own. Pausanias thinks it is ridiculous that Narcissus would not recognize his own reflection and prefers instead a lesser known version: Narcissus had a twin sister and the two bore a striking resemblance to each other; he fell in love with her, but she died; he would go to the spring and gaze at his reflection, knowing full well that it was his own; he found relief in gazing at the likeness of his beloved sister. The flower, on Pausanias's telling, has nothing to do with the man by the same name, and he does not tell us how Narcissus met his end.

Only Ovid makes the myth of Narcissus into an allegory of self-knowledge and its limits. His mother, a nymph named Liriope, brought Narcissus to the blind seer Tiresias to ask whether her boy would live to a ripe old age. "Yes," he replied, "if he never knows himself."[3] Narcissus went on to treat his many admirers, male and female, with cruel disdain, until at last one prayed, "May Narcissus love one day, so, himself, and not win over the creature whom he loves."[4] Again, Nemesis was listening. Narcissus lay down next to a clear pool and when he bent over to quench his thirst he was met with a new thirst, for the beautiful image that he saw. "Charmed by himself, spell-bound" Narcissus lay fixed on the water's edge.[5] In vain he kissed the water's surface and submerged his arms in hopes of an embrace, but was met with nothing more than a new reflection as soon as the stirred waters had calmed. In despair, he addressed his beloved directly, with the speech quoted above, a speech that climaxes with his realization, "He's me! I've realized it, and my reflection doesn't deceive me" *(iste ego sum: sensi, nec me mea fallit imago)*.[6] This realization, however, that the reflection is his own, that he and his beloved are one and the same, did not break the grip of his love. Still he lay by the edge of the pool, where he eventually wasted away, slowly consumed "by the hidden fire of passion."[7] In the place of his body, the mourning nymphs found instead a flower, a circle of white petals around a yellow center, to which is now lent his name. Tiresias's prophecy was thus proven true: self-knowledge was the end of Narcissus.

INTRODUCTION   3

Ovid's transformation of the myth of Narcissus into an allegory of self-knowledge is very likely a critical commentary on Plato, specifically on those dialogues (*Phaedrus* and *Alcibiades I*) in which Plato has Socrates recommend that lover and beloved look into each other's eyes, as if into a mirror, in which they will each see themselves reflected, not only as they are, but more importantly, as they should be.[8] For Plato, this mirroring of self and other serves to erase the difference between the two, as the lovers' souls conform ever more to each other, and the pair of them to the divine spark in them, their intellect or *nous*. In other words, knowledge of another resolves into knowledge of oneself, which in turn resolves into knowledge of (and conformity to) the intelligible world of the Forms.

Ovid's Narcissus is a sharp rebuke to this view that one can come to know oneself through an encounter with one's mirror image or double. But Ovid's is not the only Narcissus, and his is not the only verdict on mirrored doubling. Writing the *Metamorphoses* in the very early first century, before his exile to the Black Sea, the Roman poet stands on the cusp of an explosion of interest in the figure of the double. In the second and third centuries of the "common era," we witness the sudden appearance of a peculiar figure in the imagination of the Eastern Mediterranean: the *divine* double. We do not know the exact origin of this figure, but like ink that bleeds through the page, we find him seeping through the literature of late antiquity in all its diversity. Pausanias, a geographer widely traveled in the Eastern Mediterranean, relayed his story of Narcissus and his twin sister, and at the same time Christian authors were imagining what it might mean that the apostle Thomas, who according to Gospel of John was called the "twin," was in fact the twin brother of Jesus. Through an array of ancient sources—Christian and Manichaean, philosophical and religious, surviving often in fragments and in several languages—runs this single thread: the notion that each individual has a divine twin, counterpart, or alter ego whom he or she may meet. This encounter is imagined and narrated very differently in the various sources, but it very often solicits a response not unlike Narcissus's: "He's me!" *(iste ego sum)*. This encounter and proclamation mark the beginning of self-knowledge—not the autoerotic self-knowledge that, according to Ovid, killed Narcissus; not even the knowledge of the self one thought one was (because, after all, one thought one was *one*self); but the knowledge of a new and more divine self, for which these ancient sources struggle to give an adequate name and description.

In what follows we will move carefully through the various ancient sources, working closely with them, where appropriate, in their original languages. First and foremost, we will endeavor to understand what work the figure of the divine double is doing in these different religious and philosophical texts and traditions. Three traditions will prove especially important: (1) early Christianity, which in the second and third centuries witnessed a vast diversity of thought and practice before the narrowing work of an emerging orthodoxy gained momentum (and imperial support) in the fourth and fifth centuries; (2) Manichaeism, a wildly successful missionary religion hatched in southern Mesopotamia in the third century by the self-styled "apostle of light" Mani, a religion that spread westward to the Mediterranean and eastward past the Iranian plateau within a century of its founder's death; (3) Neoplatonism, a name given to the renaissance of Platonism associated with the third-century philosopher Plotinus, who was born and educated in Alexandria but lived in and around Rome during his philosophical career. Chapters 2–5, on these three traditions, constitute the bulk of this book.[9] Chapter 1, on Plato, sets the stage for our investigations into these traditions of late antiquity—traditions for which Plato provides a conceptual framework, according to which we find ourselves in a world of images and archetypes, and where everything "here" has its intelligible counterpart "there." Chapter 6 surveys the persistence of the tradition of the divine double in Manichaeism and Neoplatonism, and its eclipse in Christianity with the rise of conciliar orthodoxy in the fourth and fifth centuries; this chapter also follows the transposition and transformation of the divine double, its hidden afterlife in Christology and theodicy. Finally, the Conclusion suggests that the significance of the tradition of the divine double lies in its centuries-long meditation on the perennial problem of identity and difference, and explores how the practices of reading and writing figure in the past and possible future of this tradition.

INTRODUCTION 5

I shall say more about each of the chapters of the book in due course, and what I think is most significant about this investigation into the divine double. In order to do that, however, I must first briefly acknowledge my debts and differences with other scholars. I am by no means the first to call attention to the widespread ancient interest in twins and doubles. Raymond Kuntzmann's *Le symbolisme des jumeaux au Proche-Orient ancien* is an ambitious investigation of the birth, function, and evolution of the symbol of the twin in the ancient Near East.[10] Wendy Doniger's *Splitting the Difference* focuses on ancient Indian and Greek sources in which characters are split and doubled along different axes (male / female, horizontal / vertical).[11] On her view, these myths of self-splitting are in fact negotiations of our universal anxieties regarding sex and death. Especially helpful for our purposes is her distinction between sloughing and dividing.[12] Sloughing names the self's splitting in the sense of the real self's emergence from its unreal exterior—much as an animal might molt. On this model, the molted sheath has nothing to do with proper selfhood. Dividing, on the other hand, names the self's splitting in two in which the two halves (however divided) are *still* constitutive of the single self. On this model, selfhood consists of the tenuous union of what has somehow been divided or split. In the chapters that follow, we shall see instances of both sloughing and dividing: most often, the self must first slough something (usually the body), only to discover that the self that emerges from that shell must then suffer, or rather enjoy, division.

Shadi Bartsch's *The Mirror of the Self* provides not only a crucial frame for appreciating Ovid's Narcissus as a response to Plato, but more generally an insightful inquiry into how selfhood is imagined in classical Greek and Latin sources as constituted (but also threatened) by the sort of self-knowledge that autoscopy ("self-seeing") makes possible through the use of mirrors or other reflective surfaces (literal or figurative).[13] Bartsch's discussions of Plato have influenced my own, especially her treatment of *Phaedrus* and *Alcibiades I*. She traces this particular discourse on selfhood into the early Roman period, but not as far as late antiquity, and not into the Christian, Manichaean, or Neoplatonic sources that will largely occupy us going forward.

Curiously, the scholar who has done more than any other to bring the tradition of the divine double to light is the twentieth-century French Islamicist, Henry Corbin, in his book *L'homme de lumière dans le soufisme iranien*.[14] He begins that short book with an exploration of what he calls "an innovation in philosophical anthropology" from antiquity, a notion that "the individual person as such . . . has a transcendent dimension at his disposal," "a counterpart, a heavenly 'partner,' and that [the person's] total structure is that of a bi-unity, a *unus-ambo*."[15] Corbin rather hurriedly traces this innovation through some of the same traditions as I shall—(1), (2), and (3) above—hurriedly because he is principally interested to show the ancient witnesses' relevance for understanding medieval Persian mysticism (which is his particular expertise). However hurried his discussion, Corbin's interest in these sources centers squarely on how they imagine the self as a *unus-ambo* or "bi-unity." This new identity

> does not correspond to a relationship of $1 = 1$, but of 1×1: the identity of an essence raised to its total power by being multiplied by itself and thus put in a condition to constitute a biunity, a dialogic whole whose members share alternately the roles of first and second person. Or again the state described by our mystics: when, at the climax, the lover has become the very substance of love, he is then both the lover *and* the beloved. But *himself* will not be *that* without the second person, without the *thou*, that is to say without the Figure who makes him able to see himself, because it is through his very own eyes that the Figure looks at him.
>
> It would therefore be as wrong to reduce the two-dimensionality of this dialogic unity to a solipsism as to divide it into two essences, each of which could be itself without the other.[16]

Corbin does not explain how the proffered mathematical formula exactly captures or clarifies this new model of selfhood.[17] What we learn is that the new self is defined by its division (and not sloughing) into alternating first and second persons, by its erasure of the difference between lover and beloved, by an autoscopy in which one sees oneself though another's eyes (except that that other is also somehow oneself).

To my mind, Corbin has put his finger on what is most interesting and significant in the texts and traditions of the divine double, namely a model of selfhood as, in his words, a *unus-ambo* or "bi-unity." Consider the following story from Aristotle's *Meteorology*: There was a man who always saw an image of himself in front of him, facing him as he walked (*Mete.* 3.4.373b). Aristotle opines that this must have been because of his poor sight, which in its weakness looked on the air in front of him as if a mirror. But what if this was, not the result of poor vision and the properties of air, but instead revelatory of the very nature of selfhood, except that one would need different eyes, in no sense weaker, to perceive one's mirror image always keeping stride? What if this man and his mirror image together were what it meant to be a self? *This* is what the texts and traditions we will soon examine put forward. One of their most curious and consistent features is the conviction that the individual who encounters his divine double comes to recognize that he is not, strictly speaking, an individual at all, but rather one half of a pair, a "dividual" (to borrow a term from the philosopher Simon Critchley).[18] In other words, these sources imagine that an individual is first initiated by the divine double into the reality of his or her false individuality, and then that the newly initiated "dividual" and the double together form a tense relationship of unity and duality, what Corbin prefers to call a "bi-unity."

The significance of this model of selfhood has at least two dimensions. First of all, most obviously, it resists a certain monism of the self, that is, the notion that the self is meant to be wholly one. On this model, to assume that one is a single self is a form of false consciousness. Rather than overcoming division, the self must first be initiated into its constitutive division, the difference between the "I" and its double. The self is not one half of the pair—*either* the "I" or its double—but is rather the pair itself, somehow preserving that constitutive difference or division in a new self, a new "I." In this way, the current investigation, *Our Divine Double*, follows on my earlier work on the early sixth-century pseudonymous mystical theologian Dionysius the Areopagite. In that book I made a case for his "apophatic anthropology," that is, the notion that the self that would unite with the unknown God (the *agnōstos theos* of Acts 17:23) must itself become unknown.[19] For Dionysius, *erōs* or love for God propels the self to stretch to the point that it splits in two, in ecstasy, and thereby opens itself to the indwelling of the unknown God as Christ. Dionysius takes Paul as the exemplary lover of the divine, and his confession that "it is no longer I, but Christ who lives in me" as testimony of Paul's suffering the ecstatic indwelling of Christ. The present book, *Our Divine Double*, then, can be understood as another installment in an ongoing investigation into the notion of the self as split, doubled, and thereby deified, under the banner "no longer I."

Second, this model of selfhood constitutes a chapter in the history of mysticism, more specifically an early version of the doctrine of deification. Corbin flags this when he describes "bi-unity" as a "state described by our mystics."[20] To borrow terms from Lloyd Gerson (see Chapter 1), this model of selfhood is not "endowed" but rather "achieved": we think we are one (our "endowed" self), but when we are initiated into the mystery of the divine, we come to realize that we are in fact two (and yet somehow also one).[21] To be ushered into this new selfhood is to be put on an itinerary of increasing conformity to the divine (our "achieved" self). Thus, this model of selfhood is not a static description but an urgent prescription: the self is an enterprise or project of becoming divine. Although stretching back into earlier centuries, the Christian doctrine of deification comes to be central for orthodox understandings of salvation with the fourth-century theologian and defender of the Council of Nicaea and its creed, Athanasius of Alexandria. For Athanasius, it is Christ the Word Incarnate (*homoousios* or "consubstantial" with God the Father) who as a sacrifice on the cross atones for humanity's sins and who in his resurrection invites us to participate in his full divinity, to become ever more like the eternal and consubstantial Word.[22] What we find in the Christian texts and traditions of the divine double is an earlier doctrine of deification, not much interested in the atoning sacrifice of Christ on the cross or his resurrection from the dead. Instead, this understanding of deification focuses on Jesus as a teacher and the apostle Thomas as the "twin" of Jesus, and imagines that all Christians are thus called to be twins of Jesus (which is to say Jesus's equals). The texts from which this understanding of deification is drawn were increasingly viewed with suspicion by the emerging orthodoxy, of which Athanasius was a chief architect and spokesman in the fourth century. Athanasius's doctrine of deification, although not explicitly part of the Nicene Creed, eventually carried the day.

In *The Foundations of Mysticism*, Bernard McGinn says of the development of the Christian doctrine of deification or "divinization" that,

> The root . . . developed by the Greek fathers on the basis of the Platonic background . . . is [to be found] in the consonance the fathers saw between the believer's identification with Christ, the God-man, as taught by Paul and John, and the teaching of the best philosophers about the goal of human existence.[23]

Although McGinn is speaking of the root among the Greek "Church Fathers" (Irenaeus, Clement, Origen) that will come to bloom in Athanasius, still his description rings true of the sources under scrutiny here. As I shall argue in Chapter 1, Plato provides the conceptual framework for the tradition of the divine double and its distinctive model of selfhood. Plato has his own doctrine of deification, that is, his own teachings about how the self can become ever more conformed to the intelligible reality of the Forms (and perhaps beyond). The most famous such statement on deification is to be found in the *Theaetetus*, where Socrates says, "Therefore we ought to try to escape from earth to the dwelling of the gods as quickly as we can; and to escape is to become like God, so far as this is possible" (176b).[24] But as McGinn remarks, while Platonism may have provided the conceptual "background," Christian theologians funded the early doctrine of deification by appeals to the writings attributed to the apostle Paul and John the evangelist. In Chapters 2–4, dealing with the Christian (and Manichaean) sources, then, we shall see how Paul and John are marshaled to articulate a distinctively biblical doctrine of deification. Plotinus, of course, inherits and innovates on Plato, and develops his own doctrine of deification, understood as the progressive conformity of our descended intellect to its undescended archetype, our return to the inner life of Intellect, and thereafter perhaps even to the embrace of the One that is beyond being.

I have been speaking of "self" and "selfhood," and we would do well to pause and consider these and related terms rather carefully. Some scholars object to any talk of the "self" in antiquity, owing largely to the fact that there is no exact equivalent in Greek.[25] The closest is the Greek pronoun *autos*, which has a range of meanings: (i) It can function as a personal pronoun, meaning simply "he" (with neuter, feminine, and plural versions); (ii) paired with a nominative and the definite article *ho*, it can be reflexive, meaning "Socrates himself" *(Sokratēs ho autos)*; (iii) with a different word order it can be intensive, meaning "the same Socrates" *(ho autos Sokratēs)*. None of these meanings exactly yield an abstract notion of the "self" or "selfhood," although of course reflexivity and identity are usually considered constitutive of the self. Nor does the word *anthrōpos* or "human," or *psychē* or "soul" exactly match. Very often these terms *(autos, anthrōpos, psychē)* and others are used together without precise definitions in discussions that we moderns recognize as being about the "self" and "selfhood." Still, I prefer the more general language of "self" and "selfhood" to that of "subject" and "subjectivity" because the latter has a more specific philosophical lineage. For our purposes, then, we are consciously clustering ancient debates together under a modern category—although even in antiquity there was no "agreement about what kind of terminology or ontology would explain human nature, subjectivity, and agency best."[26] Criticisms aside, it is a common practice, and one that in my mind reveals more than it conceals about these ancient debates, clarifies more than it obscures.

While "self" and "selfhood" are the most general terms in this investigation, there are others that will consistently appear in what follows. I have already mentioned that this tradition of the divine double imagines the self as existing in a sort of false consciousness of individuality, that is, the self thinks that it is a singular individual. With the arrival of what I am calling the "divine double," that individuality is revealed to be false, and the self understands itself now as one half of a pair. In Gerson's terms, the human "endowment" has been challenged, and the enterprise of personal "achievement" now set in motion. One of the crucial achievements, then, is the proper relationship of the self and its double, the "dividual" and its other half. I will speak of this relationship as the identity or union of the two. The texts under scrutiny will provide their own descriptions of this new identity or union, which negotiates unity and duality. This relationship of identity and difference or unity-in-duality is at the heart, then, of the reimagined self—what modern scholars such as Gerson will call the "achievement" of "personhood," Valantasis the "emergent self" resulting in a "new subjectivity," Corbin the *unus-ambo* or "bi-unity," and Derrida, in another context, "plus d'un seul seul."

◠ IT IS NO SECRET that the figure of Narcissus has been immensely important for modern theories of selfhood, most famously Sigmund Freud's.[27] For Freud, "narcissism" is a necessary developmental stage, but one to be surpassed on the way to proper adult selfhood. In his essay "The 'Uncanny,'" he conjectures that the soul was for primitive humans the original double, the second self that would "preserve against extinction."[28] This lust for life springs from the "primary narcissism [or unbounded self-love] which dominates the mind of the child and of the primitive man."[29] But over the course of human development—both humanity's collective development from its primitive roots to civilization *and* an individual human's development from infantile stages to adulthood—this double, originally benign, "reverses its aspect" and becomes a critical spectator on the original singular self:

> When all is said and done, the quality of uncanniness can only come from the fact of the "double" being a creation dating back to a very early mental stage, long since surmounted—a stage, incidentally, at which it wore a more friendly aspect. The "double" has become a thing of terror, just as, after the collapse of their religion, the gods turned into demons.[30]

The double is uncanny *(unheimlich)* because it is something once familiar *(heimisch)*—"the prefix 'un' is the token of repression."[31] In short, Freud regards the double, in its benign and malevolent versions, as a developmental stage that ultimately supports his theory of repression and his explanation for the emergence of the superego.

Freud is not alone is making the double a figure menacing to the original, singular self. While Freud draws on the myth of Narcissus and his experience of mistaking his own mirror image as an intruder, he also owes a debt (one he acknowledges) to the explosion of interest in the nineteenth and early twentieth centuries in the figure of the "doppelgänger." Freud cites E. T. A Hoffman (1776–1822), the German Romantic author, who in turn was greatly influenced by Jean Paul Richter (1763–1825), credited with coining the term "doppelgänger" in his 1796 novel *Siebenkäs*. These two more or less inaugurated an entire genre of modern fiction in which a protagonist has to contend with his or her doppelgänger or double. Eminent authors of the past two centuries have contributed to this genre, including Edgar Allan Poe, Nathaniel Hawthorne, Guy de Maupassant, Mary Shelley, Fyodor Dostoyevsky, Oscar Wilde, Henry James, Heinrich Heine, Joseph Conrad, and, recently, José Saramago (among many others). In this genre, the double is not a divine, vertical visitor, but more often a threat on the horizontal plane—someone who poses a danger to the protagonist, perhaps with the threat that the image might replace the archetype. Some of that anxiety comes through in our very terminology: If "singularity" denotes the state of being singular or one, then "duplicity" should denote the state of being doubled or two. But of course duplicity connotes deceit, deception, and dissimulation—which is precisely why it is a tradition that narrates "the dangers of the double."[32] To match this immense modern genre of fiction there has arisen an equally immense body of scholarly literature trying to take its measure.[33]

Thankfully that is not our task. If modernity seems exercised by the threat of a menacing doppelgänger, a horizontal double, then late antiquity seems equally exercised by the promise of a divine counterpart, a vertical double. The task of this book is to retrieve this tradition of the divine double from the obscurity into which it has fallen, partly owing to the heterodoxy that hovers around most of its central texts, and partly owing to the fact that the texts themselves

INTRODUCTION

are often in very bad states of transmission (the former no doubt contributing to the latter).

IN CHAPTER 1 we will survey Plato's conceptual landscape of the divine double. The first half of that chapter concerns what we might call the "comedy" of the divine double—"comedy" in the classical sense of a narrative with a happy resolution. In this case, "comedy" refers to Plato's seeming confidence that one can access one's other, better half and conform oneself to it. The divine double makes possible our progressive assimilation to the world of intelligible reality, the Forms. Under this rubric, we will first consider Plato's handling of Socrates's *daimonion* or "guardian spirit," as well as the transformation of Socrates's peculiar companion into a more universal anthropology of the *daimōn*. We will then turn to Plato's *Phaedrus* and *Alcibiades I*, where Plato has Socrates recommend that lover and beloved serve as mirrors to one another, allowing each to see not just himself, but his *best* self, reflected back to him. This autoscopy allows for the spectator to become what he sees, and thus again to conform ever more to his intelligible counterpart. The first half of this chapter thus introduces both axes of doubling—the vertical double (Socrates and his *daimonion*) and the horizontal double (lover and beloved)—and the correlation of these two axes in the service of deification.

The second half of Chapter 1 concerns what we might call the "tragedy" of the divine double—"tragedy" not because it is dismal (indeed, it can be very funny) but because it suggests the impossibility of union with one's divine double, and so the impossibility of deification. We see this clearly in Plato's *Symposium* in Aristophanes's tale of humanity's primordial severing in two at the hands of the gods, threatened by human ambition. We are, according to Aristophanes, each one half of a former whole, and long for reunion with our other half. Although we find some consolation in love (and sex), we remain forever split in two, and so ever on this side of a receding horizon of union. Ironically, this tragic (but quite hilarious) account of the human condition is delivered by Athens's most celebrated comedian. This tragedy is repeated in a very different idiom in Plato's *Parmenides*, where Plato has Parmenides deliver devastating critiques of the young Socrates's theory of Forms. The dissociation of this world from the world of intelligible reality on which it depends threatens to sever us from our divine double. In a dialectical exercise meant to train Socrates and so to salvage the theory of Forms, Plato has Parmenides run through several deductions, the first two of which have to do with something he calls "the One" and the possibility of its existence. Parmenides concludes that if the One is to be properly one, it cannot be, that is, it cannot exist; and if the One is to exist, then it cannot be one, but must always be somehow two. Strictly speaking, then, to be one is impossible, and short of that impossible end, we exist in duality, and the best we can aim for is some sort of unity-in-duality.

It is precisely these tense borderlands between the one and the two, I will argue in Chapters 2 and 3, that our earliest Christian witnesses to the divine double explore. Their exploration of this landscape is not speculative but driven by a conviction that Jesus calls his disciples to become, each of them, a unity-in-duality. Chapter 2 begins with the apostle Thomas, who in the Gospel of John is "called the Twin *(didymos)*." The very name "Thomas" is an Aramaic word meaning "twin," and this seems to have led some early Christians to conclude that this apostle was the twin brother of Jesus, named Judas (although in what sense a "twin" remains unclear). This chapter focuses on a collection of Jesus's sayings that is attributed to this very apostle, Judas Thomas the Twin. I offer a close reading of this *Gospel of Thomas*, especially a number of its enigmatic sayings about the one and the two, and what it means to become a solitary *(monachos)* and a single one *(oua ouōt)*. These sayings offer, on my reading, a coded theology of the twin, in which the reader is asked to recognize that one is not, strictly speaking, a single self, but that one has the transcendent light of Jesus within oneself. This recognition can be said to render one into two: oneself and the indwelling, luminous Jesus. These sayings also ask the reader to transform, in light of this new duality, and to become a unity that encompasses and embraces this duality. The new selfhood, a unity-in-duality, is given the name "solitary" and "single one." Those who succeed in acquiring this new selfhood are understood to be, like Judas Thomas the Twin, Jesus's equals. This coded theology of the twin, therefore, is an early doctrine of deification, running parallel to the version that will come to prevail in the fourth century. Chapter 2 concludes by wondering whether Origen, the famous third-century Christian theologian from Alexandria, was influenced by the *Gospel of Thomas* in his commentary on the Gospel of John.

Chapter 3 continues this trajectory and tracks the transformations of the divine double in other Christian sources from the second and third centuries. The first part of the chapter looks at two other early witnesses to the divine double: Tatian the Assyrian (ca. 120–ca. 180), who articulates his own distinctive version of the divine double as a "syzygy" of our soul and its lost spirit; and a pair of Valentinian witnesses, the *Gospel of Philip* and the *Extracts of Theodotus*, each of which describes how the sacraments effect a union or conjunction of the individual's spirit with his or her angelic counterpart. The chapter then shifts back to the tradition associated with Judas Thomas the Twin, and looks to three later texts: the *Book of Thomas the Contender*, the *Acts of Thomas*, and the so-called "Hymn of the Pearl" (embedded in two manuscripts of the *Acts*). Each of these texts has its own distinctive theology of the twin, and in the case of the *Acts of Thomas*, a matching theology of the bridal chamber, in which Christians are bid to become virgin brides to the one bridegroom, Christ. Whereas I argue in Chapter 2 that the *Gospel of Thomas* should not be understood as an "encratic" text, that is, as forwarding an unrelenting ethic of sexual renunciation, in Chapter 3 I agree with the scholarly consensus that the *Book of Thomas* and the *Acts of Thomas* betray "encratic" views—although I am more cautious than some scholars when using this pejorative, heresiological label. Quite apart from the question of "encratism," the *Acts of Thomas* and its embedded "Hymn of the Pearl" forward a much more elaborate matrix of divine doubles than one finds in the *Gospel of Thomas*, for instance.

In Chapter 4 we move from the Christian to the Manichaean tradition of the divine double, for which our sources are also somewhat sparse. Mani announces himself as the "apostle of light," a heavenly figure who periodically takes on a body so as to teach souls how to achieve salvation. This incarnate messenger is awakened to his mission by the arrival of his twin-companion (who goes by many names), his divine alter ego who appears to him in order to reveal his true identity and calling. But the identity that is thereby revealed is explicitly an identity that contains this crucial duality: apostle and twin-companion, Mani and his *syzygos* (as he is called in the *Cologne Mani Codex*). We begin with two "etic" or outsider sources on this twin-companion, namely a pair of medieval Muslim witnesses to Manichaean myth and doctrine, and then proceed to two "emic" or insider sources: the so-called *Kephalaia of the Teacher*, a collection dating from 400 CE that survives relatively intact in Coptic; and the *Cologne Mani Codex*, a fifth-century anthology that survives, although in much worse condition, in Greek. While most of our attention is focused on how the Manichaean tradition understands the significance of Mani's own doubled self (and that of his heavenly predecessors), we will also attempt to reconstruct an account of the divine double as it bears on everyday Manichaean practitioners (lay and elect). This chapter will also look back to the *Gospel of Thomas*, which I suspect is a source for the *Kephalaia*'s understanding of Mani as *oua ouōt* or "singular," and forward to Plotinus, Mani's contemporary, whose own version of the divine double bears striking resemblances to the apostle of light's.

Chapter 5 is the most complicated of the whole, owing to the fact that the structure of the divine double is integral to Plotinus's entire philosophical system—if indeed it can be called a "system"—as recorded in his *Enneads*. Plotinus provides an account of how everything is derived, through a complicated process of procession, from a first, transcendent principle, the One. The primordial procession—that of Intellect from the One—provides the template of all subsequent processions. Plotinus also provides an account of our return or ascent from embodiment, to the distillation of intellects within our souls, to the elevation of individual intellects to the level of universal Intellect, and finally to the undoing of the very first procession of Intellect from the One. At every one of these stages in our return, we must encounter our higher self or divine double, unite with it, and thereby ascend to the next stage. Borrowing a term from Julia Kristeva, I argue that the structure of the Plotinian enterprise is thereby "Narcissan"—that is, it depends on a perfect autoscopy and the union of an identical seer and seen. Narcissus, however, is a negative exemplar for Plotinus precisely because he fails to execute properly that union: he grasps after his image, in Plotinus's version, and so plunges to a watery death.

Plotinus's return itinerary has three principal stages. First our descended intellect must distill itself from the broader powers of soul, and recognize that it has an undescended archetype, an intellect dwelling in the intelligible heights from which it is never wholly severed. By conforming our descended intellect to its undescended archetype or divine double, the individual intellect takes its place in the inner life of Intellect, where it stands as an intellectual subject to an intelligible object—the two are "yoked together" as a self and its double. The second stage dissolves this subject-object dualism so that the individual intellect is elevated to the level of the hypostasis Intellect, which Plotinus famously describes as the vision of intelligible beauty (*Ennead* 1.6, "On Beauty"). The third, nearly impossible stage is the undoing of the primordial procession of Intellect from the One. This requires an encounter with our final divine double, a primordial "otherness" (sometimes called the "indeterminate dyad" or "intelligible matter") that first emerged from the One. But this "otherness" is *other* than the One by virtue of its desire to stand apart from, so as to see, its source. And so the ultimate step in our folding that otherness back into the embrace of the One is to release our ambition for autoscopy. Following Pierre Hadot, who has drawn criticism on this point, I suggest that for Plotinus love is the reforming force, bestowed on everything by the One itself, that allows for a final reunion with the One. We close with a consideration of what division or difference, if any, can be said to remain at this moment of mystical union—and why.

Chapter 6, shorter than the rest, asks after the afterlife of the divine double in each of the three traditions under scrutiny. Manichaeism maintains a consistent interest in the figure of Mani's twin-companion. Neoplatonism after Plotinus is riven by a debate between two of his students, Porphyry of Tyre and Iamblichus of Chalcis. Contrary to Porphyry (who follows Plotinus on this point), Iamblichus insists that our intellect fully descends, and argues instead for a divine principle within us that is totally alien to us, not the undescended archetype for our descended image. This leads him to a reformulation of the divine double: we engage and awaken the alien principle within us, inscrutable to discursive reason, by means of the alien words revealed by the gods to the ancient religious traditions. For Iamblichus, our divine double is therefore accessed through ritual and revelation, not reason.

In the fourth century, an imperially endorsed Christian orthodoxy began to take shape, as expressed in the Councils of Nicaea (325) and Constantinople (381). Associated with that emerging orthodoxy was a particular doctrine of deification, authored by Athanasius but drawing on earlier figures. The texts and traditions of the divine double, however, record an early (perhaps the earliest) doctrine of deification, an alternative to what was to become the dominant model. The hostility of many of the predecessors of conciliar orthodoxy to the texts in question (such as Tatian's, Valentinian texts, and the *Gospel of Thomas*), and the Manichaeans' growing interest in some of these same texts (for instance, the *Gospel of Thomas* and *Acts of Thomas*), meant that this early alternative's days were numbered.

But even though this figure of the divine double largely recedes from the history of Christianity with the rise of conciliar orthodoxy, I suspect that it survives in a new guise. I suggest that we can see the divine double reappear in two important discourses from late antiquity: (1) "theodicy" or the problem of evil, and (2) Christology, that is, how the Incarnate Christ is understood to be both human and divine. In the first case, I detect in the "privative" theories of evil (such as one finds in Plotinus and Proclus, and the Christian thinkers in their wake) the suggestion that the One or God has its own double, namely evil. In the second case, I suspect that the fifth-century Christological controversy—whether and how the Incarnate Christ, human and divine, is confessed as one or two—is a continuation of an earlier tradition of the divine double. Whereas the earlier tradition, traced in Chapters 2 and 3, focuses on how each Christian, as Jesus's twin or double, is both human and divine, one and two, the later tradition focuses on how Christ himself is human and divine, one and two. I sketch out both avenues of inquiry—albeit provisionally— to which I promise to return in two subsequent installments in a series continuing to explore Paul's phrase, "no longer I."

The Conclusion falls into two parts. In the first, I try once again to articulate the significance of the tradition of the divine double.

INTRODUCTION

Focusing on a pair of questions—what I call the "introverted" question of the relationship of the "I" and not-"I" and the "extroverted" question of the one and the not-one (which I regard as, in the words of the *Gospel of Thomas*, *oua ouōt* or "one and the same" question)—I suggest that the ancient sources assembled here as the "tradition" of the divine double amount to a centuries-long meditation on the relationship of identity and difference. In the second half, I return to a thread that runs through several chapters, namely, whether and how these ancient texts understood themselves as mirrors in which we might see ourselves, or our divine doubles, reflected. This raises the question of the practice of reading as a means of encountering the divine double. And with the help of Jeffrey Kripal, I pivot to questions of the practice of writing—of whether, if there is a way to *read* the divine double, so also there is a way to *write* the divine double.

⁓ ONE FINAL NOTE: each of these texts and traditions has an enormous scholarly deposit associated with it, sometimes stretching back several centuries. I have been feasting on these archives for ten years, but cannot claim to have equal mastery of all of them. Throughout the chapters, I have attempted, as much as possible, to focus on my interpretation of the primary sources and to provide a clean, readable narrative. Those more interested in scholarly debates will find much, but by no means all, of the relevant literature cited in the notes. Even in the notes I have limited my citations to those scholarly threads that have been most helpful to me in the years I have been following the trail of the divine double. Likewise, the notes presume not to be exhaustive but rather to credit, not *all* the sources I have ever read, but those that have helped me give this book its shape.

1

Reading Plato's Many Doubles

Much of what follows in this book concerns texts from the second and third centuries CE, texts that I am treating collectively as a "tradition." By "tradition" I mean only that they all witness to a peculiar figure in the religious imagination of the Eastern Mediterranean: the divine double. This book will begin, however, not in the second and third centuries CE, but in the fourth and fifth centuries BCE, in classical Athens, home to the philosopher Plato (428 / 427–348 / 347 BCE) and his teacher Socrates (ca. 470–399 BCE).[1] Plato, and in his hands the literary character Socrates, lays out the conceptual landscape of the tradition of the divine double that will occupy us in the chapters to come. Fittingly, my treatment of Plato falls into two halves: comedy and tragedy, confidence and anxiety. To understand the two halves (or, as it were, the two masks of Greek drama), I will begin with a very brief overview of Plato's metaphysics, according to which the sensible world is an image *(eikōn)* and imitation *(mimēsis)* of the intelligible world. We ourselves are images, thrown into that doubled world, and enjoined to move from the sensible to the intelligible, insofar as we can. The first half of this chapter, the comedy, is not very funny at all, but is motivated by Plato's conviction that we images can conform ever more closely to our eternal archetypes. I begin with Socrates's famous *daimonion* or "guardian spirit," who guides him with negative stimuli on a path to wisdom. The *daimonion* is also our guide upward to our "divine part," the root from which we are in fact the downward growth. Plato's discussions of Socrates's *daimonion* thus introduce two crucial axes for the tradition of the divine double: (1) the horizontal—how and why we form pairs with our fellow humans; and (2) the vertical—the disorientation and reorientation that comes when we recognize that *we* are each the derivative half of some prior pair, and how and why we can each conform to our divine half. I then take up the relationship between these two axes, the horizontal and the vertical, more directly. In *Phaedrus* and *Alcibiades I*, Plato establishes lover and beloved not only as an amorous pair, but as horizontal doubles who, like mirrors, allow each to see (what is best in) himself. Lover and beloved see each other reflected in the other, not only as they each are, but more importantly, as they each *should* be. Thus, the horizontal serves the vertical axis, as the lover and beloved enable each other's mutual deification. This discourse is comedy insofar as it suggests a happy ending, and thereby exudes confidence. Much of the subsequent tradition of the divine double is funded by Plato's comedic confidence that we can and should become as divine as our double.

But even within Plato's writings there emerges another discourse, the tragic—this will occupy the second half of this chapter. Ironically, Plato chooses as the spokesman of this tragic discourse not Socrates but rather his contemporary, Aristophanes, Athens's most celebrated comedian. For this tragic discourse we look to the *Symposium* and Aristophanes's very funny, but not at all comedic, tale about the gods slicing humans in half: we are now only half of a former whole. The gods permit each half to find its other, form a pair, and through sexual union dull the pain of primordial separation. But the gods refuse (or are unable—it is unclear) to undo the original division, to fuse the two into one, to deliver a union without remainder or gap. The sorry souls of Aristophanes's funny tale are left with the tragic knowledge that the two will never be one again. Instead, they live in a persistent and penultimate two-in-oneness, or unity-in-duality. The anxiety that this introduces into the equation is only made more acute in Plato's most difficult dialogue, the *Parmenides*. Threats abound to the comedic confidence of the first half: the sensible and the intelligible worlds threaten to decouple, and the theory of Forms is beset with criticisms Socrates cannot answer. Parmenides schools Socrates in dialectic, and then performs a dialectical exercise in eight deductions. The first two are the most famous, and they begin with the hypotheses "if (the one is) one" *(ei hen estin)* and "if the one is" *(hen ei estin)*. The result of the first deduction is that if the one is one, then it cannot *be*; the result of the second deduction is that if the one *is*, then it cannot be *one*. Although these two, and the other six, deductions are seemingly intended to salvage Socrates's teetering theory of Forms, I propose (following ancient precedent) that we read the first two deductions as a sort of philosophical allegory, not so much about the Forms as about us. If we are each of us already doubled, one half human and one half divine, then the first deduction teaches us that the union of our two halves is impossible—that strictly speaking, it cannot *be*. Short of that impossible goal—union without distinction or difference—we *are*, which is to say, we exist, as two. The second deduction concludes that the one-that-is is always two, and this is where we find ourselves, we *are* and so we are doubled, striving after the impossible union that cannot be.

Plato thus ushers us into the tradition of the divine double in the second and third centuries, into those Christian and Manichaean sources (Chapters 2 through 4) that express such a vivid interest in the borderlands between the one and the not-one, an interest mapped directly onto human selfhood. His comedy funds their confidence in union and deification, his tragedy their acknowledgment of how we fall short of that union and deification and must instead negotiate the realm of the not-one, a tense but dynamic model of selfhood constituted by an inalienable duality, a new singularity for which these sources struggle to give an adequate name. With Plotinus (Chapter 5) we come full circle, not only in his innovation on his Platonic inheritance, but also in his own peculiar account of this dynamic model of selfhood and how it fits into a larger metaphysical frame of doubles, all of which must be overcome (if they can be) in our return to the ineffable One.

The Divided Line and the Doubled Person

To appreciate the play of Plato's many doubles, horizontal and vertical, we must first appreciate that his overall metaphysical framework—the division between sensible and intelligible realities—is already a structure of doubles. This is perhaps best explored through that section from *Republic VI* where Socrates introduces the analogy of the "divided line" to explain the nature of the world, seen and unseen. First, Socrates states unequivocally that there are "two kinds of things, visible and intelligible" (509d). To explain the relationship between the two and our itinerary from the one to the other, he introduces the notion of a line divided into two unequal sections. The longer of the two sections corresponds to the intelligible world, and the shorter to the sensible world. And within each section the line is further divided in two, and according to the same proportion as the whole line was divided. So the sensible world divides in two: on the bottom of the sensible scale are "images"—"and by images *(eikones)*, I mean first, shadows *(tas skias)*, then reflections in water *(ta en tais hydasi phantasmata)* and in all close-packed smooth, and shiny materials, and everything of that sort" (509d); at the top of the sensible scale are "the originals of these images"—for example, animals, plants, and presumably also our own bodies. Knowledge of the entire sensible world has the epistemological status of "opinion" *(doxa)*, with the lower realm falling under the category of imagination *(eikasia)* and the higher of belief *(pistis)*.

But these sensible things—solid, observable things like animals and plants—are in turn "images" of the intelligible realm of the Forms. The lower domain of the intelligible realm is that of soul, and soul uses sensible things, which are themselves really images of intelligible Forms: "the soul is forced to use . . . as images those very things of which images were made in the section below, and which, by comparison to their images, were thought to be clear and to be valued as such" (511a). Using these sensible things as images, the soul reasons by way of hypotheses and reaches conclusions that have the epistemological status of "thought" *(dianoia)*. These are the "so-called sciences" or *technai* (511c). The soul, however, can vault from thought to understanding *(nous)* by shedding these images:

> It does not consider these hypotheses as first principles but truly as hypotheses—but as stepping stones to take off from, enabling it to reach the un-hypothetical first principle of everything. Having grasped this principle, it reverses itself and, keeping hold of what follows from it, comes down to a conclusion without making use of anything visible at all, but only of forms themselves, moving on from forms to forms, and ending in forms. (511b)

Dialectic, in passing beyond the use of images as hypotheses, is the true "science" or *epistēmē* and delivers the soul squarely into the realm of the Forms, where intelligibility is on offer. Ruling over this realm of the Forms is the unhypothetical first principle of everything, a kind of superform, the good itself, beyond being: "the good is not being, but superior to it in rank and power" *(ouk ousias ontos tou agathou, all'eti epekeina tēs ousias)* (509b).

This brief description furnishes us with a good picture of Plato's world as doubled or divided between the sensible and the intelligible domains, and further doubled or subdivided in each domain. What is crucial to understand, however, is that the fundamental relationship between the sensible and the intelligible worlds is one of imaging *(eikōn)* and imitation *(mimēsis)*; and furthermore that this relationship is recapitulated *intra*sensibly, so to speak, between concrete sensible things (animals, plants, and such), and the shadowy world of representation (words, painting, sculpture, and so on). Everything here is either an image of an eternal archetype (a Form or *eidos*) or an image of such an image. The great achievement of the analogy of the divided line is that it not only provides a picture of a divided world and the relationship between its two halves, but also places us in that world and puts us on an itinerary from sensible to intelligible, from image to archetype, from opinion to knowledge. What it means to be a human—or perhaps better, a *person*—is to be somewhere along this itinerary, negotiating doubles, using images and reflections in order eventually to discard them.

The distinction between a human and a person is one introduced by Lloyd P. Gerson in his book, *Knowing Persons: A Study in Plato*, whereas the human is the composite between body and soul, the person (properly speaking) is a soul.[2] Sometimes Gerson will speak of the human as our embodied *endowment*, what is given to us regardless of our efforts; and of the person, by contrast, as our *achievement*, the philosophical project of becoming a proper person or a self.[3] One of the most important, and persuasive, claims that Gerson advances is that (endowed, embodied) humans "are situated within a hierarchical metaphysics by Plato," and more specifically that "our endowment—the persons we are here below— . . . stand[s] to an ideal of achievement roughly as images stand to their eternal exemplars."[4] In other words, we are sensible objects in the world—composites of body and soul—and so occupy a place on the divided line, namely at the top of the sensible scale. We are images of the eternal Forms, as there are further derivative images of us and other sensible objects (the shadows at the bottom of the sensible scale). But we are distinct in one crucial regard: "For Plato, embodied persons [in other words, we humans] are the only sorts of images that can reflectively recognize their own relatively inferior states as images and strive to transform themselves into their own ideal."[5] I have found Gerson's distinction between human and person very helpful for interpreting not only Plato but other texts in the tradition of the divine double. However, his characterization of the arrival of the person as something "achieved" suggests a striving, almost muscular effort that, to my mind, runs counter to Plato and the texts to which we will turn in subsequent chapters. Perhaps it is better to think of the "achieved" self as the *"received"* self, because its arrival is more often occasioned by a release or a letting-go than by a grasping effort.

Many scholars, perhaps driven by Descartes's concerns rather than Plato's, focus their attention on what we might call Plato's horizontal anthropology: how he imagines the body and soul forming a composite entity in this world. Gerson suggests that this horizontal anthropology is explicitly in the service of a more urgent, vertical anthropology: "The fundamental contrast for Plato is between the ideal disembodied person or self we strive to become and its embodied image . . . it is the identity of ideal and image, not that of various diachronic images, that is primary."⁶ What it means to be a human is to recognize that one's endowed humanity is a composite and an image, from which recognition two things follow: (1) the practice of isolating the soul from the body and unifying its distinct nature—what we might call a horizontal exercise; (2) the practice of having that isolated and unified soul strive to achieve identity with its ideal or eternal archetype—what we might call a vertical exercise. Gerson is exactly right when he prompts us to ask "in what sense there is truly identity between the embodied person [with its soul isolated and unified] and that person's disembodied ideal state [the archetype of its soul]."⁷ Not only of Plato, but of all the figures and texts we will soon survey, we will want to ask how each conceives of this union or identity between image and archetype, whether and how such a thing is even possible.

What follows in subsequent sections, namely our exploration of Plato's many doubles, must be understood against the backdrop both of (a) Plato's doubled metaphysics, sensible reality as the image of intelligible reality, a world in which we are placed and then urged to move from one to the other; and of (b) the knowledge that we humans are called to become persons, to isolate and unify the soul in order that it might achieve identity with its eternal counterpart, its divine double.

Socrates's *Daimonion* as a Divine Double

Widely regarded as his first dialogue, Plato's *Apology* sets Socrates face-to-face with his assembled accusers and jury of peers. This "dialogue" in fact contains very little dialogue. It is instead an *apologia* or defense speech: Socrates stands accused of corrupting the youth and not believing in the gods of Athens. To answer this second charge, the ironist tells us that his friend Chaerophon decided, without consulting him, that he would call upon the Pythian oracle of Delphi and ask the god Apollo whether any man was wiser than Socrates. To Socrates's surprise, the oracle answered in the negative. To prove the oracle wrong, Socrates sought out eminent Athenians who were thought to be—and certainly thought themselves to be—wise. Again, much to his (perhaps feigned) surprise, he discovered that they were not. He made his way through politicians, poets, even craftsmen—none were wise. Socrates himself became, so to speak, wise to the fact that the oracle's answer may have been a provocation, a goad to get him to realize that "[only] the god is wise" and that "human wisdom is worth little or nothing" (23b). With this realization, Socrates tells his audience that he embraced his new "occupation," something between an irritant and an agitant, and devoted himself to "service to the god" (23b).

He means them to ask themselves, "How could someone who has devoted himself to the service of Apollo stand accused of atheism?" While his accusers are scratching their heads, Socrates adduces even more evidence for his piety. He addresses his principal accuser, Meletus: "Does any man believe in spiritual activities *(daimonia)* who does not believe in spirits *(daimonas)?*" "No one," Meletus concedes (27c). Meletus also concedes that spirits are "either gods or children of gods"—in any case that whatever is "spiritual" *(daimonia)* is also "divine" *(theia)* (27d, 28a). So if, as Socrates insists, he believes in spiritual things, and so also in spirits, and if spirits are gods, then he believes in the gods. This brief performance of Socratic dialectic offers a foretaste of Plato's subsequent dialogues, but in the context of the *Apology* it serves to undermine the charge leveled against Socrates, namely that he is an atheist.

This performance also serves to introduce a detail about Socrates that has intrigued ancients and moderns: the fact that he has a *daimonion* or "guardian spirit." It is not enough that Socrates confesses to some vague belief in "spiritual things" *(daimonia)* to answer the charge against him. He goes on to narrate an ongoing and intimate relationship he has with one spirit in particular: "Something divine or spiritual comes to me *(moi theion ti kai daimonion gignetai)* . . . This began when I was a child. It is a voice, and whenever it speaks it turns me away from something I am about to do, but it never encourages me to do anything" (31d).[8] Here is the famous *daimonion* of Socrates, a divine voice that has been coming to him since childhood, but a voice that never impels but only impedes his actions. "Unlike *logos*, however," Luc Brisson remarks, "this sound is not necessarily articulated . . . [rather, it is] a phonic signal that manifests a prohibition . . . something like '*mē*', 'do not.'"[9] Specifically, this voice has prohibited Socrates from entering politics, and this explains why he has persisted in "giv[ing] advice privately and interfer[ing] in private affairs" (31c).

Near the end of the dialogue, when Socrates has been convicted and sentenced to death, he speaks again of his *daimonion*. To his friends, those who voted for his acquittal, Socrates speaks not of the past, but of the present moment. He exclaims,

> A surprising *(thaumasion)* thing has happened to me, judges—you I would rightly call judges. At all previous times my familiar prophetic power, my spiritual manifestation *(hē gar eiôthuia moi mantikē hē tou daimoniou)*, frequently opposed me, even in small matters, when I was about to do something wrong, but now that, as you can see for yourselves, I was faced with what one might think, and what is generally thought to be, the worst of evils, my divine sign *(to tou theiou sēmeion)* has not opposed me, either when I left home at dawn, or when I came into court, or at any time that I was about to say something during my speech. Yet in other talks it often held me back in the middle of my speaking, but now it has opposed no word or deed of mine. What do I think is the reason for this? I will tell you. What has happened to me may well be a good thing, and those of us who believe death to be an evil are certainly mistaken. I have convincing proof of this, for it is impossible that my familiar sign *(to eiôthos sēmeion)* did not oppose me if I was not about to do what was right. (40a–c)

Notice first that Socrates offers a thicker description of his *daimonion*: it is "familiar" or "customary" *(eiôthuia, eiôthos)* insofar as it speaks to him regularly, ever since childhood; "prophetic" *(mantikē)* insofar as it foresees the consequences of his actions and warns him accordingly; a "sign" *(sēmeion)* that turns him away from (but never toward) some course of action. Notice also that Socrates tells his friends no less than four times that his *daimonion* would have "opposed" him if he were to undertake anything contrary to the good. The verb *enantioomai* means "to set oneself against, oppose, withstand, refuse, or contradict." Earlier he said that it "turns him away" *(apotrepei)* but never "encourages" *(protrepei)*. The principal function of this divine *daimonion*, therefore, is apotreptic (or op-positional), not protreptic (or pro-positional): it opposes or contradicts its earthly counterpart, and so through a series of negative stimuli steers its host toward the good. In the context of the *Apology*, what is "surprising"—or better, "astonishing" and "wonderful" *(thaumasion)*—is the fact that the *daimonion*'s present silence suggests that Socrates's death is something that he should not turn from but rather welcome. His *daimonion*'s final gift is the peace that accompanies the knowledge that Socrates's certain death is a good end.

Earlier in the *Apology* (30d–e), Socrates insists that his spirited defense is not for his own sake, but for the sake of the city of Athens, to which the god has given Socrates as if a gift. To kill Socrates would be to spurn that gift and lose its benefits. Socrates offers an analogy: he is to the city what a gadfly is to a horse. Although the god has "attached" Socrates to the city as a collective, the gadfly also lands on citizens individually, rousing, persuading, and reproaching each of them—as if he were an agitant individually tailored to each citizen's inertia. And so each citizen finds in Socrates a sort of double, paired with him "like a father or an elder brother." Two pairs of doubles emerge, then, from this account in the *Apology:* In the first pair, between Socrates and his *daimonion*, the relationship is exclusively apotreptic: his divine double opposes any misguided action. In the second pair, between the city collectively or its citizens individually and its / their divine double, Socrates, the relationship is principally protreptic: he rouses and persuades. There is also a clear relationship between these two pairs: Socrates, prohibited from entering politics by his divine double or *daimonion*, is thereby freed to be the double of each citizen, urging each to the pursuit of the good. In this case a vertical double, the *daimonion*, authorizes Socrates to serve as a sort of horizontal double, a gadfly to his fellow Athenians. Later, after he has received his death sentence, Socrates warns his accusers: "there will be more people to test you, whom I now hold back, but you did not notice it" (39d). Laying in wait for his smug opponents are a legion of gadflies, other horizontal doubles. Like a spider that in dying gives birth to a horde of offspring, or a hydra whose severed head sprouts more in its place, Socrates promises the assembled accusers that he will replicate himself in those youth he has trained in philosophy.

The *Apology* offers the most details about Socrates's *daimonion*, but later Platonic dialogues fill in the picture, albeit in sometimes confusing and contradictory ways. In the *Euthyphro* Socrates speaks of the accusation against him, that he does not believe in the old gods but introduces new ones. Euthyphro responds, "it is because you say that the *daimonion* keeps coming to you" (3b). In the *Euthydemus* Socrates says that his "customary divine sign" *(to eiôthos sēmeion to daimonion)* once prevented him from leaving a certain place (272e). In a later dialogue, *Theaetetus*, he says that his *daimonion* sometimes forbids him from associating with certain people (151a). These three citations are consistent with the account given the *Apology*. So is an episode from the *Phaedrus*, where once again Socrates tells his friend how "the familiar divine sign" *(to daimonion te kai to eiôthos sēmeion)* came to him as a voice, holding him back, forbidding him to cross a river.[10]

Things get murkier, however, when we turn our attention to two dialogues whose authenticity is disputed.[11] Until now Plato seems to have carefully chosen his words: Socrates has a *daimonion* (not a *daimōn*—more on this distinction below) that is also "familiar" or "customary" and a "sign." He describes this *daimonion* as "divine" and "prophetic," and at several points makes clear that it is his own, not shared by others. *Alcibiades I* begins in the same vein: Socrates confesses that some *daimonion* prevented him from speaking with Alcibiades. Shortly thereafter, however, Socrates speaks of "the god" *(ton theon)* himself holding him back (105d–e). This becomes even more explicit in a brief exchange between the two:

> *Socrates:* My guardian *(epitropos)* is better and wiser than Pericles, your guardian.
> *Alcibiades:* Who's that, Socrates?
> *Socrates:* God *(theos)*, Alcibiades; it was he who prevented me from talking with you before today. I put my faith in him *(hôi kai pisteuôn)*, and I say that your glory will be entirely my doing. (124c–d)

Socrates's *daimonion* is now god, or at least *a* god, and such a guardian clearly trumps even Pericles, the greatest statesman of Athens's golden age. Which god in particular Socrates does not say, but presumably it is Apollo, the very god whose Pythian oracle set him on his philosophical mission.[12]

This dialogue does not expand on the significance of this detail, but another dialogue of even more spurious authenticity can be seen to do so. At first glance, the *Theages*'s account of the *daimonion* (128d–31a) raises no eyebrows: Socrates speaks of a *daimonion*, a familiar sign, that has been coming to him since childhood, a voice that turns him away from certain actions but never prescribes anything. Socrates is trying to convince Theages that those who associate with him can receive benefits from his *daimonion*. Theages proposes a trial: he will test Socrates's *daimonion* to see if indeed he makes progress in its presence. But if he does not, Theages suggests, then they should "try to appease the divine thing that comes to you with prayers and sacrifices and any other way the diviners might suggest" (131a). The proposal is Theages's own, not Socrates's: the dialogue immediately closes with Demodocus urging Socrates not to oppose the proposal, so we never eavesdrop on Socrates's opinion of this proposal that includes a ritual propitiation of his *daimonion*. But even the suggestion that the *daimonion* is something like a traditional god, whom one appeases through prayers and sacrifices, is a significant departure from the portrait gleaned from the *Apology* and the corroborating details in other authentic dialogues. Some are eager to label this development in *Theages*—authentic or not—as a "degradation" and "retrograde movement."[13] Even if it were true that *Theages* paints Socrates's *daimonion* in new, more vulgar, colors, the more important point to register for the subsequent tradition of the divine double is that this pair of dialogues introduces the idea that Socrates's own divine double (and perhaps others' as well) is God, or at least one of the gods *(Alcibiades I)*, and so might be propitiated through sacrifices and prayers *(Theages)*.

Up to this point we have been focusing exclusively on Socrates's own divine sign. But Plato also toyed with a more universal anthropology of the divine double, whereby *every* person at least potentially has his or her own *daimonion* or *daimōn*.[14] Prior to Plato, the concept of a *daimōn* was rather loose. In classical Greek literature, *daimōn* was often used to name a divine power, an impersonal force associated with, but inferior to, a god. It also often connoted the power specifically charged with the fate of an individual human.[15] It is in this sense that it is often translated "destiny" or "fate," as in Charles Kahn's rendering of Heraclitus's obscure fragment, "Man's character is his fate."[16] We are still centuries from the early Christian use of the plural *daimones* to name evil spirits (demons). The word likely derives from the verb *daiō*, which furnishes two interesting meanings: (1) to light up or kindle, or (in the passive) to blaze; (2) to divide, or (in the middle) to distribute.[17] With *daiō* in the middle voice meaning "to distribute," the *daimōn* is conceived either as that impersonal fate that distributes an individual's lot or portion, or as a more personal divine power distributing shares of good and ill. What is most relevant for our inquiry, however, is the use to which Plato puts this rich tradition of the *daimōn*.

It is best to start with the *Cratylus*, where Plato has Socrates offer an etymology of *daimōn:* Hesiod, Socrates says, calls spirits *daimones* because they are wise and knowing *(daēmones)*.[18] According to Socrates, Hesiod and the other poets say that when someone good dies, he or she becomes a *daimōn*. Socrates adjusts this slightly, saying that "every good man, whether alive or dead, is *daimonion*, and is correctly called a *daimōn*" (398c). The first question to be asked is whether Socrates means to introduce an important distinction between *daimōn* and *daimonion*. In the passages discussed above (even the spurious ones), Plato consistently has Socrates refer to his familiar sign as a *daimonion*, and never as a *daimōn*. But *daimonion* is simply the adjectival form of *daimōn*, and Plato has Socrates use this adjective to modify the noun *sēmeion* or "sign." It is decoupled from its noun, however, and stands alone as a substantive, meaning "something spiritual or divine." As the editors of an excellent collection on Socrates's *daimonion* ask, "What is the relationship between Socrates's *daimonion* and the characterization of the *daimōn* of a person as a personal guardian or destiny we find in Greek texts as well as in many (post-Socratic) Platonic dialogues?"[19] Some scholars wish to keep the two very distinct: Pierre Destrée argues that whereas a *daimōn* is the traditional notion of a personal guardian or destiny that is different for every person, the *daimonion* is a divine sign that is (or should be) common to all of us, a spur to philosophy and the examined life, the only one worth living.[20] One of the strengths of Destrée's distinction is that it helps square Socrates's infamous remark in *Republic* 496c, "Finally, my own case is hardly worth mentioning—my demonic sign *(to daimonion sēmeion)*—because it has happened to no one before me, or to only a very few," with the more universal anthropology of the *daimon*, traces of which we find in other Platonic dialogues.[21] On this reading, Socrates is not so much bragging as he is lamenting the fact that he is the only one, or at least one of very few, who has pursued philosophy and so who has a *daimonion*. If "every *good* man . . . is *daimonion*," this reading goes, then Socrates must be one of very few good men. One of the liabilities of this same distinction between *daimonion* and *daimōn* is that Socrates does not seem to maintain it at all in the etymology of *Cratylus* 398c, where *daimonion* is used as simply the adjectival form of *daimōn*.

Let us return to the evidence. Despite the many questions that *Cratylus* 398c raises, the passage unambiguously asserts that every good human is already *daimonion*, that one need not wait until one sheds this mortal coil to know that one is (or has) a *daimōn*. Nevertheless, death may mark an important moment is one's relationship with one's *daimōn*, as this passage from *Phaedo* suggests:

> We are told that when each person dies, the guardian spirit *(daimōn)* who was allotted to him in life proceeds to lead him to a certain place, whence those who have been gathered there must, after having been judged, proceed to the underworld with the guide *(hēgemonos)* who has been appointed to lead them thither from here. (107d–e)

Here is a very clear account of the *daimōn*: everyone has one, and at death it performs a crucial function. So far, this is entirely consistent with Destrée's distinction between a properly philosophical *daimonion* and a mythical *daimōn*. For the most part, so is the evidence in Plato's *Laws*, where the anonymous Athenian character twice refers to the *daimōn* as if it were assumed that everyone has one. In the first case (732c), the Athenian advises us to avoid both excessive laughter and tears, either when "one's guardian spirit" brings prosperity or when in times of trouble "our guardians" struggle to help us through. In the second case (877a), the Athenian considers the case of someone whose luck has saved him from ruin, and refers to the man's "guardian spirit" as if it were assumed that everyone had one. Curiously, and consistent with Socrates's portrait of his *daimonion* from the *Apology*, this *daimōn* serves to prevent its earthly charge from ill-considered actions.

The height of mythical speculation concerning the *daimōn*, however, arrives at the very end of the *Republic*, in the "Myth of Er." Socrates is describing the process of *metempsychosis*, or transmigration of souls. Each soul chooses its next embodied life, which choice it makes with full cognizance of its previous embodied life. Upon choosing their new lives, all the souls process in front of the god Lachesis, who "assign[s] to each the *daimōn* it had chosen as guardian of its life and fulfiller of its choice" (620e). The pairs then travel on, passing a river from which they drink and so "forget everything" in preparation for their new embodiment. In this story, the *daimōn* is a fully external, mythical guide, unaffiliated with any philosophical mission or method. To lead an embodied life, a soul simply requires a *daimōn*, and it is therefore no achievement to have one.

Although Destrée's distinction finds support in these mythical treatments of the *daimōn*, it begins to lose its footing when we consider a final passage, from the *Timaeus*:

> Now we ought to think of the most sovereign part of our soul (*peri tou kyriaōtatou par'hēmin psychēs*) as god's gift to us, given to be our guiding spirit (*hōs ara auto daimona theos hekastôi dedôken*). This, of course, is the type of soul that, as we maintain, resides in the top part of our bodies (*ep'akrôi tôi sômati*). It raises us up away from the earth and toward what is akin to us in heaven (*pros de tēn en ouranôi syngeneian*), as though we are plants grown not from the earth but from heaven. In this, we speak absolutely correctly. For it is from heaven, the place in which our souls were originally born (*hothen hē prôtē tēs psychēs genesis ephu*), that the divine part (*to theion*) suspends our head, i.e., our root (*rizan hēmôn*), and so keeps our whole body erect. (90a)

"The most sovereign part of our soul" is, for Plato, our mind (*nous*) or rational faculty (*to logistikon*)—that which allows us to pursue philosophy and to examine our lives. But here in the *Timaeus* this faculty is explicitly said to have been given to each of us by god, and to be equivalent to our individual *daimōn*. Our kinship is in heaven, and we experience our *daimōn* pulling us homeward, up from the very summit of our bodies. Except that our experience is upside-down: we are in fact not ascending from earth to heaven, but instead *descending*. We are inverted plants, and the *daimōn*, our "divine part" *(to theion)*, is our root. We stand erect, not because our feet are firmly planted, but because we are a flowering plant whose roots are nourished in heaven.

The gap between the experience and the reality of our condition may help explain some of the questions we have been wrestling with. We can presume that very few of us understand that our perspective on reality is inverted (consider that most of us are in Plato's allegorical cave). We can also presume that, according to Plato at least, most of us lead lives of quiet desperation, sadly ignorant of our true root structure. And so although everyone may *have* a *daimōn*—as the "Myth of Er" says, every soul is assigned one prior to embodiment—very few of us know it or at least live our lives in that knowledge, guided by its apotreptic interventions. Socrates, however, did. But did Plato slip, and mean to have Socrates refer to this most sovereign part of our soul as a *daimonion*, not a *daimōn?* I think not. Rather, I think that Plato has Socrates presume to distinguish his knowledge of his own *daimōn* from common knowledge of the same, funded by the traditional myths, precisely by referring to it as *to daimonion sēmeion*, as a divine signpost. Just as a sign points or directs our attention elsewhere, Socrates's divine sign serves to reorient him. Rather than rely on Destrée's sharp distinction between *daimonion* and *daimōn*—which allows modern scholars to maintain a fully rationalist portrait of Socrates and his *daimonion* and to put at a comfortable distance the more traditional, religious connotations of the *daimōn* or guardian spirit—I think it is better to think of Plato over the course of his career as, to borrow from Nietzsche, *revaluing* the tradition of the *daimōn*. Much of the mythology he seems to keep intact: the pairing of every soul and its *daimōn*, and the *daimōn*'s fully divine source. But he wishes to freight that traditional portrait with new meaning, and new urgency: the *daimōn* interrupts our lives with a divine negation (*mē* or "no"), and contradicts what we expect of it.

The voice is not crassly prophetic, telling us what to do when, but instead silences the chatter of our senses and sensibilities, which silence allows us to awaken a slumbering dimension of ourselves: the rational, mindful, "most sovereign part of our souls." What this waking looks like on the ground, of course, is the practice of philosophy, which in its Socratic variety is "elenchic" or contradictory. Thus, the *daimon*'s "no" inaugurates an elenchic philosophy of contradiction, which in turn frees others, namely one's dialectical dueling partners, from the chatter of their own senses and sensibilities. And so it is that Socrates's divine sign or double enables him to serve as a gadfly to each Athenian citizen, and the frustrating *aporia* or impasse into which his elenchic method corners each of them in fact increases the likelihood that they will discover that they too have a *daimōn* and the promise of a divine life to lead.

The botanical figure in *Timaeus* 90a introduces a crucial detail in our deliberations on the divine double. The shift in perspective that the divine sign points toward—that our understanding is upside-down—also suggests that it is not I, here and now, who has a double per se, but rather that I *am* the double, the derivate half of some pair. The plant is *less* real than the root. As if in some nineteenth-century German novel, I discover that *I* am the doppelgänger, that *I* am the image or reflection of someone more solidly real. This ambiguity between original and derivative halves of a pair also finds expression in the tension between descriptions of the *daimōn* as internal or external to the soul. Socrates's *daimonion* is a voice that comes to him or "happens" *(gignetai)*, quite apart from his bidding, and yet no one else hears this unarticulated voice. It is an internal interruption. So too in the *Timaeus* the *daimōn* is said to be in us, "in the top part of our bodies": our mind or *nous*. And yet in other passages—in the spurious dialogue *Theages* in which the *daimōn* is a god to whom one might offer sacrifices, in the *Laws* where it is a guide helping us weather the fortunes of life, or in the Myth of Er where it is assigned to a soul—the *daimōn* appears as an external agent. On precisely this tension, John Rist remarks, "What is inside the soul should be different from what is outside; yet the word *daimon* is used for both."[22] The fact that the *daimōn* is both inside and outside of me, that the *daimōn* is I and yet is not I, is crucial for understanding selfhood as imagined by traditions of the divine double, and, to borrow from Nietzsche again, for taking up the task of becoming what one is.

Lovers, Mirrors, and Mutual Deification: *Phaedrus* and *Alcibiades I*

In Plato's *Phaedrus*, Socrates offers a speech about love to an imagined youth, a beautiful boy who is deciding whether to yield to the attentions of an older man who does not love him or to one who is madly in love with him. Socrates recommends that the youth choose the lovesick madman. To explain why, however, he must offer an elaborate description of the immortal soul and its travels before it descends into a body. We learn that every ten thousand years, all souls participate in a great celestial parade. Gods and immortal souls alike make a winged ascent to the heavens, where they contemplate what lies beyond: "a view of Justice as it is . . . a view of Self-control . . . a view of Knowledge . . . the knowledge of what really is what it is" (247d–e). These eternal intelligibles—the Forms—nourish gods and souls alike. The gods make the ascent without difficulty and are renewed by the contemplation of intelligible reality, but souls must struggle to keep up. The soul that succeeds in becoming "a companion to a god" is nourished enough by the sight of what lies beyond as to keep its wings until the next round. But those many souls who fall behind see their wings shrivel, and they sink to the earth. In the great celestial parade, each soul is in the train of one or another god (for instance, Zeus, Hera, Apollo, Ares). That affiliation persists even as the souls descend into bodies: "everyone spends his life honoring the god in whose chorus he danced" (252d). Descended, embodied souls find vocations appropriate to their incomplete contemplation of intelligible reality: not surprisingly philosophers top that list, followed by kings, statesmen, doctors, priests, poets, and farmers. Sophists are given a place at the bottom of the hierarchy, just above tyrants.

The exact correspondence of godly affiliation and earthly vocation is not spelled out, except to say that followers of Zeus become philosophers (252e): "a soul that has seen the most will be planted in the seed of a man who will become a lover of wisdom or of beauty, or who will be cultivated in the arts and prone to erotic love" (248d). Why is a philosopher "prone to erotic love"? More than any of the other Forms, Beauty shines through even in baser, more material instantiations. When the highest of the descended souls, those few philosophers, see something or someone beautiful, such as a boy, "they are startled when they see an image *(homoiōma)* of what they saw up there. Then they are beside themselves, and their experience is beyond their comprehension because they cannot fully grasp what it is that they are seeing" (250a). Madness and lovesickness in an older man is a sign of the nobility of his soul, a sign of his having once seen more of reality than most. *This* is why a beautiful boy should prefer the attentions of a lovesick madman to those of a cool but distant admirer: the lover knows the real, and both lover and beloved gain by standing in its radiance.

But before we examine how the pair—lover and beloved—stand to gain, we should pan back and remember an earlier pairing. The failed companionship but persistent affiliation between a god and a soul is the vertical axis of the divine double. We are each here now because we could not manage to be "a companion to a god." Had we managed, we would have been sustained, as the gods are, by a vision of the intelligible Forms. Socrates would have us each now seek out a horizontal double: the lover a beloved, the beloved a lover. Just as in the tradition of the *daimōn*, we witness an important relationship between the vertical and the horizontal axes of doubling. Let us attend more closely to the horizontal axis as imagined in the *Phaedrus*. Socrates tells us,

> Everyone chooses his love after his own fashion from among those who are beautiful, and then treats the boy like his very own god, building him up and adorning him as an image *(hoion agalma)* to honor and worship. Those who followed Zeus, for example, choose someone to love who is a Zeus himself in nobility of his soul. (252d–e)

The lover, in other words, finds an appropriate match: a soul like Zeus finds another soul like Zeus. He treats the beloved "as if" he were an "image" or "statue" *(hoion agalma)* of Zeus himself.[23] What might appear as shameful doting on a young man is in fact, according to Socrates, a practice of devotion to the god:

> They take their god's path and seek for their own a boy whose nature is like the god's; and when they have got him they emulate the god, convincing the boy whom they love and training him to follow their god's pattern and way of life, so far as is possible in each case . . . [they] make every possible effort to draw him into being totally like themselves and the god to whom they are devoted. (253b–c)

It is because of the lover's "driving need to gaze at the god" that he finds a beloved who is like that god and trains him to be even more divine, "so far as is possible." So the failed vertical axis of doubling (companionship to a god, access to intelligible reality) sets up the horizontal axis of lover and beloved: the earthly pair, in turn, allows for mutual deification, and so the horizontal companionship promises to restore the failed vertical companionship.

Finally the lover's gaze at the beloved, and so at the god, finds its own counterpart. Socrates explains that over time the lover's desire fills him so completely that it spills over and affects the beloved himself. Appealing to a more ethereal (but reversed) metaphor, Socrates says, "Think how a breeze or an echo bounces back from a smooth solid object to its source; that is how the stream of beauty goes back to the beautiful boy and sets him aflutter." Just as the beauty of the beloved entered the eyes of the lover, and so set him aflame with desire, now the desire "bounces back" *(anterôta)* and enters the beloved's own eyes. He is infected with desire: "It is as if he had caught an eye disease from someone else, but could not identify the cause; he does not realize that he is seeing himself in the lover as in a mirror *(hōsper de en katoptrōi)*" (255d). The figure of the mirror appears in subsequent traditions of the divine double, including Mani and Plotinus (who also has Narcissus in mind). Here in the *Phaedrus* we have quite literally a play of mirrors. The beloved, groomed as a likeness *(homoiōma)* of the god for his lover to behold, comes to see himself reflected in that lover as in mirror *(hōsper de en katoptrōi)*—all the while both of them increasingly conforming to the god himself. The horizontal dimension thus serves to further the vertical mirroring of god and their two souls—all with the aim of their restoration to divinity, and thereby their access to intelligible reality.

We find a similar pattern in *Alcibiades I*, a dialogue whose authenticity scholars continue to debate.[24] It was very likely penned, if not by Plato himself, then by someone in his school shortly after his death. Socrates's partner in this dialogue is the handsome and notorious Athenian aristocrat and statesman, who appears here as a man about to make his bold entrance into politics, brimming with confidence. Most modern readers are familiar with Alcibiades from his famous, drunken appearance in the *Symposium*. But here he is sober, as is the dialogue that bears his name. Indeed, one of the reasons scholars have doubted that Plato wrote this dialogue is its relative clarity and simplicity. But for precisely this reason the Platonic tradition, especially in late antiquity, regarded it as the perfect place for a student to begin the study of Plato's dialogues.[25] As such, regardless of its authenticity, it was widely read and therefore widely influential throughout our period.

We pick up the thread of the conversation near the end, where Alcibiades and Socrates are discussing their shared need for self-cultivation.[26] Socrates confesses to an anxiety: How do we know that we are properly cultivating ourselves if we do not know ourselves, that is, what we are?

> *Socrates:* Well, then, could we ever know what skill makes us better if we didn't know what *we* were *(agnoountes ti' pot'esmen autoi)?*
> *Alcibiades:* We couldn't.
> *Socrates:* Is it actually such an easy thing to know oneself *(to gnōnai heauton)?* Was it some simpleton who inscribed those words on the temple wall at Delphi? Or is it difficult, and not for everybody? . . . this is the situation we're in: if we know ourselves, then we might be able to know how to cultivate ourselves *(tēn epimeleian hēmōn autōn)*, but if we don't know ourselves *(agnoountes)*, we'll never know how.

> ... Tell me, how can we come to know the self itself *(auto tauto)*? Maybe this is the way to find out what we ourselves are *(ti pot'esmen autoi)*—maybe it's the only possible way. (128e–129b)

The imperative "Know thyself" *(gnōthi seauton)* was inscribed on the wall of the temple of Apollo at Delphi (the same oracle that pronounced that no one was wiser than Socrates), along with the saying "Nothing in excess" *(mēden agan)*. Classical sources imagine this self-knowledge to be largely a knowledge of limits; in Shadi Bartsch's words, "know your measure, know what you can and cannot do, know your place, know the limits of your wisdom, know your faults, know that you are mortal."[27] But Plato has Socrates bend the dictum in a new direction: we are to know "the self itself" *(auto tauto)* and "what we ourselves are" *(ti pot'esmen autoi)*.

But instead of keeping with the phrase *auto to auto* (or in its contracted form, *auto tauto*), Socrates takes a pass at answering a slightly different question, "What then *is* a human?" Three options present themselves: the human is a body, a soul, or "the two of them together *(synamphoteron)*, the whole thing" (130a). Socrates quickly dispatches the first and third options and concludes, "what remains, I think, is either that [the human] is nothing, or else, if he *is* something, he's nothing other than his soul . . . Do you need any clearer proof that the soul is the man?" (130c). Lloyd Gerson's categories are again helpful here. One could say that Socrates is now searching for a definition of the person rather than the human. Our endowed humanity, which is to say the "human condition," is quite obviously the third option, the *synamphoteron* or "composite" of soul and body. By contrast, Socrates is interested in our achieved personhood, what we *really* are (or really could and should be), and he "proves" that, at root, we are our souls. This is a very swift proof indeed, but it seems to suffice for Socrates's purposes. He acknowledges that he and Alcibiades have skipped over the question of "what the self itself is" *(eiē auto to auto)* and instead have examined "what a particular self is" *(auto hekaston . . . hoti esti)*. At this point it seems that Socrates abandons the quest for the "self itself" and is satisfied with an examination of the "particular self," which is equivalent to "what we ourselves are."

Curiously, the *auto to auto* seems to fall away from the discussion at this point.[28]

Socrates seems satisfied with the result of his definition of the human—or rather, of the *person*—as essentially a soul: "Perhaps that was enough for us, for surely nothing in us has more authority *(kyriōteron)* than the soul, wouldn't you agree?" (130d). The adjective *kyriōteron* is the same Socrates uses in *Timaeus* 90a to describe a part of the soul, namely "the most sovereign . . . god's gift to us, given to be our guiding spirit *(daimona)*." Whether the author of this dialogue means to have Socrates allude to the *daimōn* here is unclear—we will return to it below. What is clear is that Socrates's inquiry into "what we ourselves are" has yielded him a working definition of the person as essentially a soul. And this permits him to revise the Delphic dictum accordingly: "the command that we should know ourselves means that we should know our souls" (130e).

Back to self-cultivation and the relationship of lover and beloved. Precisely because the soul is the defining feature of any person, if a lover were to love Alcibiades's body (or even his body and soul together), Socrates insists, then he would not really love Alcibiades the person. Only the lover of the soul can be said to love someone:

> But someone who loves your soul will not leave you, as long as you're making progress . . . Well, I'm the one who won't leave you—I'm the one who will stay with you, now that your body has lost its bloom and everyone else has gone away . . . So this is your situation: you, Alcibiades, son of Clinias, have no lovers and never have had any, it seems, except for one only *(heis monos)*, and he is your darling Socrates, son of Sophroniscus and Phaenarete. (131d)

Socrates announces himself as the *singular* double of Alcibiades, the only one who will not leave him, will remain with him past his body's bloom. Their companionship is grounded in his love of the beloved's soul.

But how is it that Socrates might come to "know himself," that is to say, his own soul, by knowing and loving Alcibiades?

> *Socrates:* I'll tell you what I suspect the inscription means, and what advice it's giving us. There may not be many examples of it, except the case of sight.
> *Alcibiades:* What do you mean by that?
> *Socrates:* You think about it, too. If the inscription took our eyes to be men and advised them, "See thyself," how would we understand such advice? Shouldn't the eye be looking at something in which it can see itself?
> *Alcibiades:* Obviously.
> *Socrates:* Let's think of something that allows us to see both it and ourselves when we look at it.
> *Alcibiades:* Obviously, Socrates, you mean mirrors *(katoptrōi)* and that sort of thing. (132d–e)

Even the dullard Alcibiades sees what Socrates is driving at: our only analogy to self-knowledge is self-vision, and for that we require a mirror. But rather than pick up the nearest mirror, Socrates instead advises a course of action that further cements his relationship with his beloved. The pair needs no artificial instrument, for they each already have a mirror:

> *Socrates:* . . . And isn't there something like that in the eye, which we see with?
> *Alcibiades:* Certainly.
> *Socrates:* I'm sure you've noticed that when a man looks into an eye his face appears in it, like in a mirror *(hōsper en katoptrōi)*. We call this the 'pupil' *(korē)*, for it's a sort of miniature *(eidōlon)* of the man who's looking. (132e)

The eye is not so much the window into the soul of the beloved as a mirror of the soul of the lover himself. Looking into the beloved's eye—at the pupil to be exact—the lover sees himself reflected in miniature *(eidōlon)*. But of course this is an analogy, for the lover is in fact supposed to look at the beloved's soul, not the eye: "Then if the soul, Alcibiades, is to know itself, it must look at a soul, and especially at that region *(topon)* in which what makes a soul good, wisdom, occurs, and at anything else which is similar to it" (133b). Just as the eye has a pupil, so the soul has a "region," its best part *(beltiston)*, than which nothing is "more divine" *(theioteron)*, namely "the part in which knowing and thinking *(to eidenai te kai phronein)* take place" (133c). In fact, "this part of [the soul] resembles the divine *(tōi theōi)*, and someone who looked at it and grasped everything divine *(pan to theion gnous)*—vision and intelligence *(thean te kai phronēsin)*—would have the best grasp of himself as well" (133c).[29] To behold the best part of the soul of another is to behold all that is divine, and to behold such is to behold and comprehend oneself, as if in a mirror, as if seeing oneself reflected in the pupil of another's eye.

Shadi Bartsch has drawn attention to *Alcibiades I* and the theme of mirroring in Plato in her book *The Mirror of the Self*. According to her, classical and Hellenistic antiquity produced two dominant, but contradictory, moralizing discourses on mirrors and the self-reflection they made possible. On the one hand, mirrors were thought to be tools of vain self-cultivation used mostly by women and "associated (negatively) with luxury, effeminization, and a profitless love of self."[30] On the other hand, the philosophical tradition appealed to the mirror as a tool for moral self-cultivation, something that allowed for "dislocation" and "self-splitting": the viewer became simultaneously the viewing subject and viewed object.[31] This allowed the viewer to take up the arch, moralizing perspective of the community, and to discern his own flaws therefrom. This second tradition was traced back to Socrates, whom Diogenes Laertius credits with recommending "to the young the constant use of the mirror, to the end that handsome men might acquire a corresponding behavior, and ugly men conceal their defects by education."[32] Curiously, however, Plato has Socrates appeal to the mirror in a way that breaks with this twofold tradition. In *Alcibiades I*, instead of the mirror making possible a preening, ocular self-cultivation (à la Diogenes Laertius's Socrates), we witness "the idea of reflection as an impersonal way for us to 'see' the divine in all of us."[33]

> Just as the *gnothi sauton* is now taken to mean something beyond the idea of knowing the limits of one's abilities, so too the act of mirroring is no longer merely a reflection of standards of community judgment, but something that transcends what one's

peers might have to say. As such, it echoes the altered concept of self-knowledge that informs Plato's dialogues from the *Phaedrus* on, what A. A. Long has called "Plato's extraordinary answer to the self-model question . . . : Make yourself as like as possible to God."[34]

This "vertical form of mirroring in the divine" is a Platonic innovation, also attributed to Socrates, but one that does not supplant the other two moralizing discourses. Bartsch traces this revolution in reflectivity from its Platonic origins through early imperial Roman thought to Seneca. She acknowledges the omission of any discussion of "the Church fathers," and we might add of any of the religious literature of the Eastern Mediterranean, Christian or otherwise. I take this acknowledgment as an invitation to carry the conversation forward from Plato to the religious and philosophical landscape of late antiquity.

Let us return, in conclusion, to a possible allusion to the *Timaeus*. Recall that in *Alcibiades 1*, 130d, Socrates says that nothing has "more authority" *(kyriōteron)* than the soul. In the *Timaeus*, *kyriōteron* names a particular part of the soul, the "most sovereign," which is none other than the *daimōn* or "guiding spirit." Later in *Alcibiades I*, the best part of the soul is said to "resemble the divine" (133c). So too in the *Timaeus*, the *daimōn* is our "divine part" *(to theion)*, and the part that raises us up "toward what is akin to us in heaven" (90a). These two accounts are quite apposite. We each have within us a divine double, a better self. According to one account (*Timaeus*, drawing on the portrait of the *daimonion* in the *Apology*), we meet that divine double as a *daimōn*, something that is both internal and external to us, guiding us toward our "whence," our proper kinship in heaven, from whose roots we descend like an inverted plant. Once we meet this vertical double and recognize our kinship with the *daimōn* (or *daimonion*), we are able to serve as helpmates to others, as horizontal doubles to other isolated halves. According to the other account (*Phaedrus* and *Alcibiades I*), we each instead begin by finding a horizontal double, another isolated half. We each come to see in the soul of the other, as if in a mirror, a reflection of our own souls, our own vertical doubles, and we each increasingly become what we see. This mutual deification eventually dissolves the differences between the two horizontal doubles: lover and beloved each become divine, and so their roles can be exchanged, but not replaced. This is exactly where *Alcibiades I* concludes, with the notorious statesman making a promise we know he will not fulfill: "We're probably going to change roles, Socrates. I'll be playing yours and you'll be playing mine, for from this day forward I will always attend on you, and you will have me as your constant companion" (135d). We know, however, that this is not how Alcibiades will end his days, that he will break this pledge and fall very far short of deification—and this injects a measure of tragedy into the heady confidence of *Phaedrus* and *Alcibiades I*. Love should, but does not, render the two one, as one might hope on both the horizontal and vertical axes.

Aristophanes's Tragic Tale of Division

Alcibiades makes his most conspicuous appearance in the *Symposium*, where he crashes a party celebrating Agathon's victory at the Dionysia. Agathon's friends, including Socrates, had gathered at his home to toast his success and to give speeches in praise of love or *erōs*. Socrates's speech, or rather his ventriloquism of the seer Diotima of Mantinea, is the most famous. But before his speech comes an "absurd" *(geloia)*, even "ridiculous" *(katagelasta)*, tale from the mouth of the comedian Aristophanes, and one that has much to do with doubles.[35] Aristophanes begins by telling us how different our human nature once was. There used to be not two but three genders: male, female, and androgyne. And each individual was a four-armed, four-legged circular creature with two sets of genitals, topped by a single head with two faces, one on either side. An individual could be gendered thoroughly male (the sons of the sun), thoroughly female (daughters of the earth), or mixed, that is to say androgynous (offspring of the moon). We used to get about by walking, or if in a rush, by gangly cartwheels. Ridiculous as it may seem, we posed a threat to the Olympian gods by trying to storm heaven. Zeus sought the counsel of his colleagues and decided not to smite us, but instead to split us in two. With his lightning bolts Zeus cut each of us down the middle, diminishing our strength, doubling our numbers, and in so doing also doubling the worship he and the other gods receive from us: "He cut those human beings in two, the way people cut sorb-apples before they dry them or the way they cut eggs with hairs" (190c).

Zeus then enlisted the help of Apollo, who playing the plastic surgeon stitched up the gory remains of these half-humans into what we are today. He turned the face of each of us around to face our wound, which he stitched up into a navel, so that we might remember our folly and remain in line. Here is how each "dividual," so to speak, reacted to this punishment:[36]

> Now, since their natural form had been cut in two, each one longed for its own other half, and so they would throw their arms about each other, weaving themselves together, wanting to grow together. In that condition they would die from hunger and general idleness, because they would not do anything apart from each other. Whenever one of the halves died and one was left, the one that was left still sought another and wove itself together with that. Sometimes the half he met came from a woman, as we'd call her now, sometimes it came from a man; either way, they kept on dying. (191a–b)

This sad state of affairs was hardly the solution Zeus was looking for: humans, divided and docile as they now were, could not offer the gods worship if they were dying off. He devised a new solution: he moved their genitals around to their front, like their faces. Whereas before we reproduced by spreading our seed in the earth, now some men sowed seeds in women (these heterosexual couples being the primordial androgynes), while some men enjoyed sex with men, and some women with women. The "satisfaction of intercourse" and (for those who reproduced) the needs of children stemmed the tide of our despair, so that we would care to live at all. Our desire for each other, therefore, saved the species: "Love is born into every human being; it calls back the halves of our original nature together; it tries to make one out of two and heal the wound of human nature" (191d).

Aristophanes adds to the images of our doubling: we are not only cut apples or sliced eggs, but "each of us, then, is a 'matching half' (*symbolon*) of a human whole, because each was sliced like a flatfish, two out of one" (191d). In this case, a *symbolon* is a token to ensure recognition of contracting parties. A knucklebone or die is broken in two, and each contracting party is given one half. The bone breaks irregularly, uniquely, and so the *symbolon* then serves as proof of the identities of both parties to the contract. We are like that, Aristophanes says, broken irregularly and uniquely, "and each of us is always seeking the half that matches him" (191d). And when a *symbolon* finds its match, when "a person meets the half that is his very own . . . the two are struck from their senses by love, by a sense of belonging to one another, and by desire, and they don't want to be separated from one another, not even for a moment" (192b–c).

In this absurd tale, it is the gods who thwart our unity and wholeness, out of fear that we may be a threat to their sovereignty. The divine is therefore jealous of unity in this allegory, and punishes us with division and doubling, and the threat of further doubling. Zeus storms, "They shall walk upright on two legs. But if I find they still run riot and do not keep the peace, I will cut them in two again, and they'll have to make their way on one leg, hopping" (190d). Here the horizontal axis—lovesick twins seeking each other out—is a consequence of and consolation for the violence of the vertical axis. We are caught between threat and promise: the threat that "we'll be split in two again" (193a) and "the greatest hope of all: if we treat the gods with due reverence, [Love] will restore to us our original nature, and by healing us, he will make us blessed and happy" (193d). *This* is why we must praise love, Aristophanes says, because only love promises to "make one out of two and heal the wound of human nature" (191d).

But is this a promise that love can keep? Can love make the two one? Let us take the most encouraging case: two halves who have found each other and are bound together by love and desire. Aristophanes says that even such a couple as this "cannot say what it is they want from one another" (192c). Clearly they each want more than sex—but what exactly they cannot say: "but like an oracle [the soul of every lover] has a sense of what it wants, and like an oracle it hides behind a riddle" (192d). The riddle turns out to be another tale within this tale:

Suppose two lovers are lying together and Hephaestus stands over them with his mending tools, asking, "What is it you human beings really want from each other?" And suppose they're perplexed, and he asks them again: "Is this your heart's desire *(epithumeite)*, then—for the two of you to become parts of the same whole, as near as can be, and never to separate, day or night? Because if that's your desire *(epithumeite)*, I'd like to weld you together *(syntēxai)* and join you *(synphusēsai)* into something that is naturally whole, so that the two of you are made into one *(hōste du'ontas hena gegonenai)*. Then the two of you would share one life, as long as you lived, because you would be one being *(hōs hena onta)*, and by the same token, when you died, you would be one and not two in Hades, having died a single death. Look at your love, and see if this is what you desire: wouldn't this be all the good fortune you could want? (192d–e)

The lovers are not allowed to answer for themselves. Instead Aristophanes answers for them the question Hephaestus posed for them: "Everyone would think he'd found out at last what he had always wanted: to come together and melt together with the one he loves, so that one person emerged from the two *(ek dyoin heis genesthai)*" (192e). However, the promise of unity—of making the two one— remains embedded in a series of conditionals and subjunctives, ifs and woulds. The promise of a god who offers to heal the wound inflicted by another god in fact goes unfulfilled. But even hedged in conditionals and subjunctives, the promise serves to maintain hope, and hope serves to ensure reverence *(eusebeian)* of the gods, and praise for love.

And so the god's offer amounts to only that—an offer. He gives voice to the lovers' ineffable desire, but then does not deliver on it. In other words, this question of a god set to right the wrong of another god is left open, with the suggestion that the two are in fact never made one, that the god offers what he will not, or perhaps *cannot*, deliver. Aristophanes concludes his speech by begging Eryximachus not to "make a comedy of it" (193d). One could interpret him to mean that he wished Eryximachus not to ridicule it. Or one could interpret him to mean that Eryximachus should not mistake this absurd, ridiculous tale for a comedy. And what is comedy? Not, as it has come to mean for us, something funny. But rather something that has a happy ending. However humorous Aristophanes's story may be, we should not think it has a happy ending—the healing of the ancient wound, the restoration of unity from division. For where, after all, does it leave the lovers but with a picture of the human condition as unavoidably two-in-one: cut asunder, cloven, two halves of a former whole—suffering from a wound inflicted by one god and irreparable by another. Even if we chance upon our other half, our most heartfelt wish—union—remains ineffable and impossible. We continue to stand or lie opposite each other, offering each other our bodies for embrace, bodies marked by wounds, marked as a threat by a navel and as a false promise of union by genitals. It is, ultimately, a tragic vision of love, delivered by Athens's most celebrated comedian.

Aristophanes injects a dose of tragic realism into the bloodstream of the tradition of the divine double. Plato's handling of Socrates's *daimonion* and his treatment of lovers as mirrors that enable mutual deification both project an image of the vertical axis of doubling—the human and the divine—as being closely aligned with the horizontal axis, between two humans. Both suggest that the division and differentiation that obtain here and now can be overcome in the pursuit of union and deification. But in Aristophanes's absurd tragedy, the two axes are set against each other from the very start. The gods divide humanity as they jealously protect their thrones on high. Division is a punishment, and as a consequence doubling is a sort of rehabilitation. By permitting us to live our lives with our other halves, the gods grant us a measure of union. But this persistent two-in-oneness or "bi-unity" serves them as much as it does us. There is no happy ending to this tragedy, no certain healing of the ancient wound, no rendering the two one. And if Aristophanes tells of the impossibility of being one in an absurd, even ridiculous allegory, Plato himself narrates a similar truth in an entirely antithetical idiom: for that, we must turn to the *Parmenides*.

Parmenides and the Impossibility of (Being) the One

The *Parmenides* is a late and notoriously difficult dialogue. It falls into two parts, so much so that some scholars in the past have wondered whether it was perhaps stitched together from two shorter pieces. Most scholars today, however, regard it as coherent, and as one of Plato's "most important" and also "most enigmatic" dialogues.[37] The first part starts familiarly enough: Socrates, although here a youth, appears as the principal interrogator, in this case of his elder, the philosopher Zeno (of paradox fame). From earlier dialogues we fully expect Socrates to play the ironic insurgent and to reduce his interlocutor to *aporia* or impasse. But instead the philosopher Parmenides, elder to both of them, steps in and schools Socrates in dialectic, humiliating him by demonstrating that he is immature and has had too little training in dialectic to be forwarding any strong theory of the Forms.

It is fitting that the ancient subtitle to the *Parmenides* is "On Forms," because much of what Socrates forwards and Parmenides critiques is reminiscent of Plato's earlier, "middle" dialogues (*Phaedo* and *Republic*, for example), in which the Forms serve as the linchpin in many of Socrates's arguments. Having heard the young Socrates forward his theory of the Forms, Parmenides gives him a dose of his own ironic medicine: "Socrates, you are much to be admired for your keenness of argument! Tell me. Have you yourself distinguished as separate *(chōris)*, in the way you mention, certain Forms themselves *(eidē auta)*, and also as separate the things that partake of them *(ta toutōn hau metechonta)*?" (130b). Much will hinge on this notion of the "separation" between the Forms and their participants, a separation that could be understood to mean their being merely distinct, or their existing apart in space and time, or their ontological independence.[38] Parmenides will exploit the different meanings of separation as he find the joints in the armor of Socrates's argument, eventually reducing him to the sort of stammering befuddlement we are accustomed to Socrates himself bringing out in others.

Parmenides raises no less than six distinct objections, but to survey them all would take too much space here.[39] One thread that runs throughout Parmenides's sixfold examination is Socrates's failure to give a satisfactory account of "participation" (*metalambanein, methexein, koinonia*), that is, how sensible reality participates in the unchanging, intelligible reality of Forms. This persistent failure leads to the final and most worrisome consequence of Socrates's view, according to Parmenides, namely the utter separation of things here (sensible reality) from the Forms (intelligible reality). The worry is that Socrates has devised two parallel but isolated and unrelated worlds, our human world of sensible objects and the divine world of intelligible objects. The two worlds are not only distinct but also ontologically independent. The result is mutual incomprehension and irrelevance: the gods cannot know or master our world, and we cannot know or master theirs (134a–e). If there are Forms, "they must by strict necessity be unknowable *(agnōsta)* to human nature" (135a). Our knowledge of the things around us and their characters, including ourselves, does not rise to the level of true knowledge or *epistēmē*, but remains incomplete opinion or *doxa*. What "knowledge" we do have of the here and how is nebulous and fuzzy: the observable characters of things are, in Mary Louise Gill's words, "imprecise because they are determined as what they are, not by fixed relations to unchanging Forms (which we might call 'vertical causality'), but by their changing relations to other things in our realm (what we might call a 'horizontal causality')."[40]

On the one hand, Parmenides succeeds in having Socrates acknowledge that "the forms inevitably involve these objections and a host of others besides" (135a). But on the other hand, Parmenides himself concedes that if one were simply to dispense with the Forms altogether, one "wouldn't have anywhere to turn his thought *(tēn dianoian)*, since he doesn't allow that for each thing there is a character *(idean)* that is always the same. In this way he will destroy the power of dialectic entirely *(tēn tou dialegesthai dynamin)*" (135b–c). What hangs in the balance, then, is this: Socrates's understanding of the Forms risks the strict separation of the human and divine worlds, the loss of the vertical axis of causality, participation, and so deification; but without some theory of Forms we cannot be certain that things have a permanent character or form *(idea)*, and thus our thinking *(dianoia)* would be disoriented and dialectical reasoning *(to dialegesthai)* destroyed.

There is a debate as to whether these criticisms Plato has Parmenides put to Socrates signal his abandonment of the theory of Forms, and thus of the metaphysical architecture that we have come to call "Platonic," or whether they are his effort to salvage and refine that theory by subjecting it to rigorous critique. We need not decide between these two interpretations, although I am much inclined to the latter. Suffice it to say that the consequences of Parmenides's criticisms extend to our focus on the divine double, both the figure of the *daimōn* and also lovers' pursuit of mutual deification. These confident threads would unravel if, as Parmenides worries, the sensible and intelligible worlds were mutually incomprehensible, irrelevant, and inaccessible. Without the vertical axis, there can be no divine double. In other words, if participation fails to lash the sensible to the intelligible world, then we are left as prisoners in the cave, with no hope of rescue. No wonder, then, that Parmenides calls this sixth and final objection "the greatest difficulty of all" (133a).

This impasse is the hinge in the dialogue between its first and second parts. Parmenides tells Socrates that the reason he is unable to reply to his criticisms is that he has tried to forward a theory of Forms before he has been "properly trained" *(gymnasthēnai)* (136d). The second half of the dialogue is a sort of training session *(gymnasia)*, in a particular dialectical method:

> And, in a word, concerning whatever you might ever hypothesize as being or as not being or as having any other property, you must examine the consequences for the thing you hypothesize in relation to itself and in relation to each of the others, whichever you select, and in relation to several of them and to all of them in the same way; and in turn, you must examine the others, both in relation to themselves and in relation to whatever other thing you select on each occasion, whether what you hypothesize you hypothesize as being or as not being. All this you must do, if, after completing your training, you are to achieve a full view of the truth. (136b–c)

Not surprisingly, Socrates says that he does not understand the description of this method, and that even if he did, he would think it "scarcely manageable" (136c). He therefore pleads for someone to perform the exercise first so that he might learn. After some resistance, Parmenides himself agrees "to play this strenuous game" and opts to take up one of his own hypotheses having to do with "the one itself" and "if it is one or if it is not one" (137b).

Earlier in the dialogue, Socrates says to Parmenides, "You say in your poem that the all is one *(hen phēs einai to pan)*, and you give splendid and excellent proofs for that" (128a–b). In the surviving fragments of the historical Parmenides's poem in hexameter verse, however, we find no such phrase, "the all is one," nor any discussion of the consequences of "the one itself . . . if it is one or if it is not."[41] But in this staged encounter by Plato, Parmenides's dialectical examination of his own (alleged) hypothesis regarding the one and its consequences is meant precisely to push Socrates on the question of whether any Form is itself one or indeed many. The examination yields no less than eight deductions: half of whose hypotheses are positive, half negative; half of whose subject is "the one," half the "others"; half of whose consequences are positive, half negative.[42] This dizzying display of dialectic promises to yield "a full view of the truth" (136c). Quite how is unclear. Is Plato parodying other philosophers? Or does he mean this exercise to yield precisely what Parmenides promises it will?[43] Scholars argue endlessly about whether and how this exercise delivers on Parmenides's promise.

Thankfully I have a different aim in mind. It is less crucial that I speculate along with the specialists about whether and how Plato, late in his career, intended to salvage (or indeed to discard) his own theory of Forms. Suffice to note, first, that Plato has introduced a threat to the very metaphysical architecture that undergirds the tradition of the divine double, this threat Parmenides calls "the greatest difficulty" (133a). The same anxiety with which Aristophanes leaves his audience in his absurd tragedy, therefore, reappears here in the *Parmenides* in metaphysical garb. Second, we must acknowledge that we moderns are not alone in being stumped by the second part of this dialogue. The subsequent Platonist tradition—perhaps most famously Plotinus—focuses instead on the revelatory quality of the first two or three deductions, which Plotinus takes to be a description of the three hypostases—One, Mind, and Soul (*hen, nous, psychē*).[44] We shall have much to say about Plotinus and his three (or at least two) hypostases in Chapter 5. For the time being we will follow his lead and focus our attention on just the first two of the eight deductions. For they can be read as something of a philosophical allegory bearing directly on the tradition of the divine double, and raising, in an even more acute way than Aristophanes's thrilling yarn, the question of the impossibility of (being) the one.

The first and second deductions both have positive and similar (but not identical) hypotheses. The first deduction proceeds with the hypothesis "If (the one is) one" *(ei hen estin)*; the second with "If the one is" *(hen ei estin)*. The slight difference in word order and sense is, as we will come to see, of enormous philosophical significance. Without going into too much detail about the nature of the Greek verb "to be," Plato's own peculiar views of this verb (especially in the *Sophist*), or more contemporary philosophical debates about identity versus predication, perhaps it is best to convey the difference between these two hypotheses simply with italics. The first supposes "the one itself," but specified in a particular way, namely as *one*—hence the emphasis "If (the one is) *one*." The second supposes whether (but not how) "the one" *is* at all—hence the emphasis "If the one *is*." The two deductions consider the consequences of each hypothesis, but with antithetical results.

Considered from the perspective of its sheer oneness, Parmenides argues, the one is neither a whole nor a part, neither in itself nor in another (and therefore is not anywhere), neither at rest nor in motion, neither the same nor different from itself or another, neither like nor unlike itself or another, neither greater nor less than itself or another, neither partakes of nor is in time; and—finally—"the one neither is one nor is" *(to hen oute hen estin oute estin)* (142e). This conclusion seems to contradict the hypothesis, "If (the one) is one." This contradiction can be softened somewhat by thinking of the conclusion, again in italics, as "the one neither *is* the one nor *is*"—in which case the result is to deny that the one has existence of any sort. But does some notion of "is," however confused or confusing, survive so that the hypothesis may remain as it is? Here is Gill's summary of where we stand:

We are left with a puzzle at the end of the first deduction. If the one is considered as what it is solely in virtue of itself, can it *be* (timelessly) one without partaking of a character other than its own? What is the function of being, which connects the one to its character? Is it *by being* as well as *by oneness* that the one is one? If so, then the conclusion of the first deduction stands [and contradicts the hypothesis]. If the one is considered as what it is solely in virtue of itself, it cannot even be one.[45]

And here is Plato's more colorful, but no less confusing, summary, on the lips of Parmenides and his young interlocutor:

> "Therefore no name belongs to [the one], nor is there an account or any knowledge or perception or opinion of it . . . Therefore it is not named nor spoken of, nor is it the object of opinion or knowledge, nor does anything that is perceive it."—"It seems not."—"Is it possible that these things are so for the one?"—"I certainly don't think so." (142a)

Whether there is some notion of being (as self-predication) that allows us to maintain the hypothesis "If (the one is) one" *and* yet allows the one still to transcend being (as existence), or not, remains an open question, an unsolved puzzle. Regardless, Parmenides concludes this first deduction not so much in floundering *aporia* as in confident *arrēsia*, the inability to speak or name the object of his inquiry. And this speechlessness is paired with an irony heightened by his final question, "Is it possible *(dynaton)* that these things are so for the one?" This amounts to asking whether it is possible that it is impossible that the one (be) one.

If the one, considered from the perspective of its oneness, is beyond being and time, and so beyond name or knowledge, perception or opinion—is, in short, impossible—what of the one considered from the perspective of being? In other words, what "if the one *is* *(hen ei estin)*"? In the second deduction, Parmenides introduces a distinction, then, between the one and the being of the one. The one-that-is, the object of the second hypothesis, is thus a whole composed of two parts, oneness and being. The one-that-is "always proves to be two... never one" (142e). Each part, oneness and being, is itself composed of two parts, again oneness and being. Thus, the one-that-is divides itself infinitely and is "unlimited in multitude" (143a). Furthermore, even if we consider the one-that-is apart from its being, it is only so by being different from its being, and can only be different by participating in difference. And so not even this one-that-is is one, because in order to stand apart from its being as oneness, it must partake of difference, and thereby be two. For every "neither-nor" in the first deduction we find a "both-and" in the second. The one-that-is is both one and many, a whole and parts, limited and unlimited, same and different, like and unlike. Whereas the one (that is) one *(ei hen estin)* turned out to be "nothing at all, not even itself," the one that is *(hen ei estin)* turns out to be "everything indiscriminately."[46]

The conclusions of the first and second deductions clearly contradict each other. But this contradicts the so-called law of noncontradiction: an object cannot be x and not x. The one cannot be nothing and everything at the same time. The appendix (155e–157b) to the first two deductions tries to resolve this contradiction by suggesting that the two deductions are descriptions of the one in two different states, one state (call it oneness) in which it does not partake of being, and another state (call it being) when it does. How does the one change from one state to another, from oneness to being and back again? Not in time, that is for certain, because oneness does not occur in time, and so cannot change into being in time. The solution is a "queer thing" *(to atopon touto)*: the instant.

> The instant *(to exaiphnēs)* seems to signify something such that changing occurs from it to each of the two states. For a thing doesn't change from rest while rest continues, or from motion while motion continues. Rather, this queer creature, the instant *(hē exaiphnēs hautē physis atopos)*, lurks between motion and rest—being in no time at all—and to it and from it the moving thing changes to resting, and the resting thing changes to the moving. (156d–e)

The argument regarding motion and rest is then applied to being and nonbeing. There is something called the instant or "the sudden," a time outside of time wherein the one changes from "not-being" *(to mē einai)* to "coming-to-be" *(to gignesthai)*, when it transitions from its state of oneness to its state of being. In this instant, the one neither is nor is not. While it rescues the first two deductions from violating the law of noncontradiction, this "solution" violates the so-called law of the excluded middle: for any proposition, either that proposition is true or its negation is true. Here, in the instant, this law does not hold: neither the proposition "the one is" nor its negation "the one is not" is true.

But what has any of this to do with the divine double? We have already seen how the criticisms that Parmenides brings to bear on Socrates's theory of the Forms reveal that this theory runs the risk of dividing the universe into two unrelated worlds, the world of sensible reality and the world of intelligible reality (the Forms). Unless Socrates is able to respond to these criticisms, especially with a robust notion of participation, then, it is thought, we are cut off from the world of the Forms and, by extension, from our divine double. One would be unable to discern the voice of one's *daimōn* or to become ever more like our "divine part" *(to theion)*. When one looked into one's beloved's eyes, one would not see there the "best part" *(beltiston)* of the soul, that than which nothing is "more divine" *(theioteron)*. We would be held down to the horizontal axis and unable to lift ourselves up and "grasp everything divine" *(pan to theion gnous)*. This is where the first part of the *Parmenides* leaves us, anxious about our efforts and our access. And this is exactly where Aristophanes leaves us, anxious whether the gods will, or even can, restore us from duality to unity.

The second part of the *Parmenides* is, at least on one reading, supposed to salvage the theory of Forms and rescue us from this unwelcome anxiety. Whether it does or does not succeed in so salvaging I cannot say. Instead of taking it as a solution to the problems posed by Socrates's theory of the Forms, I would like to take the second part—specifically its first two deductions and concluding appendix—as a sort of philosophical allegory, not so much about the Forms as about us. What is this allegory trying to teach us about us and about our divine double? If we are each of us already doubled, one half human and one half divine, then the first deduction teaches us that the union of our two halves is impossible. Strictly speaking, it cannot *be*. For the one to be one, it cannot partake of being. Our oneness exists so to speak behind us, in the past, as an absurd tale that never was (à la Aristophanes), and in front of us, in the future, as an impossible end (à la Parmenides). Just as Aristophanes's lovers were not allowed to articulate their most heartfelt desire—union—so Parmenides concludes the first deduction by insisting that the one "is not named nor spoken of" (142a). We may move closer to this ineffable negative being of "neither-nor," but how would we even measure our distance to a oneness that is beyond being and time?

Short of that impossible end, or ignorant even of our proximity to it, we *are*, which is to say, we exist, as two. The second deduction concludes that the one-that-is is always two, and this is where we find ourselves, we *are* and we are doubled. We are a whole composed of parts, which reduce to further parts. We are internally differentiated, and with this difference we are barred from ever being the one in its oneness, of uniting our two halves without difference or remainder. To be is to be doubled. Not to be is to be absolutely single. And, so the appendix to the two deductions teaches us, "to be or not to be" is a matter of the instant or the "sudden." The transition from the oneness we enjoy now, the one-that-is and is thereby always two, to the impossible oneness for which we aim happens in precisely this instant. We are "suddenly" *(exaiphnēs)* delivered from one one to another one. The delivery rescues us from the violation of one law, noncontradiction, to the violation of another law, the excluded middle. In that instant we neither are nor are not the one.[47]

By way of anticipation of coming chapters, I have often wondered whether the *Parmenides*'s short discussion of the "instant" or "sudden" *(exaiphnēs)* funded subsequent Christian reflection on the divine double, especially the appearance of the risen Christ to Paul on the road to Damascus, as told no less than three times in the Acts of the Apostles (9:3–9; 22:6–11; 26:13–18).[48] The first two of those accounts describe the risen Christ appearing to Paul "suddenly" *(exaiphnēs)* as a blinding light. At least one Christian author, writing in the early sixth century, understood this appearance as the beginning of Christ's indwelling in Paul, which indwelling allows Paul to proclaim, "It is no longer I who live, but Christ who lives in me" (Gal 2:20). This author, writing under the name of one of Paul's own converts (Dionysius the Areopagite), wrote a short letter on the word *exaiphnēs*, which concludes by speaking in a Parmenidean spirit of "the mystery with respect to [Christ that] has been reached by no word nor mind, but even when spoken, remains unsaid, and conceived unknown."[49] This author studied Plato's *Parmenides*, as well as Neoplatonic commentaries on it, especially that of Proclus.[50] He seems to have understood the indwelling of the risen Christ as that very Parmenidean "instant" in which the God beyond being—like the "one (that is) one"—comes to dwell in one of its beings; in other words, as that very instant in which the one changes from "not being" (understood as *beyond* being) to "coming-to-be." The risen Christ is therefore for this author the divine double who "suddenly" makes the impossible possible—in Plato's terms, the coincidence of the "one (that is) one" and the "one that is." That Plato's solution violates the law of the excluded middle might make for a tantalizing Christian reappraisal of Paul's insistence that "in Christ Jesus" "you are all one" and therefore *neither . . . nor* (Gal 3:28).[51]

Reading the Unwritten Doctrines

In his *Physics* Aristotle, Plato's student and later rival, mentions that his master had not included everything in his dialogues, but that there were "unwritten doctrines" *(agrapha dogmata)*.[52] These tantalizing teachings are often supposed to reflect Plato's enthusiasm, late in life, for Pythagorean philosophy, and specifically its speculation about numbers.[53] Here again Aristotle gives us a clue. In his *Metaphysics* he reports that Plato taught of two opposed first principles: the one *(to hen)* and the indefinite dyad *(hē aoristos dyas)*.[54] The one acts as a limit *(peras)* on the limitlessness *(apeiron)* of the indefinite dyad. This dyad is pure duality, but not in the sense of a determinate number "two." Rather, the dyad is better thought of as the not-one, but also as the not-yet-two. In fact, it is only by the limiting activity of the one on the unlimited dyad that the first four numbers *(tetraktus)* come to be at all (and their sum, "ten" or the decad).

My hope is that this chapter has persuaded the reader that Plato's teachings on the one and the not-one need not be hidden behind the mists of the "unwritten doctrines," but that in fact we can read them off the pages of his own dialogues, in such discussions as these: Socrates's *daimonion* (and the question of whether and how it is and is not "I"); the mutual mirroring of lover and beloved and their progressive assimilation to intelligible reality; Aristophanes's myth about humanity's division from unity into duality and the fraught enterprise of love's unifying power; and the *Parmenides*'s tortured meditations on the one and whether it can ever (be) one. Not only *can* we read these teachings, the teaching is *in* the very reading of them.

Let me explain. To see the divine double is not easy, no less (nor more) difficult than perceiving the intelligible world of the Forms shining through our own. Plato's Socrates was acutely aware of our poor eyesight and what challenges it posed for our reeducation and rehabilitation. In the *Republic*'s famous allegory of the cave, Socrates explains that someone who had been dragged to the surface from the depths of ignorance and illusion

> would need time to get adjusted before he could see things in the world above. At first, he'd see shadows *(skias)* most easily, then images *(eidôla)* of men and other things in water, then the things themselves ... Finally, I suppose, he'd be able to see the sun, not images *(phantasmata)* of it in water or some alien place, but the sun itself, in its own place, and be able to study it. (516a–b)

The figure of the reflecting pool appears also in the *Phaedo*, where Socrates says that to look closely into reality *(ta onta,* "beings") is somewhat dangerous, akin to looking at an eclipse. Just as those who wish to see an eclipse "watch its reflection in water or some such material," so too those who wish to investigate reality should "take refuge in words *(logoi)* and investigate the truth of things by means of them" (99d–100a). Before we can look directly at the sun, before we can see our divine double, we must learn to see through images and reflections, much as Ovid's Narcissus saw himself reflected in a still pool. But for us readers, it is in words and not water that we come to see the intelligible reality shining in our world, the divine double of whom *we* are each the reflection.

But which words exactly? Again in the *Republic* Socrates acknowledges our poor eyesight and suggests that our straining to see reality is like someone straining to see small letters at a distance. But what if "the same letters existed elsewhere in a larger size and on a larger surface"? They do. In the *Republic*, the reality under investigation is justice: Whereas we must strain to see justice in an individual human being, there is more justice to be seen in an entire city. "So, if you're willing, let's first find out what sort of thing justice is in a city and afterwards look for it in the individual, observing the ways in which the smaller is similar to the larger" (368e–369a). The justice of the city is, as it were, written in larger letters. Quite literally so, for the city to which Socrates now directs their attention is explicitly a "city of words," a city that he and his interlocutors will go on to imagine and Plato will capture (or rather construct) in this very book, the *Republic*: "Come, then, let's create a city in word *(en logōi . . . polin)* from its beginnings" (369c). To learn to see, we must first learn to read, and Plato has given us the words to read in the form of this city, the soul writ large. And not just in the *Republic*, but in all the dialogues, which together constitute a world of words, a textual double of sorts, reality imaged on a page. For Plato's reader, then, the text in hand is reality writ large, legible to our weak eyes, words that train us eventually to see ourselves each reflected therein, the truth of what he calls "a single man" *(andros henos)*. Thus Plato provides not only what I have called the "conceptual landscape" of the tradition of the divine double, but also a *practice* for perceiving that intelligible counterpart: reading his world of words, which like a still pool reflect to each onlooker what he or she is, or rather should be. This is, curiously, a most apt description of the *Gospel of Thomas* (to which Chapter 2 is devoted), which explicitly desires a reader who will find his or her own reality—how one is not really oneself, but somehow one *and* two—through the very practice of reading and pondering its words, the secret sayings of the living Jesus. Insofar as it desires and imagines such a reader in search of his or her divine double, this gospel is a descendent of the dialogue.

As we have seen, scholars opine that Plato was much exercised, late in life, with the relationship of the one and the not-one (or dyad). His immediate successors at the Academy, Speussippus and

Xenocrates, seem to have shared his fascination. The Neo-Pythagoreans of the first century CE and after revived philosophical speculation about the one and the dyad in the Platonic tradition. This "Middle Platonism" would find in Plotinus, and perhaps in others before him (including so-called Gnostics), even more sustained meditations. During these early centuries of the first millennium, then, philosophers in the Platonic and Neo-Pythagorean traditions (and perhaps others) were working out their own views on the relationship between the one and the two, and the places in between.

In what follows in Chapters 2–4 on Christian and Manichaean sources, we see a keen interest in the borderlands between the one and the two. These are decidedly unphilosophical sources: a gospel, apocryphal acts of the early apostles, hagiographical anthologies of a self-described "apostle of light" (to name but a few)—and many of them exist only in translation and in incomplete states of transmission. Nevertheless, embedded in the rhetoric of their distinct genres, shining through the troubled state of their texts, is a notion that the exemplary human is one who lives in this realm of the not-one, and is in fact called there by God. One is called there first by a visit from one's divine twin or double, who initiates the individual into the disturbing truth that one is not oneself, exactly, but one half of a pair—not an individual per se but a "dividual." But this self-discovery is simultaneously a self-splitting and a self-unification: the "dividual" now moves into a new mode of existence. The way to inhabit the borderlands of the one and the two is to be simultaneously one *and* two, a *new* kind of singularity that depends on and preserves a certain kind of duality. These sources have different accounts of and different names for this new singularity. Let us now allow them to speak for themselves.

2

Thomas, Who Is Called "Twin"

In his "Letter to Marcellinus," Athanasius of Alexandria says of the Book of Psalms: "These words become like a mirror *(eisoptron)* to the person singing them."[1] To hear them sung is to recognize them "as being one's own words . . . as if they were one's own songs." The Psalter allows the reader "to possess the image *(eikona)* deriving from its words," and thus to "heal" *(therapeuein)* the soul of its wayward passions.[2] The image that one can see in the Psalter is both one's own image, as if one were looking into a mirror, and Christ's, "the image *(eikōn)* of the invisible God" (Col 1:15). Like Plato's lover looking into the mirror of the beloved's eye, or Plato's reader seeing the letters of his soul writ large in a "city of words," the Christian reader of the Psalms sees himself reflected in this book, not only as he is (with his wayward passions), but as he should be, healed and whole, like Christ.

I begin this chapter with Athanasius because he is advising a practice of private devotional reading in the context of fourth-century Egypt, recommending a book of scripture because it reflects to its reader a doubled image, his own and Christ's. We know, however, that other contemporary Christian readers in Egypt were reading other texts with this same expectation. One such text was the *Gospel of Thomas*. We have long known that there was circulating in Egypt, at least as early as the third century, a gospel attributed not to one of the canonical four evangelists—Matthew, Mark, Luke, and John—but to another apostle, Thomas. We have long known of this gospel's existence because a number of early Christian writers—whom we now, retrospectively, label as more or less "orthodox"—took an interest in it. At least one of them, Origen of Alexandria, read it.[3] The interest these authors took in the *Gospel of Thomas* was motivated, not always by intellectual curiosity, but more often by an anxiety that this gospel, and others like it, posed a threat to a proper (that is to say, their own) understanding and practice of Christianity. Apart from a stray quotation, however, this gospel was lost to us. Only in the late nineteenth and early twentieth centuries did fragmentary evidence for the *Gospel of Thomas* begin to emerge; and only in the mid-twentieth century, with the discovery of the Nag Hammadi library in Egypt, did we have a complete version of this gospel, albeit in Coptic translation.[4] I say "gospel" because that is what the text calls itself. But the *Gospel of Thomas* differs considerably from the four canonical gospels, first and foremost in that it is a collection of sayings of Jesus and *not* (as the canonical gospels are) a narrative of his life, ministry, death, and resurrection. The *Gospel of Thomas* does not call Jesus by the title *christos* or "anointed" (in Hebrew, messiah). Strictly speaking, then, the gospel does not have a "Christology." Rather, it is "the living Jesus" who speaks these "secret sayings," and speaks them to one of his disciples, Didymus Judas Thomas, who is said to have written them down.

Another distinguishing feature of the *Gospel of Thomas* is what I am calling its "theology of twinning"—perhaps our very earliest witness to a Christian tradition of the divine double. Other ancient texts from the second through the third century fill out this early tradition (some of which are also attributed to this same disciple, Judas Thomas), including Tatian's *Address to the Greeks*, the *Book of Thomas the Contender* (also part of the Nag Hammadi library), the apocryphal *Acts of Thomas*, and the so-called "Hymn of the Pearl." Each of these texts displays a slightly different theology of the twin. In this chapter we will explore the *Gospel of Thomas*; in Chapter 3 we will look at the other texts in this tradition. In the *Gospel of Thomas*, this theology of the twin is very much wrapped up in the name of the disciple Judas Thomas, as we will explore below. Let it suffice for the moment to note that the name "Thomas" in Aramaic means "twin" (as does the Greek word *didymos*, which is also attached to this disciple). In short, the *Gospel of Thomas* seems to have been the product of an early Christian tradition in which one of Jesus's closest disciples was understood to be his twin—although in what sense a twin remains unclear. Paired with the attribution of the *Gospel of Thomas* to Jesus's twin, Judas Thomas, is a theological thread that runs through many of these baffling, seemingly esoteric, sayings. Many of the sayings speak of the relationship of the one and the two, and what it means to become a "solitary" or "a single one." This chapter will attempt to isolate this thread, in light of the gospel's attribution to Judas Thomas, and so to reconstruct the gospel's distinctive account of the divine double, its theology of the twin.

This theology of twinning is very much in the tradition of Plato, for at least two reasons. First, as with Plato's dialogues, the *Gospel of Thomas* presents itself as a text that, when properly interpreted, in turns interprets the reader. The reader comes to learn that he is in a process of interpreting not only these secret sayings, but also his secret self—that the text is an image of himself, except that *he* is the obscured image of the archetype he finds in, and crucially *through*, his reading. Second, this secret self occupies what I have called the "borderlands" of the one and the two. Just as Plato, in the *Parmenides*, is interested in the transition between the one (that is) *one* and the one that *is*—a transition he calls the "sudden"—so the *Gospel of Thomas* initiates the reader into a secret selfhood, a "new subjectivity" that is both one and yet two, to which he gives the name "solitary" or "a single one."

I am by no means the first to discern a theology of twinning in the *Gospel of Thomas* or in the broader tradition into which it seems to fit. When introducing one or another of the texts in this tradition, scholars often acknowledge this theology of twinning and say a few words about it. But rarely does any scholar wish to linger over it or to say much more with confidence. Partly this is owing to the fact that the theology of twinning does not lie, as it were, on the surface of these texts to be read off clearly and legibly, but instead must be drawn forth with some care. This is precisely what I intend to do in this chapter and in Chapter 3. But before we begin this careful drawing forth, we would do well to remember a few of those scholars who have tried to give voice to this somewhat elusive theology. In his introduction to the *Acts of Thomas*, H. J. W. Drijvers remarks that "there evidently developed a form of Christianity in which the 'twin' motif was a constitutive factor. This central motif occasioned the characteristic naming of the apostle Judas, the twin brother of Jesus, or briefly Judas Thomas."[5] We will soon turn to the apostle Thomas, or Judas Thomas, but notice that Drijvers does little more than acknowledge this "motif." In his introduction to the "School of St. Thomas" (on which, see more below) in his collection *Gnostic Scriptures*, Bentley Layton picks up Drijvers's appeal to a "motif," but gives much more flesh to the bone; he writes of the "twin motif" that

> in the Thomas tradition . . . this relationship provided a profound theological model for the reciprocal relationship of the individual Christian and the inner divine light or "living Jesus": to know oneself was to know one's divine double and thence to know god; to follow the living Jesus was to know and integrate one's self. Thus the twinship and companionship of Jesus and Thomas metaphorically expressed a general model of salvation through acquaintance *(gnosis)* with god, emphasizing both practical discipleship and self-awareness.[6]

This is, in fact, a remarkably lucid summary of the theology of twinning that we find in the *Gospel of Thomas* and other texts associated with that same apostle. Risto Uro, speaking specifically here of the *Gospel of Thomas*, remarks that "salvation is understood as a process of becoming like Jesus or even better as becoming him in a process of union."[7] In what follows, we will press each text for further details on its distinctive "theological model for the reciprocal relationship" between any Christian and Jesus (through the "twin" Thomas), specifically how each text understands the "integration" of the self with its divine double, or the process of becoming Jesus even to the point of union with him. What we have in the theology of the twin, then, to anticipate for just a moment, is a model of salvation as deification that flourished in the second and third centuries of Christianity (and perhaps longer). It seems to have flourished at the edges of what we might call the emerging "orthodoxy" that was finally to prevail in the fourth and fifth centuries with imperial endorsement. But even mapping this theology of the twin onto an emerging division between "orthodox" and "heterodox" is not entirely apt, as our concluding case of Origen of Alexandria will hopefully make clear.

Who Is the Apostle Thomas?

All three of the synoptic gospels (Matthew, Mark, and Luke) provide lists of "the twelve," those disciples closest to Jesus who were "sent out *(apostellēi)* to preach" (Mark 3:14) and therefore called "apostles." All three lists include a figure named Thomas (Math 10:3, Mark 3:18, Luke 6:15), although nothing more is said of him. The name "Thomas" is a Hellenized form of the Aramaic word *tāwmā*, meaning "twin." It is not so much a name as an epithet in Aramaic, but none of the synoptic gospels pauses to explain why the apostle bears this particular epithet. Only in the Fourth Gospel, John's, do we learn anything more. When he is first introduced in 11:16, we learn that this Thomas is "called the Twin *(didymos)*." We are told the same in 20:24 and 21:2, but not *why* this apostle is called "the Twin" or whose twin he is supposed to be. To a reader familiar with Aramaic and Greek, these verses would sound as if the disciple were being called "Twin Twin."[8] This nameless Twin emerges from his synoptic obscurity and assumes a central role in the unfolding drama of the Fourth Gospel. Most (in)famously Thomas is the doubter: he questions whether his fellow disciples have in fact seen their risen Lord and then defiantly demands ocular and tactile proof of the wounds of Christ: "Unless I see in his hands the print of the nails, and place my finger in the mark of the nails, and place my hand in his side, I will not believe" (20:24). When Jesus appears again eight days later and offers the Twin precisely what he had earlier demanded—namely, his wounds—this doubting Thomas immediately relents and believes, issuing his famous confession, "My Lord and my God!" (20:28). Christian tradition, both exegetical and iconographic, has largely misread this episode and understood Thomas as having *touched* Jesus's wounds, when in fact the text is clear that it is instead Jesus's *offer* to touch them that restores his faith.[9]

Be that as it may, we are still no clearer on the identity of this apostle, "Twin Twin." Although Jesus gave nicknames to others among the twelve (Mark 3:16–17: "Simon, whom he surnamed Peter; James the son of Zebedee and John the brother of James, whom he surnamed Boanerges, that is, sons of thunder"), the apostle Thomas is alone in having *only* an epithet and no proper name. Given that his epithet is "twin," however, it is no surprise that some early Christians looked to Jesus's own family for an explanation. In Mark 6:3, members of the synagogue, upon hearing Jesus teach, ask each other incredulously, "Is not this the carpenter, the son of Mary and brother of James and Joses and Judas and Simon, and are not his sisters here with us?"[10] A similar list of Jesus's brothers is found in Matthew 13:55, with Judas listed fourth rather than third. Both lists name James first, suggesting that he is, after Jesus, the eldest. This is reflected in the traditions around James "the brother of our lord" (Gal 1:19), who is remembered as a leader in the early community of Jesus's followers in Jerusalem. Judas, by contrast, would appear to be a younger brother. Strange, then, that it is Judas who was regarded, at least by some early Christians, as the twin brother of Jesus, and so identified with the apostle Thomas or *didymos*.[11]

The prologue to the *Gospel of Thomas*, as it is preserved in Coptic and found in the Nag Hammadi library, reads, "These are the secret sayings which the living Jesus spoke and which Didymus Judas Thomas wrote down." The Greek fragment of the prologue preserves this apostle's name as simply "Judas, who is also Thomas."[12] *The Book of Thomas the Contender*, another text from the Nag Hammadi library, purports to be the "secret words that the savior spoke to Judas Thomas."[13] The *Acts of Thomas*, in its Greek version, narrates the adventures of an apostle by the name of "Judas Thomas, who is also (called) Didymus" (in its Syriac version he is "Judas Thomas the Apostle").[14] In his *Ecclesiastical History*, Eusebius of Caesarea tells the story of the correspondence between Jesus and King Abgar, and mentions along the way an apostle "Judas, who was also called Thomas."[15] Finally, the "Old Syriac" translation of the New Testament (estimates for the date of which range from the late second to the early fourth century) explicitly identifies "Judas, not the Iscariot" (John 14:22) with "Thomas, who is called the Twin" (John 11:16, 20:24–29, 21:2) by rendering the name of the apostle in 14:22 as "Judas Thomas."[16] We will get into the problems with dating these texts as we discuss each in turn, but let it suffice for the moment to say that between the second and fourth centuries we have a number of witnesses to an early Christian tradition that believed Jesus to have had a brother named Judas (not to be confused with the Iscariot), a disciple who was often (and sometimes only) called the "twin" (*didymos, tāwmā*) because he was in some way or another Jesus's twin brother.

Where did this tradition begin? In short, we do not know. The New Testament hardly furnishes the reader with the notion that Jesus had a twin brother and that his name was Judas.[17] Even if a reader were inclined to understand the mentions of a "Thomas, who is called Twin" as referring to Jesus's own twin brother (which is far from obvious), it is unlikely that he or she would light upon Judas as the most likely candidate. According to the Gospels of Matthew and Mark, Judas is almost certainly a much younger brother (by at least three years), and so not Jesus's biological twin. This, however, raises the question of whether these early Christians imagined Jesus and Judas as biological twins—as if they were identical or fraternal twins, having shared Mary's womb—or otherwise, perhaps as spiritual twins. This ambiguity will play out in the ancient sources, which we will examine closely in this chapter and Chapter 3. But it bears repeating that we do not know where this tradition exactly begins: we do not know exactly what happened between the composition of the books of the canonical New Testament in the first and second centuries that mention Thomas (the Twin), on the one hand, and the witnesses from the second through fourth centuries that understand this Twin to be Jesus's twin brother Judas, on the other. Some scholars are inclined to posit an early, oral tradition in the Christian East (although not in the West) to this effect.[18]

Some have sought to explain this early Christian tradition by positing the existence of a "School of St. Thomas" in the city of Edessa in the Osrhoene area of Syria. Bentley Layton forwards this view and includes translations of three texts he considers products of this school: the *Gospel of Thomas* and the aforementioned *Book of Thomas the Contender*, along with the "Hymn of the Pearl," an allegorical tale found in some manuscripts of the *Acts of Thomas*. These four texts form the core of the early tradition that regards Judas Thomas as Jesus's twin. But whether they reflect the existence of a school is a different matter. Layton's reasons for speaking of a school have more to do with the second-century Christian theologian Valentinus than they do with Judas Thomas. He sees the Valentinians of the second and third centuries as aspiring to produce Christian theology on the sophisticated level of pagan philosophy: "Thus the Valentinian movement had the character of a philosophical school, or network of schools, rather than a distinct religious sect."[19] Without explanation, however, Layton labels the texts associated with Judas Thomas as products of a similar, but earlier, school—this despite the fact that these texts do not seem to aspire to pagan philosophical standards of profundity or perspicacity. Nor do these texts seem to have a great deal in common apart from their connection to the apostle Judas Thomas, the twin of Jesus, and thus some particular version of the theology of twinning. As Nicola Denzey Lewis observes, "The problem with the 'school' hypothesis is that all four texts are very different in their philosophies."[20] I tend to agree with Risto Uro, then, that "there is simply too little evidence for reconstructing a particular Christian school with Judas Thomas as its founder figure," or even as its inspiration.[21]

For many of the same reasons I am skeptical of the existence of a "Thomas community," by which is meant a more or less discrete group of Christians who produced some or all of these texts for their community's own purposes. The main proponent of this view is Gregory J. Riley (on whose scholarship I rely in some other cases). If each gospel were representative of a more or less distinct community of early Christians, might we read any two gospels as reflecting two competing views of Jesus and his significance? Riley believes that the literature associated with John the Evangelist and with the apostle Thomas are representative sets of texts of "two closely related Christian communities" whose disagreements one can track by comparing the two bodies of literature in counterpoint.[22]

Riley is particularly interested in what he takes to be the Gospel of John's negative portrayal of Doubting Thomas, and wonders whether the Fourth Gospel is thereby caricaturing the community of "Thomas Christians" and their gospel—sometimes today acclaimed as the "Fifth Gospel."[23] Elaine Pagels has argued along similar lines: that the Gospel of John was composed or compiled to correct the errant views of the *Gospel of Thomas*.[24] Although I have certain reservations about the scholarly assumption that early Christian gospels represent distinct early Christian communities (for instance, "Johannine" vs. "Thomasine" Christians), both of these scholars' approaches provide an interesting and illuminating lens through which to read the two gospels in counterpoint. While there may be good reasons for thinking that a distinct community produced the Gospel of John, we would do well to keep in mind that a text does not necessarily presume a ready-made community of readers, never mind a distinct group with defined social and ritual boundaries. What we have in our case is a set of texts associated with the apostle Judas Thomas, and I think we would do well to read them each on their own terms, and to refrain from appeals to "school" or "community" to explain their relationship to one another.

So too I think we should be somewhat careful when considering geography.[25] Layton confidently names Edessa as the place of his "School of St. Thomas." Even many of those who do not endorse his school hypothesis nevertheless share his conviction that these texts emerged from an East Syrian context—this despite the fact that our only copies of the *Gospel of Thomas* hail from Egypt (albeit the dry climate of Egypt is more conducive to the preservation of texts than are the seasonal cycles of Syria). Furthermore, this geography is often used as an excuse for an overreaching interpretation of the texts in question. This is very clear in the case of "encratism," which I will discuss in much greater detail below and in Chapter 3. Suffice it to say that scholars argue that an ethic of renunciation (especially sexual celibacy) was widespread in Syria, which ethic they then, following ancient heresiologists, label "encratic." With this lens firmly in place, any text that is thought to hail from Syria is submitted to an encratic interpretation, often by filling in what is perceived to be a missing backdrop, supplying an explicitly encratic framework when none is present in the text itself.²⁶ It is my firm conviction, contrary to many (but not all) scholars, that the *Gospel of Thomas* has been subject to such an (mis)interpretation. In what follows, I will attempt to let it loose, so to speak, and to view it through a different lens, one that I regard as being supplied by the text itself.

To return to the discussion of "tradition," then, I endorse this category but define it rather minimally and handle it rather loosely. True: we have ancient textual witnesses to the notion that Judas Thomas is Jesus's twin. And so I try to take each witness on its own terms, and to discern its own particular understanding of this relationship, this theology of twinning as it were. I do not presume to tell the social history of Eastern Christianity through these texts, or to narrate with any confidence who wrote what and for whom, and against whom. Rather, I assume that each text has a view, and I work to bring that view to light. In this chapter, I will attempt to do just that with the *Gospel of Thomas*, and will conclude by considering a possible reaction to and appropriation of the gospel by the third-century Christian theologian Origen of Alexandria. In Chapter 3, I will attempt to do the same for the other texts in this tradition of Thomas, and other texts in their orbit.

The *Gospel of Thomas*

BACKGROUND

The discovery of the *Gospel of Thomas* is a story that has been told and retold many times. It is a drama in two acts, Greek and Coptic. First, in 1897 and again in 1904 two British scholars, B. P. Grenfell and A. S. Hunt, published papyrus fragments from Oxyrhynchus, Egypt, that contained sayings of Jesus preserved in Greek. The first fragment (P. Oxy. 1) consists of a single leaf from a papyrus codex and includes those sayings that have come to be numbered 26–33, and 77a.²⁷ The second and third fragments (P. Oxy. 654 and 655) are from papyrus rolls, and include a prologue and those sayings that have come to be numbered 1–7 (P. Oxy 654), and 24 and 36–39 (P. Oxy. 655).²⁸ Grenfell and Hunt estimated that P. Oxy. 1 was written in the very early third century, and that P. Oxy. 654 and 655 were written well before the start of the fourth century. Between roughly 200 and 300 CE, then, these three Greek papyri, and very likely many more, were circulating in Egypt. Given the fact that the three fragments do not overlap, however, we do not know whether they derive from a single source, or whether they represent different versions, or whether one of the three was copied from another. What we do know is simply that at least one Greek version of the *Gospel of Thomas* was circulating in Egypt by the end of the second century. Closer attention to the papyri themselves suggests that the earliest one, a codex (P. Oxy. 1), may have been used for public reading in a liturgical setting, whereas the later two, both rolls (P. Oxy. 654 and 655), "appear more at home in a private, studious milieu." Despite the small sample size, we might be witnessing "a development from the *Gospel of Thomas* as scripture to document for private study."[29]

The second act of the drama began in 1945, when a pair of Egyptian brothers discovered a cache of twelve Coptic codices near the town of Nag Hammadi. The story of the slow but dramatic emergence and eventual publication of this cache need not concern us here.[30] The second codex, *Nag Hammadi Codex II* (hereafter *NHC II*), contains a complete text entitled "The Gospel according to Thomas," with 114 sayings of Jesus preserved in Coptic translation.[31] With a complete text in hand, scholars were able to correlate the Greek fragments and number them according to their sequence in *NHC II*. But it was immediately clear that there are significant differences between the Greek fragments and the Coptic text, suggesting again that there were at least two versions of the *Gospel of Thomas*, and perhaps many more. Scholars date the Coptic manuscript to the first half of the fourth century, later than the Greek fragments.

Much of the scholarship on the *Gospel of Thomas* has focused on its date of composition and / or compilation, whether some or all of its sayings—sayings either particular to this text or variations on sayings in the canonical gospels—should be dated to the first or to the second centuries. Answers to such questions of dating are inextricably intertwined with views of how the *Gospel of Thomas* relates to the canonical gospels: Does it rely on or reveal knowledge of any of them or of the alleged sayings source "Q"?[32] Where does it fit into the relative chronology of their composition and collection? What, if anything, can it tell us about the "historical" Jesus, or about Christianity in the first or second centuries? How, in these deliberations, are we to weigh the testimony of the Coptic text against the Greek fragments? Although it is nearly certain that the Coptic text is a translation from Greek, can we be equally certain that the gospel was originally written in Greek? Could it have been written in Syriac, as many scholars think the *Acts of Thomas* were? These examples, I hope, convey the flavor of the questions that are often asked of this text, and often with an eye to bringing into sharper focus of the hazy outlines of earliest Christianity, which remain—frustratingly for so many historians and believers—ever hidden from our direct gaze.

I am principally interested in the theology of the *Gospel of Thomas*—specifically its theology of the twin and its sayings having to do with the one and the two. I will work principally from the complete fourth-century Coptic translation of what I, along with most scholars, presume was a Greek original.[33] Because my principal interest is in discerning the theology of the gospel, I am less focused on the question of the date of its composition and compilation, its relationship to the canonical gospels, or whether and how it sheds light on the history of the first two centuries of Christianity and our prospects of recovering the "historical" Jesus. Instead I am out to trace the tradition of the divine double, and this gospel is crucial for the Christian side of that story.

I should also distinguish my angle of approach from that of other scholars who have endeavored to show how the *Gospel of Thomas* fits into the vast and intricate web of religious and philosophical literature from the ancient world. The sayings find parallels, allusions, and echoes in a vast sea of such literature across centuries and languages—never mind natural, political, and even religious borders—so the potential context for interpretation is endless. Often this approach involves the isolation of a single saying, or a small group of sayings, and then the interpretation of that single saying in a very different context, amid a very different set of far-flung "intertexts." I do not deny these intertexts—these parallels, allusions, and echoes—and have in fact learned a great deal tagging along as scholars follow the trail of single sayings to sometimes surprising parallels.

But I take a different tack to this text. Although somewhat out of date, Bertil Gärtner's characterization of the field still obtains:

> A rough and ready distinction can thus be drawn between two main queries about the *GT*: one analyses the history of every *logion* in tradition, asking whence it can have originated, and what was its original meaning; the other inquires after the meaning of the sayings for the person who gathered them, and how they were interpreted in the milieu which gave them their present form. We shall follow the latter path in our investigations.[34]

I agree with Gärtner that we should focus on the text in its present form and, I would add, the experience of *reading* it in its present form. I try to read it as if I were a reader without a vast library at my disposal, as if I were a reader on whom many of the parallels, allusions, and echoes to other texts and traditions would be simply lost. Such a reader, however, is not a naïf; rather, he (in my case) approaches this text with the assumption that it will teach him what he needs to know in order to read it properly, that with his participation it will interpret itself (and, as we will see, also himself). When such a reader encounters a saying whose meaning is opaque, he first looks for clarity, not outside the text, but rather within it. Sometimes he must wait, for the text does not immediately provide the interpretive key to the lock, and so the reader is continually returning to sayings that were once opaque, and trying new keys on old locks. Sometimes he finds a key before he knows that there is a lock into which it fits. And of course sometimes there are locks without any matching keys, and keys without any matching locks. Or at least so he thinks, because he can never be sure, because part of the art is discerning locks from keys. All this to say that such a reader is constantly turned back on the text he is reading, because it is always teaching him how to read it. Another way of saying this is that such a reader is always rereading.

This may seem like a rather grand description of my approach to the *Gospel of Thomas*. It is not meant to be grand in the least, but is rather an attempt to read this text as many (if not most) readers have done and still do. Some may wish to attach a name to this approach, or even a genealogy. Allow me to indulge this desire by naming two cousins of this approach, one ancient and one modern. In antiquity, a cousin bearing a strong family resemblance to this approach was given a slogan by the Alexandrian critic Aristarchus (second century BCE): "clarify Homer with Homer" *(Homeron ex Homerou saphenizein)*. The rabbis and the church fathers followed a similar method when reading their scriptures, using passages to interpret other passages, and often passages separated by great distances from each other.[35] It shares *some* features with what in the twentieth century went under the name "New Criticism." However, while my approach puts a premium on close reading and is wary of fixing meaning to historical context, it does not eschew but embraces the response of the reader. The approach I take to the *Gospel of Thomas* is not as rigid as ancient Aristarchean criticism or modern New Criticism, and frankly I do not have an easy label to apply to it.

What I know is that I learned to read texts this way from philosophers—not dead ones, but living, teaching philosophers. For them, the task of interpretation is one of concentric circles. And the central, innermost circle is the text in hand, the physical binding of which serves as a reminder that the interpretive enterprise should focus on what the reader finds within its pages. It is not as rigid an approach as it may seem: there are, after all other, wider circles, and they are licit. But it was made clear to me that before I crossed the line between the text in hand to another text—even one by the same author, and from the same period—I should first try, and try *hard*, to exhaust what the text in hand had to teach me about reading and interpreting it. Perhaps I am simply rehearsing the difference between how philosophers and historians read.

Or am I rehearsing the difference one philosopher can make? In my case, it was Stanley Cavell, one of my early teachers. Cavell introduced me to this way of reading through his own reading of Ludwig Wittgenstein's *Philosophical Investigations*. He writes of his "recognition that . . . the role of the *Investigations*" shifted under his eyes, of "finding that an *object* of interpretation has become a *means* of interpretation, and the one because of the other."[36] In other words, he set out to interpret the *Investigations* and discovered along the way that its principal aim is to teach its reader how best to interpret it, that is, how to read it. Of course he could not have learned the means of the text without first approaching it as an object. Although Cavell's writing career is in some sense a diary of his learning to read the *Investigations* ever more deeply, he also experienced that same transformation from object to means in his reading of Thoreau's *Walden*—an experience recorded in his short but beautiful meditation, *The Senses of Walden*.[37] The fact that Cavell experiences such auto-interpretive texts as the *Investigations* or *Walden* as works of therapy suggests, by way of anticipation, how I think the *Gospel of Thomas* understands itself to work on its reader.

I understand why some historians regard this philosophical approach as constraining and narrow. But it certainly did not feel that way when I was learning to read this way, and it certainly does not feel that way now as I read the *Gospel of Thomas*. On the contrary, only when I surround this text with the four walls of its binding do I feel that I can stop its meaning from seeping away into the vast, porous canvas of ancient contexts; only then do I feel that this text, now closed, is finally open.

PROLOGUE

Let us turn to the prologue of the *Gospel of Thomas* with this background in place. The gospel presents itself as the "secret sayings which the living Jesus spoke" and which Jesus's own twin brother Judas wrote down. As we have noted, we cannot be certain that the notion of "twinning" refers principally or exclusively to a fraternal, biological relationship between Jesus and Judas. What Klijn says of the *Acts of Thomas* holds true for this gospel as well: "It is not clear in which way Judas is supposed to be the twin of Christ."[38] Apart from the prologue, the *Gospel of Thomas* does not speak again about Judas as a twin. In fact, the apostle is mentioned only one other time in these sayings, and there he is referred to not as Judas but simply as "Thomas" (§13). Some scholars regard the prologue as a later addition to this collection of Jesus's sayings, and so conclude that the *Gospel of Thomas* evinces no interest in any theology of twinship. This is, I think, a mistake and a missed opportunity, because the *Gospel of Thomas* betrays an abiding interest in such questions as the relationship between the one and the two, what it means to be a solitary or a single one, union and division—all of which, on my reading, tell us a great deal about how Judas Thomas, and perhaps also we, are understood as twins of the living Jesus.

Before we plunge into the sayings, however, a comment about the setting of this gospel is in order, much of which hinges on the interpretation of a single word: "living," as in "the living Jesus." Some scholars take this title to mean that it is the risen or resurrected Jesus whose sayings are recorded in this collection. According to this reading, Jesus has returned, risen from the dead and so "living," to sojourn with his disciples before his eventual ascension, during which time he delivers to his twin the "secret sayings" or esoteric *gnosis* that he could not (or would not) deliver during his earthly ministry.[39] This reading allows for scholars to group the *Gospel of Thomas* with other texts, several from the Nag Hammadi cache deemed (rightly or wrongly) "Gnostic," in which this post-resurrection setting is clear and unambiguous.[40] Other scholars object to this reading, for what I regard as very good reasons. Rather, they contend, the *Gospel of Thomas* presents Jesus delivering these sayings—some of them very familiar, others not so—while still very much alive and active on earth. The *Gospel of Thomas* shows little interest in the death and resurrection of Jesus, as it is narrated in the canonical gospels.[41] It is unlikely that the compiler of this text or its readers were wholly ignorant of the death and resurrection of Jesus.[42] It is more likely that the text preserves and endorses a vision of Jesus's ministry in which his death and resurrection are not regarded as particularly significant for our salvation (or "life"). In fact, the *Gospel of Thomas* has quite a bit to say about life and death, and so we would do well to allow it to teach us, its readers, what it means by its own terms and categories (such as "living") rather than to assume that we already know what it will say. For although many of these terms will be familiar from canonical and even conciliar Christianity, here they are often freighted with very different meanings.

SAYINGS 1–4

I submit that the first four sayings of the *Gospel of Thomas* serve as a sort of interpretive key for the others, that these four sayings begin to teach the reader how to read, that is, how to interpret its secret sayings. They nicely frame our inquiry into its theology of the twin and the question of the one and the two. The most important saying of the *Gospel of Thomas* is the first: "And he said, 'Whoever finds the interpretation of these sayings will not experience death.'" We might not know yet what exactly it means not to experience death, but we do know that the means to this end is interpretation. We are called to interpret these sayings—secret sayings—suggesting that the practice consists in finding the esoteric meaning of Jesus's words. From the start, then, this gospel announces to its reader both the proper end or goal—not experiencing death—and the means to achieve that end: interpretation, that is, reading and pondering the sayings of the living Jesus.

The second saying expands on the first, offering a litany of stages along the interpretive path: (§2) "Jesus said, 'Let him who seeks continue until he finds. When he finds, he will become troubled. When he becomes troubled, he will be astonished, and he will rule over the all.'" Interpretation culminates in our "rul[ing] over the all"—we will come to learn more about both this reign and "the all" as we move through these sayings. This reign, however, is not placid or static: the interpreter will be "troubled" and "astonished." The Greek fragment, P. Oxy. 654, concludes with an additional phrase, "And [once having ruled], he will attain rest." Even this rest *(anapausis)* is humming with a kind of energy, as we learn in a much later saying where Jesus tells his disciples that "the sign of your father in you . . . is movement *(kim)* and repose *(anapausis)*" (§50).

So far, the end on offer—not experiencing death, ruling over the all, an energetic rest—remains somewhat mysterious, drawing the reader in. But already the fact that these sayings are attributed to "the living Jesus" suggests that our not experiencing death is somehow equivalent to our becoming like this living Jesus, that is, to our being alive in whatever distinctive way he is. We should not immediately think that this refers to some resurrection following death, because as we have already noted, nothing in this gospel indicates that "the living Jesus" is a resurrected Jesus. Instead, this living Jesus is he who lives and speaks with his disciples, and offers some life-giving teaching. Furthermore, if ruling over the all is equivalent to not experiencing death, then we readers might surmise that being ruled or subjected is equivalent to experiencing death. If so, then death is a state of subjection—but to whom or to what? That Jesus is said to be "living" suggests that he (alone) is not subjected, that he alone rules. But as we will see, he welcomes his disciples into that same life and rule.

The link between "living" and "ruling" carries the reader directly into the third saying:

> (§3) Jesus said, "If those who lead you say to you, 'See, the kingdom is in the sky,' then the birds of the sky will precede you. If they say, 'It is in the sea,' then the fish will precede you. Rather, the kingdom is inside you, and it is outside of you.
>
> When you come to know yourselves, then you will become known, and you will realize that it is you who are the sons of the living father. But if you do not know yourselves, you dwell in poverty and it is you who are that poverty."

The link is clear: "he will rule" (§2)—literally "he will become king"—and the "kingdom" (§3) have the same root.[43] First, notice that while §2 encourages seeking, §3 warns against "those who lead"—thus the reader is encouraged to pursue the interpretive enterprise apart from leading authorities. This suggests in turn that "ruling over the all" and finding the "kingdom" happens only to those who refuse to subject themselves to misled or misleading leaders. Rather than look for the kingdom in the sky or the sea, Jesus says that "it is inside you, and it is outside of you." This is the first of many opposed pairs that will confront the reader of the *Gospel of Thomas*. Already it suggests that finding the kingdom by way of interpretation will have something to do with opposed pairs, with wrestling with and overcoming perceived contraries such as inside / outside (and later, the one and the two).

This suggestion is strengthened by what immediately follows: "When you come to know yourselves, then you will become known."

First of all, following on the heels of the inside / outside distinction, this remark suggests that finding the kingdom will consist in simultaneously knowing oneself and having oneself known, in overcoming the disjunction between what we might call an interior and an exterior perspective on oneself.[44] Second, the fact that interpretation of written sayings yields self-knowledge suggests an analogy between self and text. In other words, it suggests that the reading and interpretation is not strictly about these secret sayings, but also is about our so-to-speak secret selves—that we, like these sayings, are in need of reading and interpretation. Thus, by the third saying, an astute reader is prompted to begin questioning any sharp distinction between himself and the text in his hands, and as a result any sharp distinction between what we might call "anthropology" and "textuality."

There are good reasons to regard the first three sayings, not four, as constituting the interpretive key for the rest of the gospel. The first three sayings offer what is to my mind a tight theological précis of what is to come. Through our reading and interpretation, we have already learned that we are invited into an interpretive enterprise, a means to an end—life, a life that Jesus possesses, as does "our" father. Through a simultaneous reading of text and self and an interpretation thereof that may be troubling, we will emerge knowing and known, astonished, having found or entered into a kingdom in which we ourselves rule and yet enjoy energetic rest. But entry into this kingdom seems to require our overcoming perceived contraries, such as inside and outside, specifically what is inside and outside ourselves.

The fourth saying, however, narrows our gaze and focuses our attention on perceived contraries and their overcoming: (§4) "Jesus said, 'The man old in days will not hesitate to ask a small child seven days old about the place of life, and he will live. For many who are first will become last, and they will become one and the same.'" For many scholars, what catches their eye in §4 is a detail about the small child, namely that he is seven days old. They wonder about the secret significance of this detail. But for an uninitiated reader the most significant feature of this saying is surely the inversion, namely that an old man is asking a small child about "the place of life." This phrase recalls the only other "place" to which the reader has yet been introduced, namely the "kingdom" (§3)—where we will live, rule over the all, and realize that we are sons of the living father. In other words, the old man asks the small child about the kingdom. The unsettling image of an old man asking an infant about matters of life and death sets up the next line, "for many who are first will become last." This suggests another inversion: the old man and the small child will exchange places.[45] The final line transforms the force of the saying—"and they will become one and the same." This suggests not just the exchange of the two positions, an exchange that would keep each distinct and intact, but the collapse or combination of the two into "one and the same" *(oua ouōt)*.

With this phrase—"one and the same" in Coptic *(oua ouōt)*, which translates "a single one" in Greek *(heis monos)*—we land upon a fundamental tension in the gospel. On the one hand, there is a clear endorsement of unity, of our becoming one—though in exactly what sense "one" requires further investigation. On the other hand, there is a clear understanding that unity is forged from duality, and that duality that does not disappear in the unity, that the one preserves the two.

This brings us back to where this chapter began: to Athanasius's claim that the Psalter is like a mirror *(eisoptron)* of its reader, reflecting his very own "image" *(eikōn)* back to him in words. Or for that matter to Socrates's discussion in the *Phaedrus* of how the beloved sees himself in the lover "as in a mirror" *(katoptron)*, and the reverse in *Alcibiades I*: how the lover sees himself in "miniature" *(eidōlon)* in the beloved's soul, again as if in a mirror *(katoptron)*. In both dialogues, the play of mirrors enables the lover and beloved's mutual deification. We will see in Chapter 5 how Plotinus internalizes this entire erotic optics, making lover and beloved and the play of mirrors an interior drama of the aspiring intellect. But notice that the *Gospel of Thomas* can be seen as a descendant of Plato's dialogues: the image of its own reader, its words the mirror that will reflect back to the reader his true self—and appropriately enough for a self known through a mirror, a true self that is one and yet two.

THE ONE AND THE TWO:
THE "ENCRATIC" INTERPRETATION

Many scholars have drawn attention to the gospel's meditations on the one and the two, and I will follow suit. But before I can forward my own interpretation of that meditation, I will have to introduce, and humbly question, a rather long-standing and influential interpretation. There are eight sayings in the Coptic version of the *Gospel of Thomas* that speak directly of the one (*oua / heis*), the two (*snau*), the "one and the same" or "single one" (*oua ouōt / heis monos*), and the "solitary" (*monachos*):

> (§4) Jesus said, "The man old in days will not hesitate to ask a small child seven days old about the place of life, and he will live. For many who are first will become last, and they will become one and the same *(oua ouōt)*."
>
> (§11) Jesus said, "This heaven will pass away, and the one above it will pass away. The dead are not alive, and the living will not die. In the days when you consumed what is dead, you made it what is alive. When you come to dwell in the light, what will you do? On the day when you were one *(oua)*, you became two *(snau)*. But when you become two *(snau)*, what will you do?"
>
> (§16) Jesus said, "Men think, perhaps, that it is peace which I have come to cast upon the world. They do not know that it is dissension which I have come to cast upon the earth: fire, sword, war. For there will be five in a house: three will be against two, and two against three, the father against the son, and the son against the father. And they will stand solitary *(monachos)*."
>
> (§22) Jesus saw infants being suckled. He said to his disciples, "These infants being suckled are like those who enter the kingdom." They said to him, "Shall we then, as children, enter the kingdom?" Jesus said to them, "When you make the two *(snau)* one *(oua)*, and when you make the inside like the outside, and the outside like the inside, and the above like the below. And when you make the male and the female one and the same *(oua*

ouōt), with the result that the male not be male nor the female female; and you fashion eyes in places of an eye, and a hand in place of a hand, and a foot in place of a foot, and a likeness *(ikōn)* in place of a likeness *(ikōn)*, then you will enter [the kingdom.]"

(§23) Jesus said, "I shall choose you, one *(oua)* out of a thousand, and two *(snau)* out of ten thousand, and they shall stand as a single one *(oua ouōt)*."

(§49) Jesus said, "Blessed are the solitary *(monachos)* and elect, for you will find the kingdom. For you are from it, and to it you will return."

(§75) Jesus said, "Many are standing at the door, but it is the solitary *(monachos)* who will enter the bridal chamber."

(§106) Jesus said, "When you make the two one *(snau oua)*, you will become the sons of man, when you say, 'Mountain, move away,' it will move away."

What to make of these eight baffling sayings? To put it mildly, "the language of these sayings is . . . cryptic and open to more than one interpretation."[46] As I mentioned above, some scholars believe that such sayings are so obscure that we have to supply a relevant backdrop if we are to have any hope of understanding their meaning. They ask, in other words, "What kind of mythology constitutes the symbolic world behind the sayings?"[47] One prominent and influential answer to this question is what I am calling the "encratic" interpretation of the gospel—"encratic" (from the Greek *enkrateia* or "self-control") because it reads the gospel as forwarding an unyielding virtue of sexual renunciation. The most conspicuous spokesman for this view is Gilles Quispel, who argues that the author of the *Gospel of Thomas* was himself celibate and "taught that only bachelors go to heaven."[48] I wish to focus instead on another spokesman, A. F. J. Klijn, who argues that the "symbolic world" that makes sense of these sayings and in fact the entire gospel is early Jewish exegesis of Gen 1–2 that interprets Adam as having been originally androgynous and asexual.[49] With such a mythology in place, Klijn believes, the following conclusions follow:

a. The word "single one" is equivalent to the elect and saved ones. b. Originally man was a "single one," but he became "two." In order to be saved he has to become a "single one" again. This means that he has to return to his original state. c. The original "single one" has become "two" by becoming male and female. As a result we may say that the *Gospel of Thomas* speaks about salvation as a return to the original state and that it rejects the division into male and female.[50]

In the Jewish literature Klijn has in mind, Adam's fall is regarded as a fall into sexual differentiation. The two sexes—male and female—and any sexual behavior between them are themselves the result of Adam's primordial sin.[51] Klijn is largely content to "give only a general picture" of this backdrop—in effect a pastiche of quotes from a variety of sources. But he drills down a bit deeper when he explores the "striking agreement" between the *Gospel of Thomas* and the first-century Jewish philosopher and exegete Philo of Alexandria. Philo envisions our return to the original androgynous state of Adam, in which our "oneness" or *monas* will once again reflect the oneness of God.[52] According to Klijn, this eventual return to "oneness," in both Philo and the *Gospel of Thomas*, necessitates the rejection of sex and marriage in this world.

April DeConick has recently endorsed a similar, encratic reading of the *Gospel of Thomas*, or rather of part of it.[53] DeConick divides the sayings into the original "kernel" sayings and the subsequent "accretion" sayings. She then labels all the sayings (or portions thereof) that speak of the one and the two as encratic accretions, textual layers added to the original collection. Whereas the original Thomas community believed in the imminent advent of the kingdom, DeConick argues, subsequent generations of the community suffered "while the messiah tarried," so to speak, and recast the imminent kingdom as an immanent kingdom. In other words, Thomas Christians no longer believed that they had to wait on the kingdom, but that the kingdom was waiting on them, if only they would embrace an "encratic regime."[54] She suggests that in addition to Philo, the Alexandrian encratites (whom we know from Clement of Alexandria's *Stromata*) serve as the crucial backdrop to the *Gospel of Thomas*—or at least to those sayings that DeConick identifies as encratic accretions.[55]

On the encratic reading, the eight sayings that speak of the one and the two are really speaking about humanity's lamentable division into male and female and exhorting the reader to return to his or her original oneness by rejecting marriage and rendering oneself "a single one" or celibate. Perhaps the saying that speaks most in favor of this reading is §22. Klijn offers up this selective string of phrases: ". . . When you make the two one . . . and when you make the male and the female into a single one . . . then shall you enter the Kingdom."[56] But the problem with this selection is that it obscures the fact that making the male and female into a *oua ouōt*—a "single one" (à la Klijn) or "one and the same" (à la Lambdin)—is just one in a series of cryptic conditions ("When you . . ."). The full saying reads:

(§22) Jesus saw infants being suckled. He said to his disciples, "These infants being suckled are like those who enter the kingdom." They said to him, "Shall we then, as children, enter the kingdom?" Jesus said to them, "When you make the two *(snau)* one *(oua)*, and when you make the inside like the outside, and the outside like the inside, and the above like the below. And when you make the male and the female one and the same *(oua ouōt)*, with the result that the male not be male nor the female female; and you fashion eyes in places of an eye, and a hand in place of a hand, and a foot in place of a foot, and a likeness *(ikōn)* in place of a likeness *(ikōn)*, then you will enter [the kingdom.]"

This saying is a considerably harder nut to crack when you acknowledge its full and baffling series of exhortations. Of course DeConick includes the entire saying in her translation and commentary, but she, like Klijn, takes the phrase "when you make the male and the female one and the same" as the interpretive key for everything else.[57] On their reading, the suckling infant becomes a figure for the androgynous Adam, and the litany of body parts that are to be replaced becomes a figure for the resurrected body that is on offer if only the reader will renounce gendered sexuality.

More to the point, the encratic reading depends on "twoness" standing for sinful separation and gender differentiation and "oneness" standing for the prelapsarian unity to which we should return. But it does not seem to me that this is consistently reflected in the sayings themselves. I will follow a different path through these sayings, and so attempt to draw forth a different theology, one not of encratism but of twinning.

THE ONE AND THE TWO: UNITY-IN-DUALITY

In order to follow the thread of the gospel's theology of the twin and its meditation on the one and the two, we will have to jump from saying to saying, and often double back. Whereas earlier I offered a sustained reading of the first four sayings, now I will cut an uneven path through these sayings—some of them notoriously opaque—in order to make my case. A good number of these sayings and even central themes of the gospel will be left untouched as we attempt to discern an esoteric thread running through the whole.

Perhaps the best place to begin is §11:

> Jesus said, "This heaven will pass away, and the one above it will pass away. The dead are not alive, and the living will not die. In the days when you consumed what is dead, you made it what is alive. When you come to dwell in the light, what will you do? On the day when you were one, you became two. But when you become two, what will you do?"

In the interests of keeping on the trail of the one and the two, we will have to skip over the first half of this saying and what it has to teach the reader about life, death, resurrection, and the passing away of the heavens. For our purposes, the crucial detail is the parallel between the two temporal clauses: "When you come to dwell in the light" and "when you become two." The parallel is confirmed by the repetition of the question "what will you do?" The parallel suggests that dwelling in the light is somehow the equivalent of becoming two. What would it mean if the day when you become two is the same as the day when you come to dwell in the light?

This is the first mention of light in the *Gospel of Thomas*, but a more robust discussion comes much later, in §77:

> Jesus said, "It is I who am the light which is above them all. It is I who am the all. From me did the all come forth, and unto me

did the all extend *(pōh)*. Split *(pōh)* a piece of wood and I am there. Lift up the stone, and you will find me there."

We learn that it is Jesus who is the light in which we might come to dwell, and so become two (§11). He simultaneously *is* and is *above* "the all." This echoes §2, where the end on offer is "ruling over the all," suggesting again that the goal is to take up the position of Jesus *above* the all, ruling rather than being ruled. Jesus is figured here as the comprehending source of everything, a beacon of light that both is and exceeds that which "comes forth" from him and "extends" back to him. If we take the parallel in §11 seriously, then to dwell in the light, to stand in the place of Jesus, the comprehending source of all, is to become two. Jesus recommends two curious ways of finding him, namely splitting wood and lifting a stone (§77), the first of which is quite obviously an act of making something that is one into two.[58]

If §77 figures the light as a transcendent, comprehending source, then §24 brings the light into the most immanent and intimate realm:

(§24) His disciples said, "Show us the place where you are, since it is necessary for us to seek it." He said to them, "Whoever has ears, let him hear. There is light within a man of light, and he lights up the whole world. If he does not shine, he is darkness."

Here is that "place" again—the kingdom, the place of life. Just as in §3, the disciples seem to expect that the place "where you are" is some determinate place, here rather than there. But when asked where to seek him, Jesus does not answer directly, but tells his disciples that there is light "within a man of light." Of course this light is none other than Jesus himself: the transcendent, comprehending source of all is now said to be within us. And the disciples are directed to seek him by finding this interior light, and letting it shine. There could be no clearer restatement of §3: "the kingdom is inside you, and it is outside of you."

More importantly, however, this is the key to understanding how dwelling in the light is equivalent to becoming two. The light within the man of light is Jesus the transcendent, comprehending source of all. When one finds this light, one realizes that one is not entirely oneself, not entirely *one*, but has *another*, namely Jesus, already inside. This is the splitting, the doubling, the becoming two that marks the entry into the kingdom, the place of life, from which vantage point one rules over the all—not from a place of distance from the all, but from a place of intimacy within the all, paradoxically embedded in a world that issues forth from a source within you.

In §16 Jesus hints that his hearers will not be attuned to his (quite literally) divisive message:

> (§16) Jesus said, "Men think, perhaps, that it is peace which I have come to cast upon the world. They do not know that it is dissension which I have come to cast upon the earth: fire, sword, war. For there will be five in a house: three will be against two, and two against three, the father against the son, and the son against the father. And they will stand solitary *(monachos)*."

Some scholars regard this saying as an especially early one, attesting to the historical Jesus's vibrant apocalyptic imagination. On this reading, Jesus's mention of fire, sword, and war is equivalent to his issuing a threat (or promise) of trial and tribulation prior to the advent of a new age. But this eschatological interpretation overlooks how this saying functions within the *Gospel of Thomas*, where fire, sword, and even war carry a very different set of connotations. Take fire, for example. At first §10 would seem to endorse the eschatological interpretation: "Jesus said, 'I have cast fire upon the world, and see, I am guarding it until it blazes." But if we allow the *Gospel of Thomas* to tell us what it means by its own words, we come to see that far from being a threat of an eschatological burn, fire is another name for Jesus himself, the light that is above the all and yet in humans of light: "Jesus said, 'He who is near me is near the fire, and he who is far from me is far from the kingdom'" (§82). Simply put, fire=Jesus=kingdom. So when Jesus says in §10 that he is casting fire upon the world and fanning the flames, he is setting souls ablaze with the divine light that is already within them. Fire is not a purifying punishment, but a deifying reward.

Even though the sword may be an instrument of war, here at least it is more precisely an instrument of division, of cutting in two. Five will be divided, three against two and vice versa, father against son and vice versa. And so divided, they will all "stand as solitary ones" (*ᵉm-monachos*). The Coptic translator has used a Greek word *monachos* here, meaning "solitary" or "single one."⁵⁹ It is the word that will come to be applied to Christian ascetics starting in the fourth century, namely "monk."⁶⁰ It is not clear, however, what the *Gospel of Thomas* means by "solitary." Consistent with her encratic interpretation, DeConick narrows the interpretive scope by translating *monachos* throughout as "celibate." It is better, I think, to leave it as Lambdin translates it, "solitary," because the reader is then free to ponder how someone who is "solitary" or "single" is also "one" or "two" (or both at once). §49 offers its own beatitude for the "solitary": "Blessed are the solitary (*monachos*) and elect, for you will find the kingdom. For you are from it, and to it you will return." We know from our discussion above, however, that to enter the kingdom—to "rule the all" as Jesus does—is first to recognize that one is not strictly speaking *one*, but one has *another*, namely Jesus, inside and outside of one, just as the kingdom is both inside and outside. Jesus the transcendent light is also the intimate light, the fully interior divine double. And if this is what it means to be *monachos* or "solitary," then it is a strange kind of solitude, becoming solitary only with the recognition of one's inner double.

Shifting from the more common language of kingdom and rule, however, §75 brings the "solitary" into the bridal chamber: "Many are standing at the door, but it is the solitary (*monachos*) who will enter the bridal chamber." Again, the encratic reading would have this saying suggest that only the celibate is fit to enter the bridal chamber or kingdom. Some scholars think that the Syriac title *īḥīdāyā* is behind the *Gospel of Thomas*'s Greek term *monachos*. And because *īḥīdāyā* or "single one" was used from the fourth century onward to describe consecrated Christian celibates, male and female, these scholars opine that the *Gospel of Thomas* is using this term in a similar way. However, as Sidney Griffith has argued, *īḥīdāyā* is first and foremost a Christological title:

> In Syriac ascetical texts the denotation of the term *īḥīdāyā* is not limited to the notion of singleness that bespeaks celibacy of

religious bachelorhood. Rather, it includes the element of singleness of purpose *(monotropos)*, along with the clear claim that a person called single for ascetical reasons is thereby also said to be in a special relationship with Jesus the Christ, the "Single One," the single son of God the Father (*John* 1.14, 18, 3.16, 18). This latter sense of the term may have been the primary one for the Syrians.[61]

Risto Uro has argued it is not "methodologically sound to read all of the later technical meanings of *ihidaya* [as referring to consecrated celibates] into the *monachos* of the *Gospel of Thomas*." Instead, it may be the earlier and broader connotation of *īhīdāyā*—namely, a "special relationship" with Jesus, the *Īhīdāyā*—that is relevant for understanding the use of *monachos* in the *Gospel of Thomas*. Rather than a celibate, the "single one" (*monachos* or *īhīdāyā*) may be he or she who has realized that special relationship. What exactly this special relationship is, and how singleness is constitutive of it, remains to be seen. But, following Uro, I will argue that singleness has much more to do with "unification"—and more specifically a unity-in-duality—than it does with renunciation or separation.[62]

Speaking of union, two of the sayings include the phrase "When you make the two one *(snau oua)*." As we have discussed, Klijn and DeConick regard duality (gender differentiation) as the problem, and unity (primordial androgyny) as the solution. Celibacy is the means of solving the problem. Their strongest evidence is in §22, where we read, "when you make male and female one and the same *(oua ouōt)*, with the result that the male not be male nor the female female . . . then you will enter [the kingdom.]" They take this injunction rather literally to mean that the *Gospel of Thomas* would have its readers renounce their gendered differentiation and live celibate lives anticipating their androgynous (re)entry into the kingdom. But if the reader is to take this literally, how is he or she to take the other injunctions, namely to make the inside like the outside and vice versa, the above like the below and vice versa, or to fashion eyes in place of an eye, a hand in place of a hand, a foot in place of a foot, and a likeness in place of a likeness? If we step back for a moment, this saying enjoins the mutual likeness of contraries (inside / outside, above /

below), the overcoming of our most fundamental embodied difference (gender), and a substitution of (parts of) one body for another. And if we take the injunction about making the male and female one and the same in this broader context, it seems that entry into the kingdom is much more about realizing the coincidence of opposites, or perhaps the failure of these contraries to obtain as real, than it is about a life of celibacy. To enter the kingdom, on this reading, is to fail (or rather, to succeed) in keeping one thing distinct from its contrary (the above from the below, the inside from the outside, male from female)—to bend the law of noncontradiction to its breaking point, to overcome contraries, and to realize a unity-in-duality. Recall that in Plato's *Parmenides*, the "instant" or "sudden" *(exaiphnēs)* is introduced as that transitional time that is not in time wherein we hover between the one and the not-one, violating no longer the law of noncontradiction but the law of the excluded middle: we neither are nor are not the one.[63]

It is important to underscore, however, that the unity imagined here is not one that fully overcomes or annihilates duality. In other words, "when you make the two one *(snau oua)*," the resulting "one and the same" *(oua ouōt)* is a tense unity-in-duality, humming with possibility, much as the energetic rest that marks our rule in the kingdom: recall that "the sign of your father in you" is precisely "movement *(kim)* and repose *(anapausis)*." In §23 Jesus says, "I shall choose you, one *(oua)* out of a thousand, and two *(snau)* out of ten thousand, and they shall stand as a single one *(oua ouōt)*." This phrase is not merely some "common expectation in apocalyptic literature," namely "the eschatological selection of the few."[64] The phrase may function that way in other contexts (Irenaeus, Epiphanius, Pistis Sophia, Mandaeism), but here in the *Gospel of Thomas* the message is quite clear: Jesus will choose one *(oua)* and two *(snau)* and they—the one and the two—will be "one and the same" *(oua ouōt)*. The unity that is captured by the phrase *oua ouōt* is one that preserves the two.

This unity-in-duality is in fact the theme on which a short sequence of sayings (§§47–50) meditates. §47 begins with a wariness of duality: "It is impossible for a man to mount two *(snau)* horses or to stretch two *(sᵉnte)* bows. And it is impossible for a servant to serve two *(snau)* masters; otherwise, he will honor the one *(oua)* and treat the other one *(pkeoua)* contemptuously." This serves as a warning: a certain kind of duality can ruin you by rendering you divided. But the warning about duality leads to a vision of unity-in-duality. In the very next saying Jesus encourages us, "If two *(snau)* make peace *(ᵉr-eirēnē)* with each other in this one house, they will say to the mountain, 'Move away,' and it will move away" (§48). Moving mountains would be familiar to the reader from §106, where Jesus says, "When you make the two one *(snau oua)*, you will become the sons of man, when you say, 'Mountain, move away,' it will move away." It is crucial to understand, then, that making the two one *(snau oua)* is the equivalent of "two *(snau)* mak[ing] peace with each other in this one *(ouōt)* house." The unity imagined here is one in which two "make peace with each other" and so become one, or more precisely, "one and the same" *(oua ouōt)*. And immediately on making clear that this unity is a unity-in-duality, Jesus offers an appropriate beatitude: "Blessed are the solitary *(monachos)* and elect *(et-sotp)*, for you will be find the kingdom. For you are from it, and to it you will return" (§49). The word "elect" here *(et-sotp)* is the same word that Jesus uses when he speaks in §23 about choosing the one and the two and having them stand as "one and the same" *(oua ouōt)*. In summary, the "solitary one" *(monachos)* or "one and the same" *(oua ouōt)* are the names given, not to celibates, but to those in whom the one and the two coincide, or coexist in peace. They are from the kingdom, and to it they will return (§49). The meditation series concludes with the saying we have already discussed, but I will now quote in full:

> (§50) Jesus said, "If they say to you, 'Where did you come from?,' say to them, 'We came from the light, the place where the light came into being on its own accord and established [itself] and became manifest through their image.' If they say to you, 'Is it you?,' say, 'We are its children, and we are the elect of the living father.' If they ask you, 'What is the sign of your father in you?,' say to them, 'It is movement *(kim)* and repose *(anapausis).*'"

With this saying we return to some of the themes raised by the first four sayings of the gospel: Jesus the light, who rules over the all, whose "place" is the kingdom. The blessed, elect, solitary ones are those in whom the one and the two coincide, those in whom contraries like movement and rest can coincide.

So far I have marked my reading in contrast to one influential interpretation, what I have called the "encratic" reading offered by Quispel, Klijn, and DeConick. Richard Valantasis, however, offers an interpretation of the *Gospel of Thomas* that aligns nicely with mine, especially on the matter of the one and the two. Valantasis regards the gospel as an "ascetical" text, by which he means that it "revolves about the intentional reformation of the self through specific practices."[65] Rather than define asceticism narrowly in terms of specific renunciatory practices—such as celibacy—Valantasis argues, following its etymology, that asceticism is about the practice or exercise (Greek *askesis*) of transforming the self: "No particular action in itself constitutes an ascetical one, but the intention of specific actions to create an alternative identity within a larger social or religious setting does."[66] Traditional renunciatory practices—such as fasting, celibacy, social isolation—are in fact rather absent in the gospel, and the "encratic" interpretation depends on supplying a backdrop such that opaque sayings can be decoded and their renunciatory message made clear. But the single most important practice that the *Gospel of Thomas* endorses is not any sort of renunciation but rather the *interpretation* of Jesus's secret sayings. Whatever else Jesus would seem to have his audience do or not do, the gospel is clear about the importance of interpretation.

What is the "new subjectivity" that the *Gospel of Thomas* is attempting to realize in its readers, who are ascetics by virtue of the fact that they are interpreters? Crucially, Valantasis recognizes that the reader's itinerary from "renounced self" to "emergent self" is not reducible to the singular vector of the two becoming one, as it often is on the encratic reading. He underscores the tension in many of the sayings between "singularity" and "duplicity" (his preferred terms for unity and duality). In other words, the *Gospel of Thomas* does not endorse a selfhood of simple singularity or easy integration.

While he thinks that "there is no clarity about the precise referent to [the one and the two]," nevertheless he insists that "the newly emerging subjectivity" is realized precisely through "playing with the transformation of the one into two and two into one."[67] Following Valantasis, then, I suspect that the practice of interpreting the secret sayings of Jesus invites the astute, ascetic reader into the play between the one and the two, but a play that takes place simultaneously on the page and in his or her own self. Thus, the practice of interpreting the gnomic sayings regarding the one and the two, the "single one" and the "one and the same," serves to transform the reader into what Henry Corbin calls a *unus-ambo*, a one-yet-two.

Where I differ slightly with Valantasis, however, is on the matter of "the precise referent[s]" of the one and the two. He writes, "It can categorically be stated that the new subjectivity promulgated in these sayings revolves about singularity and duplicity even when it is not clear to what these categories refer."[68] I think we can push further and find greater clarity. Let us recall that §50 (and the short meditative series on unity-in-duality, which it concludes) returns the reader to some of the central themes of the first four sayings. The kingdom is the place of light, our whence and our whither, and the sign of paternity is the coincidence of movement and repose. We also know that Jesus is that light, both the transcendent source of the all and the intimate light illuminating us, the sons of the living father. Thus Jesus, like the kingdom, is inside and outside of us. All this helps us get further clarity on what the one and the two mean. On the one hand, to make the one two is to realize that this light within oneself is Jesus, and thereby to realize that one is no longer strictly speaking *one*self, but somehow also two. On the other hand, to make the two one is to hold this duality together in peace, to be a one that is also two, a unity-in-duality, and so to bear the name "solitary" or "single one." In other words, the categories of the one and the two are not simply abstractions that the reader is supposed only to ponder, but instead refer precisely to the indwelling of Jesus in oneself (the one self becoming now two) and the self's negotiated identity as a unity containing but not annihilating that duality (the two becoming one). Interpreting these secret sayings not only discloses the truth of who we are, but realizes that truth in us. The gospel imagines its readers not only learning that Jesus is the light in them, but in fact awakening Jesus in them.

BECOMING THOMAS, BECOMING JESUS

What has any of this to do with the apostle Judas Thomas the twin (*tāwmā / didymos*)? How does the indwelling of Jesus that renders oneself a unity-in-duality relate to the apostle to whom Jesus spoke these secret sayings, the apostle who is said to be the very twin of Jesus? Are they distinct discourses, the meditation on the one and the two and the theology of twinning? To answer these questions, we will have to look closely at another handful of sayings:

> (§13) Jesus said to his disciples, "Compare me to someone and tell me whom I am like."
> Simon Peter said to him, "You are like a righteous angel."
> Matthew said to him, "You are like a wise philosopher."
> Thomas said to him, "Master, my mouth is wholly incapable of saying whom you are like."

Jesus will go on to praise Thomas for his confession of impotence and ineffability. Perhaps the key to understanding Thomas's confession is to be found in another saying: "Jesus said, 'I shall give you what no eye has seen and what no ear has heard and what no hand has touched and what has never occurred to the human mind'" (§17). What does Jesus give except his own light and life, the knowledge of our whence and whither (the kingdom) as children of light? This gift can be specified only by a series of negations of sight, hearing, touch, and thinking. If Jesus is the transcendent light—ruling the all, shining inside the children of light—it should come as no surprise that Thomas "is wholly incapable of saying whom [he is] like," for he is beyond any simile. In response to his confession, Jesus praises Thomas:

> (§13) Jesus said, "I am not your master. Because you have drunk, you have become intoxicated from the bubbling spring which I have measured out."

> And he took him and withdrew and told him three things. When Thomas returned to his companions, they asked him, "What did Jesus say to you?"
>
> Thomas said to them, "If I tell you one of the things which he told me, you will pick up stones and throw them at me; a fire will come out of the stones and burn you up."

The reader is never told what Jesus said to Thomas as they withdrew in private. Some might think that the gospel suggests that this dangerous secret is itself ineffable, or that the author of the gospel did not wish to put this esoteric revelation on the page, preferring to have it delivered orally to a ready adept. I am inclined to think, rather, that the careful reader of the gospel can infer what three things Jesus told Thomas.

The first hint is Thomas's claim that the other disciples would stone him if he were to divulge the secret. Stoning was a punishment reserved by Jews for severe crimes, with none more severe than blasphemy. Following Nicola Denzey Lewis, I suggest that a reader of the *Gospel of Thomas* would infer from this saying that Jesus told Thomas, "I am God."[69] The second hint is Jesus's immediate reaction to Thomas's confession. "I am not your master"—what could this mean except that Thomas is Jesus's equal: both of them "rule over the all" (§2). He goes on to say that, "because you have drunk, you have become intoxicated from the bubbling spring which I have measured out." Again, the careful reader will straightaway recall §108, where Jesus says, "He who will drink from my mouth will become like me. I myself shall become he, and the things that are hidden will be revealed to him." More than merely equals, Jesus and Thomas begin to merge into a single entity—on my reading a unity-in-duality, a "single" or "solitary" one (*oua ouōt* or *monachos*) that makes the two (*snau*=Jesus and Thomas) one (*oua*). Again, following Denzey Lewis, I suggest that a reader of the gospel would infer that the second thing Jesus told Thomas was "I am you." Notice that when Jesus speaks from the first person singular—"I myself"—he suggests a future identity between Thomas and himself: "I shall become he." But when he speaks from the third person singular—"He who"—he suggests not a future identity but a likeness: "he will become *like* me." This is not a fully reciprocal relationship, not an identity that can be rendered $1=1$.[70] For one who has drunk from the ecstatic cup of self-knowledge, Jesus *is* his innermost self such that Jesus can say, "I am he" or "I am she." But the same one—whom Jesus can claim to be—can only say "I am *like* Jesus." The one who comes to realize that he is two—himself and Jesus—does not therefore entirely annihilate the difference between the two. The gap between identity and likeness persists, and it is the persistence of this gap or difference that ensures that the resulting one carries always the trace of the two. I have already suggested that the name for the one that carries the trace of the two is precisely and paradoxically the "single" or "solitary" one (*oua ouōt, monachos*). I wish now to suggest that "twin" (*didymos / tāwmā*) is another name for this same one, namely that one (in whom remains the trace of the two) who is drunk from the ecstatic cup of self-knowledge, who knows that Jesus is his innermost self who can claim identity with him, but with whom he can claim only progressive likeness. Here is where the discourse of the one and the two and the theology of twinship meet and merge.

There remains the third and final thing that Jesus told Thomas in secret—what might it have been? The answer brings us back to the very first saying, and what is on offer to the reader, the interpreter: "And [Jesus] said, 'Whoever finds the interpretation of these sayings will not experience death.'" According to Denzey Lewis,

> Thomas is twins with Jesus, but he is also twins with someone else: whoever reads and understands the words of the living Jesus. One who understands these words, in the end, is returned to the primordial light. In effect, she, or he, understands that they too, become Christs [*sic*].[71]

The third saying would, on this reading, suggest to Thomas that not only he, but also all who hear (and later read) these secret sayings, and find their proper interpretation, are twins of Jesus. The third saying extends the gift of twinship to the community of readers, of interpreters. The ever-expanding community of twins, of those in whom the primordial light of Jesus shines, of those who have made the one two and the two one, is the realization of the kingdom.

Hence Denzey Lewis opines that the third saying might have been, "We are the Kingdom of God." The "radical" question posed by the *Gospel of Thomas*, then, is simply, Can we all become Thomases? Can we, too, all become Christs?

IMAGE AND LIKENESS

There remains one final secret saying to which we now turn—like so many others, a "difficult" saying offering only "aphoristic clues" as to its meaning.[72] It reads,

> (§84) Jesus said, "When you see your likeness *(eine)*, you rejoice. But when you see your images *(ikōn)* which came into being before you, and which neither die or become manifest, how much more will you have to bear!"

Jesus's distinction between image and likeness quite obviously has something to do with Gen 1:26, "Then God said, "Let us make man in our image, after our likeness."[73] Exactly what is unclear, however, because the distinction between image and likeness spurred endless commentary by Jews and Christians alike. A plausible interpretation of §84 would suggest that the "likeness" refers to our human form, the sort of thing we see reflected in an everyday mirror. Like Ovid's Narcissus, we "rejoice" at this likeness because we recognize and esteem this surface self.

By contrast we each have an "image" that came into being before us, before, that is, we had the human forms we now recognize as our likenesses. This is almost certainly meant to be the image of God imprinted on all humans, as told in Gen 1:26. It never dies nor becomes manifest. And yet it is still something to behold; that is, we are meant to *see* this image, which is presently hidden from us. In *Seek to See Him*, DeConick has collected an impressive array of ancient sources as witnesses to this theme in "vision mysticism."[74] Again, following Quispel, she imagines the Platonic tradition of the *daimōn* merging with Jewish angelology to form "the idea of a heavenly double [that] was a major constituent of primitive Jewish-Christian dogma."[75] She reads the *Gospel of Thomas* as exemplary of this "primitive Jewish-Christian" matrix. I wonder, however, on the basis of our discussion above of the living Jesus as the indwelling light, and the coincidence of the one and the two, whether the obscured "image" imagined here in §84 is Jesus, to whom, like Judas Thomas, we are called to become twins. It is not so much that we each have an individual divine double. On the contrary, our primordial image is uniform: it is Jesus, the Son whom Paul in Col 1:15 described as "the image of the invisible God." To see that image, to become Jesus's twin, is to become children of light.

The question for me is not so much *who* or *what* this image in §84 is—I think it refers to Jesus the transcendent light—but rather *how* we can see it. It seems crucial that in both cases, image and likeness, we are seeing our own reflection. In the case of the likeness, we use an everyday mirror to see a reflection of our surface self, which gives us joy. In the case of the image, however, we must find a different reflecting surface, a mirror that reflects something hidden deep within us. What sort of mirror could reflect our secret self better than these secret sayings? What sort of tool could unearth this deeply embedded image except one that promises its user that he will seek, find, become troubled and astonished (§2)? Jesus's warning in §84—"how much more will you have to bear!"—is a warning not only of how difficult it will be to bring this secret self to light so as to see it, but also that this vision of oneself or "autoscopy" will inaugurate a progressive and painful assimilation to that image. This is why I think Athanasius's understanding of the Psalter is a good contemporary analogue to the *Gospel of Thomas*'s understanding of the work it does on its readers: it is the mirror in which the reader sees his dual image, both the unblemished image of God and its sorry state now, and inaugurates the difficult therapy of making the latter like the former. The notion that autoscopy is ambivalent will return in Chapter 5, where I will argue that Plotinus's disappointment in Narcissus's "Narcissism" reveals his own commitments to a thoroughgoing "Narcissan" dialectic of progressive self-seeing and (re)union with the self seen. And if Athanasius on the Psalter is a close contemporary analogue to the *Gospel of Thomas*'s self-understanding, then they are both also children of Plato, descendants of the dialogue, in which the text becomes the mirror in which the reader sees his image, real and ideal (and the gap between).

Origen of Alexandria: Becoming John, Becoming Jesus

This chapter began with a consideration of the apostle Thomas, who emerged from his synoptic obscurity to prominence with the Gospel of John, where he appears as a more central character, Thomas who is "called the Twin *(didymos)*" (11:16, 20:24, 21:2). It is only fitting, then, that we conclude with the Gospel of John. Recall that certain scholars have argued that the Gospels of Thomas and John are representatives of more or less distinct communities of early Christians, communities in sharp disagreement on certain points. However, I wish to return to the Gospel of John from a different angle. Recall that the Greek papyri fragments of the *Gospel of Thomas* (P. Oxy. 1, 654, and 655) date to third-century Egypt. Scholars date the full Coptic version of the gospel, discovered near the town of Nag Hammadi in Egypt, to the first half of the fourth century. At a minimum, then, we know that the *Gospel of Thomas*—whenever and wherever it was first composed or collected—was circulating in Egypt between the years 200 and 350 CE. Egypt's capital city, Alexandria, was home to a great many intellectuals during this period—Christian and otherwise. I wish to focus on one in particular: Origen, born in Alexandria in 185 CE, where he lived until 234, when he moved to Caesarea in Palestine. He died in 254 or 255 CE from injuries sustained under torture during the Decian persecution several years earlier. During his Alexandrian tenure, probably in 231, Origen began work on a commentary on the Gospel of John, on which he would continue to work for much of his remaining life.

The commentary begins slowly: Book 1 purports to cover the first half verse. In his preface to the commentary, Origen insists that the four gospels are "the first-fruits of the entire Scripture," and furthermore that the Gospel of John is "the first-fruits of the gospels."[76] It is so superlative a document that no one can "understand *(labein ton noun)* this gospel unless he reclines on Jesus's breast and unless he accepts Mary from Jesus as one who has become his own mother."[77] The first condition is an allusion to "the beloved disciple," an unnamed disciple in the Gospel of John who is said to have "reclined on the breast of Jesus" at the Last Supper (John 13:23). Origen follows the mainstream tradition in identifying the beloved disciple as John, the apostle and evangelist. The second condition also has to do with the same figure: the Gospel of John tells us that at the cross were gathered Jesus's mother, Mary, his mother's sister (also named Mary), Mary Magdalene, and finally the beloved disciple. The gospel continues, "When Jesus saw his mother, and the disciple whom he loved standing near, he said to his mother, 'Woman, behold your son!' Then he said to the disciple, 'Behold, your mother!' And from that hour the disciple took her to his own home" (19:26–27). For Origen, both episodes feature John, the beloved disciple, and it is this John whom the reader must become in order to understand or "receive the mind" *(labein ton noun)* of this gospel. He explains,

> And, in order to become another John, he must become such a person that, like John, he has been designated by Jesus as one who is Jesus. For no one but Jesus was a son of Mary according to those who soundly glorify her, but when Jesus says to his mother, "See, your son" (Jn 19:26), rather than, "See, this man is also your son," it is the equivalent of saying, "See, this man is Jesus whom you bore." For everyone who is perfected "no longer lives, but Christ lives in him" (see Gal 2:20), and since Christ lives in him, Christ says to Mary concerning him, "See, your son."[78]

Notice first that Origen disowns the possibility that Mary had any other children—in other words he confesses her perpetual virginity, here and elsewhere.[79] For him, Jesus was Mary's only child, conceived by the power of the Holy Spirit. James or for that matter Judas (Thomas) could only be Jesus's brother in a loose sense of the term: they were the sons fathered by Joseph from a previous marriage.

To understand the gospel, Origen insists, one must become "another John," that is, he must become the beloved disciple, reclining on Jesus's breast and standing at the foot of the cross. But to become John is to be "designated *(deichthēnai)* by Jesus as one who is Jesus." This is what Origen takes Jesus to have done from the cross. His injunction to John and his mother Mary is not figural, but quite literal. "Woman, behold your son" does *not* mean merely that Mary should treat John as a son, and he her as a mother. Rather, it means that John *is* Jesus, the very son whom Mary bore and now weeps for on the cross. By his words from the cross, Jesus replicates himself. Origen then pivots to the apostle Paul to help explain this point. John is perfected, and this means that John, like Paul, can confess that "it is no longer I who live, but Christ who lives in me" (Gal 2:20). John, like Paul, is another Jesus, so much so that Jesus can say to Mary, "Behold your son."

This is a rather striking parallel with the *Gospel of Thomas*, in that Origen suggests that a Christian may, indeed must, become another apostle (in this case John) and thereby another Jesus. Recall that in §108, Jesus says, "He who will drink from my mouth will become like me. I myself shall become he." The reader in the *Gospel of Thomas* is invited to take up the place of Thomas, to be the twin of Jesus. To be the twin is to know (a) that Jesus is already one's innermost self and (b) that one is becoming ever more that innermost self. Origen demands that anyone who wishes to understand the Gospel of John first become John, who has already become Jesus.

It is tempting to imagine that Origen is here responding to the *Gospel of Thomas* and its theology of twinning. We know, after all, that he read the *Gospel of Thomas*. In his first homily on Luke, Origen complains about the proliferation of gospels:

> The Church has four gospels. Heretics have very many. One of them is entitled *According to the Egyptians*, another *According to the Twelve Apostles*. Basilides, too, dared to write a gospel and give it his own name. "Many have tried" (Lk 1:1) to write, but only four Gospels have been approved. Our doctrines about the Person of our Lord and Savior should be drawn from these approved Gospels. I know one gospel called *According to Thomas*, and another *According to Matthaias*. We have read many others, too, lest we appear ignorant of anything, because of those people who think they know something if they have examined these gospels. But in all these questions we approve of nothing but what the Church approves of, namely only four canonical Gospels.[80]

His *Homilies on Luke* were written just after he wrote the preface to his *Commentary on John*, probably early in the period from 231 to 244 CE.[81] Thus, we cannot be certain that Origen had read the *Gospel of Thomas* by the time he wrote his commentary. But the striking parallel suggests that he had, perhaps before he moved to Caesarea, and that it made an impression on him. He seems to disapprove of the *Gospel of Thomas*, although he does not explain exactly why. We can conjecture that he would object to the gospel's self-presentation as having been written by Jesus's twin brother Judas. He could only tolerate the title "twin" if he understood it as figural rather than literal. But is it possible that he was rather taken with the idea that a Christian is called to become Jesus through taking up the position of one his most cherished disciples? Is it possible that Origen borrowed the idea from the *Gospel of Thomas*, but rendered it in a way more palatable to his canonical conscience and his firm belief in Mary's perpetual virginity? In short, I wonder whether he borrowed the structure of the divine double that he finds in the *Gospel of Thomas*, stripped it of the theme of "twinning" associated with the apostle Judas Thomas, and transposed it onto the beloved disciple, John. This scenario would be in keeping with Origen's "ambivalent attitude" to the *Gospel of Thomas*.[82] For although in this homily on Luke he dismisses it, in other homilies from his Caesarean period he seems to quote a saying of Jesus from it, not mentioning its (suspect) source but allowing for the possibility that "this may be truly what he said."[83] If he was bold enough to quote from the *Gospel of Thomas*, I wonder whether he was bold enough to appropriate its theology for his own exegetical purposes in his *Commentary on John*.

It may very well be that this is not a case of direct influence, as I have suggested. But even if it is not, the parallel between the *Gospel of Thomas* and Origen's *Commentary on John* is simply evidence for the further proliferation of the divine double. If the one did not influence the other, then they each stand as distinct examples of a Christianized divine double in the third century. Whether or not Origen's theology of "becoming another John" was influenced by the *Gospel of Thomas*'s theology of twinning, the fact remains that the Christianized divine double does not remain entirely on the heterodox fringe of third-century Christianity, as some might prefer it would so as more easily to dismiss it. On the contrary, the divine double, in the guise of the beloved disciple John, finds a beachhead in the preeminent theologian of "proto-orthodox" Christianity in the third century.

I HAVE PROPOSED a reinterpretation of the *Gospel of Thomas* centering on its theology of the twin and the relationship of the one and the two. My reinterpretation has required drawing forth an admittedly esoteric teaching from a number of opaque sayings. And yet I would submit that the *Gospel of Thomas* authorizes the reader to do precisely this, rather than to impute to it an external interpretive frame, as I believe the "encratic" reading does. On my reading, the *Gospel of Thomas* is perhaps our first, but more importantly our most profound, Christian witness to the divine double. The reader is invited to interpret these secret sayings, and to realize that Jesus the transcendent light is his innermost self. Thus rendered two, he must now make those two one: he and his divine double must make peace in a single house. The self who succeeds in finding the identity or union of the two is named a "single one" *(oua ouōt)* or a "solitary" *(monachos)*. And that self thereby takes up the position of Judas Thomas, Jesus's twin *(didymos)* or equal. This self-knowledge—that one is not only one but also two, a "single one" *(oua ouōt)* or a "solitary" *(monachos)*—is a knowledge hard earned through a process of reading and interpretation. These secret sayings become the mirror in which the reader comes to see his secret self reflected back to him: his innermost image, the living Jesus, the image of the invisible God.

3

Syzygies, Twins, and Mirrors

IN CHAPTER 2 we looked closely at what is perhaps the earliest Christian witness to the divine double: the figure of Judas Thomas, the twin of Jesus, who is mentioned in the Gospel of John and whose legacy is associated with another gospel bearing his own name. This chapter looks beyond the *Gospel of Thomas*, both to other early witnesses to the divine double and to later elaborations of the Thomas tradition. The first half of this chapter examines two early witnesses: Tatian the Assyrian, a Christian author from the second century and contemporary with the circulation of the *Gospel of Thomas* in the Eastern Mediterranean, who imagines a "syzygy" or conjunction of each human soul with its divine spirit, which spirit it lost after the fall; and the second-century Christian theologian Valentinus and even more so later Valentinian sources (the *Gospel of Philip* and the *Excerpts of Theodotus*) that imagine, each in their own way, the sacraments as effecting a union between us and our angelic counterparts, images and their archetypes. Attending to these early sources makes it clear that the figure of the divine double is not limited to texts associated with Thomas. The second half of this chapter continues to mine the vein of the Thomas tradition and considers in turn the later texts that comprise it: *The Book of Thomas the Contender*, the apocryphal *Acts of Thomas*, and the "Hymn of the Pearl" embedded therein. We will be looking to see how the divine double finds different expressions in these various texts, and how the themes of "syzygy," twins, and mirrors are threads that run through both halves of the chapter.

We would do well, however, to ask again what exactly we mean by "tradition" here (see the earlier discussion of "school" and "tradition" from Chapter 2). To be clear, we have now three texts that are closely associated with the apostle Judas Thomas, twin brother of Jesus: the *Gospel of Thomas*, *The Book of Thomas*, the *Acts of Thomas*—and if we consider it apart from the *Acts* in which it is embedded, the "Hymn of the Pearl."[1] At a minimum, then, "tradition" means only this: these three (or four) texts and no more. This is, first and foremost, what I mean when I appeal to the Thomas "tradition"—a group of texts bound together not only by their association with the apostle Judas Thomas but also, so I insist, by their participation in yet another, and broader, "tradition" of the divine double—broader because it reaches back before Christianity and extends well beyond its borders. The Thomas tradition's variation on the divine double is principally a theology of the twin and secondarily a theology of the bridal chamber. Both are present in the *Gospel of Thomas*, as we saw in Chapter 2. In this chapter we will see the theology of the twin and of the bridal chamber developed each in its own right and correlated to the other.

Tatian's Divine Double: The Syzygy of Soul and Spirit

What little we know with confidence of Tatian (ca. 120–ca. 180) comes from the conclusion of his own single surviving work, the *Oratio ad Graecos* (or *Address to the Greeks*): "All this, men of Greece, I have compiled for you—I Tatian, a philosopher among the barbarians, born in the land of Assyria, and educated first in your learning and secondly in what I profess to preach."[2] From the *Oratio* we gather that he was born in Assyria (the land east of the river Euphrates) to pagan parents and received a traditional Hellenistic education or *paideia*—exactly where, we do not know. Eusebius of Caesarea (ca. 260–339) describes him as "a man distinguished in Greek learning and memorable for his writings" (*Ecclesiastical History* 4.16). After extensive travels, he found himself in Rome, where he became a student of Justin (ca. 100–ca. 165), who would go on to earn the title

"Martyr." Tatian refers to his teacher as "the most admirable Justin," and Whittaker credits the martyr with converting Tatian to Christianity.[3] This would make sense, because like Justin, Tatian understands his conversion as one to a new "philosophy," except that this "barbarian philosophy" is very ancient, and certainly older than the Greeks'.[4] The twofold apologetic aim of the *Oratio* is, in one scholar's words, "to convince the Greeks of the error of their ways (worship of their false gods) and to badger them into discovering the truth as Tatian himself has already done."[5]

The *Oratio* also forwards a version of the divine double, although in a very different idiom than the *Gospel of Thomas*. Commenting on John 1:1 ("In the beginning was the Word"), Tatian calls the Word *(logos)* the "firstborn" *(prototokon)* of God the Father.[6] Tatian marks his own rebirth to the original birth of the Word: "so I too, in imitation *(mimesis)* of the Word, have been reborn and have obtained understanding of the truth."[7] In other words, Tatian understands himself as a *logos* in imitation of the eternal *Logos*. Regarding this passage, H. J. W. Drijvers says, "Man can be born again, as the first-born Son was born, and through this they become identical with one another. The term *mimesis* signifies a precise relationship . . . the reborn man and the first-born of God are twins."[8] By speaking of this relationship explicitly as one of "twins," Drijvers is anticipating the *Acts of Thomas*. Although Tatian does not speak of twins per se, Drijvers thinks that Tatian's notion of the human as a son of God, in imitation of the eternal *Logos* and Son of God, makes of them twin brothers, both sons of God the Father. In other words, Tatian, like Origen after him, is developing a theology of the divine double in dialogue with the Gospel of John (see Chapter 2): whereas Origen looked to the beloved apostle John at the foot of the cross as the model for doubled discipleship, Tatian looks to the prologue and the rebirth of every human in imitation of the eternal birth of God's Word.

But this theology of the divine double soon gives way to another and in yet a different idiom. Tatian describes how Satan led his fellow angels and humanity astray. All these crestfallen creatures were banished by God, and in exile each of them lost their "more powerful spirit."[9] What or who is this spirit or *pneuma* that abandoned each creature upon its exile? Tatian explains,

> [There are] two different kinds of spirits, one of which is called soul, but the other is greater than the soul; it is the image and likeness of God. The first humans were endowed with both, so that they might be part of the material world, and at the same time above it. This is how things are.[10]

Humans have now only their own soul as a spirit; the second spirit, the one greater than soul, has abandoned them. This other spirit is the image and likeness of God (like the "image" in §84 of the *Gospel of Thomas*), and so without it humans are bereft of the divine, or nearly so. Left to its own devices, the soul will dissolve with the body at death, and rise again at the appointed time either to suffer "immortal punishment," or to live:

> Because of this if [the soul] lives alone it inclines towards matter and dies with the flesh, but if it gains union *(syzygian)* with the divine spirit it is not unaided, but mounts to the realms above where the spirit leads it; for the spirit's home is above, but the soul's birth is below. So the spirit became originally the soul's companion *(syndiaiton)*, but gave it up when the soul was unwilling to follow it. The soul kept a spark *(enausma)*, as it were, of the spirit's power, yet because of its separation it could no longer see things that are perfect, and so in search for God went astray and fashioned a multitude of gods, following the demons and their hostile devices. God's spirit is not given to all, but dwelling among some who behaved justly and being intimately connected with the soul *(symperiplekomenon tēi psychēi)* it revealed by predictions to the other souls what had been hidden. The souls which were obedient to wisdom attracted to themselves the kindred spirit *(epeilkon to pneuma syngenes)*, but those which were disobedient and rejected the servant of the suffering God were clearly shown to be enemies of God rather than his worshippers.[11]

The fallen soul is not entirely bereft of the divine because it keeps a divine spark of the spirit's power. This spark is an ambivalent remainder: it fires souls to worship false gods, more precisely to worship fallen angels (demons) as if they were gods. But by kindling this spark with a life of righteousness, the soul draws down its former companion *(syndiaiton)*, its kindred spirit *(to pneuma syngenes)*.

That wise and righteous soul who succeeds in attracting its kindred spirit forms with it a "union," which is how Whittaker renders *syzygia*. Formed from the prefix "together" *(syn-)* and the word "yoke" *(zygos)*, a *syzygia* is, at its most literal, a conjunction of two cattle "yoked together," forming a pair or a couple.[12] English cognates include "conjugal" (by way of Latin) and "zygote," a single cell formed from two gamete cells in sexual reproduction. If this *syzygia* is a "union," then, it is one that preserves the distinctions between its constitutive pair, as is the case with not only cattle under a single yoke, but also spouses in a marriage or twins in a womb. In fact the adjectival form, *syzygos* (which is often used as a noun), refers to one half of the conjoined pair, and can mean "spouse," "comrade," or "companion." We shall see *syzygia / os* appear in this and following chapters: It is a central feature of Valentinian cosmology and, so I will suggest, anthropology. It is one of the titles by which Jesus addresses Judas Thomas in *The Book of Thomas the Contender*, the "union" between the bride and Jesus in the *Acts of Thomas*, and the twin-companion of the third-century Mesopotamian "Apostle of Light" Mani (Chapter 4). And Plotinus often uses a verbal form *(syzeugnumi)* to describe how an intellectual subject is joined to an intelligible object in the inner life of universal Intellect (Chapter 5). It is therefore one of the lexical threads that weaves its way in and out of the different traditions of the divine double.

Back to Tatian: he insists that although it may be that only some souls have preserved this *syzygia* or conjunction with their spirit, the possibility is open to all humans: "It is possible for everyone who is naked to get this adornment, and race back to his ancient kinship."[13] And so he shifts from exposition to exhortation: "We ought now to search for what we once had and have lost, and link *(zeugnumai)* the soul to the Holy Spirit and busy ourselves with the union *(syzygian)* ordained by God."[14] Notice the language of linking and union—all from the root *zyg-* or "yoke." But notice also that here the spirit to which we are each called to unite is explicitly the Holy Spirit. This raises a question, a version of which we have encountered in the *Gospel of Thomas:* Do we each have an individual divine double, or is there a single divine serving as the double for each of us? The *Gospel of Thomas* imagines each of us taking up the position of Judas Thomas, and so becoming the twin of Jesus, the light that dwells in every human, who renders each one of us two, and then again a solitary or single one. In other words, in the *Gospel of Thomas* there is only one divine double, Jesus, and he invites everyone to be his twin. In Tatian we see much the same: We each have lost our spirit companion, and now struggle to kindle the spark of it in our dark lives. Although we may each experience its loss and recovery as very much individual, the spirit whom we attract and with whom we unite is the very same spirit with whom everyone unites, the one Holy Spirit. This also introduces a horizontal dimension to the vertical divine double: If we are each joined to a single divine double by way of this vertical axis (*mimēsis* of the eternal Word or *syzygia* with the Holy Spirit), then we are all joined to each other on a horizontal axis, just as students are bound to each other by virtue of a shared teacher, or children by virtue of shared parents.

Tatian's theology of the divine double begins with an account of how we are each reborn in imitation of the birth of the eternal *Logos*, and how thereby the two are twin siblings of sorts, both children of God the Father. He then expands that notion of the divine double by appeal to a fallen division between the soul and the spirit (which is identical to the Holy Spirit), a division that is to be overcome in a restoration of our prelapsarian syzygy. This is perhaps best captured in the following line from Tatian's *Oratio*, which we could well imagine included among the secret sayings of the *Gospel of Thomas:* "You ask continually who God is, and overlook what is in you."[15] *What is in you*. Recall that when Origen explains that the beloved disciple at the foot of the cross has already become Jesus himself (such that he is Mary's very own son), he appeals to Paul's famous line from his Letter to the Galatians, "it is no longer I who live, but Christ who lives in me" (Gal 2:20). Tatian is probably also alluding to Paul when he remarks, "you overlook what is in you." Regardless, it is nearly certain that Tatian's framework for the divine double—namely, the loss and recovery of the prelapsarian spirit—owes to

Paul's distinction between soul and spirit (Heb 4:12), or between the psychic *(psychikos)* and the spiritual *(pneumatikos)* human (1 Cor 2: 9–16). Already we have seen, then, three early Christian witnesses to a notion of the divine double appealing to at least three different threads from the New Testament: the *Gospel of Thomas* to Judas Thomas the twin of Jesus; Tatian to the (re)birth of the *Logos* and the soul's loss and recovery of its *syzygos* spirit; and Origen to the beloved disciple John's having become Jesus himself, on the model of Paul's having confessed to the indwelling of Christ.

Valentinus, Valentinianism, and the Union of the Image and the Angel

We turn now to a contemporary of Tatian's by the name of Valentinus (100–170 CE): born in Egypt, educated in Alexandria, a convert to Christianity, and a teacher first in Alexandria and thereafter in Rome. Due to the fact that he was retroactively identified as a heretic, first by Irenaeus of Lyons (ca. 130–ca. 202 CE) and then by other heresiologists, most of his writings are now lost. But in his monumental work, *Against Heresies*, Irenaeus also tells us a great deal about Valentinus, his followers, and their distinctive theology—although his account does not square with the surviving sources in the Valentinian tradition.[16] Central to the Valentinian system, at least as told by Irenaeus, is the notion that the cosmos is organized into an emanating series of male / female syzygies or pairs.[17] The first two syzygies—(1) the Ineffable and the Silence and (2) Parent and Truth—exist in a wholly transcendent realm called the *bathus* or "deep." From them emanate, respectively, two more pairs, and the whole of them constitute what is called the primary "Ogdoad" or eight. And from the last of them in turn emanate another series of twelve and ten, the "Dodecad" and "Decad." All told, then, there are thirty divinities or "aeons" (fifteen syzygies) that make up this divine realm, called the Pleroma or "Fullness," balanced equally between male and female.

The balance of the Pleroma was upset by a single female aeon, Sophia, who left the divine realm and gave birth apart from her appointed *syzygos* or consort. This turn away from the Pleroma set in a motion a series of events that led to the creation of the material world by a demiurge, a figure borrowed from Plato's *Timaeus*. The surviving texts (especially Irenaeus's *Against Heresies*) offer very different accounts of the story of the creation of the world and humankind, their plight, and the efforts of the savior, Christ, to restore spiritual *(pneumatikoi)* humans to the Pleroma. However, neither the horizontal syzygies that populate the Pleroma nor the different mythological narrations of the creation of the world and humankind are entirely relevant for our purposes.

What *is* relevant is later Valentinian reflection on the sacraments as effecting a conjunction or union of each individual with his or her angelic counterpart. We will look first to a text called the *Gospel of Philip*, which follows immediately after the *Gospel of Thomas* in Codex II of the Nag Hammadi library.[18] It is an anthology consisting of some one hundred short excerpts "pertaining to the meaning and value of sacraments within the context of a Valentinian conception of the human predicament and life after death."[19] No one knows exactly when or where it was compiled (never mind the excerpts themselves), although it must have been well before it was translated into Coptic in the mid-fourth century. The text names five sacraments: baptism, chrismation (anointing), eucharist—all of which are familiar, at least in name—as well as two less familiar: "redemption" and the "bridal chamber."[20]

Though it is difficult to summarize a wandering anthology, one leading scholar has tried:

> According to this gospel the existential malady of humanity results from the differentiation of the sexes. When Eve was separated from Adam, the original androgynous unity was broken (68,22–26). The purpose of Christ's coming is to reunite Adam and Eve (70,12–17). Just as a husband and wife unite in the bridal chamber, so also the reunion effected by Christ takes place in a bridal chamber, the sacramental one (70,17–22), where a person receives a foretaste and assurance of ultimate union with an angelic, heavenly counterpart (cf. 58,10–14).[21]

Here we have an explicit mythology of primordial androgyny—precisely the sort of mythology that some scholars have used (in my view, misused) to read the *Gospel of Thomas*'s opaque sayings on the one and the two, the solitary and the single one. This mythology informs the excerpts' reflections on the meaning and value of the sacraments.

In one of the most famous passages from the *Gospel of Philip*, Jesus speaks to a divine addressee in the midst of a "thanksgiving" or eucharist: "You who have joined *(hōtr)* the perfect light with the holy spirit, unite *(hotr)* the angels with us also, as being the images *(ikōn)*" (58,11–14). Here Jesus is praying that by the power of the eucharist we here, who are images, might be united with our angels. This is in contrast to the *Gospel of Thomas*'s appeal to "image" in §84, where it is our divine double, Jesus the light, who is the image.[22] For the *Gospel of Philip*, it is *we* who are the images, and the angels who are, as it were, our archetypes. The union or conjunction hoped for here is described in Coptic with a verb *(hōtr)* that is perhaps translating the original Greek *syzeugnumi*, "to yoke"—the verbal form of the noun *syzygos* or *syzygia*. If this is right, Jesus is offering up a eucharistic prayer that each of us images may form a syzygy with our angel.

Later the *Gospel of Philip* warns its reader of evil spirits who come in male and female forms. These evil spirits prey on us: the male spirits on women and the female spirits on men. The only sure defense against these spiritual predators is for each of us to take on our gendered opposite: "a male power or a female power, the bridegroom and the bride.—One receives from them the mirrored bridal chamber" (65,9–12). It is tempting to think that the union imagined here as sure defense against the evil spirits is the union of a husband and wife—after all, this follows on an earlier proclamation, "Great is the mystery of marriage!" (64,32–33). But recall that this text names the "bridal chamber" as the fifth and final sacrament in Valentinian initiation (67,27–30). Mention of our each taking a male or female *power* suggests that something more is at work than a simple marriage between husband and wife. "Power" suggests that we are each uniting to an angelic counterpart, and that it is *this* union that protects each of us from spiritual predators. This is strengthened by the fact that the bridal chamber is described as "mirrored" *(ikonikos)*, that is, it is the space in which we images meet and recognize our angelic archetypes. It may be that in the earthly bridal chamber we unite male and female, husband and wife, in such a way as to anticipate, or even to solicit, the union of our individual image (gendered male or female) with its angelic counterpart (gendered male or female), and thus to heal the breach between Adam and Eve. Whatever the exact shape of this sacrament, and the correlation between earthly marriage and heavenly union, the point is made clear when this excerpt concludes by repeating the language from our first excerpt (58,12–14): imagining a union of image and angel (65,24–25).[23]

We find a different, but complementary, picture in another Valentinian text, namely the *Excerpts of Theodotus (Excerpta ex Theodoto)*.[24] These are excerpts from the writings of a second-century Valentinian teacher in Alexandria, preserved in Greek as citations by Clement of Alexandria (ca. 150–ca. 215). Like the *Gospel of Philip*, these excerpts reflect on the theology behind the sacraments, in this case the sacrament of baptism. We pick up the thread where Clement is explaining how Valentinians such as Theodotus interpret Gen 1:27, "So God created man in his own image, in the image of God he created him; male and female he created them." This verse, he explains, refers to the first "emanation" *(probolēn)* from Sophia, the last of the thirty aeons: "Now the males of that emanation are the elect, but the females are the called, and they call the male beings angelic, and the females themselves, the spiritual seed" (21,1). We go on to learn that when Adam and Eve were split, the male aspect of that emanation stayed with Adam, while the female aspect or seed became Eve, "from whom come women just as men" (21,2). This marks a first important difference with the *Gospel of Philip*.[25] In that text, we are each essentially either male or female (and this seems to correspond to our being men or women here on earth) and our angelic counterparts in turn are essentially either male or female. Accordingly, we each have to unite with our angel, gendered opposite. In this text by contrast we are all, men and women alike, essentially the female half of the primordial androgyne: we are the spiritual seed seeking our male counterparts. In both cases, however, there is a union of gendered pairs.

The excerpts go on to explain that the males "are drawn together *(synestalē)* into the Word," whereas "the females, becoming males, will be united *(henoutai)* to the angels and dwell in the Pleroma"

(21,3). Here is a second difference with the *Gospel of Philip:* whereas that text spoke of the union of image and angel as a conjunction (*hōtr*, perhaps translating *syzeugnumi*), these excerpts speak in stronger language of the union *(henōsis)* of the male and female, of the angels with the seed, which union will mark our (re)entry into the Pleroma. They make clear in what follows that baptism is the sacrament of this union. To Paul's question from 1 Cor 15:29, "If the dead do not rise, why are we baptized?," the text supplies an answer: "We rise, then, and becoming like angels are restored to the males, members to members, into unity *(eis henōsin)*" (22,3).

As we have seen, the males, or angels, are "drawn together into the Word" (21,3). The Word is none other than the savior, Jesus, and so the angels exist *in nuce* in Jesus. This helps explain why the excerpts insist that these angels were baptized with Jesus in the Jordan (21,6). According to Einar Thomassen,

> the angels who are baptized together with Jesus represent the participation of each individual baptizand in the baptism of Jesus. Thus the notion of a re-enactment of, and identification with, the Saviour's baptism is translated into a re-enactment of, and identification with, the baptism of the baptizand's individual angel.[26]

By virtue of the fact that the angels, drawn together into the Word, were baptized together with Jesus *then*, we who are baptized *now* are reunited with our angelic counterparts, female seeds to our male partners. But curiously, the baptism that enables the reunion is as crucial for the male elect as it is for the female seed.

> For they pray and plead as for parts of themselves, and, being held back because of us while eager to enter [sc. the Pleroma], they ask forgiveness for us, that we may enter together with them. For it is almost as if they need us in order to enter, since without us this is not allowed them (35,3–4).[27]

Just as we are cut off from our higher selves, our angelic counterparts, so even they are barred from entry into the Pleroma. Our reunion in baptism makes possible our restoration, and theirs. Not that baptism was thought to effect immediately this restoration and reentry: it "only prefigures and makes possible a union which will only be ultimately realized eschatologically."[28]

There is one final excerpt that bears directly on our broader inquiry into the divine double, and the question of the one and two.

> Now they say that our angels were emanated in unity *(en henotēti)*, and are one *(heis ontes)*, in that they came forth from one *(apo henos proelthontes)*. Now since we were divided, Jesus was baptized so that the undivided should be divided until he should unite *(henōsēi)* us with them in the Pleroma so that we who are many may all become one in the one *(hen genomenoi pantes tōi heni)* which was divided for our sakes. (36,1–2)

Thomassen calls this the *Excerpta*'s meditation on "the dialectic of the one and the many."[29] Our divine doubles, our angelic counterparts, emerge as mediating the singularity of the savior and the multiplicity of the spiritual seed. The angels were originally an emanation in unity, having come forth from the one. They were not yet *our* angels, because *we* had not yet emerged into multiplicity. With our separation from this first emanation, our splitting the female from the male, multiplicity enters the scene. The savior descends in baptism, along with his angelic emanation, and divides that angelic emanation to match our condition, differentiates it so that each of us might have a counterpart, every female a male. This differentiation is salvific, but it is also instrumental, and temporary: the differentiation enables us to (re)unite with them, and this reunion allows us "who are many all [to] become one in the one." In other words, the dialectic of the one and the many resolves to a dialectic of the one and the not-one: all that remains is, on the one hand, the one from which all else came forth, and on the other, what comes forth in unity from that one. We are still very much in Plato's company, and awaiting the arrival of Plotinus. Notice also that, just as with the *Gospel of Thomas* and Tatian's *Oratio*, the appearance of individuated divine doubles resolves to a singular divine double: Jesus the light in the *Gospel of Thomas*, the Holy Spirit in Tatian's *Oratio*, and the unity of the angelic emanation in the *Excerpta*.

The *Book of Thomas* and the Achievement of Twinship

Tatian and the Valentinian sources stand as further early Christian witnesses to the divine double. The Thomas tradition continued to develop its theology of the divine double centered around the figure of Judas Thomas the twin of Jesus. Of the thirteen Coptic codices discovered near the town of Nag Hammadi, Egypt, in 1945, one has been particularly relevant for our purposes: Codex II contains not only a complete version of the *Gospel of Thomas* (as discussed in Chapter 2), and the *Gospel of Philip* (discussed above), but also another text entitled *The Book of Thomas the Contender Writing to the Perfect* (Tractate II.7, hereafter the *Book of Thomas*).[30] Whereas prior to 1945 we had known of the existence of a gospel attributed to Thomas from several ancient witnesses and the modern discovery of papyri fragments at Oxyrhynchus, the *Book of Thomas* was, as with so many others in the Nag Hammadi cache, a complete surprise. The foremost expert on this text suggests that it was written sometime in the first half of the third century, that is, 200–250 CE.[31] This would put it just after the *Gospel of Thomas*, which we know was circulating in Egypt by the turn of the third century. Like the *Gospel of Thomas*, it was almost certainly composed in Greek and then translated into Coptic. And like the *Gospel of Thomas*, the *Book of Thomas* opens:

> The secret words that the savior spoke to Judas Thomas which I, even I Mathaias, wrote down, while I was walking, listening to them speak with one another. (138.1–3)

What follows is a text very likely stitched together from two earlier sources, now set on the eve of Jesus's ascension. The risen savior delivers his last will and testament to Judas Thomas. The message includes a rigid ethic of renunciation: "Everyone who seeks the truth from the true wisdom will make himself wings so as to fly, fleeing the lust that scorches the spirits of men" (140.1–3). Later this scorching lust is called simply the "fire": it bestows on the unsuspecting a false beauty and imprisons them "in a dark sweetness and captivate[s] them with fragrant pleasure" (140.21–24). From this fire Jesus offers release and "rest"—recalling the *Gospel of Thomas* and its promise of rest or *anapausis* (§§2, 50). Unlike the *Gospel of Thomas*, then, but very much like the *Acts of Thomas* (to which we will turn next), the *Book of Thomas* can fairly be classified as encratic, not because it is necessarily the product of a distinct religious group of "encratites" but rather because it forwards an unambiguous ethic of sexual renunciation.

But apart from its encratism, how does the *Book of Thomas* as we have it present the relationship between Jesus and Thomas? The answer comes at the very start:

> The savior said, "Brother *(psan)* Thomas, while you have time in the world listen to me, and I will reveal to you the things you have pondered in your mind.
>
> "Now since it has been said that you are my twin *(soeiš)* and true companion *(šbᵉr)*, examine yourself and learn who you are. In what way you exist, and how you will come to be. Since you will be called my brother, it is not fitting that you be ignorant of yourself. And I know that you have understood, because you had already understood that I am the knowledge of the truth. So while you accompany me, although you are uncomprehending, you have (in fact) already come to know, and you will be called 'the one who knows himself.' For he who has not known himself has known nothing, but he who has known himself has at the same time already achieved knowledge about the depth of the all. So then you my brother Thomas have beheld what is obscure to men, that is, what they ignorantly stumble against." (138.5–21)

It is clear that we are dealing here with another text that regards Judas Thomas as Jesus's twin brother. Gregory Riley has conjectured that the original Greek would have read, "You are my twin *(didymos)* and my true companion *(syzygos)*."[32] Recall that *didymos* or "twin" is the Greek title (and equivalent to the Syriac word *tāwmā*) that is given to Thomas in the Gospel of John and in the opening of the *Gospel of*

Thomas, sometimes yielding a triple name / title: Didymus Judas Thomas. While the Coptic word *soeiš* can mean "twin" and so is a good translation of *didymos*, the more general meaning is one half of a pair, and so can also in this context be translated as a "double."[33]

But Jesus adds another title to Thomas here in the *Book of Thomas*: *šbᵉr*, or, if we accept Riley's conjecture, *syzygos*. This is the adjectival form of the word *syzygia* that Tatian used to describe the conjunction between the soul and its recovered spirit—the bond we form with our divine double. When used as a noun, as it is here in the *Book of Thomas*, *syzygos* can mean spouse, comrade, companion, or even twin. The Coptic word *šbᵉr* means much the same—companion, friend, comrade—but without the connotation of a shared yoke. In the *Book of Thomas*, however, Jesus says a good deal more than just to invoke these two titles, "twin" and "companion." First of all, he says of these titles, "it has been *said* that you are my twin and my true companion," and shortly thereafter he says, "you will be *called* my brother" (my emphasis). The fact that the *Book of Thomas* has Jesus first address Judas Thomas as brother makes it clear that it regards him as Jesus's brother Judas, the very one mentioned in Mark 6:3 and Matthew 13:55. And the fact that Judas is *said* to be Jesus's twin and true companion and *called* brother probably reflects the language from the Gospel of John, where Thomas is introduced as he "who is called *(legomenos)* the Twin *(didymos)*" (11:16, 20:24, 21:2). But in the context of the *Book of Thomas* this might serve to suggest, in addition, that Judas Thomas's twinship, companionship, and even brotherhood are not (borrowing Gerson's language again) something only *endowed* at birth, but rather *achieved* over time. In fact, the *Book of Thomas* seems staged at just the moment when Jesus will tell his brother how it is he can earn the titles twin, companion, and brother: "Now since it has been said that you are my twin and true companion, examine yourself and learn who you are. In what way you exist, and how you will come to be. Since you will be called my brother, it is not fitting that you be ignorant of yourself." The tenses are hard to make sense of: Judas *will* be called Jesus's brother, except that he has *already* been called brother by Jesus himself; Judas is *already* said to be Jesus's twin and companion, but seems somehow *not yet* to have earned those titles. The goal is very clearly self-knowledge: "who you are, in what way you exist, and how you will come to be." But just how much Judas Thomas knows himself is unclear, as the tenses continue to baffle: "And I know that you have understood, because you had already understood that I am the knowledge of the truth. So while you accompany me, although you are uncomprehending, you have (in fact) already come to know, and you will be called 'the one who knows himself.'" Thomas already understands or has come to know something, but all the while still not comprehending something else. He knows that Jesus is the knowledge of the truth (whatever that means), but still falls short of full self-knowledge. Judas Thomas is on the threshold, knowing something without knowing that he has known it.

I take it that this second-order knowing is what constitutes full self-knowledge. And to fall short of it is rather serious, "for he who has not known himself has known nothing." On the other hand, "he who has known himself has at the same time already achieved knowledge about the depth of the all." According to what Jesus says later, to know oneself is to be perfect, and those who do not are only "babes" (139.12). The exhortation to know oneself is therefore an exhortation to grow up, that is, one might say to *earn* brotherhood rather than merely to *inherit* it by virtue of sharing a mother. Thus, Judas Thomas stands on the cusp of earning that with which until now he had only been endowed: to become a full, mature twin and companion of his brother Jesus. To know oneself as Jesus's twin and companion is to have "achieved knowledge about the depth of the all." This recalls the *Gospel of Thomas*, where Jesus says, "It is I who am the light which is above them all. It is I who am the all. From me did the all come forth, and unto me did the all extend" (§77). Later in the *Book of Thomas*, Thomas addresses Jesus as "our light," bidding him to "enlighten" him, to which Jesus replies, "It is in light that light exists" (139.21–22). This too recalls the *Gospel of Thomas*, where Jesus says, "There is light within a man of light, and he lights up the whole world. If he does not shine, he is darkness" (§24). These allusions in the *Book of Thomas* bring it more obviously in line with the theology of the twin we discerned in the *Gospel of Thomas*.[34] Self-knowledge is knowledge of Jesus, who is the depth of the all, the light that shines in us. To know *this*, that Jesus is one's innermost self, is to become his twin, to earn the title *didymos* and *syzygos*.

So to repeat: the *Book of Thomas* does exhibit its own theology of the twin. It is found in the very opening of the dialogue between Jesus and Judas Thomas, and centers on the achievement of self-knowledge. It is not, at least on my reading, as robust a theology of the twin as one finds encoded in the *Gospel of Thomas*. But certain allusions to that gospel suggest that the *Book of Thomas*'s theology of the twin is largely consonant with it. What marks the *Book of Thomas* as distinctive is its emphasis on what I am calling (following Gerson) the tension between the *endowment* and the *achievement* of twinship and companionship.

The *Acts of Thomas* and the Multiplication of Doubles

After the *Gospel of Thomas*, the most significant witness to the Thomas tradition is an apocryphal collection called the *Acts of Thomas*, which narrates Judas Thomas's evangelism in the East, especially in India. Most scholars now think that the *Acts* were composed first in Syriac, but soon thereafter translated into Greek.[35] But most scholars also give priority to the Greek translation because the Syriac version that has come done to us shows signs of having been altered to make it align with emerging orthodoxies. In other words, the Syriac original has been lost, and what we have at places reads more as "a catholicizing revision."[36] It is thought to have been composed in the early third century, and so is roughly contemporaneous with the *Book of Thomas*.

The *Acts* are a drama in thirteen episodes, spanning Jerusalem to India, which conclude with the martyrdom of the main character, Judas Thomas. The narrative is lively and quick paced, and might lead one to think that the *Acts* were unsophisticated "popular" literature. Drijvers, however, insists that what might appear as "a motley mixture of miracle stories, fantastic deeds of the apostle, conversions, nature miracles and stories of demons, which are akin to the novelistic narrative art of the ancient world," is in fact an "artfully worked out literary structure," and decidedly *not* "popular literature."[37] "Rather," he goes on to say, the *Acts* "came into being in a learned milieu," which produced this tight "literary, symbolic, and typological structure, which is welded into a unity, as it were subterraneously, by all kinds of allusions."[38] In what follows, we will give priority to the Greek translation, although with appeal to the Syriac, and following Drijvers's lead, assume that the *Acts* forward a relatively coherent theology.[39]

By way of anticipation, we could say that the theology of the *Acts* is "resolutely soteriological" and weaves together two dominant themes.[40] The first, in keeping with the Thomas tradition, is a theology of the twin, the aim of which is self-knowledge understood as knowledge of the self as the twin of Jesus, to whom the *Acts* apply more familiar titles such as "Lord" and "Christ." This theme runs "subterraneously" throughout the *Acts* and so, just as in the *Gospel of Thomas*, must be brought to the surface through a close reading. The second is a theology of the bridal chamber, according to which one must renounce worldly sex and marriage in order to become the bride of Christ, the one true bridegroom. These two theologies, of the twin and of the bridal chamber, are both variations on the tradition of the divine double: in both cases one endeavors to unite to one's divine double, who is none other than Jesus Christ, either through the figure of a fraternal twinship or through the figure of a consummated union. Each theology in the *Acts* features its own representative hymn: the theology of the bridal chamber has Thomas's wedding hymn, and the theology of the twin has his famous "Hymn of the Pearl." We will examine the former below; the latter will be given its own section in this chapter, owing to the fact that it was likely a freestanding text subsequently woven into the *Acts*.

ACT 1: JUDAS THOMAS, TWIN AND SLAVE OF CHRIST

Let us turn to the first act, then, over which we will linger because it introduces so many of the central themes of the remaining twelve.[41] We begin in Jerusalem, after the death and resurrection of Jesus, with the eleven apostles (without Judas Iscariot) gathered together to divide the world by lots into regions for evangelizing. "According to lot, India fell to Judas Thomas, who is also (called) Didymus."[42]

Judas—or, as he is more often called, Thomas or "the apostle"—objects to his assignment, so much so that Jesus appears to him at night to persuade him, promising even that "my grace is with thee."[43] Thomas stubbornly resists, until Jesus devises a scheme: he approaches a merchant named Abban who is visiting Jerusalem on behalf of his king Gundaphorus in India, and who is in need of a carpenter. Like his twin brother Jesus, Thomas is skilled in carpentry, a trade they both learned from their father, Joseph. Jesus then sells Thomas into slavery, writing up a bill of sale: "I, Jesus the son of Joseph the carpenter, confirm that I have sold my slave, Judas by name, to thee Abban, a merchant of Gundaphorus the king of the Indians."[44] Notice two details: first, although the *Acts* refer to Judas Thomas very often by his title, Thomas (Didymus), the bill of sale makes clear that his name is Judas, that is, Jesus's brother who is mentioned in Matthew 13:55 and Mark 6:3; second, the merchant does not remark, either at the sale or upon receipt of Judas Thomas, that the two look at all alike, never mind identical. It would certainly be odd if someone were to sell his identical twin into slavery, and no doubt would rouse the suspicions of the buyer. Within the logic of the narrative, therefore, we should assume that Jesus and Thomas do not look alike, at least not at this moment.

The sale succeeds in overcoming Thomas's resistance to his apostolic assignment. But he carries with him not only the grace of his risen Lord (and brother), but also his own price, that is, the silver Jesus received in exchange for him. The apostle is thereby free to buy his own freedom, but he does not. In fact, he remains a slave so that he might free others. The first stop on their voyage to India is a city called Andrapolis, perhaps meant to be somewhere on the Red Sea. There Thomas and the merchant Abban are invited to the local king's palace to celebrate the wedding of the king's daughter. Thomas begrudgingly obeys, but sits sullen in a corner, eating and drinking nothing. After suffering a blow from a passing waiter, Thomas predicts that the assailant's offending hand will soon be dragged across the floor by dogs. He then stands and delivers a long song, a wedding song about a maiden, "a daughter of light," "her chamber full of light," waiting on her bridegroom.[45] It is quite obviously an allegory, and a critical commentary on the wedding he is attending—although no one but a single flute girl can understand him, because his song is in Hebrew. She, however, understands him and "loves him greatly" for "in appearance he was comely above all that were present."[46] Soon enough Thomas's earlier prediction comes true—the waiter is slaughtered outside by a lion, and his dismembered hand is dragged through the feast by dogs. The guests recoil in horror, but the flute girl tells them all of the apostle's earlier prediction, and exclaims, "This man is either a god or an apostle of God."[47]

Curiously, the king responds to this bizarre episode by inviting the foreigner to pray over the young bridal couple. Thomas is forced to comply, and issues a prayer, presumably now in Greek, because the couple seems to understand him, calling on "My Lord and my God, the companion (*synodoiporos*) of his servants, who doth guide and direct those who believe in him."[48] The Syriac version of this prayer is much longer, and includes this line addressed to "Our Lord": "you are one with two names."[49] This proves truer than perhaps Thomas even anticipated, as we shall see in a moment. The word "companion" (*synodoiporos*) means "a fellow traveler," and this too anticipates what happens next.[50] For the king now asks Thomas to leave the young couple and he complies. But when the bridegroom, now all alone with his bride, lifts the veil to behold her, he sees sitting next to her "the Lord Jesus in the likeness of the apostle Judas Thomas."[51] Having just seen Thomas leave the room, the young man is confused; Jesus tells him, "I am not Judas who is also Thomas, I am his brother."[52] Jesus has proven himself a companion or fellow traveler indeed, appearing now, in a foreign land, in the likeness of his own brother and apostle. To the young couple, he is indeed one man with two names. Whereas earlier at the sale to Abban Jesus and Thomas did not resemble each other, here they do, so much so as to be identical. Jesus, then, can and does take the likeness or form of Thomas—but why?

In short: so as to teach them. Specifically, he would have them "abandon this filthy intercourse" on the precipice of which they now stand. Instead, he would have them "become holy temples, pure and free."[53] According to Jesus, to be a pure temple is to refrain from marriage, sex, and childbirth. These end only in grief and anxiety.

The reward of refusing marriage *here* is the promise of an "incorruptible and true marriage" *there*, "that bridal chamber <which is full of> immortality and light."⁵⁴ This promise is persuasive, and when the parents arrive the next morning, the bride confesses:

> Truly, father, I am in great love *(agapē)*, and I pray to my Lord that the love which I experienced this night may remain with me, and I will ask for the husband of whom I have learned today ... And that I have set at naught this man, and this marriage which passes away from before my eyes, (is) because I am bound in another marriage. And that I have no intercourse with a short-lived husband, the end of which is <remorse and bitterness> of soul, (is) because I am yoked *(synezeuchthēn)* with <the> true man.⁵⁵

Jesus in effect persuades the young lovers to abandon their earthly beloveds, and instead to enter the bridal chamber where he himself will join with each of them in an endless intercourse. Notice that the bride uses a verbal form of *syn+zygos* to name this union: "I am yoked" *(synezeuchthēn)*—the same root that Tatian uses to describe the syzygy of soul and spirit, and Jesus in the *Book of Thomas* to address his brother Judas (see also Mani and Plotinus in Chapters 4 and 5).

Immediately following the bride, the bridegroom also confesses in thanksgiving:⁵⁶

> I thank you, Lord, who through the stranger [Thomas] was proclaimed and found in us ... that by setting me beside your greatness you might unite me with yourself; who did show me to seek myself and to recognize who I was and who and how I now am, that I may become again what I was; whom I did not know, but you did seek me out; of whom I was unaware, but you did take me to you; whom I have perceived, and now cannot forget; whose love *(agapē)* ferments within me, and of whom I cannot speak as I ought, but what I can say about him is short and very little and does not correspond to his glory; but he does not blame when I make bold to say to him even what I do not know; for it is for love of him that I say this.⁵⁷

Here is one place in the *Acts* where the theology of the bridal chamber and the theology of the twin seem to cross paths. The bridegroom thanks the Lord for the couple's finding Jesus (already) in them, and for Jesus's uniting with him—in effect, for exchanging roles with him: the bridegroom becomes the bride, and Jesus the heavenly bridegroom. But this theology of the bridal chamber is crossed with a theology of self-knowledge: I did not know who I was or how I came to be me; but the Lord has taught me that I was once united to him—as the bride says, in a syzygy—and will be again. Love is the bond of this union, a union of which "I cannot speak as I ought" because the precise unity-in-distinction of such a syzygy (of Christ and his twin, the bridegroom and the bride) is beyond the ken of language.

Only now, in retrospect, can the reader fully understand Thomas's wedding hymn as an allegory: the song celebrating the maiden, the daughter of light, in her chamber waiting on the arrival of her bridegroom, is of course no celebration of the earthly wedding about to take place. It is on the contrary an anticipatory rebuke of that wedding, which is a corrupted copy of "that incorruptible and true marriage" with "the true man," Christ the bridegroom. The Syriac version of the wedding hymn changes the allegory by specifying that the daughter of light is not the individual soul united to Christ in a syzygy, but is instead "my church."[58] This displaces the *Acts*' theology of the bridal chamber from the dangerously individual union to the safer ecclesial context, and interrupts the logic that binds the theologies of the twin and the bridal chamber together.

Furthermore, at the close of the hymn, the Greek and Syriac diverge again. The Greek reads, "And they [the bridal party] glorified and praised, with the living Spirit, / The Father of Truth and the Mother of Wisdom."[59] This mention of a divine father and mother is replaced in the Syriac version with a Trinitarian formula more palatable to the tastes of emerging orthodoxy:

> and have glorified the Father, the Lord of all,
> and the only(-begotten) Son, who is of Him,
> and have praised the Spirit, His Wisdom.[60]

The divine mother appears in two other prayers in the Greek *Acts*.[61] In the second act, Thomas prays as he anoints recent converts with oil, "Come, compassionate mother . . . Come, mother of the seven houses, that your rest may be in the eighth house."[62] Even more striking is the prayer he offers in the fifth act, which includes the lines "Come . . . Holy Dove / That bears the twin young; / Come, hidden Mother."[63] These lines have baffled some scholars, one going so far as to say that the title of a dove bearing twin young "cannot be explained with any confidence."[64] Drijvers, however, believes that these lines preserve an early and distinct Trinitarian alternative, according to which "the Holy Spirit, the Mother, . . . gives birth to the Son, whose divine Mother she is, and also gives birth to the new man, the twin brother of the Son."[65] The twin young are the Son (like Tatian's eternal *Logos*), who becomes incarnate as Jesus, and his twin brother Judas. If Drijvers is right, then the *Acts*' theology of the twin stretches up as far as its doctrine of a triune God.

ACTS 2–13: THE DYOMORPHIC THOMAS AND THE MATRIX OF DIVINE DOUBLES

We will have to pick up the pace if we wish to see how the remaining episodes, all of them set in India, unfold the two theologies of the divine double. In the second act, Abban and his slave Thomas arrive in India, in the realm of King Gundaphorus. In the third act, after having successfully baptized King Gundaphorus and his family, the apostle is led out of town to a place where he finds the corpse of a young man. Led there by his Lord, Thomas announces to those who are following him that this corpse is the work of the enemy. Immediately a great serpent slithers out of its hole and confesses to the crime: he lusted after a young woman, and following her, discovered that she had a young lover. He then lay in wait for the young lover, and killed him with his venomous bite. In his confession, the serpent adds, "I know that you are the twin *(didymos)* of Christ."[66] He is, of course, no ordinary serpent, but the very enemy of all humankind: "I am he who entered through the fence into Paradise and said to Eve all the things my father charged me to say to her."[67] This enemy, therefore, recognizes what humans do not at first: that Judas Thomas is the twin of Christ.[68]

We witness their twinship immediately dramatized. Thomas forces the serpent to suck its venom from the young man, restoring him to life and causing the serpent to explode with its own black gall. Straightaway the young man recognizes Thomas and exclaims, "You are a man that has two forms *(dyo morphes)*, and wherever you will, there you are found, and you are restrained by no man, as I see."[69] The young man has just been summoned from some afterlife or realm of the dead where he saw Thomas. Thomas has "two forms," because he is simultaneously present in that world and in this world to which the young man has just been restored. Furthermore, Thomas's second self or double is accompanied in the afterlife by someone to whom the young man refers to only as "that man." But it is clear that this nameless man is Christ. The young man explains to the apostle,

> I saw how that man [Christ] stood beside you [Thomas], and said to you: "I have many wonders to show through you, and I have great works to accomplish through you, for which you shall receive a reward; and you shall make many love, and they shall rest in eternal light as children of God. Do you, then," he said, speaking to you of me, "revive this young man stricken by the enemy, and become at all times his guardian." You [Thomas] have done well to come here, and again you shall do well to depart to him [that man, Christ], for indeed he never leaves you at all.[70]

Nothing suggests that Thomas knows of his double in the other world; rather, he seems to be learning about his own double from the testimony of the recently resurrected youth. He learns, then, not only that he has, so to speak, an avatar in the afterlife, but that his double is accompanied there by none other than Christ. Thomas learns that Christ never leaves his second self, that Jesus is his constant companion.

The theology of the twin dramatized here does not pertain only to Jesus and Thomas. The young man, restored to life and freed from the lust that led him to his end, speaks of how "light shone upon me (so that I am now free)" and says, "I found that figure of light to be my kinsman *(syngenē)*."[71] It is revealed that not only Thomas, but also the young man, is Christ's kin. Having been restored to life, he now longs for his kinsman,

> the Son of Truth, who is kinsman *(syngenē)* of concord, who driving away the mist enlightens his own creation, and healing its wounds overthrows its enemies. But I pray you, man of God, make me to look upon him again, and to see him who is now become hidden from me, that I may also hear his voice, the wonder of which I cannot express; for it is not of the nature of this bodily organ.[72]

Through Thomas, his twin, Christ reveals that he is all of humanity's kinsman. We may not be aware of that kinship, as even Thomas is not, or at least not the full scope of it. And having once met his kinsman Christ, the human longs to see Christ's enlightening face and hear his otherworldly voice.

The sixth act reprises this episode. Thomas raises from the dead a young woman who was killed by her lover. Her lover had heard Thomas preach sexual renunciation and was persuaded to pursue purity and holiness in a chaste union with his beloved; when she refused this arrangement, he slew her. Upon her resurrection from the dead, she says to Thomas, "I pray you, my Lord, where is that other who was with you, who did not leave me to remain in that dreadful and cruel place, but delivered me to you?"[73] She then narrates her journey into a dark world of dead souls, all suffering terrible punishments at the hands of demons. Having received a tour of these torments, she is given back the one "who is like" Thomas, who in turn delivers her to Thomas, saying, "Take her, for she is one of the sheep that have gone astray."[74] Having been received by *that* Thomas, there in other world, she finds herself delivered to *this* Thomas, in this world.

Thomas says in the wake of the young woman's testimony, "Walk rather in faith and meekness and holiness and hope, in which God delights, that you may become his kinsmen *(oikeioi)*." Here "kin" means specifically those who live in God's house *(oikos)*, members of his household *(oikeioi)*. Later in that same speech, the language of kinship reappears, but tethered to the notion of race or kind *(genos)*: "Look upon us, Lord, because we have left those who belong to us by race *(kata genos)*, that we may be united with your kindred *(syngeneia)*."[75] In fact, we have already encountered this term: the young man recently resurrected speaks of Christ as "the Son of Truth, who is kinsman *(syngenē)* of concord"; a fantastic ass's colt with the power of speech addresses Thomas as "kinsman *(syngenēs)* of the great race *(genous)*."[76] This cluster of ideas of household, kinship, race, and kind runs throughout the *Acts*. There are three households, or more often races or kinds: (1) the *genos* of evil spirits or demons; (2) the *genos* of humans; and of course (3) God's own *genos* (or *oikos*). Humans have both their own proper *genos*, humankind, and also a *genos* with which they can freely affiliate, the demonic or the divine. The persistent struggle in these *Acts*, then, is to rescue humans from a demonic affiliation, to which sex and procreation commit them, and to welcome them instead into the divine household, where they can be, according to the theology of the twin, like Judas Thomas twin brothers of Jesus, or, according to the theology of the bridal chamber, brides to the one bridegroom Christ.

Acts 7–13 take place in the kingdom of Misdaeus. Much of the drama of these episodes centers around Thomas's converting first the women of a household, and then the men, to a life of "holiness." As Thomas teaches, "holiness appeared from God, abolishing fornication, overthrowing the enemy . . . Abide therefore in holiness . . . Holiness is a temple of Christ."[77] The villains in this drama are King Misdaeus and his friend Charisius, both of whose wives are converted to lives of holy renunciation. As punishment for his turning their wives against them, the villains imprison Thomas and put the women under house arrest. At one point, however, the women appear at the prison, much to Thomas's surprise. When he asks them how they escaped house arrest, they, equally surprised by his question, explain that he himself freed them, brought them to the prison, and then disappeared. When it is clear to them both that Thomas has a double prowling the area, the women proclaim, "Glory be to you, Jesus of many forms *(polymorphe)*, glory to you who does appear in the guise of poor manhood."[78] They do not take Thomas's doppelgänger to be Thomas's second self exactly, like the one the young man and woman raised from the dead claim to have seen in the afterlife, but instead they take him to be a polymorphic Jesus *(polymorphos Iēsous)*.[79] Like the episode early in the *Acts* where Jesus appears in the bridal chamber in the likeness of Thomas, here he appears as Thomas to aid in the spread of his gospel of holiness, ensuring that the women who have chosen to follow Thomas can do so, free of the intervention of their lascivious husbands. Thomas's divine double here is not his astral avatar, but rather his own twin Jesus assuming his likeness.

The picture that emerges from the *Acts* is a complicated matrix of divine doubles (see figure) that goes well beyond what we have seen in the *Gospel of Thomas* or the *Book of Thomas*. If we permit the matrix to organize the *Acts*' disparate testimonies, at least four relationships of doubling present themselves: on the horizontal axes, (1) Thomas^1 to Jesus^1 and (2) Thomas^2 to Jesus^2; on the vertical axes, (3) Thomas^1 to Thomas^2 and (4) Jesus^1 to Jesus^2. The first of these relationships is the theology of the twin: Thomas *here* is the twin brother of Jesus *here*. Jesus is able to assume the likeness of his twin and so is acclaimed as polymorphic: a shape-shifter of sorts, or doppelgänger. The second of these relationships is the theology of the bridal chamber: by Thomas^1 renouncing sex and marriage *here*, Thomas^2 becomes the bride *there*, consummating a union with the eternal bridegroom Christ (Jesus^2). Witnesses also testify to the fact that Judas Thomas and Jesus are already constant companions in the afterlife. The language of kinship and household can be seen to apply to both horizontal relationships: twin brothers are kin and are under the roof of one house, their father's (or parents'); bride and bridegroom are united as kin and share a house just as they do a bed. Let us turn to the vertical plane: the third relationship is that between a doubled Thomas, here and there. The name given to this is dyomorphy, or having two forms—although this vertical dyomorphy should be distinguished from Jesus's horizontal polymorphy. The fourth and final relationship, then, is between a doubled Jesus, here and there. It is unclear how sharply distinct these two are, the human and the divine, and if distinct, how exactly they are thought to relate. The sharp articulation of how the human and

There Thomas² (bride⇒)	 Jesus² (⇐bridegroom)
Here (dyomorphic⇑) Thomas¹ (twin⇒)	 (⇐polymorphic) Jesus¹

divine natures of the Incarnate Christ coexist and relate will have to wait for the fifth century and its fractious controversies. It is curious, however, that the human parallel, the relationship between Thomas here and there, is framed in the *Acts* as dyomorphy. This pairs well with the Antiochene ("Nestorian") and thereafter Chalcedonian orthodox insistence on the two natures of the Incarnate Christ: dyophysitism (see Chapter 6).

The "Hymn of the Pearl," or Rather of the Royal Garment

The *Acts of Thomas* is well attested, with something on the order of seventy-five Greek and six Syriac manuscripts. But in only one of the surviving Greek manuscripts, and again in only one of the surviving Syriac manuscripts, do we find a hymn (or in Greek a "psalm") inserted into the *Acts*, what has come to be known as the "Hymn of the Pearl."[80] The Syriac manuscript provides its own title, "The hymn of Judas Thomas, the Apostle, when he was in the country of India" (the Greek provides none).[81] In both cases Thomas offers up this hymn or psalm in the long ninth act, when he is imprisoned by King Misdaeus. The 105 verses that follow were, like the rest of the *Acts*, almost certainly composed in Syriac. They fit well into the Syriac genre of liturgical hymns or *madrashe*, and several scholars have analyzed their meter within the conventions of that genre. Unlike the rest of the *Acts*, however, most scholars regard the Syriac manuscript as preserving the earlier and less adulterated version of the hymn. The very fact that the hymn appears in only two manuscripts suggests that it was not original to the *Acts* but inserted later; by whom and exactly why remains a matter of dispute. If it was inserted somewhere in the redaction history of the *Acts*, the hymn may have originally stood on its own as an independent composition. The fact that it contains no obviously Christian content, moreover, raises the question of whether it originated in a different religious milieu and was subsequently repurposed for a Christian audience in these apocryphal *Acts*.

A good deal of scholarship has focused on discerning the precise provenance of the original hymn: What sort of religious milieu produced it, and when? However, there is little agreement on this question. Some regard it as a classic Gnostic allegory, of either Iranian or Egyptian origin; others as a Christian *midrash* on certain parables from the synoptic gospels; others as an ancient fairy tale with no religious import at all; and others still as a Manichaean allegory inserted into the *Acts of Thomas* when they appropriated that text for their own use. There is slightly more agreement, but alas little precision, on the question of the date of its composition: although some outliers argue for the first century, most opinions range from the second through the fourth centuries. And as with almost every text we have discussed in relation to the Thomas tradition, scholars are inclined to suggest that it was composed in the environs of Edessa.

The cloud of questions that hovers over the hymn may seem at the very outset to obscure our view and so thwart our interpretation. On the contrary: we can disperse this obscuring cloud easily enough by insisting that the original composition and provenance of the hymn are not of paramount importance to our interpretation of it in situ in the *Acts of Thomas*. Following Gerard P. Luttikhuizen, I suggest that we "focus on the question of what the text means when it is read *within the context of the ATh*."[82] The text is quite obviously an allegory: in fact it allegorizes itself.[83] I will first offer a brief summary of the hymn's plot and then focus on understanding its allegorical dimensions. Our gaze will be further focused by our interest in the divine double—or as is the case here, doubles. Having that in place, we will then pan back and consider whether and how the hymn's allegory of divine doubles fits with the theology of the twin on offer in the *Acts* in which it is embedded.

The hymn is told in the first person: a young man speaks of his royal family in the East, a father, mother, and brother. Let us call him a prince. He is stripped of his royal garment and sent to Egypt to retrieve a pearl guarded by a serpent. He travels west to Egypt, at first accompanied by guardians and then alone, and finds there the serpent he is seeking. He meets a countryman from the East, but adopts the dress of the Egyptians so as to blend in. The Egyptians see through his disguise, however, and make him eat of their food, which makes the prince forget his parentage and his mission to acquire the pearl. His parents learn of his troubles and send a magical letter to awaken him: it does so, and he in turn lulls the serpent to sleep and recovers the pearl. On his way home he is greeted first by the magical letter, and then his royal garment. Finally, he returns to his father's kingdom, with the pearl in hand and enveloped in his royal garment.

Any allegory of the hymn must ask who or what this prince is supposed to signify. There are two common interpretations. The first interprets the prince as a savior or redeemer figure who is sent into the world to rescue the human soul (the pearl) but becomes ensnared in that world and so in need of saving himself. This is often alleged to be a fundamental Gnostic myth of the "redeemed redeemer" or *salvator salvandus*. There is, in my view, little to recommend this interpretation of the hymn. Much more compelling is a second interpretation, according to which the prince is not the savior but the human spirit (or soul) that departs its heavenly origin (the East) and descends into embodiment (Egypt). The drama is therefore the spirit's return: how its divine kin recall it from its exile and restore it to its divine home. One problem with this second interpretation, however, is that it does not furnish an obvious meaning for the pearl. On this reading, the pearl and the serpent principally serve to explain how the human spirit finds itself in exile. The real interest of the allegory, then, is how the spirit comes to realize its divine parentage and return home. This interpretation understands—correctly in my view—that "the letter and the garment ... are much more important to the development of the story" and that "the pearl plays only a supporting part in the story, just as the serpent does."[84] The scholarly convention of labeling this interpolated hymn the "Hymn of the *Pearl*," therefore, is somewhat unfortunate insofar as it leads the reader to think that the drama centers on the young man's recovery of the prized pearl from the serpent. Merely counting the verses should push back against that conclusion: whereas the young man's recovery of the pearl is narrated in a few short verses, the hymn devotes almost twenty verses to his parents' letter to him, and nearly thirty-five to his return home, including detailed descriptions of how the letter and especially his royal garment go out to meet him. In short, this is a hymn, not of the pearl, but of the letter and the garment.

Before we examine the hymn's treatment of the letter and the garment, we should linger over the cast of characters. The young man tells of his parents, the king and queen of the East, who in turn tell of "your brother, our second in command [with whom] you will be heir in our kingdom."[85] The Syriac word *trayānā* means "second" but also "double," suggesting an ambiguity between the brother as a "viceroy" or a twin.[86] We do not learn much more about this brother other than that he remains in the kingdom while the young man ventures out to Egypt. But the very fact that we have a royal couple, a king and queen, and a pair of brothers neither of whom is specified as elder, marks an interesting analog with the Trinitarian portrait we examined above in the Greek *Acts*, in which the Spirit is described as a mother who "bearest the twin young."[87] Recall that Drijvers conjectures that the Greek *Acts* bear traces of an ancient Trinitarian formula in which God the Father and the Holy Spirit as Mother have twin boys, the eternal Son (who becomes incarnate as Jesus) and his twin brother Judas. The case of the hymn would seem to reinforce that family portrait, especially because it is Judas Thomas who sings the hymn and thus makes the prince's voice speaking in the first person—the brother in exile in Egypt—his own. It could well be that whoever first included the hymn in the *Acts* intended to have the royal family in the hymn mirror the *Acts*' portrait of the Trinity. Subsequent changes to both the *Acts* and the hymn have perhaps made that mirroring more difficult, but not impossible, to discern.

The parents promise the young man that with his brother he "will be heir *(yārut)* in our kingdom."[88] If the young man signifies the human spirit and his brother signifies Christ, then the promise of such an inheritance should recall Paul's promise, best captured in these lines from Romans:

> When we cry, "Abba! Father!" it is the Spirit itself bearing witness with our spirit that we are children of God, and if children, then heirs *(klēronomoi)*, heirs of God and fellow heirs *(synklēronomoi)* with Christ, provided we suffer with him in order that we may also be glorified with him." (Rom 8:15b–17)[89]

In short, before we learn anything of the letter or the royal garment, an astute reader of the *Acts* will have gathered that this hymn celebrates a drama in which the human, who is none other than Judas Thomas, speaks of his or her struggles in exile and imprisonment, and looks forward to a time when he will become co-heir with his (twin) brother, who is none other than Jesus Christ.

Let us now look more carefully at the drama. As we will soon see, there is a sudden proliferation of doubles in this hymn. First, the young man is accompanied on his journey abroad by two "guardians" or "companions," who both depart from him as he enters Egypt.⁹⁰ Who or what this first pair of companions is remains unclear. But whoever or whatever they are, their departure leaves him "single *(ḥad)* and alone *(mshāwḥad)*" and a "stranger" to his "fellow-lodgers."⁹¹ It is when he is "single and alone" that he is most vulnerable; in other words, he is in need of a double. He receives some comfort in the form of a countryman from the East, "a son of my race, a son of freedom . . . a youth handsome [and] lovely, a son of the anointed ones."⁹² He is said to have "recognized" this countryman:

> And to me he came and followed.
> And I made him my intimate friend,
> a companion with whom I shared my merchandise.⁹³

This friend and companion "follows" the young man, although curiously this verb *nqep* also means "to cleave or adhere to." Whatever bond they form, it is for their mutual anonymity and protection as strangers in a strange land. And just as suddenly as he appears, this countryman companion disappears, never again to be mentioned in the hymn. Instead, the young man from the East says that he was fooled into eating the Egyptians' food, forgot who he was and his mission, and "fell into a deep sleep."

Their son being once again single and alone, the king and queen devise a plan to rescue him: they compose a letter enjoining him to "awake" and "remember" who he is and what he was sent to do.⁹⁴ The letter also reminds him of his "glorious garment" and his "brother, our second in command, [with whom] you will be in our kingdom."⁹⁵ The letter flies to him in the form of an eagle, and then "all of it became speech (words) to me": "And according to what was inscribed in my heart / were the words of my letter written."⁹⁶ This is a very curious verse: it is not that the young man inscribes the message of the letter on his heart, as one might expect. On the contrary, the letter merely repeats what is already inscribed in his heart.⁹⁷ The letter is his textual double, as it were: it mirrors back to him his inner inscription, which text had been obscured by exile. The young man is something of a palimpsest, and his textual double renders his inner inscription once again legible.

Immediately he remembers who he is and his mission, which he accomplishes swiftly and without difficulty. Again, the hymn does not linger over the significance of the mission (the recovery of the pearl), but rather frames its fulfillment by a long account of the letter, his textual double, and then his journey home. On his way home he encounters the letter once again: "And as with its voice it had awakened us, / so also with its light it was leading me."[98] The shift from the first person plural (us) to singular (me) has led some to wonder whether the reader is meant to infer that the young man has his anonymous countryman with him—the "intimate friend" who appeared and disappeared suddenly in the narrative. In other words, are there are now two doubles: the countryman and the letter? In any case, a second (or third) double enters the scene: the "royal silk," "my glorious garment," begins to entice the young man, urging him homeward with its "appearance," "voice," "guidance," and "love."[99] It goes out to meet him, on the road:

> And I was not remembering its fashion,
> for in my childhood I had left my father's house.
> Then suddenly *(men shelyā)*, as I received it,
> the clothing seemed to me like a mirror of myself.
> I saw all of it in myself,
> and also I received all in it,
> because we were two in distinction,
> but we were also one in form.
> And also the stewards,
> who brought it to me, I saw them,
> to be two, [and yet] one in form,
> for one sign of the king was inscribed on them.
> . . .
> I also saw that all over it,
> the motions of knowledge were stirring.[100] (75–80, 88)

The most striking feature of this description, of course, is the prince's remarking that his royal garment "seemed to me like a mirror of myself." Just as the letter reflected the prince's inner inscription, so the garment reflects his outer appearance back to him.[101] But then the very distinction between the inner and the outer seems to break down, as the prince says that he "saw all of it"—his own mirror reflection—"in myself," and furthermore "I received all in it." What does it mean to see a reflection of oneself, and then to see and receive that mirror reflection into oneself? Clearly the hymn is trying to narrate figuratively a profound autoscopy, and with it self-knowledge. As we have seen, the mirror is one of the consistent tropes in the tradition of the divine double, from Plato (Chapter 1), to the *Gospel of Thomas* (Chapter 2), and, we will see, in Mani (Chapter 4) and Plotinus (Chapter 5). The hymn's notion that the letter is a mirror that reflects not our outward appearance but some inner image follows closely §84 in the *Gospel of Thomas*, where, so I argue, the gospel itself becomes the mirror in which the reader sees, not his "likeness" *(eine)* or outer human form, but his "image" *(ikōn)*. Here is another way, then, in which the hymn embedded in the *Acts* (which in turn quotes the *Gospel of Thomas*) begins to resonate, as hymns are wont to do, with the texts with which it is paired.

Similarly, the adverb "suddenly" (Syriac *men shelyā*, Greek *exaiphnēs*) marks the most freighted encounters with the divine double. In Plato's *Parmenides*, it is only in the "instant" or "sudden" *(to exaiphnēs)* that we move from the one (that is) one and so is not to the one that is and so is always two (Chapter 1). And the Acts of the Apostles says that Christ "suddenly" appears to Paul on the road to Damascus, inaugurating his new self as "no longer I"—no longer one—"but Christ who lives in me"—two-in-one. And in fact some similar unity-in-distinction is what the prince says of himself and his garment: "We were two in distinction, but we were also one in form." As is fitting for a hymn, the precise meanings of "distinction" *(pūrshānā)* and "form" *(dmū)* are not given, and so the reader is left only with the knowledge that the prince and his garment are somehow one and yet two. This goes as well for the stewards who brought his garment to him: "two, [and yet] one in form, / for one sign of the king was inscribed on them."[102]

Adorning himself with the royal garment, the prince is welcomed back to his father's kingdom. There is no explicit mention of his brother in this reunion. Instead, the prince bows his head and worships "him, the brightness *(zīwā)* of my father who sent [the garment] to me."[103] One might be tempted to think that this is a reunion with the king himself, but I think it is clear that the "brightness" or "countenance" of his father refers not to the king but to his son, the prince's (twin) brother who remained in the kingdom throughout his exile. After all, this "brightness" promises the prince that he will accompany him to "the place of the king of kings"—God the Father—and that the prince "should appear with him (the brightness) before *our* king."[104] There is, therefore, a reunion with the brother, but because the hymn ends here, we do not learn of their appearance, the two of them, before their king.

Let us now, as promised, consider how this hymn, understood allegorically, functions in the apocryphal *Acts* themselves. Embedded in the drama of Judas Thomas, the hymn comes to serve as a sort of textual double for the *Acts* themselves. The reader is asked to interpret the hymn in light of the *Acts* and its braided theology of the twin and the bridal chamber. But the reader is also asked to interpret the *Acts* in light of the hymn, and so to reconsider which pieces in the drama are the most salient for salvation. Judas Thomas sings this hymn, in the first person, while languishing in prison and expecting to die. The prince's story becomes his story, thus more or less making clear that the prince is not the redeemed redeemer, but instead a tale of humanity's exile and return. In light of the *Acts'* theology of the twin, according to which Judas Thomas is the twin of Jesus Christ, the brother in the hymn stands for Christ. The pearl, I would submit, is best understood as holiness, that is, a life of sexual renunciation that, according to the *Acts'* theology of the bridal chamber, renders one a bride ready for the bridegroom Christ. But unlike the rest of the *Acts*, the hymn is less concerned with the recovery (or preservation) of holiness, and more interested in how the divine double calls the human home, how Christ calls Judas Thomas home, by reminding him of who he is and what his mission is, and by leading him back. We noted that there is a proliferation of divine doubles in the hymn: companion, countryman, letter or facing page of an inner inscription, and of course the royal garment. But in an important sense these are all the same: they are a series of divine doubles sent by the prince's one divine double, who is of course Judas Thomas's twin brother Christ. On the eve of his death, Judas Thomas sings this song to celebrate and also to solicit his divine double, his twin brother, who will lead him homeward.

Conclusion

This chapter has surveyed a number of Christian witnesses to the divine double from the second and third centuries. The first half of the chapter looked at two streams from the second century: Tatian the Assyrian and his notion of a syzygy of soul and spirit and Valentinian reflection on the sacraments as effecting a union of us and our angelic counterparts, images to our archetypes. The second half followed the trail of the Thomas tradition further into the third century, considering in turn each of the texts of that tradition: the *Book of Thomas*, the *Acts of Thomas*, and the "Hymn of the Pearl." There are undoubtedly other witnesses to the divine double from these same centuries, including not only other Christian sources but also Jewish, Hermetic, and Sethian sources that would only enrich this historical narrative. But my aim in this chapter has been not merely to document *all* the witnesses, but rather to convey a sense of the cluster of concerns that animate this sampling and how these concerns follow on the heels of Plato and the *Gospel of Thomas*. We see Plato's mirror appearing again and again: both in the sense that our divine double is our mirror image, or rather that we are *its* mirror image, and in the sense that the text itself can be a mirror—in the most recent case, the *Acts* and the "Hymn" mirror each other, and we the reader, poised between those two mirrors as if in a *mise en abyme*, can begin to see, to know, our own twin or double. We see the persistent effort to name the union or conjunction between ourselves and our doubles, an effort troubled by the fact that such a union occupies the borderlands between the one and the not-one, or presumes to preserve the one and the two in some unity-in-distinction. The notion of our being a twin is one attempt to capture that unity-in-distinction, as is the notion of our being a bride to a bridegroom, conjoined and yet distinct. The theme of the bridal chamber, present already in the secret sayings of the *Gospel of Thomas*, is reimagined in both the *Gospel of Philip* and the *Acts of Thomas*. Another and new attempt to name that unity-in-distinction appears in Tatian and Valentinus: the syzygy. It becomes one of the threads of the tradition of the divine double moving forward, weaving its way not only through Valentinian sources and the *Acts of Thomas*, but, as we will soon see, through the *Cologne Mani Codex* and even Plotinus's *Enneads*.

4

Mani and His Twin-Companion

ONE OF THE SEVERAL Manichaean texts that survive only in Coptic translation preserves a humorous anecdote about an exchange Mani had with one of his disciples. Mani was staying in the Persian capital, Seleucia-Ctesiphon, and on a single exhausting day he was called no less than three times for private audiences with King Shapur I (r. 239–270). Upon Mani's third and final return to his congregation, a disciple by the name of Aurades remarked, "Pray, Lord Mani, let us have two Manis after your likeness who come down as you did, one Mani to stay with us and another to go to Shapur."[1] His seems an innocent enough request: a disciple, jealous of his master's time and attention, jokes about having another Mani to occupy the king. But Mani refuses Aurades's rhetorical request, and gently rebukes him, "What then, if two Manis had come into this world? Which place could bear them and which country would admit them?"[2] On the surface, his reply suggests merely that the world can seem barely to tolerate *one* Mani, never mind two. But beneath the surface a much more serious point is being made. Mani insists, with a good dose of insider irony, "I am the *only* Mani."[3] The insider would of course understand that Mani has a twin or companion, a divine double who has nearly as many names as there are surviving sources—a Socratic *daimōn* of sorts who has been with him since childhood. Mani, the third-century man raised in a baptist sect in southern Mesopotamia, is acclaimed by his disciples as the "Apostle of Light" precisely because he alone is *not* Mani—Mani, rather, is a composite, a human and his divine counterpart.[4] In other words, Mani is already two, and so cannot be duplicated further. As Albert Henrichs puts it, "To duplicate the one (the Apostle of God) or the other (a figure with a definite, historical background) would have meant to do away with him."[5] The disciple's innocent request is remembered and rebuffed so as to reinforce Manichaean doctrine about the very doubled selfhood of the apostle. What Mani declares here and six further times in the space of two pages is, in Coptic, *anak ou-manichaios en-ouōt*. "I am the *only* Mani" is a permissible translation, as is "I, a single Mani" or "I, one Mani alone." Embedded in this first-person declaration is the phrase *oua ouōt*— "one and the same" or "a single one" (which is familiar to us from the discussion of the *Gospel of Thomas* in Chapter 2). This anecdote thus functions like an insider joke operating on two levels: first, Mani cannot be duplicated precisely because he is already doubled; second, in his rebuff to duplication Mani appeals to his own singularity (his being *oua ouōt*), but a singularity that conjoins two, he and his double.

The aim of this chapter is to unpack and understand the two dimensions of this joke. Through the surviving witnesses, I will trace the figure of Mani's twin or companion: How was this figure described, and how was his union with Mani imagined? I will begin with some general background on Mani's life and career and the religion he founded in third-century Mesopotamia, a religion that was destined to spread as far west as Roman North Africa and as far east as China. I will then begin our investigation into the sources, which survive in a wide array of languages, genres, and states of transmission. First on the agenda will be the medieval Islamic sources, al-Bīrūnī and Ibn al-Nadīm, who, despite their prejudices against Mani and his religion, are crucial witnesses to the figure of his twin or companion. For corroboration of their etic descriptions, I will turn to the emic descriptions in the surviving Manichaean sources, focusing our attention on two Western witnesses: (1) the *Kephalaia of the Teacher*, a collection of Mani's teachings surviving in Coptic translation, which includes the anecdote above; and (2) the

Cologne Mani Codex (CMC), probably the single most important surviving Manichaean text for our purposes. Confirming but deepening the Arabic sources, the *Kephalaia* introduce Mani's twin or companion as the Paraclete whom Jesus foretold in the Gospel of John and who is identified in other Christian traditions with the Holy Spirit. Moreover, the *Kephalaia* figure this Paraclete as Mani's image or *eikōn*, with Mani insisting that the two of them form "a single body with a single spirit."[6] This phrase includes the now-familiar construction *oua ouōt*, and thus serves to unpack the anecdote with which we began: Who is Mani, who is his double, and how are the two of them *oua ouōt* or "one and the same"? These questions will lead us into the so-called *Cologne Mani Codex*, a miniature fifth-century book discovered in Upper Egypt several decades ago. This codex also confirms and deepens what we knew from the Arabic sources about Mani's upbringing among the baptists of southern Mesopotamia, and makes it clear that he was raised in a Christian environment and understood himself as not just *a* but *the* exemplary Christian. For our purposes, however, it is relevant because it provides the most sustained descriptions of Mani's companion, whom he names his *syzygos*.

We come to learn from these sources that Mani's selfhood was consistently understood, perhaps by himself but certainly by his disciples, as constituted by the coincidence of the one and the two: to be the "I" Mani is to be his human self (an "Apostle of Light" sojourning in a body) and his *syzygos* (sent to inaugurate his apostleship) together. As is captured in the anecdote above, the name given to this doubled selfhood is "one," "alone," or "solitary" (Coptic: *oua ouōt*, Greek: *monos, monēros, monogenēs*; Syriac: *had, mshāwhad, īhīdāyā*). These names, especially in Coptic (*oua ouōt*), call to mind the *Gospel of Thomas* and raise the question of whether and how Mani's doubled selfhood is related to that of the apostle Judas Thomas, twin *(didymos)* of Jesus. The possible connection to the *Gospel of Thomas* also raises the question of whether in Manichaeism we find a universal or a restricted anthropology of the divine double. Whereas the *Gospel of Thomas* imagines that *all* Christians are called to become twins of Jesus, and thus to become "solitary" ones precisely because they welcome the indwelling of the light of Jesus, it is unclear whether the Manichaean sources believe that everyone has a divine double, or whether such a selfhood is restricted to Mani and his forerunners, other incarnations of the Apostle of Light. We will see that there is something of a universal anthropology of the divine double in Manichaeism, but that it is two tiered: differentiating the divine double in the case of Mani and his ilk from the divine double of the regular Manichaean faithful.

Introduction to Mani and Manichaeism

In much of what follows I will adhere closely to a handful of ancient primary texts, attending to the peculiarities of their treatment of Mani's divine double.[7] But for the benefit of the reader who may not be familiar with Mani or the religion he founded, let us pan back and view him and his faith with a wider angle. Introductions to Manichaeism tend to focus on the man or the mythology, Mani himself or the dizzying cosmic drama into which he believed we are thrown. This focus has come at a cost, namely the danger of "losing the Manichaeans" themselves, as Jason David BeDuhn has warned in his book *The Manichaean Body*.[8] By looking only at the life of the founder or the system of belief he preached, we blind ourselves to the lives of those who made up these communities, *their* practices and rationales. Certainly BeDuhn's is the best account of what it means to *be* Manichaean, to find oneself in history in "a unified Manichaean tradition of practice."[9] But our interest in Mani and Manichaeism is somewhat different, more specific, and may permit our return to the more traditional focus on the man and the mythology. For to understand Mani's divine double, we need to know something both about his life, as remembered by largely hagiographical sources, and about the mythology that explains Mani's own identity and that of his twin or companion (and how the two are in fact one).

Mani was born in the year 216 to a father named Pattek (Arabic, Futtuq; Greek, Pattikios; Middle Persian, Ptyg) and a mother probably named Maryam.[10] Although he was descended from royal blood of the Arsacid dynasty that ruled over the Parthian kingdom (247 BCE–224 CE), he grew up in the shadow of the Arsacids' successors, the Sassanians, several of whose kings he was destined to know and advise (including Shapur I, mentioned above as eager for his company). His mother cared for him in his first four years. According to legend, his father was told by a divine voice in a temple in the capital city, Seleucia-Ctesiphon, that he should abstain from meat, wine, and women. In response he abandoned his wife and joined a community of "baptists" living in southern Mesopotamia, taking with him his young son, who would spend the next twenty years of his life with them. We will explore who these "baptists" were in greater detail and why Mani broke with them at the age of twenty-four. According to the sources examined closely below, Mani was visited at least twice by a heavenly messenger, whom he called his "twin" or "companion." This divine double became for Mani a kind of alter ego, the other half of his whole self, protecting and guiding him throughout the rest of his life. It was this heavenly twin-companion who persuaded Mani to break with the baptists, strike out on his own, and preach his own enlightening gospel.

When he did so, his father joined him as his first disciple. Mani himself wrote a canon of scriptures, as well as extracanonical commentaries;[11] established a two-tiered community structure of catechumens ("hearers") and elect, each with its own incumbent rites and responsibilities;[12] preached far and wide, and in different idioms to diverse audiences; and reached out to political powers to help ensure that his fledgling faith could survive in the Persian empire with its newly ascendant Zoroastrian ideology. Indeed, "he may be said to have combined the charisma of Jesus, the missionary purpose of Paul, and the doctrinal stringency of an Augustine."[13] Underlying all his efforts was a conviction, seconded by his twin-companion, that his message was a universal one, the culmination of previous prophecies, practices, and teachings—in other words, the universal truth. Mani seems to have regarded himself as the final incarnation of a heavenly figure, the Apostle of Light, sent to successive generations to reveal the truth, which was veiled according to need and circumstance. Previous incarnations included Zoroaster, Buddha, and Jesus (among others). Mani's good news spread throughout the Persian empire, and well beyond, eventually stretching the full latitude of the known world, east to west. His success won his share of friends at the Sassanian court, as well as enemies. When Bahram I ascended to the throne in 274 (r. until 276 or 277), he rescinded the support that his brother Hormizd (r. 272–273) and his father Shapur I had lent Mani, and with the help of the chief Magian or *mobad* named Karder, arranged to have Mani imprisoned. After a month in chains, during which time he was able to receive visitors and arrange for the survival of his communities after his departure, Mani died in the year 276 or 277 (scholars debate the exact date).

Mani probably understood himself as a Christian, and his universal message as the truth of Christianity, restored after successive generations of corruption. "Manichaeism"—derived from the Syriac title "Mani the living" *(Mani hayya)* or in Greek, *Manichaios*—is a name used first by Christian heresiologists and then by modern scholars to distinguish it sharply from forms of Christianity more familiar to us from the early centuries of the common era. In today's parlance, the adjective "Manichaean" connotes absolute dualism— good and evil, light and darkness—and is as often applied to political views as it is to religious ones. Dualism has a home in Mani's teaching, but we would do well to approach it carefully. Although Mani is said to have received his revelation explaining the totality of the world directly from his twin-companion, the story that is recorded in the various sources is very likely the result of systematizing efforts on the part of the first generations of Mani's followers. What he taught, *in nuce*, was "an analysis of the causes and nature of evil and suffering in the world, the predicament in which human and all life are entangled," "the divine nature of the soul," and finally "a practice for the salvation of the divine in the universe."[14] In other words: how the world came to be, and us in it; how the divine, including our soul, is caught in this world; and most importantly, how to free what is divine in us and in the world, and thus contribute to the salvation of the world. His teaching is often summarized by the motto "The two principles and the three times." The two principles—here is Mani's dualism—are light and darkness, two separate and eternal realms, roughly equivalent to good and evil. To say that these are separate, however, brings us to the matter of the three times: at first light and darkness were separate; now they are mingled; once again they will be separate—in other words, beginning, middle, and end.

That relatively simple scheme, however, gives way to an elaborate account of the drama that led to the mingling of light and darkness, the shift from the first to the second ages. The realm of darkness, seething in its dark desire, randomly groped after the realm of light. Sensing the threat, the Father of light, who preferred to remain distant and hidden from the conflict, called forth a number of divinities that advance the drama, often by calling forth ever-new divinities according to certain patterns. The Father sent as a sacrifice his own Son (or First Man), who in apparent defeat was trapped by the forces of darkness—this was the first emanation. But this was an elaborate trap set by the forces of light. In the second emanation, the First Man was rescued and his captors slayed. But the dead matter of the slain was used to create the universe and to house the light that is still held captive there: thus, the universe was created by the forces of light as a mixture of light and darkness—a mixture, though, that would ultimately need to be separated. This slow separation happens through a third emanation, divinities not of creation but of salvation. The gods of salvation managed to release some of the light from its captors by appearing naked before them, thus prompting the forces of darkness to ejaculate light particles. The forces of darkness, however, created humans to entrap light even further: humans were made in the image of the gods of salvation who appeared naked before the forces of darkness, but made by them so as to lust and so multiply. With every new generation born of sex the light in humans is further divided and distributed, ensuring its perpetual imprisonment in dark matter.

Here is where the narrative becomes more familiar, and more relevant to our purposes. A divinity by the name of Jesus the Splendor descended to save Adam and his ilk, to rescue them from the sexual reproduction that keeps light imprisoned. To do so, Jesus called forth another divinity called the Light Mind, which, as we will see when we turn to the *Kephalaia*, differentiated itself into three further entities: (1) the Apostle of Light, a heavenly being who becomes incarnate on earth in successive generations to save Adam's offspring, most famously as Zoroaster, Buddha, Jesus of Nazareth, and now Mani; (2) the companion, counterpart, or twin, who appears to the incarnate apostle, awakening him to his apostolic mission; (3) something called the Light Form, which is paired with the soul of every Manichaean, and which meets that soul upon death.

There are, then, three paths for humans to take. They can choose to ignore the Apostle of Light, in which case when light is finally separated from darkness once and forever more, they will be cast into the realm of darkness. They can choose to follow the Apostle of Light as catechumens or "hearers": they may reproduce, but in so doing ensure that the light within them will not escape this world, but will be reborn, and further distributed. The consolation for these *auditores* is that they support those who choose to lead a life devoted to the salvation of the world, the release of imprisoned light. These "elect" do not reproduce, and their diet is strictly limited to certain fruits and vegetables that contain more light than others. By consuming and digesting these foods, the elect become in effect factories for the liberation of light. This peculiar alimentary regime, and the soteriology on which it is based, has been reconstructed with great care by BeDuhn.

This condensed introduction, I hope, will go some distance in helping to situate Mani and his divine double. It is an understanding of selfhood that appears in Manichaean mythology to explain how the gods descend to save Adam's woeful offspring: the Apostle of Light and his companion, counterpart, or twin. But it is also an understanding of selfhood that appears very much in this world, both in the figure of Mani himself (and his forerunners) and in the promise of what the Manichaean faithful can hope for, after death, in the case of their own souls.

The Arabic Sources: Al-Bīrūnī and Ibn al-Nadīm

We turn now to two etic or "outsider" sources, in this case two medieval Islamic authors writing in Arabic.[15] The first of the two is the scholar al-Bīrūnī (973–1050). His first great work was an encyclopedia of calendars and eras he prepared for the sultan, his patron, entitled *The Chronology of All Nations*.[16] Chapter 8 (of 31) is devoted to "the eras of the pseudo-prophets" and includes a discussion of Mani among the litany of false prophets. Mani is traditionally credited with authoring his own canon of seven scriptures, all of them in his native language, Syriac. However, none of these seven texts has survived in anything more than fragments or a loose quotation. Somewhere between the year 240 and 250, at the height of his influence at the Sassanian royal court, Mani composed an extracanonical work, not in his native Syriac but in Middle Persian, the language of the empire. Titled *Shabuhragan*, "Dedicated to Shapur," the work presents Mani's theology in terms legible to an imperial Zoroastrian audience.[17] In chapter 8 of his *Chronology* al-Bīrūnī quotes from Mani's *Shabuhragan*:[18]

> In the beginning of his book called *Shābūrkān* [*Shabuhragan*], which he composed for Shāpūr b. Ardashīr, he says: "Wisdom and deeds have always from time to time been brought to mankind by the messengers of God *(rusul allah)*. So in one age they have been brought by the messenger *(rasūl)* called Buddha, to India, in another by Zarādusht [Zoroaster] to Persia, in another by Jesus to the West. Thereupon his revelation has come down, this prophecy *(nubūwwa)* in this last age through me, Mānī, the messenger of the God of truth *(rasūl ilāh al-haqq)* to Babylonia." In his gospel, which he arranged according to the twenty-two letters of the alphabet, he says that he is the Paraclete announced by the Messiah, and that he is the seal of the prophets *(khātam al-nabiyīn)*.[19]

Most important for our purposes is the fact that Mani speaks here of his "revelation," one delivered "in this last age." After this citation from the *Shabuhragan*, al-Bīrūnī tells us that Mani "received the first divine revelation in his 13th year, in the year 539 of the Babylonian astronomers, in the 2nd year of Ardashīr [=228 CE], the King of Kings."[20] There is no mention of a second divine revelation (to which some other sources attest), but the fact that the revelation was "first" suggests that there were others. Al-Bīrūnī does not tell us about the nature of this revelation. All we learn from al-Bīrūnī in his paraphrase from one of Mani's seven canonical works, *The Great Gospel*, is that Mani claimed in that work to be "the Paraclete announced by the Messiah." We will return to the Paraclete below when we turn to the *Kephalaia*. Later in the *Chronology*, after listing several of Mani's other books, al-Bīrūnī writes that Mani "maintained that he had explained *in extenso* what had only been hinted at by the Messiah."[21] Neither of these crucial claims is substantiated by al-Bīrūnī, and so these titillating details take us deeper into the ancient witnesses, turning now to al-Bīrūnī's own double, Ibn al-Nadīm.

Ibn al-Nadīm (d. 995 or 998) was, like al-Bīrūnī, a medieval Islamic encyclopedist. His *Kitab al-Fihrist* was intended as an index of all books written in Arabic. In the ninth of its ten chapters, al-Nadīm documents the doctrines of the nonmonotheistic creeds, including the Manichaeans (and others whom he regarded as dualists). Although he is, no less than al-Bīrūnī, largely a hostile witness to Manichaeism, nevertheless his encyclopedic aims seem to keep his own orthodoxy (he was a twelver Shi'ite) largely in check as he preserves what has been described as "the most complete heresiological account of [Manichaeism] in any ancient tradition (Christian, Zoroastrian, or Islamic)."[22] Ibn al-Nadīm provides a much more detailed biography of Mani than does al-Bīrūnī: we learn that his father Futtuq left the capital city of Seleucia-Ctesiphon and joined a group in the marshlands of southern Mesopotamia called "the Mughtasilah" or "washers," whose founder is alleged to be someone named *al-Hasīh* (see below). Mani was brought up in this community, although al-Nadīm does not tell us any more about the community's beliefs or practices apart from what we can infer from their name and their founder. Instead he relays this account of Mani's first revelation:

> Even when young, Mani spoke with words of wisdom and then, when he was twelve years old, there came to him a revelation. According to his statement it was from the King of the Gardens of Light and, from what he said, it was God exalted. The angel bringing the revelation was called the Twin *(at-tawm)*, which is a Nabataean word meaning "Companion" *(qarīn)*. He said to him, "Leave this cult, for thou art not one of its adherents. Upon thee are laid purity and refraining from bodily lusts, but it is not yet time for thee to appear openly, because of thy tender years."

When he had completed his twenty-fourth year, the Twin *(at-tawm)* came to him saying, "The time is fulfilled for thee to come forth and to give the summons to thy cause."[23]

This aligns with al-Bīrūnī's account: when Mani had completed his twelfth year (al-Nadīm), and so was in his thirteenth year (al-Bīrūnī), he was visited by an angel of "God exalted." Apart from the issues of exact chronology, there are more serious questions about the names al-Nadīm uses to introduce this heavenly messenger. First, he is called "the Twin" *(at-tawm).*[24] This seems straightforward enough, except that *tawm* is not a Nabataean word. "Nabataean" *(nabat)* strictly refers to the Aramaic-speaking populations of Arab ethnicity associated with their famous capital Petra, but in medieval Arabic *nabat* is also used to refer to the indigenous Aramaic-speaking population of southern Mesopotamia (for instance, the Mughtasila), as opposed to the later Arab settlers from the Arabian Peninsula.[25] Thus, "Nabataean" here probably means some southern Mesopotamian dialect of Aramaic, except that this very ordinary Arabic word *tawm* ("twin") is not exactly Aramaic either and it does not mean "companion" *(qarīn)*. François de Blois has suggested a very convincing emendation to the text. He remarks that all the manuscripts of al-Nadīm's *Fihrist* derive from a single master copy in which the author left many blank spaces for words and dates, apparently intending to fill them in later. De Blois suggests that this is one of those cases, and so proposes the following reconstruction:

> And the angel who brought him the inspiration was called the twin *(at-taw'am)*, but in Nabataean (i.e., Babylonian Aramaic) he is < . . . >, which means the companion *(al-qarīn)*.[26]

If we follow de Blois, then it seems that the word that the master copy omits is some variation on the Syriac word *zawgā*, meaning spouse or companion (the natural equivalent to the Arabic *qarīn*). Aramaic dialects (such as Syriac) have in fact borrowed this word from the Greek word *zeugos*, which we have encountered in previous chapters: the *zyg-* root meaning "yoke," from which we have "syzygy" or "conjunction." The importance of de Blois's philological reconstruction is that it promises to recover the two terms with which Mani's messenger is traditionally described: (1) twin and (2) companion. The surviving Western, largely Egyptian, sources (such as the *CMC*, to which we will soon turn) often recall Mani's messenger largely in the second register, as a companion (for instance, *syzygos* in the *CMC*), whereas the Eastern sources (Parthian, Middle Persian, Sogdian, Turkish, Chinese) often recall him in the first register, as a twin (Parthian *yamag*, Middle Persian *nar-jamīg*, and so on). This Arabic source (the *Fihrist*), poised between the East and West, the Iranian and the Aramaic traditions, thus includes both, at least according to de Blois's reconstruction.

Putting the philological reconstruction to one side, let us return briefly to the *Fihrist*. We learn that in his twelfth year Mani was visited by a messenger who was both his twin and his companion. The twin-companion first tells him to leave the cult of the Mughtasila, but not until he has passed out of his tender years. The twin-companion returns twelve years later and inaugurates Mani's mission with these words:

> Peace be upon you, oh, Mani, from me and from the Lord who sent me to you. He has chosen you for his mission, and commanded you to summon in your own right, to preach the gospel of truth as from his presence, and to carry on in this [mission] with all of your perseverance.[27]

This is the mandate delivered by Mani's divine double. We also learn from al-Nadīm, echoing al-Bīrūnī, that Mani "asserted that he was the Paraclete about whom Jesus, for whom may there be peace, preached."[28] Admittedly, the composite portrait of Mani's divine double is still very sketchy. If we merge the two medieval Islamic accounts, we can surmise that Mani received two revelations from a visitor sometime during or just after his twelfth and twenty-fourth years, a visitor who is called both a "twin" and a "companion." The revelation inaugurates his religious mission, which necessitates his breaking with the community in which he was reared, and which is meant to make explicit Christ's (heretofore implicit) teachings. Furthermore, a key to Mani's identity is a figure whom Jesus foretold in the Gospel of John, the Paraclete, and it is this suggestion that leads us from our two Arabic sources to the Coptic *Kephalaia*.

The *Kephalaia of the Teacher* and the Paraclete

In the early fourth century Eusebius of Caesarea accused Mani of "pos[ing] as Christ": "At one time [Mani] proclaimed himself the Paraclete—the Holy Spirit himself—conceited crackbrain that he was."[29] But who, or what, is the Paraclete? The word *paraklētos* is a noun with a passive sense formed from the verb *parakaleō*, meaning literally "to call *(kaleō)* to one's side *(para)*."[30] The noun accordingly means "someone who appears in [sic] another's behalf, mediator, intercessor, helper."[31] The word appears in those writings in the New Testament associated with the apostle John. In 1 John we read, "We have an advocate *(paraklētos)* with the Father, Jesus Christ the righteous" (2:1). Here Jesus Christ himself is understood as the *paraklētos* or "advocate." But in the Gospel of John, Jesus speaks of "another *paraklētos*":

> And I will pray the Father, and he will give you another counselor *(paraklētos)*, to be with you for ever, even the Spirit of Truth, whom the world cannot receive, because it neither sees him nor knows him; you know him, for he dwells with you, and will be in you. (14:16–17)

The Gospel of John goes on to equate this Paraclete with the Holy Spirit or Spirit of Truth (14:26, 15:26), which Spirit has traditionally been understood as having been given to the apostles by the resurrected Jesus upon his first appearance to them after his death: "Jesus said to them again, 'Peace be with you. As the Father has sent me, even so I send you.' And when he said this, he breathed on them, and said to them, 'Receive the Holy Spirit'" (20:21–22).

Although the Gospel of John identifies the Paraclete with the Holy Spirit, and many early traditions follow suit, some early Christians may have understood these passages to foretell the arrival of another figure, who would somehow serve in Jesus's stead as a sort of replacement or regent. The most famous but controversial instance of this is the case of "Montanism" or the "New Prophecy," a second-century movement centered on gifts of the spirit that emerged from Phrygia in Asia Minor.[32] Heresiologists used the name of one of its early leaders, Montanus, as a label for the entire movement—a standard strategy for suggesting that any heterodox group can be traced back to a single heretical author or "heresiarch." Eusebius of Caesarea devoted a good deal of attention to these "false prophets" and tells us that "some of these sectarians slithered like poisonous reptiles over Asia and Phrygia, boasting that Montanus was the Paraclete and that his female followers Priscilla and Maximilla were his prophetesses."[33] There is no doubt that the New Prophecy was associated with the Holy Spirit and its gifts, and so with the Paraclete. It is less clear, however, whether the prophets (Montanus, Priscilla, or Maximilla) simply understood themselves as recipients of the Holy Spirit—that is, literally *inspired* by the Paraclete-Spirit—or whether one or more of them actually understood him- or herself to *be* the Paraclete, *the* figure whom Jesus foretold. Eusebius reports that at least some of their followers boasted as much, but we have good reasons for doubting Eusebius's reporting of the New Prophecy. Whether Montanus or any of the other early leaders of the New Prophecy claimed to be the Paraclete, Eusebius accuses Mani (to whom he devotes much less attention) of doing so, and of "pos[ing] as Christ."[34]

As we have seen, both Arabic sources say that Mani understood himself as the Paraclete: al-Bīrūnī reports that in his gospel Mani "says that he is the Paraclete announced by the Messiah"; al-Nadīm reports that Mani "asserted that he was the Paraclete about whom Jesus, for whom may there be peace, preached."[35] Given that al-Bīrūnī and Ibn al-Nadīm were not likely reading Eusebius, we have to look to the Manichaean sources themselves to confirm their report. In fact, we need look no further than the so-called *Kephalaia of the Teacher*. In 1929 local workmen digging for fertilizer in the ruins of an ancient house in Medinet Madi in the Fayum oasis in Egypt discovered seven papyrus codices, each preserved in its wooden cover. These Coptic texts are unquestionably Manichaean, date from about 400 CE, and are translations of Syriac originals "that reach back to Mani himself . . . or to the first generation of the church."[36] These texts did not originate from the Fayum: their Coptic script suggests that they came from Asyut (Lycopolis) in Upper Egypt, an area where Manichaeans enjoyed success in their early evangelization efforts. A fourth-century Neoplatonist by the name of Alexander of Lycopolis wrote a treatise against Manichaeism in which he attests to its spread in this region of Egypt.[37] The most important work from this Medinet Madi discovery is a text called the *Kephalaia* or *Chapters*, split now between collections in Berlin and Dublin. The Berlin half is entitled *The Kephalaia of the Teacher*, and it is on this codex that we shall now focus.

The Berlin *Kephalaia* contains over two hundred chapters, each of which "purports to be the verbatim record of a lesson by Mani, yet it is apparent that it is a constructed text in the process of evolution."[38] It seems to have been a document for internal use, perhaps for catechetical purposes. The codex begins with a brief rehearsal of the grand cosmic drama, the birth and battle of the world caught between the powers of light and darkness. Next comes a list of the Manichaean canon, and an explanation for the text in hand. Whereas Mani was careful to compose his own canon, he is quoted in the introduction explaining that his disciples should collect and preserve his extracanonical commentary—these very chapters. The first chapter offers a history of Mani's predecessors, the succession of apostles who attempted to preach the truth to other ages and places. This list includes Buddha, Zoroaster, and Jesus, and thus confirms al-Bīrūnī's citation of Mani's *Shabuhragan*. But here this triumvirate is expanded to include such figures from the Hebrew Bible as Sethel, Enosh, Enoch, and Shem; and along with the Buddha in the East is included another figure named "Aurentes." This and other Manichaean lists of apostles are meant to buttress Mani's universalism, but it is interesting that the only figure from this list to whom the *Kephalaia* gives any substantial attention is Jesus.

We will return to the first chapter in just a moment. But let us page ahead briefly to the seventh chapter, famous for its clear and complete account of Manichaean myth, specifically the dizzying succession of divinities who advance the plot in light's slow triumph over darkness. Our interest is in the figure called the "Light Mind" who "chooses all the churches":

> And, again, [the Light Mind] too summoned three powers after the pattern of Jesus.
>
> The first power is the Apostle of Light; the one who shall on occasion come and assume the church of the flesh, of humanity; and he becomes the inner leader of righteousness.
>
> The second is the counterpart, who shall come to the apostle and appear to him, becoming companion to him, sticking close to him everywhere; and providing help to him all the time, from all afflictions and dangers.
>
> The third is the Light Form; the one whom the elect and the catechumens shall receive, should they renounce the world. (36,2–8)

This is an unusually clear taxonomy. The Light Mind summons three further figures, all of them "after the pattern of Jesus." The first figure or "power" is the Apostle of Light: Mani, of course, but before him Buddha, Zoroaster, Jesus, and others—all sent "on occasion" to "assume the church of the flesh, of humanity." Behind all the various personages, though, is a single agent, the Apostle of Light. Next comes the "counterpart" and "companion" to the Apostle of Light. We know of this companion from Mani's life, at least from Ibn al-Nadīm. But according to the *Kephalaia*, each Apostle of Light has had a counterpart and companion (although those encounters have not here been narrated). The third power is the Light Form, which both ranks of the Manichaean community—elect and hearer—receive upon their renunciation of the world. We will have occasion to return to this third power when we consider whether and how Manichaeism has a universal anthropology of the divine double, or whether it is restricted to the Apostle of Light, such as Mani and his forerunners.

With this taxonomy in place, let us return to the first chapter, where Mani narrates the arrival of his own counterpart and companion. The single most significant feature of the *Kephalaia*'s version of this episode from Mani's life is that it presents his companion as the Paraclete.

> [Wh]e[n] the church of the savior was raised to the heights, my apostolate began, which you asked me about! From that time on

was sent the Paraclete, the Spirit of Truth; the one who has co[me] to you in this last generation. Just like the savior said: When I go, I will send to you the Paraclete. [Whe]n the Paraclete comes, he can upbraid the world concerni[ng sin, and] he can speak with you on behalf of right[eou]sness, and [about] judgment, concerning who believe. (14,4–10)

The first chapter of the *Kephalaia* adheres closely to the Gospel of John: the "other" Paraclete whom Jesus "the savior" foretold (Jn 14:16) is identified with the Holy Spirit (Jn 14:26) or Spirit of Truth (Jn 15:26). It is this Paraclete who came to Mani to inaugurate his apostolate of light. Although anticipating the next section, we should note here that the *Cologne Mani Codex* confirms the *Kephalaia* (and also al-Bīrūnī and al-Nadīm) in that it mentions the Paraclete no fewer than four times.[39] The dilemma is that the sources speak sometimes of Mani's companion as the Paraclete, and sometimes of Mani himself (or his mind or *nous*) as the Paraclete. Johannes van Oort attempts to resolve the "seeming contradiction":

> The dilemma of the church fathers as well as the seeming contradiction that both the *Nous* and the Suzugos are called "Paraclete" may be solved by a further examination of the Manichaean (and typical Gnostic) concept of the Suzugos. When Mani, i.e., the *Nous* of Mani, was sent into the world, a mirror image of this *Nous*, i.e., his *alter ego*, remained behind in heaven. One ego, Mani's Light-*Nous*, was imprisoned in his body and thus forgot his mission. Then the Suzugos, the *alter ego*, was sent from heaven ... The *Nous* of Mani and his *suzugos* should therefore be treated as two complementary aspects of Mani's identity.[40]

Strictly speaking, Mani's undescended *Nous* and his companion are two faces of the same divine agent. Once the companion (Paraclete) has visited the incarnate Mani to awaken him to his apostolate, then he (Mani) can also be said to be the Paraclete, precisely insofar as the companion has been conjoined to its counterpart, the now-embodied Apostle of Light. Thus, the resolution to the "seeming contradiction" reinforces the essential, doubled nature of Mani's selfhood, once he is visited by (and so becomes) the Paraclete.

Van Oort's mention of a "mirror image" takes us back to the first chapter of the *Kephalaia*, where a second pass at describing Mani's revelation provides somewhat more detail:

> At that same season he [. . . 10 lines largely illegible . . .] my image *(tah-ikōn)*, I assuming it in the years of Arta[b]anus the [ki]ng of Persia, I was tended and grew tall and attained the ful[lne]ss of the sea / [so]n. In that same year, when Ard[ashi]r the ki[ng was c]rowned, the living Paraclete came down t[o me. He sp]oke with me. He unveiled to me the hidden mystery, the one that is hidden from the worlds and the generations, the myster[y] of the dep[ths] and the heights. He unveiled to me the mystery of the light and the darkness; the mystery of the calamity of conflict, and the w[ar], and the great [. . .] the battle that the darkness spread about. Aft[erwards], he unveiled to me also: How the light [. . .] the darkness, through their mingling this universe was set up [. . .] H[e o]pened my eyes also to the way that the ships were constructed; [to enable the go]ds of light to be in them, to purify the li[ght from] creation. (14,27–15,10)

The *Kephalaia*, as far as it is legible, does not seem to differentiate between a first and second revelation of the companion (as al-Nadīm does). This second account follows directly on the heels of the first, and situates the revelation not so much in Mani's own life but in the life of the Persian dynasty. It also provides a short précis of Manichaean myth: the mystery of the light and the darkness. Perhaps most tantalizing is the mention of "my image" *(tah-ikōn)*. The verb is no longer legible in this line, and this passage follows on ten lines of which only fragments are legible. Nevertheless, it seems clear that the Paraclete is meant to be in some sense "my image" (Gr. *eikōn*) and that Mani is saying that he "assumed" that image when he had grown to maturity. This is, of course, quite a departure from the Gospel of John. Nowhere does Jesus say that the Paraclete will be an image or *eikōn*. But as we will see in the next section, this tantalizing detail in the *Kephalaia* finds confirmation in the *Cologne Mani*

Codex, where Mani proclaims, "Then, at the time when my body reached its full growth, immediately there flew down and appeared before me that most beautiful and greatest mirror image *(katoptron)* of [my self]" (*CMC* 17,1). We will also consider the ways that this "image" and "mirror image" may allude to Paul (and his concept of *eikōn*), Plato (lovers serving as each other's mirror), and the *Gospel of Thomas* (the "image" as opposed to "likeness" in §84).

We go on to learn from Mani that the Paraclete revealed to him everything that had happened and would happen, and that Mani, for his part, understood everything: "I have seen the totality through him!" (15,23). Perhaps more significant than even this realization are the next lines, "I have become a single body, / with a single spirit!" What does this mean? On the one hand, Mani already had a body and a spirit—or at least so he thought. But upon the arrival of his counterpart and companion, the Paraclete who is also his image, Mani is offered the opportunity to become singular in a new sense. The phrases "a single body" and "a single spirit" provide the key. "A single body" in Coptic is *ou-sōma en-ouōt;* likewise "a single spirit" is *ou-pneuma en-ouōt.* You can see in each the repetition of a construction, *oua ouōt,* that is familiar to us from the anecdote with which this chapter opened: there, Mani responded to his disciple's request for two Manis by saying, "I am the *only* Mani" or *anak ou-manichaios en-ouōt.* As I said at the start of this chapter, Mani's retort functions almost like a joke operating on two levels: first, Mani cannot be duplicated precisely he is already doubled; second, Mani insists on his singularity (his being *oua ouōt*) but a singularity that conjoins him and his double. It is the second dimension of the joke, then, that Mani's comment in this first chapter corroborates: "I have become a single body, / with a single spirit!" For it is precisely in having a counterpart and companion, a Paraclete who is also his image, that Mani can be said to be singular ("a single body with a single spirit"), not only in the sense of alone and unique, but singular in that he, Mani, conjoins, contains, preserves the two. As Albert Henrichs remarked over thirty years ago,

> Mani's awareness of, and insistence on, his own singularity is the basis of his self-conception . . . The fact that Mani possessed

an alter-ego in form of the Twin of Light makes him a split personality in the literal sense of that term rather than an individual: his human existence was nothing but a briefly reflected image of its true and eternal counterpart.[41]

In other words, Mani's singularity is marked by a split, a distinction between himself and his twin, a distinction that is never erased such that Mani becomes an individual per se. He is, as it were, singular, but not exactly one (if we mean by "one" something incompatible with two). He is an "I" whose singularity preserves its duplicity.

Mani's *Syzygos:* The *Cologne Mani Codex*

The *Kephalaia* has yielded great insights into the nature both of Mani's twin-companion (imagined as the Paraclete) and of their union as a singularity. We now turn to the *Cologne Mani Codex,* the most important text for our purposes, and the one to which we will devote most of our attention in what remains of this chapter.[42] In 1969 a tiny Greek codex, no larger than a matchbox, was discovered somewhere in the area of Asyut (Lycopolis) in Egypt—the same place where the Medinet Madi codices were found. The exact provenance of the codex is unknown, as is the exact means by which it was acquired by and conveyed to the Institut für Altertumskunde at the University of Cologne in that same year. The codex was in very poor shape, but Anton Fackelmann, "an eminent restorer of ancient manuscripts," managed to separate out ninety-six damaged leaves from an unknown total, which leaves were then transcribed by Albert Henrichs and Ludwig Koenen.[43] Over the course of the 1970s and 1980s, the surviving, legible text of the *Cologne Mani Codex* (as it was now called, owing to its new home) was published (by Henrichs and Koenen, and later by Henrichs, Koenen, and Römer), at first serially and then in a complete critical edition.[44]

The text in fact offers up its own title, "On the Origin of His Body" *(peri tēs gennēs tou sōmatos autou):* "his" referring of course to Mani; and "body" being taken in two senses. First, "his body" refers to Mani's own body, that in which the Apostle of Light sojourned on earth. Second, "his body" *can* be understood in terms of Paul's Christology *(soma christou)* to refer to Mani's mystical body, that is, his church.⁴⁵ The *Cologne Mani Codex* (hereafter *CMC*) is often called Mani's biography, but in fact it is more properly an anthology: a collection of excerpts from the writings of Mani's earliest disciples, which an anonymous editor has arranged into chronological order.⁴⁶ The codex itself has been dated to the fifth century, although scholars agree that the anthology was probably compiled much earlier, perhaps soon after Mani's death. Scholars also agree that the anthology is a Greek translation of a Syriac original. Due to the damage to the codex, the text suffers from many lacunae that disrupt the continuity of the narrative. Nevertheless, the chronological frame survives in the following sections: (1) pages 1–13 offer an account of Mani's childhood; (2) pages 14–44 focus on the two revelations of Mani's *syzygos* (and thus will be of great interest to us); (3) pages 45–72 are a digression in which Mani's own revelations are set against the backdrop of his predecessors, including five unattested apocalypses and the apostleship of Paul; (4) pages 72–99 deal with those southern Mesopotamian baptists who raised Mani and with whom he broke after his second revelation; (5) pages 100–116 narrate this break and his subsequent move to Seleucia-Ctesiphon; (6) pages 126–145 narrate Mani's early missionary activity and travels, including his conversion of a hermit covered entirely in hair, and of a local king; (7) pages 146ff are badly damaged and largely illegible.

The *CMC* offers a wealth of information on Mani and early Manichaeism, but perhaps the most significant feature of this discovery for the history of religions is what it revealed about Mani's background among the baptists. In his *Fihrist*, Ibn al-Nadīm reports that Mani's father joined "a group of people in the environs of Dastumīsān known as the Mughtasilah."⁴⁷ Later, al-Nadīm tells us that these "Mughtasilah" or "washers," also called Sabians of the Marshlands, were first established by a figure he calls *al-Hasīh*.⁴⁸ Scholars were wary of trusting al-Nadīm's report, but the *CMC* confirms it. In the long, relatively well-preserved section of the *CMC* that deals with Mani's tensions with his baptist brethren, he refers to a certain Alchasai *(alchasaios)* as "the founder of your law" (94,10–11). Alchasai is a figure well known from Christian heresiological reports: *Elchasai* (Hippolytus), *Elksai* (Epiphanius), *ho Elkesaios* (Methodius of Olympus), *Elkesaios* (Pseudo-Epiphanius), *'Iks'* (Theodore bar Konai)—all of these are variations (including al-Nadīm's *al-Hasīh*) on a Syriac name, or more properly a title, *hayla kasya* or "Hidden Power."[49] The *CMC* largely confirms these patristic sources: Alchasai was a Christian (fl. first to second century) who assumed the title "Hidden Power" and established in Mesopotamia an exclusively male, celibate community centered around repeated ritual baptism. Mani was probably raised in a third-century community descended from Alchasai's original community. His community was characterized by (1) a ritualistic conception of piety; (2) the keeping of the Sabbath; (3) baptisms or repeated ritual ablutions of the whole body in running water; (4) celebration of the Eucharist with unleavened bread and mere water; (5) the rejection of certain parts of the Old and New Testaments, including all of the apostle Paul; (6) abstention from meat, wine, and women ("encratism"); (7) the cyclical incarnation of the True Prophet or Apostle (i.e., Alchasai); (8) a belief in the resurrection of the body understood as a "resting of the garment" *(anapausis tou endymatos)*.[50] All told, it is abundantly clear from the *CMC* that Mani was raised in a Christian community, albeit one at the far margins of the emerging orthodoxy of the third and especially fourth centuries.

The *CMC* settled a debate that had been raging throughout modern scholarship as to whether Manichaeism was best understood as emerging from Christianity or from Zoroastrianism (the latter would help explain its dualism). Because Manichaean writings themselves reflect the "cultural triangulation" of Semitic, Greek, and Iranian influences, and because we have a very poor understanding of how exactly Jews, Christians (in all their local variety), and Zoroastrians interacted in Mesopotamia in the second and third centuries, scholars often settled for classifying the Elchasaite baptists and therefore also Mani as "syncretists" and "Gnostics" (whatever that might mean in this case).[51] Many scholars still fall back on the rather imprecise label "Jewish-Christian" to describe the baptists' particular Christianity, presumably to mark it as heterodox. This despite the fact that, as Guy Stroumsa has observed, Manichaeans "considered themselves to be Christians, nay, *the* true Christians, while they condemned the Catholics for 'judaizing,' and hence for being unfaithful to the true doctrine of Christ."[52] On the basis of the evidence in the *CMC*, Nicholas Baker-Brian has recently argued persuasively that we should cease applying to Manichaeism the labels "syncretism" and "Gnosticism"—and I would add the increasingly troubled, hyphenated label "Jewish-Christian"—and instead think of Mani as "a reforming Christian who sought to reclaim a more ancient and more authentic form of religious belief than the one that he had encountered during the formative years of his life."[53] In other words, we would do better to think of the Mesopotamian baptists as Christians of a particular kind, and Mani as a reforming Christian from within their ranks, whose reforms also impinged on the emerging Christian orthodoxy of the third and especially fourth centuries, and also on the other religious traditions of the region: Judaism, but especially Zoroastrianism, and later Islam and Buddhism. The irony of this is that it means that the Christian polemicists were right: Manichaeism *was* a Christian heresy in the sense that it was a variation within third-century Christianity—a judgment we can make without assuming the truth of the position that regarded this particular variation as a deep perversion.

Our interest in the *CMC*, however, has less to do with these questions and much more to do with questions about Mani's twin or companion, here named the *syzygos*. While there is an entire section (pp. 14–44) of the *CMC* devoted to the revelations of Mani's *syzygos*, in truth the figure appears throughout the narrative, even before we have a proper name for him. In the first section (pp. 1–13), devoted to Mani's childhood, we learn that Mani was "protected [through] the might of [the] angels and the powers of holiness" (3,2). We go on to read that "sometimes like a flash of lightning he [came]"—but who is this *he*? (It cannot refer to Mani, because he is speaking). Whoever he is, the fact that he comes "like a flash of lightning" will prove important, as Mani's predecessors also experienced (as we will see shortly) a "rapture" and "revelation" accompanied by lightning. After a break in the text, we pick up on the next page that this nameless one "was reassuring also about this power which is steadfast in affliction" and that he showed Mani many visions and great sights throughout his youth (4,3–11). Finally, we learn that the "light-angels and exceedingly strong powers" who are guarding over the young

Mani are under the explicit command from "Jesus, the Splendor" (11,8–13). Without going into great detail about Manichaean mythology, suffice to say that this figure, Jesus the Splendor, is a cosmic being, an emissary from the realm of light, who is sent to reveal himself and saving knowledge to Adam, who is trapped in darkness. A specific quality or function of Jesus the Splendor is then hypostasized and named the Light-Nous or Light Mind, whose specific charge is the salvation of other souls. It is Jesus the Splendor, as the Light Mind, who, according to the *Kephalaia*, summons and sends into the world both the Apostle of Light (who sojourns, for example, as the Buddha, Zoroaster, or Jesus of Nazareth) and then the counterpart or companion to inaugurate that apostleship and protect the apostle. It seems, then, that the unnamed "he" in this first section of the *CMC* is under the command of Jesus the Splendor, and so is in all likelihood the counterpart or companion—the one Mani will soon name the *syzygos*. Before he has even been properly introduced in the narrative, such as we have it with its many lacunae, we can appreciate that Mani's twin-companion is active in his early life as a revealer of visions and great sights, and one whose arrival is marked by lightning.

In the last two pages of this first section, Mani provides two other details about his twin-companion. First, in his fourth year Mani tells how "[from] the waters [a face] of a man appeared to me" (12,1–2). The *CMC* does not connect this image of a face in the water with the *syzygos*.[54] But in his historical novel about the life of Mani, entitled *The Gardens of Light*, the French-Lebanese writer Amin Maalouf uses this single detail to frame the first revelation of Mani's companion. The young Mani, twelve in Maalouf's telling, throws himself down at the riverbank in despair. Mani closes his eyes as if in a daze, opens them to speak to himself, but discovers that the image reflecting back at him in the water does not speak as he does. In fact, the image smiles silently at him, and Mani follows suit. Maalouf explains, "It was no longer the water which reflected his appearance, but it was his own face which mimicked the other self which he perceived in the water."[55] Admittedly, Maalouf's restaging assimilates this detail about the face in the water, supposedly from Mani's fourth year, to the better-known "first" revelation in or after his twelfth year. But Maalouf's treatment includes two aspects worth noting. First, Mani's encounter with his image in the water is an inverted Narcissus episode: whereas Ovid's Narcissus had failed to know himself through the contemplation of his own image in the water, it is precisely his own image in the water that brings Mani face-to-face with his double, and so with himself. Second, what seems to differentiate Narcissus from Mani is how each understands the image before him. Narcissus, according to Ovid, finally recognizes the image as an image—his very own—and yet he cannot pull himself away from it and so dies by the edge of the water. Mani, on the other hand (at least in Maalouf's hands), comes to see that the face in the water is *not* an image, but rather the archetype of which *he* is the image (like the *Gospel of Philip* in Chapter 3, in contrast to the *Gospel of Thomas* §84 in Chapter 2). It is precisely by encountering a mirror in which one learns that the image (appearance) one perceives is itself the archetype (reality) that one begins to know oneself at all, that is, to know oneself as two. Such a mirror does more than reflect: it reverses the priority between image and archetype.

On the final pages of this first section devoted to Mani's childhood, we read, "At another time a voice *(phōnē)*, like that of the *syzygos*, spoke to me out of the air, saying: 'Strengthen your power, make your mind firm, and receive all that is about to be revealed to you'" (13,2–8). First, though Mani's twin-companion is largely phanic (that is, he *appears*—from the Greek *phaino*), he is also phonic: he has a voice *(phōnē)* and speaks to Mani as early as his childhood. This, of course, immediately calls to mind Socrates's *daimōn* (see Chapter 1), except that, according to Plato, the *daimonion* was exclusively phonic, not phanic, and the voice that Socrates heard was always apotreptic (op-positional)—issuing a series of guiding Nos—and never protreptic (pro-positional).[56] Second, notice that the narrative refers to the *syzygos* as if he had already been introduced. This leads me to think that he had already been so in the narrative, somewhere in the text's many lacunae. Again, that would help explain the references to the nameless "he" who is said to have come like lightning, revealing many visions and great sights, and under the command of Jesus the Splendor. All this would suggest that the *CMC* regards

Mani's twin-companion as having been active well before the two discrete revelations in his twelfth and twenty-fourth years.

Thus, there is something of a tension within the anthology: on the one hand, the twin-companion's presence in Mani's early life is constant and pervasive; on the other hand, there are traditions of two discrete revelations of Mani's *syzygos*, collected in the second section (pp. 14–44) of the *CMC*. From the authority of Baraies the Teacher, we read:

> ... and from all laws, and (that) he might free the souls from ignorance by becoming paraclete and leader of the apostleship in this generation. Then, at the time when my body reached its full growth, immediately there flew down and appeared before me that most beautiful and greatest mirror-image of [myself] *(katoptron tou prosōpou mou)*. (17,1–16)

And again on the following page,

> [When] I was twenty[-five] years old [...] the most blessed Lord was greatly moved with compassion for me, called me into his grace, and immediately sent to me [from there my] *syzygos*, [appearing in] great [glory] ... (18,1,10–16)[57]

These would seem to correspond to the two discrete revelations attested by Ibn al-Nadīm: one at age twelve (17,8–10: "at the time when my body reached its full growth") and another at age of twenty-four (18,1) or twenty-five (73,5–6). The first revelation is of "*that* most beautiful and greatest mirror-image of [myself]" (18,13–16). Again, the fact that this revelation is introduced with the demonstrative pronoun "that" *(ekeino)* suggests the figure has already been introduced.[58] Perhaps *that* "mirror image" was introduced in a section now lost or illegible. Or perhaps *that* "mirror image" is meant to refer back to the face of the man in the water (12,1–2), a figure whom I am inclined to identify as the twin-companion.

Some may wonder, given the prominence of the apostle Paul in the *CMC*, whether the notion of a mirror image *(katoptron)* of a face *(prosōpon)* is an allusion to Paul's famous line in 1 Cor 13:12: "For now we see in a mirror *(di'esoptrou)* dimly *(en ainigmati)*, but then face to face *(prosōpon pros prosōpon)*." There are at least two problems here. First of all, there is the fact that Mani and Paul use slightly different terms for mirrors: *katoptron* versus *esoptron*. Second and more importantly, the point that Paul is making seems at odds with the story about Mani. Paul is contrasting our knowledge now *(arti)* with our knowledge then *(pote)*. The appeal to a mirror is meant to suggest our partial knowledge now: we do not see reality directly or "face to face" but only indirectly, as we see someone who is out of our direct line of sight (say, around a corner) by using a mirror. In the case of Paul, the appeal to the mirror is not so that we can see ourselves face-to-face, but that we can see a reflection of someone else, until such time as we round the corner and see him or her face-to-face. In other words, the mirror is an accommodation to our present position. But Mani suggests that the revelation of his twin-companion is precisely an encounter face-to-face, an encounter in which the *syzygos* himself *is* the mirror, reflecting Mani's image back to him. This autoscopy is not some second-order accommodated knowledge, but true self-knowledge.

The more relevant comparison for Mani's *katoptron* would seem to be with Plato. In Chapter 1 we considered Plato's appeals to the mirror in *Phaedrus* and *Alcibiades I*. In *Phaedrus*, the beloved comes to see himself reflected in the lover as if in a mirror *(hōsper de en katoptrōi)* (255d). In that case, the horizontal mirroring of lover and beloved serves to restore the vertical mirroring of their two souls and intelligible reality, the Forms. In *Alcibiades I*, Socrates appeals to the analogy of two lovers staring into each other's eyes: "when a man looks into an eye his face appears in it, like in a mirror *(hōsper en katoptrō)*" (132e). But the analogy of the eye is meant to apply to the soul: a lover looks into a beloved's soul and finds therein a mirror image of himself, or rather an image of a "more divine" *(theioteron)* version of himself (133c). In both cases, *Phaedrus* and *Alcibiades I*, to see your mirror image is to be, on the one hand, rendered two: image and archetype, except that the mirror image is in fact the archetype of which you are the image. But on the other hand, to be rendered two in autoscopy (self as both viewer and viewed) makes possible the progressive return of the one to the other, as the image conforms ever more closely to its archetype. This would seem the more relevant context than Paul for Mani's encounter with "that most beautiful and greatest mirror-image of [myself]." He and his *syzygos* play the part of Plato's lover and beloved (and vice versa): he beholds his own image and is thereby rendered two, but he is also set on a path of progressive conformity with that "most beautiful and greatest" version of himself.

Perhaps, though, we should not discount altogether Paul's relevance for Mani's *katoptron*. Recall that in the *Kephalaia* Mani refers to "my image" *(tah-ikōn)*. As in so many other cases, Coptic here borrows a Greek word for image, *eikōn*. Hans Dieter Betz suggests that Mani's companion appearing to him as his *katoptron* or "mirror image" in the *CMC* is somehow connected with Paul's concept of the icon.[59] Several of Paul's many appeals to *eikōn* could inform our understanding of Mani's companion as his mirror image.[60] Rom 8:29 speaks of God's foreknowledge and predestination of some to be conformed to the image of his Son: perhaps Mani understood Paul as referring to himself and his fellow Apostles of Light. 1 Cor 15:49 contrasts our having once "borne the image of the man of dust" with the future in which we will bear "the image of the man of heaven": Mani's *syzygos* is certainly a heavenly mirror image. The most compelling comparison to be made, however, is 1 Cor 3:18: "And we all, with unveiled face *(prosōpōi)*, reflecting *(katoprizomenoi)* the glory of the Lord, are being changed into his image *(eikona)* from one degree of glory to another, for this comes from the Lord who is the Spirit." Here in one verse we have mention of "image" *(eikōn)*, à la the *Kephalaia*, and also of "reflecting" or "mirroring" *(katoprizō,* a verb formed from *katoptron)* an "unveiled face" *(prosōpon)*, à la the *CMC*. Mani or his followers could well have understood him and his *syzygos* as being reflections of each other's face, mirror images or icons of one another, and of their divine origin in the realm of light. Finally, whereas Paul says unequivocally "we *all* . . . ," it is unclear how universal an anthropology of the divine double we find in Manichaeism. Do only Mani and his forerunners reflect the glory of the Lord, and so change into his image? Or is there a manner, according to Mani himself or his followers, in which this is available to everyone?

So much for Mani's first revelation in the form of his mirror image, at the age of twelve. The second revelation comes in his twenty-fourth (18,1) or twenty-fifth year (73,5–6), and the visitor is explicitly named a *syzygos*. I have refrained from translating *syzygos* as "twin" largely because this seems to confuse matters. As de Blois points out, the Manichaean tradition remembers this visitor under two distinct but related clusters of titles: those having to do with twinning and those having to do with companionship or partnership.[61] *Syzygos* falls squarely into the latter category. De Blois argues that the Western sources largely remember Mani's double as a companion, and the Eastern sources as a twin (and that al-Nadīm preserves both). In light of this, it seems more prudent to translate *syzygos* as "companion" than as "twin."

Syzygos appears only once in the New Testament, in Phil 4:2–3, where Paul writes: "I entreat Eudoia and I entreat Syntyche to agree in the Lord. And I ask you also, true yokefellow *(syzyge)*, help these women, for they have labored side by side with me in the gospel together with Clement and the rest of my fellow workers *(synergōn)*, whose names are in the book of life." This is somewhat baffling: the letter is addressed to "all the saints in Christ Jesus who are at Philippi, with the bishops and deacons," which is condensed to "my brethren" throughout the letter. Who then is this addressee in the second person singular—"you"—who moreover is described as a *syzygos* (rather than the more common Pauline title *synergos*)? Scholars, ancient and modern, are at a bit of a loss: might it refer to Paul's wife (as Clement and Origen opined)? Could *syzygos* be a proper name, someone in the community of Philippi? No one really knows.[62] In any case, it is possible that the *CMC* took the name for Mani's companion from Paul's cryptic address to a "true *syzygos*."[63]

The *syzygos* is given other titles, including "my ever-vigilant *syzygos*" (22,16–17), "that all-glorious and all-blessed one" (26,9–10), "a good counselor of all counsels" (32,14–16), "ally and protector" (33,4), and "my most unfailing *syzygos*" (69,14–15), among others. But more important than any title is what the *syzygos* does for Mani and, moreover, teaches him. His most important intervention, of course, is his having separated Mani from the baptists: "drawing [me to the divine] side" (20,1–17). Having brought him face-to-face, and arm in arm, with his mirror image, the *syzygos* teaches him, in Mani's words,

> who I am, what my body is, in what way I have come, how my arrival into this world took place, who I am of the ones most renowned for their eminence, how I was begotten into this fleshly body, by what woman I was delivered and born according to the flesh, and by whose [passion] I was engendered. (21,2–16)

This instruction in Mani's cosmic whence and whither centers on his sojourn in the body—recall that the title of the *CMC* is "On the Origin of His Body" *(peri tēs gennēs tou sōmatos autou)*. But the more precise constitution of this "I" is also a central piece of the curriculum: "concerning me, who I am, and who my inseparable *suzugos* is; moreover, concerning my soul, which exists as the soul of all the worlds, both what it itself is and how it came to be" (23,4–11). This lesson in Mani's theological anthropology is hardly systematic, but a good deal can be gleaned from the following:

> I acquired [the *syzygos*] as my own possession. I believed that he belongs to me and is (mine) and is a good and excellent counselor. I recognized *(epegnōn)* him and understood that I am that one from whom I was separated. I testified that I myself am that one who is unshakeable. (24,3–15)

On the one hand, Mani's relationship to his *syzygos* is one of possession: the *syzygos* belongs to him. The *syzygos*'s relationship to Mani, on the other hand, is one of counseling. The relationship is not entirely symmetric, despite the *syzygos* being Mani's mirror image. Furthermore, the *syzygos* is someone whom Mani must recognize, and recognition *(epignōsis)* consists in Mani's understanding that he, Mani, is identical with that one, his *syzygos*, from whom he was separated. The *CMC* does not narrate this cosmic separation, but if we appeal to the *Kephalaia*, we might think that the separation referred to here is the Light Mind's differentiation of itself into, first, the Apostle of Light, who will be incarnated as Mani, and second the "counterpart" or "companion" who appears at the appointed hour to inaugurate that apostleship. The identity is made clear in the closing testimony: "I myself am that one" *(egō ekeinos autos eimi)*.

We have from Mani (whether it be the historical Mani or the hagiographical character) no clearer an "I" statement than this.[64] It is important to realize that this lesson in Mani's theological anthropology comes as part of a confession of faith: Mani says, "I believed ... I recognized ... I testified." Mani's selfhood is a matter of some doctrinal urgency, as evidenced by his negative reaction to the request made by his disciple to duplicate in that telling tale from the *Kephalaia*. The disciple's innocent request is remembered in order to underscore the nature of Mani's "I." Henrichs judges the constitution of Mani's "I" as "far from ... original, [but rather] well known as the classical Gnostic expression of *Selbstfindung*"— *Selbstfindung* or "self-discovery."[65] While we might, in the wake of recent scholarship, be somewhat more circumspect about the category of "Gnosticism" (and whether Manichaeism is to be included in it), nevertheless Henrichs's formulation is apt.[66] The revelation of Mani's *syzygos* is a moment of *Selbstfindung* (self-discovery); but precisely the moment of *Selbstfindung* is simultaneously a moment of *Selbst-spaltung* (self-division) and of *Selbst-einigung* (self-unification). In other words, it is precisely the coincidence of division and unification that constitutes Mani's distinctive selfhood.

I take this coincidence of division and unification to be the backdrop to Mani's further first-person declarations in the *CMC*: "I am solitary *(monērēs d'egō)* ... I, alone against all *(monos ōn para pantas)*" (31,1–9). In its immediate context, these "I" statements contrast Mani with "the multitude," the errant crowd of baptists and "the ordinances of that teaching in which I was reared" (44,4–6). Mani "became like a stranger *(othneiōi)* and a solitary *(monērei)* in their midst" (44,6–8), but his estrangement and solitary selfhood are made possible only by his union with his double, his *syzygos*. Much later in the *CMC* Mani worries, "I am alone *(egō de monogenēs)*" (104,8–9), in contrast to the many "kings and dynasts of the world and the founders of the sects" (103,21–104,3). But then "the splendid one" reassures him, making clear that because he (Mani) has his (the *syzygos*'s) help, he "alone" (that is, with his companion) will triumph over these many powers. The contrast between Mani and the multitude, then, is not between the one and the many, but between the "solitary"—understood as Mani's being one and yet two—and the many. In other words, the only way to contend against the many is not to be merely one, but to be one *and* two, to be the Mani whose singularity includes himself and his double. The three Greek terms that Mani uses to describe his singular or solitary selfhood here (*monos, monēros, monogenēs*) probably translate three of Mani's own terms from Syriac (*ḥad, mshāwhad, īḥīdāyā*).[67] In the *Kephalaia* all three terms are rendered in Coptic with *ouōt*, and with an indefinite article as *oua ouōt*.

When Mani responds to his disciple's request that he duplicate, he says over and over, *anak ou-manichaios en-ouōt:* "I, a single Mani" or "I, one Mani alone." As we noted at the beginning of this chapter, embedded in this first-person declaration is the phrase *oua ouōt*—"one and the same" or "a single one." And the same phrase appears in Mani's declaration that with his companion, the Paraclete, he has "become a single body *(ou-sōma n-ouōt)* with a single spirit *(ou-pneuma n-ouōt).*" The phrase should be familiar to us: *oua ouōt* or "one and the same" is a phrase that appears often (along with *monachos* or "single one") in the *Gospel of Thomas*. In Chapter 2 I argued that the *Gospel of Thomas* forwards a particular understanding of selfhood, according to which one first discovers that one is in fact two because Jesus the light dwells within oneself, whereupon the ascetic enterprise is living into the reality of this unity-in-duality—and that the Gospel's consistent name for this new selfhood is both *monachos*, "solitary," and *oua ouōt*, "a single one." This is not a unity that annihilates duality, but rather one that depends on and preserves it.

Scholars have long debated whether Mani or his followers were familiar with the *Gospel of Thomas*. Cyril of Jerusalem (ca. 313–386) insisted that the *Gospel of Thomas* was authored by "one of the three wicked disciples of Mani."[68] Because the *Gospel of Thomas* almost certainly predates Mani, the more relevant question is whether Mani or his followers made use of the gospel. Henrichs is skeptical, deeming it "rash to assume that the *Gospel of Thomas* was known to Mani."[69] More recently W.-P. Funk has asked the question anew, and argued that three *logia* from the *Gospel of Thomas* influenced Manichaeism:

of the three (§§5, 23, and 44), §23 seems the most relevant for our purposes.[70] It reads, "Jesus said, 'I shall choose you, one *(oua)* out of a thousand, and two *(snay)* out of ten thousand, and they shall stand as a single one *(oua ouōt)*.'" The *Kephalaia* has two passages that echo this saying: *Kephalaion* 76, "I choose a few from among the many" (187,32–188,1); *Kephalaion* 119, "two in ten thousand after the likeness of the Primal Man" (285,25). Funk judges the first instance of selecting a few from many to be too generic to serve as evidence of influence; but the second seems to him legitimate proof that the Manichaeans borrowed this phrase from the *Gospel of Thomas*.[71] Regardless of one's assessment of his conclusions, it is surprising that Funk's argument does not focus on the second half of §23, "and they shall stand as a single one *(oua ouōt)*." As we have seen, this phrase is crucial for Mani's own "I" statements. Curiously, before and immediately after Mani says, "I choose a few from among the many" (187,32–188,1), he issues two such first-person statements, "I, a single Mani" *(anak ou-manichaios en-ouōt* [187,27; 188,2], also "this single Mani," *enp-manichaios en-ouōt* [188,13]). Given the preponderance of the phrase *oua ouōt* in the *Kephalaia*, three instances of its close proximity to a possible echo of the *Gospel of Thomas*, and the centrality of the phrase to the gospel's understanding of selfhood, I would think that the investigation of the possible influence of the gospel on Manichaeism should focus precisely on this.

Although I recognize that the evidence suggests that influence was "a possibility, but only that," I suspect that Funk is correct that the *Gospel of Thomas* did influence Manichaeism, perhaps even Mani himself.[72] If my suspicion is correct, then Mani's "I" statements from the *Kephalaia* and the *CMC*—confessions of his being "one," "alone," or "singular" (Coptic: *oua ouōt*, Greek: *monos, monēros, monogenēs;* Syriac: *ḥad, mshāwḥad, īḥīdāyā*) should be understood as appropriating and developing the *Gospel of Thomas*'s peculiar understanding of selfhood as *monachos* and *oua ouōt*. According to this logic, Mani, an Apostle of Light at first ignorant of his apostolate, is visited by own image, his own counterpart and companion the Paraclete, and discovers that he is not merely one, but has a double. This recognition inaugurates his becoming a new self: in his own words a single body and spirit, but words we should read in light of the *Gospel of Thomas*'s meditation on the one and the two. If this is right, then Mani and his followers would regard him as the exemplary "solitary" or "single one," as described in the *Gospel of Thomas*, precisely because he is doubled. But in the end I am less interested in arguments about influence and genealogy. In other words, if my suspicion that the Manichaeans were influenced by the *Gospel of Thomas* were to be proven wrong, it is still abundantly clear from the Manichaean sources themselves that Mani and his faithful flock conceived of him as being "singular" (and so, "the one complete Mani") only because he was already doubled.

A Manichaean Anthropology?

Up to this point we have been focused on the constitution of Mani's own self, the fact of *his* being doubled and simultaneously "singular." But to what degree is Mani's selfhood understood as exceptional, and to what degree is it meant to be revelatory of selfhood more generally? In other words, is Mani the model for a universal Manichaean anthropology? Can other Manichaeans hope for a visitation from their divine double or twin-companion, their heavenly counterpart who will awaken them to the knowledge of their whence and whither? In a fascinating article that plots the connections between Mani's and Plotinus's respective accounts of the self, Leo Sweeney answers in the negative.[73] Despite the fact that both Mani and Plotinus conceive of the self as, in Plotinus's words, "a couple" *(to synampho)* composed of the "higher" and "lower man," Sweeney argues that the most significant difference between their anthropologies is precisely the fact that for Plotinus this model holds for all persons whereas for Mani it holds only for him: "In the Manichaean world-view . . . only Mani as the new and final prophet has a Twin, whereas every Plotinian human soul has an intellect, which remains There."[74] If Sweeney is correct, then only Mani has a divine double, and everyday Manichaeans—"hearers" and even the "elect"—have no share in that doubled selfhood.

We would do well to test Sweeney's confident, negative conclusion against the evidence of the sources, beginning with the *CMC*. In the third part of that text we have something of an editorial digression in which Mani's own revelations are set against the backdrop of his predecessors, including five prophets and the apostle Paul. This genealogy is provided to dispel any doubt that Mani's "apostleship of the Spirit, the Paraclete," is mere "boasting" (46,1–7). The first five forerunners to Mani are Adam, Sethel, Enosh, Shem, and Enoch, and the sixth is Paul. What follows is an explanation of how each of these "forefathers" was privileged with his own "revelation" *(apokalypsis)* and "rapture" *(harpagē)*, and how each spoke and wrote about that experience.[75] Some of Mani's forerunners were visited by angels: Adam, for instance, was visited by an angel who calls himself Balsamos (49,3–4); Sethel by an unnamed angel (50.12); Enoch by no fewer than seven angels (58.20). Enosh, for his rapture, was "snatched up" by the "Spirit" (53,15), and his successor Shem by the "Living Spirit" (55,16–17). Paul's revelation, of course, came from "Jesus Christ" (62,20; cf. Gal 1:11–12), and subsequently he was "snatched up into Paradise" (61.8; 2 Cor 12:1–5).

None of the forefathers' revelations or raptures, however, is described as a visitation from a *syzygos*. Perhaps this is evidence for Sweeney's claim that the revelation of a divine double is reserved for Mani alone. But perhaps not: Mani, after all, describes his *syzygos* as an angel, that is to say, a messenger. Recall that the appearance of Mani's visitor was accompanied by lightning: "For sometimes like a flash of lightning he [came] . . ." (3.2). Similarly the face of the angel who came to Sethel was "nothing other than flashes of lightning" (50,16); so too with Shem: "the image of the form of his face was lovely and fresh, more so than the gleaming splendor [of the sun] still more than [lightning]" (56,20). Finally, and perhaps most importantly, the accounts of Enosh and Shem both describe their visitors as "Spirit" and Shem adds the adjective "Living." These titles can clearly be squared with the notion that the prophets' visitor is the Paraclete, the Holy Spirit. By drawing on the accounts of previous revelations, the *CMC* gives the impression that Mani is not the first to have been visited by a heavenly counterpart; all of his predecessors have been visited by their *syzygoi* as well. For it is precisely the visitation by one's heavenly counterpart that reveals one's whence and whither and inaugurates one's saving mission. This interpretation finds confirmation in the teaching of the *Kephalaia*. The Light Mind differentiates itself into, on the one hand, the Apostle of Light, who sojourns in a body ("assumes the church of the flesh"), and, on the other hand, the counterpart or companion, who appears to the embodied apostle to inaugurate his mission. If we use the *Kephalaia* to interpret the *CMC*, then Adam, Sethel, Enosh, Shem, Enoch, and Paul are various incarnations of the Apostle of Light. And as such, they must each be visited by a counterpart-companion, one of whose Greek names is *syzygos*.

At the very least, then, Sweeney must revise his negative conclusion. Mani is not the *only* figure whose self is, like Plotinus's, a "couple," a pair of "twins." Certainly Mani's followers (and probably Mani too) understood this to be the case for his prophetic predecessors, his "forefathers," as well. Van Oort argues that all the prophets were visited by one and the same twin—variously called Jesus Christ, Jesus the Splendor, the Paraclete, the Living Spirit, the Light-Nous—because all these prophets are essentially one and the same individual, sent in each generation to teach others.[76] But if Mani's anthropology holds for himself and his predecessors, what of his disciples: Did they hold out hope for visitations from *their* heavenly counterparts? In other words, can we generalize from the experience of the Apostle of Light and articulate a universal Manichaean anthropology?

To answer this question we must return to the *Kephalaia*. Recall that the Light Mind produces a third version of itself, namely the Light Form:

> The third is the Light Form; the one whom the elect and the catechumens shall receive, should they renounce the world. And also the fifth father is this Light Form; the one who shall appear to everyone who will g[o] out from his body, corresponding to the pattern of the image *(ikōn)* to the apostle; and the thr[ee] great glorious angels who are come with her. (36,9–15)

It is this Light Form on which we need now to focus in order to understand whether there is a universal Manichaean anthropology of the divine double. Here we learn that the Light Form will appear to both tiers of the Manichaean community—catechumens or "hearers" and the elect. This Light Form "corresponds to the pattern of the image *(ikōn)* to the apostle." We have already seen how Mani's companion or counterpart is understood as his image: "my image *(ikōn)*" *(Kephalaia* 14,28); "that most beautiful and greatest mirror-image of [myself] *(katoptron tou prosōpou mou)*" *(CMC* 17,1–16). Here we learn that the relationship of the apostle to his companion is repeated at the level of the Manichaean faithful: the Light Form appears to the faithful just as his image appears to the apostle.

But when exactly does it appear, and how? The preceding passage suggests that the descent of the Light Form happens at death: "should they renounce the world . . . to everyone who will go out from his body." In other words, the faithful can expect to meet their divine double only at their release from this body and this world. The Light Form understood in this way seems very close to the notion of the *dēn* or *daēnā* in Zoroastrianism: "the sum of man's spiritual attributes and individuality . . . [his] inner self," which inner self is personified as a woman—a beautiful woman or heinous hag depending on the human's conduct.[77] Upon death, a soul meets its divine double, the *daēnā*, who ushers it into heaven or hell. If this is the whole of the story, then there is a universal Manichaean anthropology of the divine double, but it is available to the faithful only upon death and significantly conforms to a mythological figure from Zoroastrian sources.

The Light Form or *morphē*, however, may have another dimension.[78] Elsewhere in the *Kephalaia*, Mani speaks of how the Apostle of Light, before he is incarnate (say, as Mani, Jesus, Zoroaster, or Buddha) selects the souls who will constitute his faithful, his church. He selects these souls by "freeing" their "forms":

> Now this is how it is for you to understand (about) the souls of the [ele]ct and the catechumens that shall receive the hop[e of] God and enter the land of the living, so that their forms could be chosen in the heights: Before he is born in this human flesh and befo[re the A]postle is manifested in the flesh, still abid[ing . . .] he shall choose the forms of his entire church and make th[em] free, whether of the elect or of the catechume[ns]. Now when he chooses the forms of the elect and [the] catechumens, and

> makes them free from abov[e], afterwards he shall come down immediately and choose them. (90, 224.28–225.5)[79]

This happens with each successive Apostle of Light and his church: "When the Apostle will be raised up to the heights, he and his church, and they depart from the world, at that instant another Apostle shall be sent to it, to another chu[rch . . .]. Yet, first, he shall make the forms of his church free in the heights, as I have told you" (1,12.1–6). Only those souls whose forms are freed can then be chosen for membership in the earthly church that the apostle establishes. The question is whether the *morphē* that the apostle frees in order to select that soul as a Manichaean is the same as the *morphē* of the Light Form, who meets the Manichaean at death. If these two forms *are* the same, then it would appear that the divine double frames a Manichaean life: in its pre-incarnate state an individual soul's *morphē* is freed so that that soul can become a Manichaean catechumen or elect on earth, and in its post-incarnate state that soul is reunited with its *morphē*. A soul's earthly sojourn, then, is a period of separation from its double understood as its proper *morphē* or form.

The evidence suggests, therefore, that Manichaeism offers up a two-tiered anthropology of the divine double (which does not, however, correspond to its well-known two-tiered community structure of hearers and elect). The top tier is the selfhood of the Apostle of Light, who periodically becomes incarnate—as, say, Mani, Jesus, Zoroaster, or Buddha (or according to the *CMC*, as Adam, Sethel, Enosh, Shem, Enoch, or Paul). The apostle is paired with a companion or counterpart, who goes under various names (such as *syzygos*) depending on the text and tradition in question. The two of them—the apostle and his *syzygos*—form a singular self, a *oua ouōt*, that depends on and preserves its fundamental duality. The second tier is the selfhood of the faithful, whose souls each have forms, forms that the apostle frees in order to become incarnate on earth and form the Manichaean church (hearers and elect). These souls live their lives sadly shorn of their divine doubles, with whom they are reunited at death, very much like the Zoroastrian concept of the *daēnā*. In this two-tiered anthropology, the single most significant difference is whether one can expect to have one's double as a part of one's life, or whether one must wait for death to enjoy such a reunion.

Conclusion

With Mani we follow the trail of the divine double outside the boundaries of early Christianity, or at least what we are accustomed to regard as those boundaries: Mani, after all, thought of himself as a reforming Christian. Be that as it may, we can see the Manichaean inheritance and innovation of earlier themes and threads in the tradition of the divine double. The most obvious is the theme with which this chapter began, that at least one Manichaean source (the *Kephalaia*) articulates Mani's doubled selfhood by appealing to the same language as the *Gospel of Thomas:* he is a *oua ouōt* or "single one," a unity (one) that contains and preserves distinction (two). Of course, the cosmology and mythology in which that confession of Mani's doubled selfhood is embedded is very distinctive: the notion of the Apostle of Light, serially embodied so as to save his elect, whose apostolic mission is inaugurated by his twin-companion. These two terms for the divine double—twin (such as the Arabic *at-tawm*) and companion (such as the Greek *syzygos*)—reach back to the sources we have explored in Chapters 2 and 3: the *Gospel of Thomas*, Tatian's *Oratio*, the *Gospel of Philip* and the *Excerpta ex Theodoto*, the *Book of Thomas*, the *Acts of Thomas*, and the "Hymn of the Pearl." The appeal to image and mirror reach back even farther, to Plato (*Phaedrus* and *Alcibiades I*, see Chapter 1) and to the apostle Paul (especially 2 Cor 3:18). The mention of a face in the water (*CMC* 12,1–2) might even be an appropriation of Ovid's myth of Narcissus, with whose failed autoscopy we began this book. We have seen how several of the Christian witnesses to the divine double draw on the Gospel of John: the *Gospel of Thomas* on the figure of "Thomas, who was called Twin" (John 11:16, 20:24, 21:2); Origen of Alexandria on Jesus's designating John as Mary's own son and so, for Origen, another Jesus (John 19:26–27); Tatian on the birth of the *logos* in the individual, in imitation of the eternal birth of the *Logos* from God the Father (John 1:1). To that list we now add the Manichaean appropriation of the figure of the Paraclete (1 John 2:1, Gospel of John 14:16–17, 26; 15:26), a name now given to the twin-companion and, once it is conjoined with the Apostle of Light, also to that conjunction. Finally, we have seen how the Manichaean tradition, situated in an Iranian context, appropriates the Zoroastrian notion of the *dēn* or *daēnā* to explain the divine double on offer to the everyday faithful, hearers and elect alike. Just as Manichaean theology and mythology are omnivorous and accumulative, but also innovative, so is its tradition of the divine double.

5

Plotinus and the Doubled Intellect

IN THE YEAR 243 the young emperor Gordian III, barely eighteen years old, marched against the Sassanians and their king, Shapur I. The campaign ended badly for Gordian, who was killed (perhaps by his own troops), and his successor, Philip the Arab, was forced to sue for an unfavorable peace. Somewhere in the Roman force was a thirty-nine-year-old philosopher from Alexandria by the name of Plotinus (ca. 204/205–270). At this same time Mani, the Apostle of Light (together with his twin-companion), was in the royal entourage of King Shapur. It is tempting to imagine these two, the philosopher and the apostle, meeting amid the cacophony of that campaign, facing off as rivals, or perhaps as a pair, as counterparts. Certainly it was what Plotinus was hoping for: his student Porphyry tells us that he was "eager to make acquaintance with the Persian philosophical discipline and that prevailing among the Indians."[1] Alas, such a meeting was not to be, and Plotinus was lucky to escape with his life to nearby Antioch. He then quit the Roman East, and at the age of forty made a new home for himself in Rome.

He spent the following nineteen years in the capital, forming around himself a "school" of philosophy—more of an extended circle of students and supporters than a proper school with a set curriculum. He died in 270 of a painful and hideous illness; in his last moments he was visited by his longtime friend and physician

Eustochius, to whom he is reported to have said, "I have been waiting a long time for you. Try to bring back the god in us to the divine in the All."[2] After his death, Porphyry, whom Plotinus had sent away to Sicily to recover from his suicidal depression, took up the task of editing and arranging Plotinus's writings—a task to which he was entrusted, so he says, by Plotinus himself. Porphyry arranged the fifty-four treatises of wildly uneven length into a neat scheme of six sets of nine—hence the title *Enneads* or "nines." Porphyry's division into six "nines" was according to theme, and in doing so he mixed up the chronology of the treatises—which chronology, however, Porphyry dutifully (if not indubitably) records in his *Life of Plotinus*. All that we know of Plotinus comes from this hagiographical vita; but as is the case with all late antique biographies of holy men and women, we should not take it as an entirely reliable historical source (even if it is our only one). Like any student or disciple, Porphyry may have various aims in representing his teacher to a wider literate audience, some of which aims may be at odds with historical veracity.

A. H. Armstrong, whose English translation of the *Enneads* is still standard, says of Plotinus's writings that they are "an unsystematic presentation of a systematic philosophy."[3] I myself am somewhat uncertain about the latter claim, but the former is beyond question: the *Enneads* are something of a jumbled mess—some of that owing to Porphyry's strong editorial hand (which in certain cases interrupts the flow of Plotinus's argument) and some to Plotinus's own opaque prose and seeming equivocation on central points of his teaching. In this chapter I have the challenge of trying to isolate one piece of this allegedly systematic philosophy, namely Plotinus's understanding of the self as doubled.[4] Isolating Plotinus's understanding of selfhood, however, cannot be done with surgical precision. The doubled self is not strictly an issue of anthropology, but reaches up, so to speak, the great chain of being all the way to the three hypostases: the One, Intellect, and Soul. In other words, anthropology is tied up with metaphysics, specifically with protology and soteriology—Intellect's emergence from the ineffable One and the possibility of our return thereto.

PLOTINUS AND THE DOUBLED INTELLECT 187

It is entirely commonplace to say that Plotinus regarded the self as doubled, as constituted by some identity of an undescended intellect, feasting on the intelligible Forms, and a descended intellect, a soul occluded by its sojourn in a body. The identity of the two intellects (which are really *one* intellect)—what Plotinus calls their "coupling" *(synampho)*—is a "dynamic monism," or, if you will, a sort of anthropological "dynamonism." This feature of Plotinian anthropology will occupy us in the middle of this chapter, as will two other related issues: (1) how Plotinus understood Plato's discussion of the *daimōn* and adapted it to fit his own philosophy; and (2) whether Plotinus believed there is an intelligible Form that corresponds to each individual intellect. Plotinus's overriding concern is to see us isolate our intellect from the broader powers of our soul, burdened with the care of a body, and thus to ascend up (or rather in) to Intellect and possibly even the One.

In what follows, I will traverse Plotinus's "system" from top to bottom and back again, beginning with the primordial procession of Intellect from the One and the inner life of universal Intellect; and then to the nature of the doubled self, the unity of the undescended and descended intellect (along with the *daimōn* and the possibility of Forms of individuals). I will then turn explicitly to the possibility of our return by focusing first on a reading of the figure of Narcissus in "On Beauty" (1.6), an ambivalent figure for Plotinus precisely because our return requires a perfectly staged "Narcissan" autoscopy or "self-seeing." Finally I will explore the precise choreography of our return to the One, or "mystical self-reversion," in which we must encounter and unite with three successive divine doubles: first, our undescended intellect; second, the intelligible object to which we are each "yoked" in the inner life of Intellect; and third, the primordial otherness that first emerged from the One and was instantiated as Intellect. The encounter and union with these three divine doubles will leave us on the very cusp of an annihilating union with our ineffable source. I will conclude by exploring how love reforms whatever is wayward in that primordial otherness, and so allows us to fold back into the embrace of the One.

The One and the Intellect

PRIMORDIAL PROCESSION

Plotinus's metaphysics is famous for, among other things, a graded triad of hypostases or principles: the One, Intellect, and Soul. A question that occupies Plotinus throughout the *Enneads* is how anything should have emerged from the One in its splendid, transcendent isolation. Understanding how something other than the One comes into being is crucial for Plotinus for two reasons. First, the inaugural or "primordial" procession of Intellect from the One is the model for all that comes after. All subsequent processions, from Soul down to the furthest extremity of matter, are recapitulations of this same procession, albeit weakened with each reiteration. So understanding procession is key to understanding the emergence of everything. Second, the procession of Intellect from the One is urgent for Plotinus because the return of our intellect to the One follows this same itinerary in reverse.

All too often Plotinian procession is reduced to "emanation," understood as an inscrutable, automatic generation.[5] Plotinus himself contributes to this view when he speaks of the procession of Intellect from the One as "radiation" *(perilampsis)*, as the sun gives off light or a fire heat (5.1.6.28). Or when he speaks of superabundant overflow: "The One, perfect because it seeks nothing, has nothing, and needs nothing, overflows *(hypererruē)*, as it were, and its superabundance *(to hyperplēres)* makes something other than itself *(autou . . . allo)*" (5.2.1.8–9). Radiation and overflow are important in procession, but they are only one step in an elaborate choreography. But often Plotinus gives a more precise parsing of procession. The very first stage is what might be called the activity *of* the One: its own isolated and disinterested transcendence or "self-creative freedom." The second stage, the activity *from* the One, is, in the words of two modern scholars, "an exceedingly great *energeia*" or an "indeterminate vitality."[6] Sometimes Plotinus speaks of radiation and overflow to describe this second stage, which is a movement outward from the One. More often, however, he parses it with even greater precision: something emerges from within the One that is somehow other than the One, but not yet defined as anything else, and it stretches forth. This leads to the third stage, in which this primordial, indeterminate "otherness" turns back to the One from which it is emerging and attempts to contemplate its source; it is unable to do so fully, and so becomes instantiated and defined as Intellect, a first declension of the One.[7]

Let us focus more closely on what first emerges from the One. It is at this stage that Plotinus will speak of "overflow," and what flows out is simply "something other than itself" *(autou allo)*. Plotinus speaks of this primordial otherness sometimes in an Aristotelian idiom as "intelligible matter" and sometimes in a Platonic and Neo-Pythagorean idiom as the "indefinite dyad." I wish to focus on the latter for two reasons. First, "intelligible matter" is a notoriously difficult topic in Plotinian metaphysics and raises more generally the specter of matter and its relationship to evil.[8] Second, given our interest in the divine double, the figure of the dyad (and its relationship to the One) is especially important. At the outset, however, we need to acknowledge the impossibility of speaking in exact terms about this primordial otherness. For Plotinus, language is equipped only to speak of things that are—that is, the sensible world and the intelligible world of which it partakes. But the One and the primordial procession of an otherness therefrom is entirely antecedent to the intelligible world, the realm of beauty, being, and the Forms. This goes some distance in explaining why Plotinus takes so many passes at describing this primordial procession, and avails himself of so many different models and figures.

In *Ennead* 6.8, "On Free Will and the Will of the One," he speaks of "something like Intellect in the One which is not Intellect; for it is one" (6.8.18.21–22). We are dealing here with some sort of proto-Intellect, embedded in but emerging from the One, from which it is not yet distinguished, for it is *still* in some sense one. Plotinus speaks of this emergence as an "intellectual power" *(noēra dynamis)* revolving around the One as radii do the center of a circle. Insofar as it is an indeterminate power, it is not yet the image of the One it will be when it becomes defined as Intellect. We are still antecedent to the establishment of the image (Intellect) and archetype (One) relationship. We find something similar in 6.9, "On the Good or the One," where Plotinus says that "there must be something before Intellect which wants to be one, but is not one, but in unitary form" *(henoeidous)* (6.9.5.25–26). Here too this unnamed something, prior to Intellect, haunts the borderlands between the One and what will eventually be Intellect. It is no longer the One but wants *(boulomenou)* to be the One. This wanting or willing may be the key to understanding its emergence from the One, because the One does not need, never mind want, for anything. And perhaps it is also, then, the key to understanding how we return to the One. We shall see that Plotinus faults Narcissus for wanting to seize *(labein bouletheis)* the image on the water. And it is the proto-Intellect's "wanting," I suspect, that explains what Plotinus means when he says that "it did somehow dare *(tolmēsas)* to stand away *(apostēnai)* from the One." Keep this in mind, for I suspect that the return to the One will require our somehow overcoming this audacity *(tolma)* to revolt *(apostasis)*.

The name Plotinus often attaches to this primordial otherness is the "indefinite dyad," a concept he borrows from Plato and the Neo-Pythagorean revival of number theory in the first several centuries CE. For Plotinus, neither the One *(to hen)* nor the indefinite dyad *(hē aoristos dyas)* is a number per se: they are both prior to number. This dyad is not exactly two, but rather the not-One that emerges from within the One: "For number is not primary: the One is prior to the dyad, but the dyad is secondary and, originating from the One, has it as definer *(horistēn)*, but is itself of its own nature indefinite" (5.1.5.6–8). The dyad is "indefinite" (*a*, "without"+*horistos*, "definition") because it only receives such definition when it turns and contemplates the One. This turn and contemplation of the One is what brings about numbers, in all their multiplicity, and the Forms: "from the Indefinite Dyad and the One derive the Forms and Numbers: that is, Intellect" (5.4.2.7–8).[9] Elsewhere he describes the emergence of the proto-Intellect as "sight not yet seeing" (5.3.11.5): in other words, eyes that have yet to turn back to their source as an object of sight. In sum, then, what emerges from the One is something other than the One, an intellectual power, the indefinite dyad (not-One) that wants to be one, a kind of proto-Intellect that extends out from the One and wishes to see.

Let us now move on to the turn and contemplation of the One. Plotinus asks plainly, "How then does [the Good or One] generate Intellect?" The answer seems simple: "Because by its return to it, it sees: and this seeing is Intellect" (5.1.7.6–7). This passage poses a challenge (common enough with Plotinus's prose): how best to interpret and translate the pronouns, implicit and explicit? A plain reading of the question and answer would suggest that the subject remains the same in both, in which case it should read: "How does [the Good] generate Intellect? Because by the Good's return to itself the Good sees: and this seeing is Intellect" (my translation). Armstrong does not like the implications of this reading, and proposes instead a sharp and unmarked change in subject between question and answer.[10] It seems that he wants to preserve the transcendent One (or Good) from any suggestion that it stretches to the point that it sees itself, because any autoscopy (being simultaneously seer and seen) would seem to disqualify the One as One. However, I think the tension can be resolved apart from abruptly changing the subject from question to answer. We have just seen Plotinus struggle to find adequate language for the primordial otherness that first emerges from the One. We have seen how this otherness, this dyad (not-One), is also still very much (part of) the One: "unitary in form" *(henoeidous)* or still "one" *(gar hen)*. In some sense, until that ineffable otherness is defined and instantiated as Intellect, it is still (part of) the One, such that Plotinus can speak of the One's return to itself. But at precisely the "moment" when the One turns on itself and beholds itself, at precisely that moment it becomes Intellect, defined now as seeing *(horasis)*—"seeing sight" now rather than "sight without seeing" or "unformed sight" (5.3.11.5, 10–12). There may even be some wordplay at work here: only when the One turns and sees *(horasis)* itself is it defined *(horistos)* as Intellect.

When the indeterminate otherness turns so as to contemplate the One, it cannot take in the sight of its source: "For when it contemplates the One, it does not contemplate it as one" (3.8.8.31–32).[11] Like light refracted through a prism into a full color spectrum, the sheer simplicity of the One, when seen, is split into the many. Intellect's seeing is like a screen or a grid that breaks the singular source into an articulated manifold: "Intellect sees, by means of itself, like something divided proceeding from the undivided" (5.1.7.17–18). The indeterminate otherness is thus "overcome by many and into many and so becoming Intellect" (6.8.18.28–29). In 3.8, "On Nature and Contemplation," Plotinus writes that "beginning as one it did not stay as it began, but, without noticing it, became many, as if heavy, and unrolled itself because it wanted to possess everything" (3.8.8.32–34). Here (again, anticipating our discussion of Narcissus), Intellect's "wanting to possess" is both an explanation for the first declension from the One and an obstacle to its return to the One. Curiously, Plotinus also says that the Intellect "became many, as if heavy": this verb *bareō* means to "weigh down" and in the passive means not only "weighed down" or "heavy" but also "pregnant."[12] On this reading, the sight of the One so to speak "impregnates" Intellect with a fully articulated intelligible world. This is corroborated in a passage from *Ennead* 6.7:

> Intellect therefore had the power *(dynamin)* from [the Good] to generate *(to gennan)* and to be filled of its own offspring *(gennēmatōn)*, since the Good gave what [the Good] did not itself have. But from the Good itself who is one there were many for this Intellect; for it was unable to hold the power which it received and broke it up and made the one power many, that it might be able so to bear *(pherein)* it part by part ... And so, if one likens [Intellect] to a living richly varied sphere, or imagines it as a thing all faces *(pamprosōpon)*, shining with living faces. (6.7.15.18–23, 25–27)

The image of a sphere teeming with living faces may strike us merely as a colorful description of the intelligible world. However, I think this description is actually meant to give a more precise account of Intellect's inner articulation.

THE INNER LIFE OF INTELLECT

What is the inner life of Intellect, the second hypostasis or *archē*? It is extremely difficult to get a clear picture from Plotinus, and experts differ on this question. On my best reading, the *archē* or universal principle Intellect is the collective of all individual intellects, which are just above figured as "living faces." Think of every living face as an intellectual subject, locked eye-to-eye with another face, an intelligible object. The name Plotinus elsewhere gives this relationship is syzygy: every intellect is "coupled" *(synezeuchthai)* to an intelligible (3.8.9.8, 9; 5.5.1.23, 24). Such a duality or syzygy is the basic structure of Intellect, which forever differentiates it from the One (recall all the uses to which this term, *syzygia*, and its cognates [such as *syzygos*] have been put in the Christian and Manichaean traditions). The intellectual object here is a Form. This would suggest that the inner life of Intellect is constituted of subjects and objects, individual intellects and Forms—and the whole humming sum is Intellect. But Plotinus seems unhappy with that division between intellects and Forms, and the figure above, after all, does not differentiate between living faces. Elsewhere Plotinus says, "Intellect as a whole is all the Forms, and each individual Form is an individual intellect" (5.9.8.3–4).[13] If this is so, then the inner life of Intellect is *not* constituted by two distinct classes of entities: intellects and Forms (subjects and objects). Rather, individual intellects *are* Forms, such that there is only one class of entity in Intellect.[14] This also raises the question, to which we will return below, of whether individual, embodied intellects—we, in other words—each have a Form.

To return to the figure of the richly varied sphere of living faces, every face is an intellectual subject *(nous)* serving as an intelligible object *(noēton)* to another intellect or Form. Thus, the individual intellect-Forms are thinking each other, and the whole collective is Intellect. This is Plotinus's appropriation of the Aristotelian definition of god in his *Metaphysics* L.9: "Therefore it thinks itself, (since it is the most excellent) and its thinking is the thinking of thinking" *(auton ara noei, eiper to kratiston, kai estin hē noēsis noēseōs noēsis)* (1074b33–34). Plotinus has appropriated the Aristotelian god, identified it with Intellect, and subordinated it to the One. He has also wed this notion of thought thinking itself *(hē noēsis noēseōs noēsis)* with Plato's realm of the Forms. It is, in Gerson's words, "a remarkable act of syncretism."[15] Every Form is an intellect *(nous)* thinking *(noēsis)* another intellect-Form as an intelligible *(noēton)*, and this relationship is a coupling or syzygy.

Here is another rather stirring picture of the inner life of Intellect, in which Plotinus is speaking of the individual intellects or Forms as "gods":

> [The gods] see all things, not those to which coming to be, but those to which real being belongs, and they see themselves in other things; for all things there are transparent, and there is nothing dark or opaque; everything and all things are clear to the inmost part to everything; for light is transparent to light. Each there has everything in itself and sees all things in every other, so that all are everywhere and each and every one is all and the glory is unbounded. (5.8.4.3–9)

On this description, the intellects or Forms are indistinguishable from each other, and they see themselves in the other intellects. The world of Intellect, teeming with living faces, is thus like a giant hall of mirrors, except that what each face sees is not the surface of its own or another face, but rather its entire interior. This bears a striking resemblance to the letter to the prince in the "Hymn of the Pearl," which becomes a mirror by which the prince sees his own inner image, reads his own inner inscription; so too the royal garment, a mirror of himself: "I saw all of it myself, and also I received all in it."[16] As Remes puts it, in the "self-reflexive state of the Intellect . . . the relation of subject and object is one of identity"; and although "each intellect is two, inasmuch as it can be conceptually divided into the thinker and the things thought . . . [each intellect is also] identical to its objects of thought which are internal to it."[17] The reflections of intellectual subject and intelligible object are entirely without blemish, with every subject enjoying a full view of its object. This is related to what Gerson calls "the eternal interconnectedness of Forms," which Gerson explains thus: "Forms do not contain each other as proper parts, but each one is 'transparent' to all the rest because in Intellect they are identical with a single activity . . . The Forms are not really distinct entities, but really distinct aspects of Intellect."[18] Jean Trouillard suggests that there is a kind of intersubjectivity among the individual intellects, which suggestion Armstrong follows in speaking of the "interpenetration of a community of living minds."[19]

This affords us a chance to step back and consider what the procession of Intellect from the One, and the inner life of Intellect, have to do with the divine double. Primordial procession is itself something of an encounter between the One and its double. Indeterminate otherness or the indefinite dyad emerges and then turns toward its source from which it is not yet distinct. Its own turning instantiates it as fully other than, an image of, the One—its derivative double, Intellect. The inner life of Intellect is another iteration of the divine double, as Plotinus appropriates and subordinates the Aristotelian god—thought thinking itself—as the second hypostasis, Intellect, after the One. Intellect is the collective of all individual intellects, which on my reading are identical with the Forms, beholding their fellow minds as intelligible objects. The intellectual subject and intelligible objects are "yoked together." Here, however, the syzygy between intellect and intelligible is a horizontal relationship between, in Schroeder's phrase, "ontic equals," that is, the intellect-Forms themselves.[20] Finally, the intellect-Forms are said to be fully "transparent," a sphere of living faces all seeing into each other, without hindrance or distortion—as Plato has Socrates advise that we look into the eye, but really the soul, of another and so see ourselves, but really our best selves, reflected there as if in a mirror.

We will soon turn from the lofty heights of the One and Intellect to Plotinus's view of human nature. But in truth we will not leave these lofty heights entirely behind, because Plotinus believes that we individual, embodied intellects "here" enjoy an unbroken relationship with our individual, disembodied intellects "there." In this section we have focused on the doubled structure of the primordial procession and of the inner life of Intellect. Next we will see it in Plotinus's account of how the human is simultaneously here and there. And to return from here to there—what Zeke Mazur calls "mystical self-reversion"—will require that our doubled intellects (to which we now turn) overcome that split between here and there and then, having ascended to Intellect, overcome the inherent duality in Intellect's inner life (syzygy). Only upon first overcoming these two can we finally, and if it all possible, overcome the primordial procession itself, and return the ecstatic plenitude of Intellect to the ineffable source from which it first sought to stand apart as other.

The Doubled Self

THE DESCENDED AND UNDESCENDED INTELLECT

To move from the primordial procession of Intellect from the One and the inner life of Intellect to the nature of human selfhood is to skip several crucial links in the great chain of being, including: the procession of the universal principle Soul from Intellect and with it the emergence of time from eternity; the twin births of the world soul and the host of individual souls; and the descent of individual souls into bodies. Let me attempt the impossible and treat those links *very* briefly. If the activity of Intellect is eternal "self-reflexive intellection," then the activity of Soul is life *(bios)* in time. And whereas in Intellect each individual intellect succeeds in fully thinking its intelligible fellow—a full transparency without blemish—in Soul there is a gap between aim and achievement, between desire and fulfillment.[21] Another way to put this is that the activity of Intellect is intransitive (because self-contained), whereas the activity of Soul is transitive.[22] Inherently oriented outward, Soul serves as "the mediator of Forms [that is, Intellect] to the sensible world" and thus its "function is rather 'demiurgic.'"[23] If Intellect created the sensible world on its own, without the Soul's action in time, that world would be frozen, a sort of snapshot of the intelligible world. The *archē* or hypostasis Soul has two children: (1) the world soul and (2) the host of individual souls—and the two are "sisters" (4.3.6.13; 2.9.18.16). The individual souls are the descended instantiations of individual intellects. The world soul in a sense prepares the way for the descent of individual souls into bodies, for the body into which an individual soul descends is composed of matter and the informing work of the world soul. When an individual soul does descend, then, the resulting "composite" *(to synamphoteron)*—a human being, for example—is not individual soul+matter (as it is in Aristotle), but rather soul^1 (individual soul)+body, in which the body is already soul^2 (world soul)+matter.

One last note before we turn to the relevant texts: any discussion of human selfhood in Plotinus can be tripped up by his seeming imprecision. Whereas he is usually very clear in distinguishing the hypostasis Soul from the hypostasis Intellect, he is not so when it comes to individual souls and intellects. An individual embodied soul is the locus of a number of activities: chief among them is the activity of intellect (although we often neglect our intellects), but other activities (cognitive, affective, reproductive, vegetative, and so on) are included as well. When Plotinus speaks of a soul performing its highest function, intellection *(noēsis)*, he sometimes speaks of it as still a "soul" although in point of fact it is more properly understood as an intellect. Conversely, he will sometimes use *noēsis* to speak not only of intellection of the Forms but also of the sort of discursive thinking that an embodied soul engages in, which is more properly referred to as *dianoia*.

Plotinus's simplest and clearest definition of selfhood is this: "For every human is double *(dittos)*, one of him is the sort of compound being *(to synamphoteron)* and one of him is himself *(autos)*" (2.3.9.31–32). The compound being or composite is an individual embodied soul: individual soul (soul^1)+body (soul^2+matter). This is of course a kind of dualism, "a crude dualism of body and soul," but it is not the dualism Plotinus thinks is most important.[24] The individual soul (soul^1) is *itself* double, and *this* is the crucial dualism for Plotinus. As he writes in 3.8,

> The first part of the soul, then, that which is above and always filled and illuminated by the reality above, remains There; but another part, participating by the first participation of the participant goes forth, for soul goes forth always, life from life; for actuality reaches everywhere, and there is no point where it fails. But in going forth it lets its prior part remain where it left it, for if it abandoned what is before it, it would no longer be everywhere, but only at the last point it reached. But what goes forth is not equal to what remains. (3.8.5.10–18)

Here is an example where Plotinus uses "soul" capaciously to include intellect. For insofar as an individual "soul" is "above and always filled and illuminated by the reality above, remains There," that "soul" is thinking the Forms and is therefore an individual intellect enjoying the inner life of Intellect. The point, however, is that Plotinus regards every individual soul or intellect as already divided, or at least bi-located: one part of it is here, having descended into the composite, and another part of it is there, eternally fed on the vision of intelligible beauty.

This doctrine of the undescended intellect appears throughout the *Enneads*; here are two further examples:

> Our soul does not altogether come down, but there is always something of it in the intelligible. (4.8.8.2–4)

> The human, and especially the good human is not the composite *(to synamphoteron)* of soul and body; separation from the body and despising its so-called goods make this plain. (1.4.14.1–4)

There are therefore two dualisms in Plotinian anthropology: the "apparent" dualism of body and soul, and the "real" dualism of lower and higher, descended and undescended, intellect.[25] Our descended intellect is an image of our undescended intellect, and thus again we are in a position of conforming the image ever more to its archetype. Plotinus famously appeals to an Orphic myth about how the Titans lured the child Dionysus away with a mirror *(katoptron)*: distracted by his own image, Dionysus was helpless as they slew him and then ate him (4.3.12.1–3). We are like the god Dionysus, Plotinus says. Intellects see their images *(eidōla)* and plunge down to the level of that reflection, that is, they descend: "But even these are not cut off from their own principle and from intellect. For they did not come down with intellect, but went on ahead of it down to earth, but their heads are firmly set in heaven" (4.3.12.2–6). The crucial point here is that the undescended intellect erred: it saw its own image and descended in pursuit of that image, into embodiment. The difference is that part of that intellect remains "firmly set in heaven," and thus we are doubled. And to overcome our constitutive division, we have to reverse the Titans' mirror trick. Here Plotinus figures matter as a kind of mirror that threatens to capture the intellect's attention by showing it its own image. But once intellect has descended into embodiment, it still needs another mirror to show it its true image, or rather, to show it that it is the image of an undescended archetype.

For Plotinus, this doctrine of the undescended intellect solves a problem that Plato identified in the *Parmenides* (133b–134b), namely, the threat of the separation of the sensible and the intelligible worlds, a separation that would threaten not only certain knowledge (*epistēmē*) but also our progressive ascent to intelligibility. By having the intellect straddle the intelligible world (undescended) and the sensible world (descended), Plotinus might think to have "solved" the problem, but in fact he has only made the individual intellect do the work of holding the two worlds together. In other words, Plotinus is forced to account for the identity of the descended and the undescended intellect. There is a concern, then, that "the Plotinian picture [of the 'double self'] may remain disunified."[26] To answer this worry, Plotinus is led to modify his view of doubled selfhood into one of tripled selfhood, and so to articulate a mediating self, a "center of consciousness" that might help hold together the sensible and intelligible worlds.

We see the seeds of this view in his famous treatise "Against the Gnostics": "There is one intellect, unchangeably the same, without any sort of decline, imitating the Father as far as is possible to it: and that one part of our soul is always directed to the intelligible realities, one to the things of this world, and one is in the middle between these" (2.9.2.3–6). That "middle" part will become in Plotinus's later treatises a developed philosophy of the "we"—a term he uses to describe the discursive reasoning (*dianoia*) that operates between bestial sense perception and angelic intellection (see 5.3.3, for instance). The level of discursive reason is "the summit of the sensible man."[27] Whether this discursive reasoning or "we" serves to lash together the sensible and intelligible realities sufficiently to "solve" the problem of the separation of the two worlds that Parmenides pointed out to Socrates, I do not know. What is more interesting to me is that the concept of the "we" gives the reader of the *Enneads* a place to stand, and in which to recognize him- or herself: neither a beast nor an angel, but a human in community and sharing a sensible world—hence *we* (not I). As Pauliina Remes puts it,

This given relation to the world that all human souls share may be expressed by Plotinus's choice of the plural "we" *(hēmeis)* in place of the modern singular "I" in posing the central question: "Who are we?" For him, as for most ancient philosophers, each consciousness grasps, ideally, the very same world.[28]

We know vividly from Porphyry's *Life* that Plotinus lived among a vibrant and mixed community of men and women who were philosophers, physicians, politicians, and such. By speaking of "we" rather than "I," I suspect that Plotinus is appealing to this community for the task ahead: the elevation of discursive reasoning to intellection. For as John Dillon points out, although the "we" is not identical with intellect, "it can become so, and that is what we have to work toward."[29] The "we" is, in the words of H. J. Blumenthal, "mobile."[30] Thus, some of the rhetorical, if not exactly philosophical, significance of the appeal to the "we" is that it presents us at a crossroads, with a choice to incline upward or downward. And in effect, the threefold model of selfhood again resolves into the twofold model, as the philosophical enterprise is to make the "we" conform to the undescended intellect.

But how do "we" ascend, how do "we" incline upward to our intellect? To answer this question we have to look at one of Plotinus's descriptions of the descent of the soul or intellect. In the myth of the mirror of Dionysus, it is the image of the intellect that beguiles the intellect such that it plunges downward. In this next account of descent, something seems to reach up to the intelligible and pull it down:

> But we—who are we? Are we that which draws near and comes to be in time? No, even before this coming to be came to be we were there, humans who were different *(alloi)*, and some of us even gods, pure souls and intellects united with the whole of reality; we were parts of the intelligible, not marked off or cut off but belonging to the whole; and we are not cut off even now. But now another human *(anthrōpos allos)*, wishing to exist *(einai thelōn)*, approached that man; and when he found us—for we were not outside the All—he wound himself round us and at-

tached himself to that man who was then each of us . . . and we have come to be the pair *(to synampho)* of them, not the one which we were before—and sometimes just the other one which we added on afterwards, when that prior one is inactive and in another way not present. (6.4.14.18–32)

This description should be familiar to us by now: pure souls or intellects feasting on the intelligible—that is who we really are. But somehow "another human," whose distinguishing mark as an outsider is his wishing (for there is no distinction between desire and fulfillment at the level of the Intellect), finds us there. He penetrates into the eternal realm and wraps himself around each of us—like a lamprey on a host or a tumor around an organ. He makes of us a pair, and his wishing weighs us down. Yes, "we are not cut off even now," at least not entirely, but we now wax and wane between him and our true self. What is perhaps most surprising in this description is that the lower self initiates the descent of the higher: it reaches upward and pulls it down.

What is even more important in the description of the descent, however, is that the union or identity of the two—the higher and lower humans, the undescended and descended intellects—is a named a "pair" or *synampho*. Any individual self—insofar as the self is the soul or intellect—is an individual only insofar as he is a "dividual," divided between higher and lower halves.[31] The *synampho* is thus the Plotinian equivalent of Mani's *oua ouōt:* a singularity preserving, indeed pulsing with, duality. Leo Sweeney says of Mani's and Plotinus's parallel accounts of selfhood that "each formulated a monism which is dynamic rather than static"—we might call it "dynamonism."[32] And if the power or *dynamis* of this monism consists in the two halves held together, we might further specify it as "dyadic" dynamonism.

Despite this striking parallel, however, there is still a crucial difference between Mani and Plotinus on how the lower half ascends. The reader may recall that the *Kephalaia* explain how the Apostle of Light sojourns on earth in different bodies at different times in order to free the light of souls entrapped in bodies. It is then the twin-companion who descends to awaken the apostle to his divine mission. In other words, the initiative is on the part of the divine double, not the earthly sojourner (similarly with the "Hymn of the Pearl"). In Plotinus, however, the undescended intellect cannot show such initiative or interest in what is beneath it. Of our intellect Plotinus says that "it is separate *(chōristos)* because it itself does not incline towards *(prosneuein)* us, but rather we look up *(eis to anō blepontas)* towards it" (5.3.3.43–45). The undescended intellect cannot descend so as to save us, as Mani's twin-companion does for him. One "half" of our intellect is enjoying the self-contained inner life of Intellect. The other, lower "half" suffers the misfortune of descent into embodiment. Our salvation consists not in our rescue by our higher power per se, but by our struggling to see the archetype of which we are the sad image: "The more [the soul] is directed to that contemplation [of that which is before it, that is, its higher half], the fairer and more powerful it is. It receives from there and gives to what comes after it, and is always illuminated as it illuminates" (2.9.2.17–19).

"ON OUR ALLOTTED GUARDIAN SPIRIT"

The doubled structure of the self finds expression in two other contexts in the *Enneads*, both of which have occasioned much commentary: (1) Plotinus's adaptation of Plato's discussion of the *daimōn* for his own purposes; (2) his views on whether there are Forms of individuals. Plotinus devotes an entire short treatise (3.4) to the *daimōn* or "guardian spirit." We saw in Chapter 1 that there is a tension within Plato between his description of Socrates's peculiar *daimonion* and his more universal account of the *daimōn*, which weaves traditional mythical themes into a philosophical anthropology. One possible way to render the two consistent is to suggest that although the philosophical anthropology of the *daimōn* is universal—that is, everyone has (but perhaps does not use) a "most sovereign part of the soul"—Socrates's *daimonion* is the sign given only to those who use that sovereign part—that is, everyone *could* have a Socratic *daimonion*, but they quite evidently do not.[33] What is immediately striking about Plotinus's innovation on this Platonic inheritance is that he more or less completely ignores Socrates's *daimonion* and instead attempts to appropriate only Plato's universal philosophical anthropology of the *daimōn*. Why the oblivion of Socrates's *daimonion*? It is hard to say, but Rist argues that it has to do with the philosophical tradition between Plato and Plotinus (starting with Xenophon and the spurious Platonic dialogue *Theages*), where he sees a consistent "retrograde movement" (a "debasing," "degradation," "vulgarization").[34] On this reading, Plato's account of Socrates's *daimonion* is reduced to the level of "superstition," subject to the enthusiasms of third-century CE magic and theurgy. For Rist, Plotinus is turning his nose up at this tradition, which surrounds him on all sides, and attempting instead to preserve Plato's more pristine philosophical perspective. This puts Rist squarely in a long-standing debate about Plotinus's view of magic and theurgy, which thankfully we need neither rehearse nor resolve.[35]

Rather, we are concerned with what Plotinus does with those Platonic sources with which he *does* choose to engage. His treatise "On Our Allotted Guardian Spirit" inquires into the *daimōn* against a backdrop of reincarnation. Given that the soul's powers include growth (plants), sense perception (animals), and rationality (humans), what determines what the soul will become once it is free of its particular body after death? Any human who "guards the human" in him—whatever that means—becomes human again. But what about ascent and descent through reincarnation? Plotinus's answer to this question relies on Plato's discussion in the *Phaedo* (107c–e), where Socrates speaks of how the soul's afterlife depends on its conduct in this life, and distinguishes between three "allotted" or "appointed" spirit-guides: (1) the spirit *(daimōn)* allotted to us in this life; (2) the guide *(hēgemon)* appointed to lead our soul after death to the underworld; (3) another guide *(hēgemon)* appointed to lead us back to life here. Plotinus seems relatively unconcerned with (2) and (3), and instead focuses on the figure of the *daimōn* "allotted in life," and specifically whether anyone after death can become a *daimōn*.

> Who, then, becomes a spirit *(daimōn)*? He who was one here too. And who a god? Certainly he who has one here. What worked *(energēsan)* in a man leads him [after death], since it was his ruler and guide here too. Is this, then, "the spirit to whom he

> was allotted while he lived?" No, but that which is before the working principle; for this presides inactive *(argoun)* over the man, but that which comes after it acts. If the working principle *(to energoun)* is that by which we have sense-perception, the spirit *(daimōn)* is the rational principle *(to logikon)*; but if we live by the rational principle, the spirit is what is above this *(to hyper touto)*, presiding inactive *(argos)* and giving its consent to the principle which works. So it is rightly said that "we shall choose."[36] For we choose the principle which stands above us according to our choice of life. (3.4.3.1–10)

This is a difficult passage, one where Plotinus makes a crucial distinction between (i) the "working principle" *(to energoun)* in each of our lives and (ii) that which is above this working principle, presiding inactive *(argos)* in each of our lives, and which he equates with the *daimōn*. We choose our own way of life—that is, we choose its governing principle: for example, whether to live according to sense perception (like an animal) or according to our rational part *(to logikon,* like a human). Whichever we choose, our *daimōn* is one level above that *(to hyper touto)*. In other words, wherever we find ourselves, we have a higher self above us. The structure of the self, on this picture, is always doubled, although that doubled structure shifts up and down a scale.

What does the higher self do for the lower self if it remains inactive *(argos)*? It is said to give its consent to the lower principle: the verb here, *synchōreō*, means literally to give or cede *chōra* or "space." It seems to be in that ceded space, then, that the lower principle experiences the freedom to choose.

> But if a man is able to follow the spirit which is above him, he comes to be himself above, living that spirit's life, and giving the pre-eminence to that better part of himself to which he is being led; and after that spirit he rises to another, until he reaches the heights. (3.4.3.18–21)

Clearly disturbed by Socrates's description of the allotment of a *daimōn* of one sort or another to an undeserving individual, Plotinus bends the *Phaedo* into alignment with the *Republic*, where Socrates insists that "virtue knows no master; each will possess it to a greater or lesser degree, depending on whether he values or disdains it. The responsibility lies with the one who makes the choice; the god[dess Lachesis] has none" (617e). The *daimōn* or higher self can be said to "lead" *(agein)* only insofar as it is always above *(hyper)*, but the choice whether to incline upward to it (or not) is always one's own.

The choice on which Socrates insists in the *Republic*, however, is not one made in this life, but one made prior to embodiment before the goddess Lachesis. Plotinus responds by interpreting this prior choice as "a riddling representation of the soul's universal and permanent purpose *(proairesin)* and disposition" (3.4.5.2–4). The word translated "purpose" here *(proairesis)* denotes the choice *(hairesis)* one makes for *(pro)* something. Plotinus seems to suggest, then, that Socrates is not so much describing an actual choice that souls make prior to embodiment as he is offering an allegory to explain how a soul is disposed over the course of its many embodiments: some are disposed to decline and others to incline. This is not strict determinism, for each soul has the capacity to adjust its course. Rather, it suggests that an embodied soul makes a decision informed by its past, by its patterns of disposition. The soul is a like an object moving through space: its trajectory is established, and any change in that trajectory must contend with its momentum.

Plotinus frames this tension as the dialectic between the soul's sovereign decision *(to kurion)* and its character *(ēthos)*, and this leads back to a discussion of the *daimōn* and to what degree it is or is not one's own:

> Plato gives the power of decision *(to kurion)* rather to the souls, which adapt what is given to them to their own characters *(ta autōn ēthē)*. For that this guardian spirit is not entirely outside but only in the sense that he is not bound to us, and is not active in us but is ours, to speak in terms of soul, but not ours if we are considered as men of a particular kind who have a life which is subject to him [the guardian spirit], is shown by what is said in the *Timaeus*. (3.4.5.17–23)

Our *daimōn* both is and is not "ours." From our embodied perspective *here*, we live subject to or simply "under" *(hypo)* the *daimōn* (because it is that which is above us or *to hyper touto*), often unknowingly, and thus we do not consider it our own, but rather something else, superior to and distant from us. From our disembodied perspective *there*, the *daimōn* is not active in our lower, embodied life, but is our own nevertheless—or perhaps better, we belong to it. Plotinus then refers to *Timaeus* 90a, which makes clear his point:

> Now we ought to think of the most sovereign part of our soul as god's gift to us, given to be our guiding spirit *(daimōn)*. This, of course, is the type of soul that, as we maintain, resides in the top part of our bodies. It raises us up away from the earth and toward what is akin to us in heaven, as though we are plants grown not from the earth but from heaven. In this, we speak absolutely correctly. For it is from heaven, the place in which our souls were originally born, that the divine part suspends our head, i.e., our root, and so keeps our whole body erect.

I discussed this passage in some detail in Chapter 1. Plotinus points his reader to it to help answer how the *daimōn* both is and is not our own. From our disembodied perspective *there*, it is the *daimōn* and not our embodied soul that is our true self, "the most sovereign part of our soul." The *daimōn* is our root, and what we typically know as ourselves—our embodied soul—is in fact a downward plant growth from that root structure. The *daimōn* is thus more "us" than "we" are, and in this way is indisputably ours.

To recap, then: We can descend and ascend through reincarnation; whatever life we lead now is a dialectic between our sovereign decision and our soul's long-standing character; whatever life we lead, our *daimōn* exists above our life by one level; thus a man who lives according to sense perception has his *daimōn* at the level of reason *(to logikon)*, and a woman who lives according to reason has her *daimōn* at the level of intellect *(nous)*.[37] But what about a "nobly good" person *(spoudaios)*? Intellect is active in such a person, which is to say that it is the governing principle of his or her life (3.4.6). But the *daimōn* cannot be a partner *(synergos)* in such a person's life; the *daimōn* must surpass the active principle, in this case intellect. According to Plotinus, then, such a person has a god beyond intellect as his or her *daimōn*. A god beyond intellect can mean only one thing: the One itself. In other words, Plotinus imagines that there are sages who have completely activated their intellect (that is, who have conformed their descended intellect to its eternal archetype) and so, having done so, have the One itself as their *daimōn*.[38] But precisely because the *daimōn* is said always to be inactive *(argos)* in our lives, and compounded by the fact that the One exists in splendidly isolated transcendence, it is unclear what it means for such a person to have the One as its guardian spirit. As Rist puts it, "Plotinus tells us little about how such guidance is transmitted."[39]

FORMS OF INDIVIDUALS?

In the section above titled "The Inner Life of Intellect," I described Intellect as the collective of all individual intellects, and argued that individual intellects are equivalent to Forms—in Plotinus's figure, faces contemplating each other. As I flagged there, this is connected to the question of whether Plotinus thought that each individual embodied intellect has its own Form. This question has an important genealogy in Plato and his own changing theory of Forms. Plato is generally thought to have posited Forms as "one over many," that is, a causative principle of many particular instantiations: the Form of horse, for example, is the causative principle of all horses. In other words, "there is a Form, according to the *Republic* (596a5-7), corresponding to every set of things that have a common name."[40] After the *Republic*, however, Plato's theory of the Forms underwent many changes and challenges, principally in such dialogues as the *Parmenides*, *Sophist*, *Timaeus*, and *Philebus*. Nowhere in Plato, however, nor in any of the early Platonists, do we find a version of the theory that suggests that there are Forms for every individual or instantiated particular.[41] In fact, one of Aristotle's many objections to the theory of Forms is that it leads to this view—but it is a view no Platonist accepts (*Metaphysics* 990b14).[42] No Platonist, it seems, except Plotinus.

To say "seems" here is not simply academic equivocation: the question of whether Plotinus did or did not hold this view—so peculiar for Platonists—has generated a storm of scholarly debate. There have been at least two fronts to this storm: the first in the 1960s and 1970s, the second in the 1990s.[43] The problem is that Plotinus seems to contradict himself on this very question: in treatises 5.9 ("On Intellect, the Forms, and Being") and 5.7 ("On the Question of Whether There Are Ideas of Particulars"). Again, "seems" is appropriate because some scholars argue that there is a coherent view to be had if only we read Plotinus correctly. The fact that treatise 5.9, where Plotinus seems to reject the notion, comes well before treatise 5.7, where he seems to endorse it, suggests to some scholars that the contradiction can be resolved by appealing to a development in Plotinus's view: in effect 5.7 abrogates 5.9.[44] Others think the matter much murkier, owing to the fact that Plotinus discusses the issue at several points, and equivocates throughout, such that if we were to arrange his verdicts chronologically, his testimony would amount to: no in 5.9 [5], yes in 5.7 [18], no in 6.4–5 [22–23], perhaps yes in 4.3 [27], no in 6.7 [38], and perhaps yes again in 3.2 [47] (with the chronology of composition included in brackets).[45] The most prominent skeptic, H. J. Blumenthal (who assembles the chronology of verdicts), throws up his hands in the face of this alleged inconsistency.[46]

The loose consensus of the second wave of scholarly debate in the 1990s, however, is that Plotinus *did* in fact hold some version of this view.[47] It is not my intention to wade into these troubled waters to offer a new resolution to the debate. Rather, leaning lightly on this somewhat hesitating consensus, I wish to ask: *Why* might Plotinus hold the peculiar view that there were Forms of individuals or, put another way, that *each* individual intellect had an eternal archetype in the intelligible realm? Wouldn't it be more elegant if there were a finite number of more general Forms that caused all particular instantiations? After all, weren't Forms introduced by Plato precisely to explain the specificity of our world by appeal to a set of more general, intelligible principles? Furthermore, if, as we have discussed above, all intellects are Forms, and there is in the universal Intellect an identity of subject and object, in what sense can we really say that the individual intellect-Forms are *individuals?* What differentiates one intellect-Form from another?

Answers to these questions, of course, are hard to come by. Perhaps Plotinus's "radical innovation" was his conviction that individuality so to speak *mattered*, mattered so much in fact that individuation must be native to the intelligible realm rather than the result of some successive stage in its instantiation.[48] But why might individuation matter so much? I suggest that Plotinus takes this peculiar stand on the Forms of individuals because he is concerned ultimately about our return to the realm of Intellect and, beyond even that, to the One. I am not alone in this regard. Paul Kalligas writes, "It is the ability of each individual human being to return to his intelligible origin by making use of the essential features that makes it necessary to postulate a *different* form for each human being."[49] Evidence for this can be found in the very opening of treatise 5.7: "Is there an idea of each particular thing? Yes, if I and each one of us have a way of ascent and return *(anagōgēn)* to the intelligible, the principle of each of us is there" (5.7.1.1–3). Our return to our "whence" depends on, and so demands, that some version of ourselves, namely the Form of our individual intellect, is already there.

Plotinus describes a cyclical universe, in which each cycle sees a finite number of Forms cause a finite number of individuals.[50] We individual intellects each have an eternal archetype in the realm of the intelligible, and in the universe's next cycle that eternal archetype will generate a new image, a new individual intellect. Our connection to that subsequent individual intellect in the next age is not horizontal but vertical: we are connected only by virtue of the fact that we are two images of a single archetype. The two images could (but need not) differ radically from one another across two cycles, much as Plato describes changes in a soul's embodiment through reincarnation.

Kalligas supplies a reconstruction of Plotinus's argument for the Forms of individuals from another treatise (1.1), borrowing from Aristotle and a fragment of Proclus's otherwise lost commentary on the *Enneads:*

		(1)	Every essence is a form
	(1) →	(2)	Whatever is the same as its essence is a form
		(3)	Everything simple is the same as its essence
		(4)	The (higher) soul is simple
(3) + (4) →		(5)	The (higher) soul is the same as its essence
(2) + (5) →		(6)	The (higher) soul is a form[51]

Plotinus has borrowed Plato's definition of the human as the soul (as opposed to the body or the composite of the two) from *Alcibiades I* (130c). But in Plotinus's scheme, the essence of the soul is its highest register, intellect. He writes, "If . . . soul and essential soul are one and the same, soul will be a kind of Form" (1.1.2.6–7). In other words, the individual soul has a Form—that Form being its essence as intellect. In our highest register, we each exist "there" as a Form.

There are a few passages where Plotinus seems to disown or at least question the view he articulates in 5.7. We will pass over these passages, however, not because we wish to pretend that they do not exist or that they necessarily, when correctly understood, align with his views in 5.7, but rather because we are principally concerned to appreciate Plotinus's aims for holding the view that there *are* Forms of individuals. In 5.7 he refuses the idea that there could be a single Form, human, that causes all individual humans: "Humans are not related to their form as portraits of Socrates are to their original." This finds corroboration in a passage we have already discussed:

> But we—who are we? Are we that which draws near and comes to be in time? No, even before this coming to be came to be we were there, humans who were different *(alloi)*, and some of us *(tines)* even gods, pure souls and intellects united with the whole of reality; we were parts of the intelligible, not marked off or cut off but belonging to the whole; and we are not cut off even now. (6.4.14.17–22)

Notice that this description of our prior, pre-embodied life as intellects insists that we were in the plural even there. There we were *tines*, that is, distinct intellects. There is not a single Form from which we are derived; rather, we are the furniture of universal Intellect, "parts of the intelligible" but "belonging to the whole." When Plotinus says that we were different *(alloi)*, he means that we were different from what we are now, after our "coming to be" and descent into bodies. But the fact that we are called "different" raises the question of whether and how the intellect-Forms can be said to be individual. In other words, in what ways, if any, do the intellect-Forms differ from one another?

The short answer is that they do not: intellect-Forms are identical to one other. And yet, although identical, they are still distinct. Plotinus speaks of this unity-in-distinction in a rather riddling way: "The soul when it is altogether apart [from the body] is particular without being particular . . . it is part, not the whole, though even so it is in another way the whole" (6.4.16.32–34). What does it mean that the soul, become intellect, is particular without being particular? It seems that the intellects' distinctiveness consists only in their numerical rather than qualitative difference. Their identity consists in their being indistinguishable parts, and the sum of these identical parts is universal Intellect. In other words, individual intellect-Forms differ from each other only insofar as there are many of them. The individuality of an undescended intellect consists in this and only this. What we typically regard as individuality is a matter of qualitative difference (a particular), which according to Plotinus begins to adhere to individual intellects only as they begin their descent as souls into bodies.

With this, however, we return to the pressing question of why Plotinus held to this view, and the suggestion that it is necessary to account for our return to the intelligible realm and beyond. Most importantly, this view ensures that there is an unbroken line between the undescended and descended intellect, that our doubled self is lashed together. We can be confident of our return to our whence precisely because our essential selves, our souls distilled into intellects, are already there, numerically individuated intellect-Forms. As we have noted above in contrast to Mani, however, the placement of our higher half "there" does not imply that the intellect-Form can descend to elevate or "save" us from the burden of embodiment.

The initiative for our return, so it seems, must be our own. But the fact that there are Forms of our individual intellects also means that for Plotinus Plato's famous descriptions of our ascent to the contemplation of the Forms—in the *Symposium* and *Phaedrus*, for example, or the allegory of the cave in *Republic* (514a–520a)—can be understood as our ascent to ourselves.

But before we turn the page on the question of Forms of individuals, we should consider whether and how the numerical individuation of intellect-Forms bears on our return to the universal Intellect and beyond. Rist calls attention to the fact that whereas Plato speaks of our deification as "becoming as like God as possible" *(homoiōsis theōi kata to dynaton)*, Plotinus often drops the limiting condition, "as possible."[52] Does this mean, then, that the intellect that would unite with the One can do so without distinction, without *kata to dynaton*? In the very last section of the *Enneads*, 6.9.11, Plotinus writes:

> Since, then, there were not two, but the seer himself was one with the seen (for it was not really seen, but united to him), if he remembers who he became when he was united with that, he will have an image of that in himself. He was one himself, with no distinction in himself either in relation to himself or to other things . . . but there was not even any reason or thought, and he himself was not there, if we must even say this. (6.9.11.4–9, 11–13)

Plotinus is describing the union of the purified intellect with the One: *after* its union the intellect retains an "image" *(eikōn)* of the One in itself; but *in* the moment of its union to the One, is the intellect in any way distinct from the One, especially if the intellect is said not even to be there? This is where numerical individuation is crucial. Plotinus describes union with the One with words (*synaphē, synousia, parousia*) whose prefixes (*syn-*, "together"; *para-*, "alongside") suggest that this union preserves, in the words of R. Arnou, "a certain duality."[53] Rist remarks that "this duality is not, of course, in the One. There is no duality in the One; all duality and otherness is in the others." His answer to his conundrum is that the only way for Plotinus to safeguard the transcendence of the One is to suggest that in such a union the intellect differs from the One only numerically, not qualitatively: "Hence we may conclude that the very means which enable Plotinus to solve his difficulties about Forms of individuals are relevant also to this fundamental problem of how the soul can be held to attain union with the One without the loss of the One's transcendence."[54]

On Beauty, Autoscopy, and Narcissus

With this section and the next, we turn explicitly to the theme of our elevation to the level of Intellect and our return to the One, that is, the mystical enterprise that on my view drives Plotinus's metaphysics. Our return itinerary includes several stages or steps: (i) Our intellect must distill itself from the broader powers of our soul, and that descended intellect must assimilate to its undescended archetype; (ii) restored to its place in the inner life of Intellect, the individual intellect-Form must overcome the syzygy of subject and object, and thus be elevated to the level of the hypostasis Intellect; (iii) the elevated intellect must finally overcome or reverse the primordial procession of Intellect from the One (this last stage we will examine in the next section). This return itinerary, however, betrays the same structure or staging throughout, namely that the self must encounter itself in an autoscopy or "self-seeing" and then overcome that staged duality of seer and seen so as to be elevated to the next stage.

This structure demands that we back up and consider the first *Ennead* Plotinus composed, namely 1.6, "On Beauty," an intense and rousing meditation on beauty in this sensible world, its participation in intelligible beauty, and our life's calling to behold this "absolute beauty" *(auto to kalon)*. Our interest in this treatise includes not only how it narrates our elevation to a vision of intelligible beauty (ii), and a glimpse of what lies behind beauty's veil (iii), but also its famous allusion to the figure of Narcissus. Although relying on a different version of the myth than Ovid's, Plotinus appeals to the figure of Narcissus as a negative exemplar. My suspicion is that Narcissus exemplifies precisely the kind of staged autoscopy that our elevation and return requires on several levels, but is a *negative* exemplar because he fails to overcome the duality of subject and object and so be raised to the next level.

"On Beauty" begins with a question familiar from Plato's two dialogues on beauty, the *Symposium* and *Phaedrus:* What makes something beautiful? And it supplies an equally familiar answer: Whatever is beautiful is so by virtue of its participation *(metoxē)* in the Form of beauty (1.6.2.13). Whatever is fully intelligible is truly beautiful, and vice versa, and only Forms are fully intelligible and so "really exist" *(onta ontōs)* (1.6.5.20–21). Everything else exists as a derivative participant, including us *here.* But we can be fully sustained by a vision of beauty *there:* the goal is "to win this and only this," the "blessed sight" (1.6.7.36–37,34). We come to this by an abandonment or letting-go of our senses, and "wak[ing] another way of seeing, which everyone has but few use" (1.6.8.27–28). We turn this way of seeing on ourselves, as if we were each a sculptor freeing the inner form from its excess of stone:

> Go back into yourself and look; and if you do not yet see yourself beautiful, then, just as someone making a statue *(agalmatos)* which has to be beautiful cuts away here and polishes there and makes one part smooth and clears another till he has given his statue a beautiful face, so you too must cut away excess and straighten the crooked and clear the dark and make it bright, and never stop "working on your statue" *(tektainōn to son agalma)* till the divine glory of virtue shines out on you, till you see "self-mastery enthroned upon its holy seat" *(sōphrosynēn en hagnōi bebōsan bathrō).* (1.6.9.7–16)

The quotations in this passage are both from Plato's *Phaedrus.* The first, "working on your statue" *(tektainōn to son agalma),* is familiar to us from Chapter 1: Plato describes how "everyone chooses his love after his own fashion from among those who are beautiful, and then treats the boy like his very own god, building him up and adorning him as an image *(hoion agalma tektainetai)*" (252d7). The second quotation comes from a passage when the mad lover sees the face of a beautiful boy: "his memory is carried back to the real nature of Beauty, and he sees it again where it stands on the sacred pedestal next to Self-Control" *(kai palin eiden autēn meta sōphrosynēs en hagnōi bathrō bebōsan)* (254b7). Both of these quotations are pulled from Plato's account of the charged, erotic tension between lover and beloved, the tense horizontal axis that makes possible the restoration of the vertical axis or mutual deification. By subsuming the horizontal double of lover and beloved, and all that comes with it (lust, struggle, restraint, cultivation, mirror reflection, images conforming to their archetypes) into the self's relationship to itself, Plotinus has essentially internalized the fragile and fraught dynamics of Platonic *erōs*.[55] All the energy of *erōs* stirs beneath the surface of his placid, almost pacific, description of the sculptor learning to free the form from the stone. Nevertheless some of that passion breaks through earlier, when Plotinus exclaims, "If anyone sees it, what passion *(erōtas)* he will feel, what longing *(pothous)* in his desire to be united with it, what a shock of delight *(ekplagein meth'hēdonēs)*!" (1.6.7.13–14).

At this point in the analogy, the sculptor is working to make the sculpture his perfect likeness and thus to stand before himself, simultaneously seer and seen. The climax of "On Beauty" follows directly on the heels of this staged scene:

> If you have become this, and see it, and are at home with yourself in purity, with nothing hindering you from becoming in this way one, with no inward mixture of anything else, but wholly yourself, nothing but true light . . . when you see that you have become this, then you have become sight; you can trust yourself then; you have already ascended and need no one to show you; concentrate your gaze and see. This alone is the eye that sees the great beauty. (1.6.9.16–25)

Only when the sculptor and the sculpture are one and the same, only at the moment of an autoscopy earned through the practice of *aphairesis* or "clearing-away," does the scene shift from one of seer and seen to one of pure, transparent vision. This passage provides the inspiration for Pierre Hadot's beautiful book *Plotinus, or the Simplicity of Vision*, and also for Ralph Waldo Emerson's description in *Nature* of becoming "a transparent eyeball."[56]

The ascent to the blessed sight of intelligible beauty, however, depends on a perfectly staged autoscopy, one that will give way to pure vision—perfectly staged because pitfalls abound. We must not run after the beauty in bodies, but must know

> that they are images *(eikones)*, traces *(ichnē)*, shadows *(skiai)*, and hurry away to that of which they are images *(eikones)*. For if a man runs to the image and wants to seize it as if it was the reality *(hōs alēthinon)*—like a beautiful reflection *(eidōlou kalou)* playing on the water, which some story somewhere, I think, said riddingly a man wanted to catch *(labein boulētheis)* and sank down into the stream and disappeared—then this man who clings to beautiful bodies and will not let them go, will, like the man in story, but in soul, not in body, sink down into dark depths where intellect has no delight, and stay blind in Hades, consorting with shadows there and here. (1.6.8.6–16)

This is a very clear allusion to the figure of Narcissus, with whom we first began our inquiry into the divine double. Narcissus here is clearly a negative exemplar—but why exactly? Was it that he was running after a beautiful body? Arnold I. Davidson thinks so: "Narcissus represents a moral and spiritual state, the result, after the constitution of the sensible world, of what transpires when the soul *directs its attention toward the body*."[57] Plotinus says that Narcissus wanted to catch *(labein boulētheis)* a reflection shimmering on the water. Was his error, then, that he mistook that image for a body? Perhaps, and if so, the lesson is simple enough: we must discern the difference between image (body) and reality (soul), as Narcissus failed to do.

I suspect, however, that the allusion to Narcissus yields more. Curiously, the word Plotinus uses, *eidōlon* (here rendered "reflection"), is the word Plato uses when he has Socrates tell Alcibiades what we see when we look into the pupil of another's eye, that is, a miniature mirror-image or *eidōlon* (*Alcibiades I* 132e). For Plato, this serves as an analogy for how we come to know ourselves: one looks into another's soul and sees one's *eidōlon* or reflection and this allows for mutual cultivation and deification. I do not think Plotinus's choice of words here is a coincidence, and this leads me to wonder again: How did Narcissus err? Consider in comparison the case of the sculptor: he is removing the excess stone and, quoting *Phaedrus*, "working on the statue," that is, working to free the *agalma* within. Success for the sculptor is to stand before an image or *agalma* of himself, not shimmering on water but standing before him in stone, face-to-face. Hadot insists that the practice results in the sculptor and sculpture being identical, for only if identical can they both dissolve into pure vision. If this is right, then Narcissus was no fool to contemplate his reflection playing over the water's surface. He was in fact on the threshold of a proper autoscopy. His error, then, was not to seek out his own beautiful image, but rather what he did when we saw it: he wanted to seize or catch it *(labein bouletheis)*. Whether the erring had more to do with grasping or with willing (or whether the two can be distinguished), I do not know; but perhaps *this* was his downfall, quite literally.

To invoke Narcissus here is also to insert myself, somewhat reluctantly, into a conversation between Richard Harder, Pierre Hadot, and Julia Kristeva. Harder first raised the question of whether Plotinus was guilty of a kind of "autoeroticism."[58] Whereas Plotinus condemns Narcissus for his fascination with the image of his beautiful body, Harder wonders whether Plotinus replaces that sensible autoeroticism with an intelligible one. After all, the soul is explicitly enjoined to behold itself, beautiful in soul. Is this not merely "a higher kind of autoeroticism"?[59] In her *Tales of Love*, Julia Kristeva follows Harder's lead. First, she takes Narcissus's error to be his failing to see that the image on the water is his own image:

> In this instance the error lies, therefore, in failing to see that the reflection is of none but the self; Narcissus after all is guilty of being unaware of himself as source of the reflection. Let us accept that charge, which indicts Narcissus as being guilty of not knowing himself: he who loves a reflection without knowing it is his own does not, in fact, know who he is.[60]

This is curious, because Ovid, on whose *Metamorphoses* she depends here, is clear that Narcissus *did* realize that the image was his own:

> iste ego sum: sensi, nec me mea fallit imago;
> uror amore mei: flammas moveoque feroque.⁶¹
>
> He is myself! I feel it,
> I know my image now. I burn with love
> Of my own self; I start the fire I suffer.

Kristeva understands Plotinus as "violently antinarcissistic," that is, he is opposed to our mistaking the body for the soul, and thus opposed to our loving the body rather than the soul. But still, she thinks, Plotinus is "Narcissan" if not "Narcissistic."⁶² "Narcissus has been transcended" in that the autoeroticism of the body has been overcome. But Narcissus has been preserved not only on the level of the soul's contemplation of itself (such as in the sculptor / sculpture analogy), but also on the level of the One (to which we will return in the next section).

Kristeva alleges to have drawn on Hadot's work in her interpretation of Plotinus. Davidson, however, has sought to use Hadot to critique Kristeva's charge that Plotinus is a "Narcissan." At issue, it seems, is what we mean by "self" here. Hadot, Davidson insists, is very clear that for Plotinus the soul or the "self" is not first and foremost my particular, individual self. Plotinian autoscopy operates on the level of the self entirely shorn of its individuating qualities:

> In the works of Plotinus, individuality and totality are radically opposed, they mutually repudiate one another: "In becoming 'someone,' one becomes not-All, one adds a negation to the 'All.'" . . . "To seek one's own beauty" does not mean: to see a beauty that pleases "me" because it is "my self," but to see in my "self," that is to say, thanks to my conversion toward interiority, the Beauty that is nothing other than the All in its noetic necessity.⁶³

Hadot (and Davidson) are right that when the seer (self) and seen (beauty) are identical, the "self" is unindividuated. But this dissolution of the individuated self does rely on a face-off between the self and its image (*agalma* or *eidōlon*). When that self and its image are individuated, then the structure is, in Kristeva's terms, Narcissan: a soul beholding its own beauty. But as that self and its image conform to the unindividuated, absolute beauty of intelligibility (as the sculptor / sculpture figure suggests it will precisely by removing the individuating encumbrance of stone), then the autoscopy—at its height—dissolves (or resolves) into a panoscopy, the All's seeing of itself, or pure vision. It seems to me, however, that Kristeva is on to something, namely that the staging of the autoscopy is Narcissan: the self beholds its own image. But Hadot (and Davidson) are right that this Narcissan staging, far from being Narcissistic, sets up a dissolution of seer and seen, self and beauty, into transparent, pure vision. The error of Plotinus's Narcissus, then, is that he was Narcissistic precisely at the moment when he needed to be Narcissan: just as he beheld himself as an image shimmering on the water, he failed to conform himself and his image to absolute beauty, and so instead of dissolving seer and seen into pure vision, he grasped after beauty and sunk down to his death.

We may thus appropriate and apply Kristeva's language of the "Narcissan" structure of Plotinus's metaphysics and mysticism without endorsing her critique of that structure as part of her grand narrative about interiority in the West.[64] Every stage of our return itinerary—(i) through (iii) above—depends on the self's encountering itself as outside itself, as an object to a subject. And if the self is to ascend to a new level, then at every stage the autoscopy in which the self is simultaneously seer and seen must give way to a dissolution of that dualism of subject and object. It would be as if Narcissus beholding his reflection in the water had merged with that image rather than vainly grasping for it.

"On Beauty" mostly narrates that operation at the level of the individual intellect-Form being elevated to the vision of intelligible beauty—in other words, stage (ii) above. But the same structure obtains at the lower level, where the descended intellect must see and recognize itself in its undescended counterpart, the *nous* feasting on the Forms: this encounter gives way to the lower intellect's assimilation to and union with its higher half. That reunified intellect then forms a new subject, which in turn faces its own new object, another intellect-Form, as intelligible object. This new encounter in turn gives way to the intellect's assimilation to and union with the intelligible: this is pure vision, the elevation of the individual intellect to the simple beauty of universal Intellect.

"On Beauty," however, does not stop with the climax of pure vision, with the imperative, "concentrate your gaze and see." We learn, only in the very last lines, that there is something beyond this blessed sight, something beyond intelligible beauty, beyond that which really exists, beyond "the Forms *(ta eidē)* . . . the Ideas *(tas ideas)*" (1.6.9.35–36): "That which is beyond this *(to de epekeina toutou)* we call the nature of the Good, which holds beauty as a screen *(probeblēmenon)* before it . . . the Good is that which is beyond, the 'spring and origin' of beauty" (1.6.9.37–39, 42–44). The Good is that which is defined by its being "beyond" *(epekeina)*. Just as often Plotinus names this beyond "the One," although it is of course beyond all names, including these two.[65] He says that the Good (One) "holds beauty as a screen before it." The verb here is a common enough one, *proballō*, meaning "to throw before." But here it means to throw in front of oneself, perhaps as protection or concealment, as one would a veil or a screen. What we see when we see beauty, even at the height and simplicity of vision, it is still a screen. We cannot see what lies behind the screen because the screen is, so to speak, the very condition of sight. But on this threshold we stand to move from pure vision to union, a movement that follows in reverse the primordial procession of Intellect from the One.

Our Return Home

THREE STAGES (I–III) AND THREE MOVEMENTS (A–C)

Nowhere does Plotinus lay out, once and for all, a clear itinerary for our return home to the One. On my best reconstruction, our return itinerary has three stages, which repeat in reverse the stages of procession and our descent into embodied souls, and each of which overcomes a crucial duality: (i) the overcoming of the difference between the descended and undescended intellect; (ii) the overcoming of the subject and object dualism in the inner life of Intellect; and (iii) the overcoming of the primordial procession of Intellect from the One. In all three stages, the itinerary requires that the self encounter and contemplate its double. For this reason I think it is apt, following Kristeva, to characterize Plotinus's mysticism as "Narcissan," for it is Narcissus who stages this autoscopy but (due to his "Narcissism") fails to follow through on it. To succeed in overcoming the duality is to unite the self to its double, but not as Narcissus sought to do by grasping.

Just as we analyzed the procession of Intellect from the One into a discrete choreography, so too we can analyze the stages of our return itinerary. The scholar who has most successfully mapped (or reconstructed) this itinerary and its choreography is, to my mind, Zeke Mazur.[66] He documents how each stage in our return involves at least three discrete movements, which I adapt as follows: (a) self-reversion: the self turns to face itself in the form of its double; (b) autophany / autoscopy: the double reveals itself to the self; (c) self-unification: the self and the double merge or, to use one of Plotinus's favorite geometrical figures, their two centers join. Narcissus can be understood as having stood on the threshold of return because he succeeded in (a) and (b) but failed in (c).

Let us apply this tripartite choreography to the three stages of our return. The first stage of our return (i) is the distillation of our intellect from among the broader powers of the soul. That distilled intellect then turns in on or reverts to itself, only to discover that its eternal archetype, the individual intellect-Form, exists above it, so to speak, in the intelligible realm. Like a sculptor it frees the form from the encumbering stone and stands before its perfect likeness, its double. This is the moment of autoscopy, or in Mazur's terms, autophany: the face-off of the self and its double before the two unite. The second stage of our return (ii) repeats this choreography but within the inner life of Intellect. The individual intellect-Form, restored to its undescended state, encounters its identical double in the face of another intellect-Form. This is what Plotinus calls a sphere of shining faces, in which each intellectual subject is joined in a syzygy with another intelligible object—again a perfectly staged autoscopy. The subject and object perspectives then unite or merge and the individual intellect is elevated to the pure vision of Intellect, the sum of all individual intellectual subjects and intelligible objects.

This choreography is very clear in 1.6, "On Beauty." Plotinus enjoins his reader to "go back into yourself and look" (1.6.9.7): self-reversion (a). After the figure of the sculptor, he describes how the self stands before its perfect likeness, its double: "if you become this, and see it, and are at home with yourself in purity" (1.6.9.16–18): autophany (b). Finally, the self and its double merge: "with nothing hindering you from becoming in this way one, with no inward mixture of anything else, but wholly yourself, nothing but true light" (1.6.9.17–18): finally, self-unification (c).

This tripartite choreography—(a), (b), and (c)—remains consistent throughout the stages. But something shifts at the end of the second stage. At the height of the ascent in "On Beauty," Plotinus announces to the aspirant, "You have already ascended and need no one to show you; concentrate your gaze and see. This alone is the eye that sees the great beauty" (1.6.9.23–25). The hypostasis Intellect is characterized by determination, that is, it is the collective sum of all the Forms, which are defined and determined as beautiful and intelligible. What is most surprising, then, in "On Beauty" is that the individual intellect elevated to the level of the hypostasis Intellect is described in a manner that breaks with Intellect's perfectly self-contained and determined beauty: "wholly yourself, nothing but true light, not measured by dimensions, or bounded by shape into littleness, or expanded to size by unboundedness, but everywhere unmeasured, because greater than all measure and superior to all quantity" (1.6.9.18–22). As Mazur notes, this description echoes the description of the One of the first deduction of the *Parmenides* (139b–140d), which Plotinus himself adapts to his own account of the transcendent One.[67] Why is it, then, that at the height of our elevation to the level of Intellect, the self begins to show signs of a boundlessness more becoming of the One than of Intellect? Why do cracks begin to appear in the crystalline structure of Intellect?

THE FINAL DIVINE DOUBLE: PRIMORDIAL OTHERNESS

This question brings us to the third stage of our return itinerary (iii), namely, the overcoming or undoing of the primordial procession of

Intellect from the One. Recall that Plotinus speaks of a primordial "otherness" that emerges from the One, turns back on its ineffable source, and in (imperfectly) contemplating its source instantiates itself as Intellect. Plotinus speaks of this primordial otherness as both an "indefinite dyad" (following Platonic and Neo-Pythagorean terminology) and as "intelligible matter" (following Aristotelian terminology). Prior to its turn and instantiation as Intellect, this "otherness" exists as, in Mazur's words, a "liminal, pre-noetic efflux of the One."[68]

Why is this rehearsal of the primordial procession important for understanding our return itinerary? Precisely because the individual intellect-Form that has been elevated to the level of the hypostasis Intellect—that is, the intellect that has passed through stages (i) through (iii)—must again now (a) revert to itself, (b) witness an autophany, and (c) unite with its double (its higher self). The elevated intellect, when it turns inward on itself, discovers that it has one final double, and that double is none other than primordial otherness, the "liminal, prenoetic efflux of the One." In other words, Intellect contains a trace, image, imprint of the One within it, and this trace, image, or imprint is the final divine double, the "indefinite dyad" or "intelligible matter" that occupies the places in between Intellect and the One.

Mazur adduces many passages in support of this reading, but perhaps the best case is found in treatise 6.9, which Porphyry places as the final treatise in the collection. First comes self-reversion (a): Plotinus insists that the soul or intellect "must let go of all outward things and turn altogether to what is within" (6.9.7.17). The following passage speaks of the next two movements, autophany (b) and self-unification (c):

> When therefore the seer sees himself, then when he sees, he will see himself as like this, or rather he will be in union with himself as like this and will be aware of himself as like this since he has become single and simple. But perhaps one should not say "will see," but "was seen," if one must speak of these as two, the seer and the seen, and not both as one—a bold statement. So then the seer does not see and does not distinguish and does

not imagine two, but it is as if he had become someone else and he is not himself and he does not count as his own there, but has come to belong to that and so is one, having joined, as it were, center to center. For here too when the centers have come together they are one, but there is duality when they are separate. This is also how we now speak of "another." For this reason the vision is hard to put into words. For how could one announce that as another when he did not see, there when he had the vision, another, but one with himself? (6.9.10.9–21)

The intellect that turns in on itself finds and sees itself there—or rather finds that it is seen, beheld by its double. This staged autophany and autoscopy (b) then give way to a union of self and other (c), except that their union makes it difficult to speak of "self" or anything "other" than it because the two have now become one.

But who exactly is this self / other that appears and with whom the elevated intellect unites? The intellect that unites with this final double "becomes, not substance, but 'beyond substance' *(epekeina ousias)* by this converse" (6.9.11.42–43). Plato famously describes the Form Good as "beyond substance" or "beyond being" in *Republic* 509b3, which serves as a textual foundation for Plotinus's insistence on the One as beyond Intellect, Being, and Beauty. The crucial point here is that, in the final stage of the return itinerary, the intellect sees and unites with its higher self or divine double and so it is brought "beyond" *(epekeina)* the level of universal Intellect. Plotinus then says that we each have within us "a likeness *(homoiōma)* of that"—"that" referring to the One beyond being. This likeness or "image" *(eikōn)* of the One within us is that primordial otherness that is "above" Intellect but still "below" the One. In another passage, Plotinus explains that the intellect, "because it is Intellect, it sees [what is above Intellect], when it does see it, with that of it which is not Intellect" (5.5.8.23). When we converse—or better, "have intercourse" *(prosomilei)*—with that likeness in ourselves, that image within us that is not Intellect, we are united to that which is beyond Intellect.

LOVING REFORMS WANTING

But this is not the "end of the journey" (*Republic* VII 5323e3). The intellect that has united to its double, primordial otherness, is still in some crucial sense alienated from the One. Just as with the procession, so with the return: the position of primordial otherness (indefinite dyad, intelligible matter) is liminal—it is no longer simply part of the One, but it is not yet so other as to be instantiated as a distinct hypostasis, Intellect. As we noted much earlier when discussing the procession of Intellect from the One, the primordial otherness is characterized by "want[ing] *(boulomenou)* to be one but is not one" and "somehow dar[ing] *(tolmēsas)* to stand away *(apostēnai)* from the One" (6.9.5.26–27; 29–30). These few lines provide a crucial clue: the primordial otherness audaciously wants to stand apart from, and so against, its source *(apostēnai* from *aphistēmi* meaning "to revolt"). In other words, the very emergence of otherness from the One is an act of revolt, of daring *(tolmē)* to want or wish for more—but a wish for *what* more, exactly? In short, it wants *to see:* to stand sufficiently apart from itself so that it can see itself, not knowing that by standing apart, it becomes so other that when it turns and sees, it does not see itself per se because it has become a distinct hypostasis staring now not at itself, but the source from which it has become alienated.

All this is to say that the intellect that has been united to its final divine double, primordial otherness, has succeeded only in restoring itself to this primordial state of wanting, daring, and rebellion. Again, this cannot be the "end of the journey" (*Republic* VII 5323e3). To return to the embrace of the One, the intellect, united to primordial otherness, must find a way to undo its daring desire to stand apart, must release the ambition for autoscopy. We should recall that in 1.6, "On Beauty," Narcissus is faulted precisely for "wanting to seize" *(boulomenos labein)* the image of himself he sees on the water. His desire to seize it causes him to fall in and sink to his death (a different version of Narcissus's end than Ovid's). It is unclear whether it is the wanting or the seizing that is Narcissus's sin, or even if the two can de distinguished. But it is curious that both primordial otherness and Narcissus are faulted for their willing or wanting, in one case to stand apart from its source, in the other to seize rather than unite with his image-double. It is not at all clear, however, whether and how Plotinus ever explains how we should reorient ourselves to the One such that we can overcome Narcissus's cloying desire or, more acutely, the rebellious desire of primordial otherness and so fold back into the silent embrace of the One.

Let me forward one possible interpretation, inspired by Pierre Hadot. He argues that universal Intellect, including its constituents, the Forms, does not "kindle our love."[69] What animates the intelligible world of beauty and being is the grace bestowed on it by the One or the Good: "Each [form] is what it is by itself; but it becomes desirable *(epheton)* when the Good colors it, giving a kind of grace *(charitas)* to them and passionate love *(erōtas)* to the desirers *(ephiemena)*" (6.7.22.5–7). The word "grace" *(charis)*, then, is Plotinus's own, but Hadot is clearly alert to the fact that readers may accuse him of Christianizing Plotinus.[70] He insists that he is not, and that "this notion of gratuitousness" was not borrowed from Christianity, but is the only proper phenomenological conclusion of Plotinus's philosophical reflection.[71] Hadot explains, "What Plotinus calls the Good is thus, at the same time, that which, by bestowing grace, gives rise to love, and that which, by awakening love, causes grace to appear. The Good is what all things desire; it is what is desirable in an absolute sense."[72]

On Hadot's reading, then, Plotinus regards love as the only proper orientation in the world, and what orients us, ultimately, to the Good (One). But unlike Plato's homoerotic love, which uses appetitive *erōs* as a rung on the ladder of the ascent to the Forms, Plotinian love "by contrast, waits for ecstasy, ceasing all activity, establishing the soul's faculties in complete repose, and forgetting everything, so as to be completely ready for the divine invasion."[73] If Hadot is right, and the soul's ascent to the One is kindled by the grace of the Good coloring everything, then when the intellect united to its final double, primordial otherness, wishes to fold back into the One, it is this love which has sped it along that ensures the aspirant will not simply stall at the liminal level of daring, willing, and rebelling.

If the ascendant soul is "moved by [the Good] to love from the beginning," this is because the Good itself *is* love. In a remarkable passage, Plotinus writes that the Good "is beloved *(erasmion)*, love *(erōs)*, and love of itself *(autou erōs)*." Kristeva fixes on this passage as evidence that the Good's autoeroticism implies that "God is Narcissus."[74] I think this is a misreading of the significance of Narcissus for Plotinus. On the contrary, what is most significant, to my mind, is the fact that in this same treatise Plotinus considers whether and how the One might be said to be free, and along the way rejects such definitions of the One's freedom as "self-determined" and "self-ruling" because the reflexivity of those definitions contains a duality that is inappropriate to the radical simplicity of the One. In other words, the One cannot determine or rule itself because it is one. In the context of the treatise, then, what is most remarkable about the description of the Good as "beloved *(erasmion)*, love *(erōs)*, and love of itself *(autou erōs)*" is precisely that self-love does *not* seem to violate the radical simplicity of the One. In other words, there is something about the reflexivity of love, in contrast to other reflexive relationships, that is perfectly in keeping with the One's simplicity. Love is not an "activity" that, if added to the One, compromises its simplicity.[75] Rather, as Hadot says, "in the final analysis, the Good itself is Love."[76]

To return, then, to our broader aim, that is, to understand how Plotinus conceives of the final stage of our return itinerary: We were wrestling with how the intellect, united to its final divine double, primordial otherness, might avoid the alienating wishing, daring, and rebelling of that first "efflux" from the One. I have suggested, following Hadot, that Plotinus regards love as that which attracts us to the One, by virtue of the grace it bestows on everything posterior to its absolute anteriority. Any intellect that has passed through the three stages of the return itinerary has been spurred along by this divine initiative. This love, then, might be said to reorient the primordial otherness to which the intellect has finally united, to annul its ambition for autoscopy, and lead it back to its ineffable source. This love, and only this love, is capable of this final step because love is somehow the only relationship—if that is even the right word—that the One can be said to have to itself and still not compromise its radical simplicity. If this is right, then the drama of the divine double, our return itinerary, ends when love reforms whatever remains that is other than the One.

SELF-UNIFICATION = SELF-ANNIHILATION

Love is what transports the intellect from union with its final divine double, primordial otherness (the indeterminate dyad or intelligible matter), to union with the One itself. This final union, however, is distinguished from self-unification in the two previous stages along the itinerary because union here is self-annihilation, that is, "a final phase in which even this autophanous self must be dissolved ... so as to attain either absolute coalescence or identification with the supreme principle."[77] The self that unites with the primordial emergence now lovingly longs to return to the One, reforming primordial otherness's wanting to stand apart. "There is nothing in between" the intellect and the ineffable One now, "nor are there still two but both are one; nor could you still make a distinction while [the One] is present; lovers and their beloveds here below imitate *(mimēsis)* this in their will to be united" (6.7.34.13–16). Aristophanes's tragic vision from Plato's *Symposium* thus returns. Lovers seek a reunion that the gods will not, or perhaps cannot, grant them. Plotinus adapts this tragedy to his own philosophical comedy: earthly lovers may forever find reunion deferred, but lovers of the One can enjoy the archetypal reunion of which earthly love is only an image or imitation.

Such enjoyment, however, comes at the cost of soul and intellect's defining features. Plotinus speaks of the soul suffering "a kind of confusion and annihilation *(aphanisasa)* of the intellect remaining within her" (6.7.35.34–35).[78] When the Good "rests upon" this soul and its annihilated intellect—or rather they come to rest in it because it contains them—then

> the soul does not move then either, because [the Good] does not move. Nor, then, is it soul, because [the Good] does not live, but is above life. Nor is it intellect, because [the Good] does not think either; for one must be made like. [The Good] does not even think that it does not think. (6.7.35.43–45)

We must be careful here, however: What exactly do we mean by annihilation? The verb *aphanizō* literally means to render something invisible, or make something disappear. But it can also mean something far stronger: to destroy or obliterate. Following Mazur, I have translated it as "annihilate" rather than Armstrong's "annul." What might it mean here, in the context of the self's union with the One?

If the self that would unite with the One is stripped of its qualities as soul (movement, life) and intellect (thought), does it thereby cease to exist? In a sense, yes, because for Plotinus being obtains at the level of Intellect. Following Plato, he regards the Good (One) as "beyond being" *(epekeina ousias)*. Is it fair, then, to say that the self is annihilated in union with the One? Again, yes, if we recognize that the *nihil* or nothingness into which the self is ushered (in an*nihil*ation) is the "beyond being" of the One. What then remains of the self in this self-annihilating union? Mazur describes this union as "coalescence" and "identification." The "co" in coalescence should remind us of Rist's claim (following Arnou) that even, in fact especially, at the moment of union with the One, there is "a certain duality" in the union. Rist argues that the strictly numerical differentiation of otherwise identical intellects applies to the strictly numerical differentiation of the self and the One in their final union. The only "otherness" that remains, then, is the fact that *two* centers overlap. In other words, self-annihilating union of the self and the One is an identification of the two, but an identification that preserves some numerical differentiation. Rist warns that this *must* be the case lest the One compromise its transcendence.

I am inclined to agree with Rist, but with one significant qualification. Strictly speaking, we cannot even refer to the differentiation between self and One in union as a *numerical* differentiation because number properly exists only at the level of Intellect (and below). The indefinite dyad that primordially emerges from the One and is eventually instantiated as Intellect is therefore a "dyad" or "two" that is prior to any number. In this sense, we speak of the indefinite dyad not as "two" but the "not-One." Perhaps this can help us deepen our understanding of mystical union according to Plotinus. The self is stripped of its defining features as soul and intellect, annihilated or elevated to the "beyond being" of the One, and united thereto in a union in which only the thinnest of cracks can be seen—a differentiation that is prior even to number, prior to our ability to count them as two, a differentiation whose only content is the "not" in the indefinite dyad's being the "not-One." Thus even at the "end of the journey," final union with the One, there remains a hairline crack or difference between the two centers, self and One. It is a difference so subtle that we cannot even count the two centers as two because they exist prior to number, a gap so thin that there is no longer any internal "otherness" wanting to reemerge. The crack of this differentiating "not," however, preserves what Arnou calls "a certain duality" in the radical simplicity of the One, a specter or perhaps a distant memory of the divine doubles that have led the self home.

6

Whither the Divine Double?

WE HAVE LINGERED in the second and third centuries, when interest in the divine double seems to peak in the Eastern Mediterranean: Christian, Manichaean, and Neoplatonic sources (and perhaps others) evince an abiding interest in this figure. But what becomes of this interest in subsequent centuries? Does it abide or abate? The answer to that question, of course, depends on the specific religious and philosophical tradition in question. The clearest answer is the case of Manichaeism: the divine double remains at the heart of the ever-expanding tradition of reflection on the nature of Mani himself. Truth be told, in the case of Manichaeism we have not exactly been lingering in the third century, but have been relying on later sources as triangulating witnesses to the tradition's very early and widespread interest in the figure of Mani's twin-companion. The *Kephalaia* date from about 400 CE and purport to record Mani's own teachings; the *Cologne Mani Codex* dates from the fifth century, although the compilation of which it is a miniature copy may have been assembled as early as the late third century. Thus, we can confidently answer that in the case of Manichaeism there does not seem to be any cooling of interest in the figure of the divine double in the fourth or fifth centuries, or thereafter. Most of that interest centers on Mani himself, the *oua ouōt* or "single one" who is himself the union of the Apostle of Light and the twin-companion. In the *Kephalaia*, however, we have glimpsed how the tradition also shows signs of bending the divine double to bear on everyday practitioners: they too may have a cosmic alter ego, the Light Form from which they are derived and with which they will reunite after death. And while we have focused on relatively early, Western sources (such as Greek, Coptic, and to some extent Arabic), later Eastern sources (such as Turkish, Sogdian, and Chinese) also evince an abiding interest in Mani's twin-companion.[1]

The case of Neoplatonism is more complicated and consequently more interesting. At the center of Plotinus's elaborate map of our descent into bodies and our ascent to Intellect and the One is his firm conviction that our intellect never fully descends from its proper place in the intelligible heights. This is our anchor above, from which we can safely pull ourselves up out of the bodies in which our intellects sojourn. In the wake of Plotinus's death, however, a sharp disagreement erupts between two of his students over precisely this issue. Porphyry of Tyre (ca. 234–ca. 305), whom we have met as the editor of the *Enneads*, adheres to his teacher's position that the descended intellect enjoys unbroken contact with its undescended counterpart and so can ascend by its own contemplative efforts. Iamblichus of Chalcis (ca. 245–ca. 325), on the contrary, insists that the intellect descends completely into the body and is cut off from the inner life of universal Intellect.[2] Iamblichus would then seem to threaten the entire enterprise of Plotinian metaphysics and soteriology by his denial of our divine double. But in fact he does not. He too insists on a higher principle residing within us, what he calls "another principle *(hetera archē)* of the soul above all nature and generation" or simply "the one of the soul" *(to hen tēs psychēs)*.[3] The difference is that for Iamblichus this principle within us is fully alien to us, obscure to our own sight, and inaccessible to our own feeble efforts—the self is therefore profoundly "self-alienated" *(allotriōthen)* or "made other to itself" *(heteroiousthai pros heautēn)*.[4]

Like Plotinus and Porphyry, then, Iamblichus held that the self has what Gregory Shaw calls a "dual reference," but the crucial difference between the two parties had to do with how to *engage* that duality.[5] Plotinus believed that one's own contemplative efforts were sufficient to distill the intellect from the broader powers of the soul, and to conform the descended image to its undescended archetype. Consequently he put no stock in ritual practices to aid in our return; having been invited by a friend to make sacrifices at the local temples, Plotinus once infamously quipped, "The gods ought to come to me, not I to them."[6] Iamblichus, descendant of a long line of pagan priests from Syria, bristled at the suggestion that traditional religious practice might be obsolete. He also thought that such confidence in our own contemplative efforts betrayed Titanic hubris. Just as the principle within us is fully alien to us—after all, "the divine has nothing in common with us"—so the activation of that principle must come from outside us *(exothen)*.[7] Thankfully, it has, and abundantly so: the religious liturgies of Greece, Syria, and Egypt (among others)—inscrutable to our discursive reason—were given to us by the gods as the alien words that can awaken the alien principle in us. On our own, we are "weak and small, possessed by a congenital nothingness *(oudaneia)*."[8] And yet,

> the awareness of our own nothingness *(oudaneia)* when we compare ourselves to the gods, makes us turn spontaneously to prayer. And from our supplication, in a short time we are led up to that one to whom we pray, and from our continual intercourse we obtain a likeness to it, and from imperfection we are gradually embraced by divine perfection.[9]

The gods have given us the ancient prayers with which to activate our alien principle, and so we can become theurgists, that is, "chaperones" or "cooperators" as the divine meets the divine within us.[10] But unless we first accept our own nothingness, the full weight of embodiment, what Shaw enticingly calls the "wounds" of our incarnation, our Titanic ambition to storm the heavens will only keep us further enslaved in dark matter.

As it turns out, Iamblichus carried the day, and the subsequent Neoplatonic tradition increasingly embraced his theory and practice of theurgy. For our purposes, he signals an important shift in the Neoplatonic tradition of the divine double. Iamblichus imagines our divine alter ego to be more fully *alter* or "other" than Plotinus does or, for that matter, any of the other witnesses we have surveyed. He pushes the union of the self and its double more squarely into the realm of paradox, inscrutable to discursive reason, almost to a coincidence of opposites: we are fully human and fully divine, but the latter only because of the former, homeward bound only because fully exiled. And we engage that paradox precisely through ritual and revelation, not reason. The full story of this shift in the tradition of the divine double within Neoplatonism, and its obvious affinities with the Christological, sacramental and mystical theologies of Christianity in the fourth and subsequent centuries, deserves to be told in greater detail.[11]

The case of Christianity is no less complicated or interesting. Throughout this book I have sought to bring to light the peculiar notion of selfhood that runs through the ancient sources, and how it contributes to the articulation of what in Christian theology is often termed the doctrine of "deification" or "divinization" (*theosis, theopoiēsis*), that is, the conviction that we are each called upon, in the words of Plato's Socrates, "to become like God" (*Theaetetus* 176b). Texts and traditions associated with the apostle Judas Thomas the Twin are not often included when scholars tell the story of the development of the Christian doctrine of deification. That story usually centers on such figures as Irenaeus of Lyons (fl. second century) and especially the Alexandrian theologians, Clement (150–between 211 and 215), Origen (ca. 185–ca. 254), and Athanasius (ca. 293–373).[12] Clement is famous for his formula "The Word of God became a human so that you may learn from a human how a human may become God," which Athanasius sharpens as "[The Word] became human so that we might become god."[13] For Athanasius, it is Christ the Incarnate Word (the Son *homoousios* or "consubstantial" with God the Father, as the Nicene Creed of 325 insists) who as a sacrifice on the cross atones for humanity's sins and who in his resurrection invites us to participate in his full divinity, to become evermore like the eternal and consubstantial Word.[14] With the unambiguous victory of the pro-Nicene party at the Council of Constantinople in 381, Athanasius's legacy and that of his Cappadocian supporters (Basil of Caesarea, Gregory of Nazianzus, and Gregory of Nyssa) was secure. His doctrine of deification was not part of the Nicene Creed in 325 or its revision at Constantinople in 381. But his authority as the architect of and tireless advocate for Trinitarian orthodoxy lent his other views, such as the doctrine of deification, an enormous degree of prestige. By the end of the fourth century there was not much room for a competing doctrine of deification in the newly established Christian orthodoxy of the empire.

But even if there had been room, it is unlikely that the texts and traditions associated with the apostle Judas Thomas (much less Tatian and Valentinus) would have been tolerated in those circles. Already our third- and fourth-century witnesses make it clear that the *Gospel of Thomas* did not receive a warm welcome among the forerunners and architects of that orthodoxy. Such figures as Hippolytus (ca. 170–ca. 235), Origen, Eusebius of Caesarea (fl. fourth century), Cyril of Jerusalem (ca. 315–386), Jerome (ca. 347–419 / 420), and Ambrose (339–397) knew of and disapproved of the gospel.[15] Their disapproval, however, does not establish that they were much familiar with that gospel. By and large they are satisfied to name it as another instance of the proliferation of heterodox literature, another false gospel to mislead the masses. So Eusebius compiles a list of apocryphal works, "in order that we might know them and the writings which are put forward by heretics under the name of the apostles containing gospels such as those of Peter, and of Thomas, and of Matthias, and of some others besides."[16] Origen may have borrowed from the *Gospel of Thomas* in his own commentary on the Gospel of John. But even if I am right, Origen remains an outlier.

Cyril of Jerusalem is convinced that the *Gospel of Thomas* was written not by Jesus's apostle Judas Thomas, but instead by one of Mani's own disciples named Thomas.[17] However fantastic this suggestion may be, it points to an important reality for the afterlife of the texts and traditions associated with the apostle Judas Thomas. There is ample evidence that Manichaeans embraced these texts—the *Acts of Thomas*, the "Hymn of the Pearl," and perhaps even the *Gospel of Thomas*—as they sought to form a canon of Christian writings that might complement Mani's own.[18] No doubt the encratism of the *Acts* appealed to a Manichaean ethic of sexual renunciation (at least among the elect), and the notion of the "single one" *(oua ouōt)* or unity-in-duality in the *Gospel of Thomas* was, I suspect, an influence on early Manichaean reflection on the nature of Mani's own selfhood (such as one finds in the *Kephalaia*). But the most relevant point is simply that as Manichaean interest in these texts grew, their viability in Christian circles very likely diminished.

The texts and traditions of the second and third centuries associated with Judas Thomas offer, then, an early but parallel doctrine of deification. In contrast to the Alexandria tradition that finds fruition in Athanasius, however, these texts are not much interested in the atoning sacrifice of Christ on the cross or his resurrection from the dead. Instead, their understanding of deification focuses on Jesus as a teacher and the apostle Judas Thomas as the "twin" of Jesus, and imagines that all Christians are thus called to be twins of Jesus (which is to say, Jesus's equals). It also offers a theological anthropology that corresponds to this doctrine of deification. It is an understanding of selfhood as simultaneously one and two, the self and its divine double, that together constitute a new self, a unity-in-duality. But if the doctrine of deification associated with the divine double faded from the scene after the rise of conciliar orthodoxy in the fourth and fifth centuries and the appropriation of those texts associated with Judas Thomas by the Manichaeans, what became of this peculiar notion of selfhood?[19] Did it survive, and if so, how?

With this question I would like to end by proposing the transposition and transformation of the divine double into two new domains. In order even to entertain this proposal, however, we must agree to look for the divine double in a new aspect. We will not find him in his usual guise: our heavenly twin, divine alter ego, or even intelligible archetype. It is, I think, safe to say that the *figure* of the divine double does recede from view in the history of Christianity with the advent of conciliar orthodoxy. And yet I propose that although the *figure* recedes, in fact the *structure* of the divine double reappears in two important philosophical and theological discourses of late antiquity: the problem of evil or "theodicy," and Christology—specifically, how the Incarnate Christ is understood to be both human and divine.[20]

The Problem of Evil: God's Double

What is evil? When we call something "evil," what exactly in it or about it is evil? Can we isolate that and know evil *in itself*? These questions are sufficiently pressing as to be nearly ubiquitous. And however pressing they may feel, they are equally, if not more, frustrating. So frustrating in fact that we customarily group these questions and the attempted answers together as a "problem": the problem of evil. The problem of evil is most acute in a monistic or monotheistic framework, where a single first principle or god is the source of everything and—so we often worry—also somehow the source of evil. If God is good and God created everything, how and why is there evil? In modernity we have come to call this investigation "theodicy," on the understanding that it threatens to call the very righteousness *(dikē)* of God *(theos)* into question.[21] In the ancient Mediterranean world, Jewish, Christian, and "pagan" monotheists—as well as dualist Manichaeans and Zoroastrians—wrestled with this dilemma. The prophet Mani taught that good and evil are two irreducible and opposing forces or elements into whose violent drama we find ourselves thrown. The Jewish tradition, though unquestionably monotheistic, displayed a surprising comfort with the idea that evil exists as a chaotic menace that God does not so much vanquish as try to contain.[22]

I wish to focus our attention on one important and influential thread of theodicy in late antiquity where the structure of the divine double reappears, a thread that began among Platonist philosophers and continued among Christian theologians. According to this thread, evil does not, strictly speaking, exist at all. Although we can and should speak of evil things—persons, actions, or events—we cannot specify, speak of, or know evil itself. Evil is not. If we must speak of it, our speech fails us, because evil is nothing, nonbeing, and language is not equipped to speak of nothing. Evil haunts our world, reducing things that do exist to worse versions of themselves. Sometimes this approach is called a "privative" theory of evil because evil does not have its own existence, but is simply the privation of existence. The clear advantage of this approach is that, on the one hand, it exonerates God from responsibility for evil's existence, precisely because evil has none, and on the other hand, it permits us to speak of evil things, things that have fallen under the sway of nothing or nonbeing.

Although a great deal of attention has been given to this privative theory of evil, a crucial and unsettling feature of the tradition remains largely unexplored. Very often its proponents, in trying to specify evil's peculiar nonbeing, will describe evil in a manner nearly indistinguishable from God. Platonists after Plotinus agree that the first principle (the One or the Good) is the cause of all the things that are, material and immaterial, but itself transcends being. Christians insist that the one uncreated God created *ex nihilo*, that is, from out of nothing. In other words, for anything to exist, there must be something or someone outside of or beyond it who calls it into existence—this "something else" is God for the Christians, the One for the Platonists. Evil cannot have existence because, if it did, either (the One) God would have caused it, in which case (the One) God cannot be said to be good, or else some other principle or deity caused it, in which case (the One) God is not alone but has a competitor in causation (dualism). The move to deny evil any existence would seem to avoid either pitfall, but in fact, I argue, it does not. By denying evil any existence, this tradition in effect puts evil exactly where (the One) God is (or is not): outside of the category of being. The proponents of this tradition work to protect themselves from this disturbing implication by insisting that we can distinguish between the nonbeing of God and the nonbeing of evil. Their efforts are, not surprisingly, troubled by the fact that the criteria of differentiation obtain only in the world of existence.

Let me be more specific by first saying a few words about this thread in Plato and the Neoplatonists, and then turning briefly to those Christian theologians in their wake. One would be hard-pressed to find a theory of evil in the Platonic corpus, but there are a handful of relevant remarks scattered throughout the dialogues. By far and away, the most important passage from Plato dealing with evil is found in the *Theaetetus*:

> But it is not possible, Theodorus, that evil should be destroyed—for there must *(anankē)* always be something opposed *(hypenan-*

tion) to the good; nor is it possible that it should have its seat in heaven. But it must inevitably *(ex anankēs)* haunt human life, and prowl about this earth. That is why a man should make all haste to escape from earth to heaven; and escape means becoming as like God as possible *(homoiōsis theōi kata to dynaton)*; and a man becomes like God when he becomes just and pure, with understanding. (176a–b)

The end of this passage is familiar to us by now, as it contains Plato's proof-text for a doctrine of deification: "becoming as like God as possible." But notice that the imperative of deification follows on a short discussion of evil, in which two features of evil are established: first, that it is somehow necessary *(anankē)*; second, that it is opposed or contrary to the good, more precisely *sub*contrary *(hypenantion)* to the good.

Plotinus provides us our first theory of evil, and it takes up precisely these two features.[23] As for the *necessity* of evil, Plotinus takes Plato to mean that procession from the One runs its course to its very end, and at its end is matter *(hylē)*.[24] The furthest edge or extremity of procession is a stubborn substrate—but without it the universe or "the All" would be incomplete. And this necessary substrate, this "underlying matter," Plotinus insists, is evil (1.8.7). What about evil's *opposition* to the good?[25] Because matter is evil, material beings are caught between their recalcitrant material substrate and the intelligible forms that attempt to mold that stiff clay. By impeding the work of the forms, matter pulls material beings from higher to lower levels of being and intelligibility. What we recognize as evil in the world is simply the result of what we might call the "drag" of matter.

On the one hand, then, the opposition of evil to the good is an opposition of *sub*contrariety: recalling Plato's *hypenantion* or *sub*contrary, Plotinus figures it as corruption and infection. Plotinus says that the first principle, the Good, and its last procession, evil matter, together serve as "contrary principles" *(ex enantiōn)* in the universe (1.8.7). Notice that the prefix *hyp-* has been dropped and the two are no longer sub- but full contraries. The dualism is even more striking elsewhere in other passages, such as when he says that "just as there is absolute good . . . so there must be absolute evil" (1.8.3).

In what is to my mind the most remarkable passage from his treatise on evil, Plotinus asks, "How do we *know* evil? How do we *know* matter?" He is not asking how we recognize something as evil, or how we apprehend a material being. Instead, he is asking how we know evil *qua* evil, matter *qua* matter. The question is difficult precisely because one can properly know only beings. And because evil matter has a sort of form of nonexistence, falls *below* being, so to speak, strictly speaking we should not be able to know it. But of course the same is true of the One—we cannot *know* it because it is not a being. And yet, as we have seen, some of the most passionate passages in Plotinus concern precisely how we can return to the One, commune with it, unite with it. And here, in *Ennead* 1.8.9, Plotinus, it seems, is wondering whether and how we might do the same with evil.

First of all, he says, "because it is unbounded . . . we know it by removal" (1.8.9). Removal—*aphairesis* or "clearing-away"—is also a crucial practice for our return to the ineffable One. It is a sculptural term, made famous by Plotinus in "On Beauty" (1.6.9) in which he recommends that we become our own sculptors, and remove or clear away the stone that hides our divine image in the rough rock. But here Plotinus imagines us doing the same operation in order to know evil. He goes on:

> But how do we *know* what has absolutely no part in form? By absolutely taking away all form, we call that in which there is no form matter; in the process of taking away *(aphairountes)* all form we apprehend formlessness in ourselves, if we propose to look at matter. So this which sees matter is another intellect which is not intellect *(nous allos houtos, ou nous)*, it presumes to see what is not its own. (1.8.9)

Although "we call that in which there is no form matter," we could equally call that in which there is no form the One. But following him here, notice that as we pursue our knowledge of evil, and *remove* all form—again, like a sculptor—we apprehend absolute formlessness, and we apprehend it *in ourselves*. Like the One, evil matter is not an object we encounter but rather a formless reality (if that is even the right word) that we apprehend as always already in us, but exceeding us. And what allows us to apprehend this dimension is "another intellect which is not intellect," a faculty Plotinus can specify only by means of yet another negation.

The tension between affirmation and negation continues to heighten as Plotinus struggles to give voice to how we might see and so know our own innermost contrary, the darkness of ineffable evil matter.

> As an eye withdraws itself from the light so that it may see the darkness and not see it—leaving the light is so that it may see the darkness, since with the light it cannot see it; but without something it cannot see it, but only not see—that it may be able to see in the way it is possible to see darkness; so intellect, leaving its own light in itself and as it were going outside itself *(exō hautou proelthōn)* and coming to what is not its own *(eis ta mē hautou elthōn)*, by not bringing its own light with it experiences something contrary to itself *(tounantion)*, that it may see its own contrary *(enantion)*. (1.8.9)

I won't pretend to do justice to this short passage, but consider how heightened and fraught Plotinus's prose is here—his words are set against themselves: light and darkness, sight and blindness, going out and coming in. We might be forgiven if we mistook this description of our approach to evil as a description of our approach to the One. After all, this passage crescendos with a description of an ecstasy—the intellect's "going outside itself"—so as to encounter and experience its own contrary. What is its contrary? Evil of course—or is it the One? Plotinus says that to experience evil is like trying to see darkness. But let me put it to you this way: If you have been plunged into the darkness, how can you distinguish evil from the One? How do you make a distinction when you are ecstatically experiencing your ontological contrary? In the darkness, just how much weight can the prepositions *beyond* or *below* bear for distinguishing the One from evil?

Proclus offers a sharp alternative to Plotinus's view in his treatise *On the Existence of Evils*.[26] For Proclus, Plotinus has veered off course, from monism to dualism. While some admire Plotinus's subtle, sophisticated balance between a single first principle, the One, and its necessary and opposite counterpart, evil matter, Proclus regards this as incoherent. Because evil matter is the last but necessary procession of the One, Proclus understandably insists that for Plotinus the One is still ultimately the cause of evil. And according to his understanding of causality, a cause is, in a greater sense, whatever its effect is; so if the One is the cause of evil, then the One must be more evil than evil. But conversely, effects revert to their cause, that is, they strive to be more like their cause. So if the One or the Good is the cause of evil, then evil would revert to the Good, that is, it would strive to be more and more like the Good. The two horns of this dilemma are captured nicely in Proclus's critique of Plotinus: "the good, as the cause of evil, would be evil, and evil, as being produced from the good, would be good" (31,20–1).

Proclus insists that matter cannot, strictly speaking, oppose the Good, cannot stand on its own as a contrary to the Good. Anything that exists, insofar as it exists, is good. This includes matter, which, *however* it exists, certainly for Proclus still exists, and so must be good. For Proclus, like Plotinus, evil does not exist on its own, but only in or alongside other things. But he pushes back against Plotinus in part by returning to the passage we discussed earlier, *Theaetetus* 176, and calling attention to the fact that Plato specifies how evil opposes the good. As I have mentioned, when Plato says that "there must always be something *opposed* to the good," the precise opposition is *hypenantion*, a *sub*contrary. Evil does not oppose the good on equal footing, such that good and evil would be members of the same genus; rather, Proclus insists, Plato is careful to say that evil opposes good, but from *below*, not as its equal.

But where does this leave the ontology of evil? First of all, contrary to Plotinus, Proclus insists that there is no absolute evil. In fact, it is better not to speak of evil but rather of evils, in the plural, because all that we can speak about are beings in which evil appears, in or alongside them, impeding their proper being. If we are forced to speak of evil itself, then evil should be understood as a *parhypostasis*, a by-product of or a parasite on beings. This bug afflicts only certain beings, what Proclus calls "intermittent participants." No need to linger over this term, except to say that in the great procession from the One to matter, Proclus thinks that cracks, so to speak, necessarily appear in the lower orders of beings. These beings do not participate continuously in the intelligible forms, but only intermittently—they flicker, as it were, and in those breaks in their participation the parasite of evil finds its entry. This, by the way, is how Proclus explains the *necessity* of evil. So even though both Plotinus and Proclus affirm the necessity of evil and its opposition to the good, following *Theaetetus* 176, they differ on how to understand that necessity and opposition.

There is certainly something elegant in Proclus's solution. There doesn't seem to be a whiff of the dualism on offer in Plotinus, and evil's ontology becomes even more elusive than in Plotinus. You might think that Proclus has won the day, solved the problem, and sharply distinguished evil from the One. But consider the following: Yes, evil falls outside of being, below it as *parhypostasis* and subcontrary. And yet evil still haunts being, and in order to gesture at this ghostly ontology, Proclus is forced to use negations and metaphors—two of the principal linguistic strategies of any negative theology. Furthermore, Proclus insists that evils cannot exist on their own or appear as such, but can exist or appear only in or alongside beings. But this makes for an interesting parallel with the One, which also cannot exist because it exceeds existence, cannot appear as itself but only in its effects, namely beings. So it would seem that we are veiled from both, from both evil *and* the One.

Finally, Proclus even concedes that evil is "somehow" *(pōs)* uncaused *(anaition)*. Of course for it to be caused would be to reinscribe it into the order of beings, and then Proclus would find himself in the same dilemma as Plotinus. But this is a remarkable concession precisely because within Proclus's own system, only the One is uncaused. As Plato writes in the *Timaeus* (28a): "Now everything that comes to be must of necessity come to be by the agency of some cause, for it is impossible for anything to come to be without a cause." And so just as we are rescued from some of the problems inherent in Plotinus's account of evil, problems that suggested a deep and unsettling parallel between evil matter and the One, so with Proclus we are delivered again to this same unsettling parallel in which evil and the One emerge as both uncaused. For Proclus the goal is to exonerate the One from responsibility for the existence of evils in the world. But in order to do so, you might say that he has to make evil, like god, uncaused. Or to put it more bluntly: the only way to save god from evil is to make evil a god.

Plotinus and Proclus offer two alleged solutions to the problem of evil, but in both of them evil comes to look a lot like the One's double. This is, I propose, the first transposition and transformation of the divine double. In fact, the very name "divine double" is ambiguous: it could refer to our own divine double, or the divine's own double. This book is entitled *Our Divine Double* precisely to dispel that ambiguity, or rather to defer it until now, when we see that the lexical ambiguity opens up a new horizon of inquiry. Standing on that new horizon are not only these two Neoplatonists, but also a host of Christian theologians wrestling with the same problem and in some cases taking their cue from the "privative" accounts offered by these two Neoplatonists. Among the Christian theologians, of course, this question of the relationship of evil, understood as nothing, to God is made more acute by the widespread defense of the doctrine of creation *ex nihilo*: If God created out of nothing, then what is the status of that nothing, and how does it continue to bear on creation? Relevant figures to consider here will include Origen, Athanasius, Gregory of Nyssa, Evagrius of Pontus, Augustine of Hippo, Dionysius the Areopagite, and John Scottus Eriugena. An investigation into this tension in the writings of Neoplatonists and Christians would proceed under the banner of Paul's phrase, "no longer I," except that it would explore the duality of *God's* own "I" relative to evil.[27]

Christology: The Two "I"s of Christ

The fifth century witnessed a controversy over the nature(s) and person(s) of the Incarnate Christ that would result in the schism of conciliar orthodoxy into three distinct constituencies—confessional divisions that remain to this day.[28] It is extremely difficult, however, to appreciate what was at stake in this controversy, in part because the contestants cannot agree on exactly what is or should be at stake, they make a virtue of speaking past each other, and the terminology is as shifting sands beneath our feet. My suspicion, however, is that this controversy should be understood as a continuation of the tradition of the divine double, who appears here in a new guise. Whereas the earlier Christian tradition of the divine double, as we have explored it in this book, centers on how every human might him- or herself become the twin of Jesus, fully human and divine, this later tradition, becomes largely a debate about how the Incarnate Christ is fully human and divine. Whereas the earlier tradition explored how each and every Christian should aspire to a divine unity-in-duality, the later tradition explores—and differs sharply on—whether and how the Incarnate Christ is both one and two, with respect to his nature(s) and his person(s).

The controversy is often framed as a clash of titans: a *tête à tête* between Cyril (ca. 375–444), the indomitable patriarch of Alexandria, and Nestorius (d. 451), the stubborn patriarch of Constantinople whose intellect roots stretched eastward to Antioch. Nearly as often the controversy is framed as a collision between the theological commitments and exegetical traditions of two ancient sees, Alexandria and Antioch, for which Cyril and Nestorius are seen as merely the respective champions. Behind Cyril stands Athanasius, and behind Nestorius stands Theodore of Mopsuestia (ca. 350–428 / 429), who is regarded as the towering intellectual of the Antiochene tradition. What hangs in the balance, however—between Athanasius and Cyril, on the one hand, and Theodore and Nestorius, on the other—is whether Christ (and crucially, by extension, whether we) should be regarded as having a single "I" or in fact two "I"s.

Let me first try to specify what this Christological controversy was explicitly *about*, which should not be confused with what was *at stake*. All contestants agreed that Christ had both a human and a divine nature; the debate centered on how the two natures so to speak "coexisted" in the one Incarnate Christ. Nestorius famously objected to the popular title *Theotokos* or "God-bearer" for the Virgin Mary on the grounds that it confuses the human and divine natures of Christ. Mary is the mother of the man Jesus, not the mother of the Word, the Son eternally begotten from and "consubstantial" *(homoousios)* with the Father. Strictly speaking, Nestorius argued, she bears not

God the Word, but the Incarnate Christ, and so is better hailed as *Christotokos*. To preserve the distinction between and the integrity of each nature, Nestorius preferred to speak of a "conjunction" *(synapheia)* rather than a union *(henōsis)* of the two in the Incarnate Christ. For him, to confuse the divine and the human natures—as loose talk about "union" is wont to do—amounted to "nothing more nor less than to corrupt both."[29] Cyril's objections were many, and fierce. He regarded Nestorius's opposition to *Theotokos* as an attack on Mary and her popular cult. He regarded a "conjunction" of the two natures as too weak to secure the saving efficacy of the Incarnation. He feared that anything less than a natural union—or later, a *hypostatic* union—would result in a "twofold" Christ, what John McGuckin has colorfully characterized as the "bi-polar" Christ of Nestorius (to which I will return below). And finally, Cyril was anxious that Nestorius's account of the "conjunction" of the human and divine natures in Christ did not sufficiently mark Christ off as unique, that Christ appeared as a man "adopted" by God in much the way that other saints have been.

Nestorius was a student of Theodore of Mopsuestia in Antioch, who is famous not only for his sober scriptural exegesis but also for his Christology. Theodore's predecessor, Diodore of Tarsus (d. before 394), spoke of the Incarnate Christ as having two *prosopa*—two persons or "faces"—and thus sought to safeguard the distinction between the human and divine natures. The problem with each nature having its own proper *prosopon*, however, is that Diodore fumbles in his efforts to say whether and how Christ is also somehow *one*. Theodore represents the second wave of Antiochene Christology: he suggests that while Christ has two natures and two corresponding *prosopa*, the human *prosopon* or "face" so to speak lends itself as the common *prosopon* of both the human nature and the indwelling Word. But this shared or common *prosopon* of the human Jesus is something of a screen, a veil behind which lay two distinct natures and *prosopa*. Pull aside the veil and you will see two faces staring back at you.

John McGuckin regards the question of the "single subjectivity" versus the "bi-polarity" of the Incarnate Christ as the beating heart of this controversy.[30] He regards Nestorius as essentially faithful to

Theodore of Mopsuestia. As we have seen, at the heart of Theodore's Christology is the notion that two natures, human and divine, have two corresponding *prosopa* (persons or faces), which in the Incarnate Christ are united insofar as the one human *prosopon* lends its face to the irreducible duality. McGuckin is certainly right that "central to the coherence of Nestorius's thought was his belief that all Christological thinking should always begin from the concrete experience the church has of Christ in his double reality."[31] Following Theodore, Nestorius thought that we should start with, neither the man Jesus of Nazareth, nor the divine Word, but instead the one fact of the Incarnate Christ, in whom the "eyes of faith" have always recognized "two clearly observed aspects of his reality, which signify to the beholder divinity as well as humanity."[32]

Nestorius also follows Theodore in insisting that the Christological union in a single *prosopon* is a union *kat'eudokian*, by God's pleasure or grace, one in which the human nature cooperates. Crucially, this prosopic union of the two distinct natures and corresponding *prosopa* is not—and cannot be—(in McGuckin's words) "ontologically grounded."[33] There is not nor can there ever be a union of natures. This did not sit well with Cyril. Nestorius's unwillingness to ground the union of the two natures ontologically—as Cyril sought to do with the *hypostatic* union—threatens to split open what McGuckin calls the "single subjectivity of Christ." I think McGuckin has put his finger on what is at stake in the Christological controversy, namely whether Christ is—and by extension whether we each ought to be—a single "I" or not, a unified subject that brooks no interior alterity or meaningful difference (Cyril's hypostatic union), or instead an irreducible duality, dynamically bringing constitutive difference together without annulling it (Nestorius's prosopic conjunction).

I hope it is clear by now why I regard the Christological controversy as a transposition and transformation of the earlier tradition of the divine double. We see in the exchange between Cyril and Nestorius, and perhaps between the two traditions for which they are each spokesman, a sophisticated debate about the coincidence of the human and the divine in a single "individual" (be it Christ or a Christian), and how that coincidence forces upon us fundamental questions about the nature of selfhood and about unity and its relationship to duality. It should be clear that I regard the losers in this controversy, the Antiochenes, as those who seem to carry the tradition of the divine double forward: they confess a Christ who is irreducibly dual, a savior whose salvation consists of the correlation and cooperation of human and divine, two "I"s participating in a shared project of selfhood.[34]

As I said, McGuckin helps bring to light the two-subjects Christology as the Antiochene tradition's greatest defining feature. Of course, he does so precisely to discredit it: for him, "bi-polarity" is a dead end for both Christology and theological anthropology. But I believe that if the Antiochene tradition is to be resuscitated, both historically and for present use, it will be because its confession of an irreducibly dual Christ, and by extension an irreducibly dual human self, has much to recommend it. A contemporary resuscitation or retrieval may involve pushing the Antiochene position further than even its best representatives were willing to go, because they too were groping after something of which they were as yet uncertain. And I think we would do better to grope forward, as they did, rather than retreat into singular subjectivity cowed by warnings of pathology. Whether one agrees or disagrees is less important to me than securing acknowledgment that *this* is where the debate should begin, and perhaps end. Who is Christ and who am I? Am I—is he—one "I" or two, and if one or two, how? And what, after all, is an "I"? These are questions to which Antioch began to offer a distinctive answer, an answer that deserves a hearing, which I am convinced it has not yet to this day been given.

Conclusion

What am I? Where have I come from? To what end? And this feeling that I am nothing without a *not*-I which is at the same time my *own* being, is the religious feeling. But what part of me is I and what part not-I?

—Ludwig Feuerbach

The "I" and the Not-"I," the One and the Not-One

MUCH OF THIS book has been about the "I" and the paradox of how that "I" is constituted by, in Feuerbach's words, a not-"I" that is simultaneously its very own "I." It is a paradox of identity and difference: how the identity of the "I" depends on inalienable difference. The tradition of the divine double strikes me as a long meditation on this paradox, which Plato, more than any other ancient thinker, put into words. I do not mean to suggest that Plato inaugurated this paradox; I am inclined rather to think that this paradox inaugurated Plato, by which I mean that the reality of the "I" and the not-"I," perhaps first forced upon him by his teacher's *daimonion*, opened for him the question of how the one is not one. The self becomes the site of this question, and we cast about for words that can give it voice. What figure could better capture how our "I" is constituted by a not-"I" (that is also our very own "I") than a mirror and our reflection in it (for instance, *Phaedrus* and *Alcibiades I*)? What am I? Am I the archetype before whose image I now stand? Am I rather the image standing before my own archetype? Am I somehow the both of them together? Alongside mirrors and reflections, the language of love presents itself as especially apt (as in the *Symposium*): If I, a lover, seek to become one with my beloved, to what degree are we identical and to what degree different? Is sex a kind of longing for the (re)union of lover and beloved, a wish to make one out of two? We find these questions asked again in a different register, and at a different altitude in Plato's *Parmenides*. If we are (sensible) images of (intelligible) archetypes, what if the very structure of intelligibility (the Forms) itself depends on the paradox of the one and the not-one, how the one is not one?

It may well be that the first-person questions, such as Socrates's *daimonion* raises and Feuerbach rehearses, open up for us the horizon of the "larger" question of the one and the not-one (as I have suggested was the case for Plato). But like a reflection in a mirror, the larger question is both identical to and different from the first-person question, and we are not certain which is the image and which the archetype, or even if that distinction applies. In other words, we come to realize that the questions we are asking of ourselves are equally questions about whether, why, and how there is anything other than the one, or whether, why, and how the one is not one. And vice versa: the most abstract questions about the one and the not-one are equally questions about ourselves, about our own identity and difference. They may all be, in the words of the *Gospel of Thomas*, precisely "one and the same" *(oua ouōt)* question.

You may be wondering why anyone, ancient or modern, would experience such questions—either the "introverted" questions about the "I" and not-"I" or the "extroverted" questions about the one and the not-one—as urgent. If I were to appeal to experience, I might say that we often feel as if, in the words of W. H. Auden, "we are lived by powers we pretend to understand."[1] Most moderns, I would hazard to guess, imagine that the "powers" by which we feel that we are lived are our unconscious—a vertical double of sorts, a wellspring *beneath* what we typically recognize as our "I." Perhaps this is part of the reason the questions about the "I" and not-"I" and the one and the not-one, as posed by Plato and other voices from the ancient tradition of the divine double, sometimes fail to find purchase with modern readers. For the ancient witnesses assembled in the previous chapters, however, the "powers" by which we are lived are not so much *beneath* as *above* us: they are divine. Furthermore, the plural "powers" are largely reducible to the singular: we are lived by a *power* we pretend to understand, which power is simultaneously and paradoxically "I" and not-"I." The urgency enters when we realize that the question of the "I" and not-"I" or one and not-one reveals *both* that the "I" we are each accustomed to recognize is at best incomplete (and worse, is a form of false consciousness) *and* thereby that we are not each fixed in place but instead in between and on the move: in between the "I" we each thought we were and the new "I" whose identity includes the difference of the not-"I"; on our way from one to the other.

Plato speaks of this as our "becoming like God" *(theōsis)*. The Christian witnesses assembled here follow suit and give voice to a very early doctrine of deification that would eventually fade from the scene in the fourth and fifth centuries. Just as Plato cast about for words to capture the paradox of the "I" and the not-"I," the one and the not-one, so too do the Christian sources give distinctive expression to this early doctrine of "becoming like God." The figure of (Judas) Thomas supplies a vocabulary: he is a "twin" *(didymos)* of Jesus, his divine double to whom he is, in one way, identical, and from whom, in another way, different. The coincidence of that identity and difference is imagined as a new "I," a new self, for which new and paradoxical names are necessary: a "solitary" *(monachos)*, "a single one" *(oua ouōt)*, according to the *Gospel of Thomas*. And like Plato, the early Christian sources also appropriate the language of love, albeit in a scriptural idiom. The bride and bridegroom unite in the bridal chamber, and like husband and wife, they become one (for instance, Gen 2:24) and yet remain two (for instance, *Gospel of Thomas*, *Gospel of Philip*, and *Acts of Thomas*). The Christian and thereafter the Manichaean sources also introduce new vocabulary to give voice to this same paradox: a syzygy of "yokemates" *(syzygoi)* (as in Tatian, *Acts of Thomas*, and especially the *Cologne Mani Codex*). Curiously, it is the

Manichaean tradition (for instance, the *Kephalaia*) that takes advantage of Jesus's own ambiguous relationship to the figure of the Paraclete to name the identity and difference of Mani the Apostle of Light and his twin-companion. And as we have seen, the Christian and Manichaean sources make abundant use of the writings associated with the apostles John and Paul to name the divine double and the associated doctrine of deification.

My point here in rehearsing the earlier chapters is that these various vocabularies (in Plato as well as in the Christian and Manichaean sources) are attempts to find words to speak to a fundamental paradox: what I have called the "introverted" question of the "I" and the not-"I" and the "extroverted" question of the one and the not-one—which I regard as essentially one and the same question. In other words, as I hope is clear by now, I regard the tradition of the divine double as a centuries-long exploration of this fundamental problem. Philosophers are sometimes wont to reduce philosophy to a series of problems. I usually resist this characterization, since we often think that problems are in need of solutions, as we think questions are in need of answers. But if we can instead inhabit the idea that problems and questions are to be lived with, rather than solved or answered, then I think we can safely identify (or rather differentiate) the "I" and not-"I," the one and the not-one, as one of the perennial problems with which philosophy (and perhaps more so, religion) wrestles.

More often one hears of the problem of the one and the many: since the pre-Socratics, philosophers have been exercised with the question of how the vast world of multiplicity in which we find ourselves can be explained by appeal to fewer and more-fundamental principles, and those principles to even fewer and more-fundamental principles, until we arrive at a single and most fundamental principle or source, a one from which the many derive. It is the conceit of this book that the question of the one and the many is reducible to the question of the one and the not-one, that the question of how the many derive from the one follows from a more (perhaps the most) fundamental question: whether, why, and how the one became not-one. To my mind, the ancient philosopher who most powerfully explores this fundamental question is Plotinus. The question of the one and the not-one, the "I" and the not-"I," the self and its double, appears at every level of his metaphysics, from our doubled intellect, to thought thinking itself in the hypostasis Intellect, to Intellect's first emergence from the One as an indeterminate otherness or "dyad." His metaphysics are in the service of an urgent enterprise: he wishes us—we who are each always one and not-one—to return to the One from whence we have come through a process of facing a series of our own doubles, facing them and then dissolving into them.

This book has been a project of recovery, of recovering a lost tradition. In the case of Christianity, that tradition has perhaps been more buried than lost, more suppressed than simply forgotten. What we have unearthed is an understanding of the human self, who is one and not-one, as divine, who is also one and not-one. This understanding of the self and the urgent enterprise of "becoming like God" are thus not accidentally but *essentially* related: we are and must be one and not-one because (the One) God who we are becoming increasingly like is one and not-one. We have here, then, a meditation on the coincidence of identity and difference, unity and distinction, a paradox that makes a claim on me (or at least what I thought was "me") here and now and stretches me upward or inward to (the One) God. Having recovered this tradition of the divine double, not only as a "minority report" in theological anthropology and soteriology, but as a fixation on a fundamental question or problem in the history of philosophy and religion, I wonder what else it might help us to explain, or to explore.

Reading and Writing the Divine Double

Several of our sources have reflected on themselves as writings, more specifically reflected upon themselves as reflecting surfaces in which a reader might see his own image reflected in their words, as if in a mirror or a pool of still water, as he is or as he should be. Plato's city of words is like a reflecting pool in which we see our own soul, writ large. His dialogues become our textual doubles, the reading of which, like the eye of a beloved, reflects back to us our own self. So too Athanasius's understanding of the Psalter: it is the mirror in which the reader sees both his own image and that of the Christ, "the image of the invisible God" (Col 1:15). I suggested that we read the *Gospel of Thomas* in light of Athanasius's Psalter, its secret sayings as the mirror in which the reader slowly discovers his secret self, his image (as opposed to likeness), and recognizes his twin, Jesus the indwelling light. In those two manuscripts in which the *Acts of Thomas* includes the "Hymn of the Pearl," the reader is caught between two narratives of twinning and doubling that mirror each other, such that, as if in a *mise en abyme*, he stands in the midst of an infinite series of divine doubles, and in so doing has his own drawn out of him.

These examples raise for me the question of the practice of reading: to put it more sharply, whether the practice of reading is a (or *the*) way to meet one's own divine double. Consider this passage from Maurice Blanchot's *Thomas the Obscure*:

> Thomas stayed in his room to read. He was sitting with his hands joined over his brow, his thumbs pressing against his hairline, so deep in concentration that he did not make a move when anyone opened the door. Those who came in thought he was pretending to read, seeing that the book was always open to the same page. He was reading. He was reading with unsurpassable meticulousness and attention. In relation to every symbol, he was in the position of the male praying mantis about to be devoured by the female. They looked at each other. The words, coming forth from the book which was taking on the power of life and death, exercised a gentle and peaceful attraction over the glance which played over them. Each of them, like a half-closed eye, admitted the excessively keen glance which in other circumstances it would not have tolerated. And so Thomas slipped toward these corridors, approaching them defenselessly until the moment he was perceived by the very quick of the word. Even this was not fearful, but rather an almost pleasant moment he would have wished to prolong. The reader contemplated his little spark of life joyfully, not doubting that he had awakened it. It was with pleasure that he saw himself in this eye looking at him.[2]

Thomas, "reading with unsurpassable meticulousness and attention," comes to see that his are not the only eyes on the page. The words themselves, coming forth from the book, awakened by his reading but still "half-closed," consent to admit his eager eyes, to meet his with theirs: "he was perceived by the very quick of the word," and "he saw himself in this eye looking at him." Their eyes, his own and the words', meet only to exchange places, or rather occupy both places at once. As Corbin says of one's encounter with the divine double, "It is through his very own eyes that the Figure looks at him."[3] Here, in the very act of reading, the paradox of the "I" and the not-"I" is playing out on, or rather above, the page.

Jeffrey J. Kripal has called attention to the significance of the practice of reading for our encountering the divine double and has supplied another very modern instance: Harold Bloom.[4] Bloom describes his childhood reading of William Blake and Hart Crane: "In my instance at least, the self came to its belated birth (or second birth) by reading visionary poetry, a reading that implicitly was an act of knowing something previously unknown within me," namely that "the self's potential as power involves the self's immortality, not as duration but as the awakening to a knowledge of something in the self that cannot die, because it was never born."[5] Bloom describes this knowledge gained through reading, this *gnosis*, as "a mutual knowing, and a simultaneous being known, of and by God," "the act of distinguishing the *psyche*, or soul, from the deep self, an act of distinction that is also a recognition."[6] Notice that Bloom's recognition of his "deep self" is crucially an act of *distinction*—of keeping the two distinct precisely so that they can be made one.

Thus begins a new search: to look through these and other sources, ancient and modern, for further evidence for such a practice of reading, reading with an eye to encountering one's divine double. And not only to make a scholarly case, but to find exemplars, even goads, for what we might do (but often do not) when we read. And not only how we might read, but how we might write. Kripal speaks of reading and writing as "Realization" and "Authorization."[7] Realization is what happened to Bloom through his reading: he recognizes his "I" and not-"I," and thereby knows and is known. As Kripal puts it, "Realization is finally the insight that we are being written," that these texts, these cites of words, are our reality writ large, mirrors in which we can recognize ourselves.

What would it mean, however, to *write* rather than to read the divine double? What would it mean to take on authorship of our own "I" and not-"I," to become, in Kripal's words, "an author of the impossible . . . who knows that the Human is Two *and* One"?[8] I explored a similar question in some earlier work on "Pseudo"-Dionysius the Areopagite, and hunted through the history of Christianity for witnesses to writing as a mystical practice.[9] I suggested that for Dionysius the very practice of writing under a pseudonym is an ecstatic devotion seeking deifying union with the "unknown God" (Acts 17). The author renders himself, in his own words, "neither himself nor someone else," neither the sixth-century Syrian that scholars assume him to be nor the Athenian judge under whose name he writes.[10] Like the ecstatic God with whom he seeks to suffer union, as a writer he simultaneously remains where he is and stretches outside himself.[11] He writes himself *into* the reality of the "I" and the not-"I," the one and the not-one, and, by making himself a disciple of the apostle Paul, opens himself to the indwelling of Christ, which Paul famously acclaims with his own confession of doubled selfhood, "it is no longer I, but Christ who lives in me."

When I set out on the trail of the divine double, I did not expect that it would circle back to this question of writing, but it has. Dionysius's pseudonyms aside, then, we might ask: What *other* forms and practices of writing might serve to deliver us into the paradox of the "I" and the not-"I"? If the character Thomas the Obscure offers us a rousing example of one reading his divine double, does Blanchot then emerge as one writing his divine double—in Kripal's words, "an author of the impossible"?[12] And if not Blanchot, then who are the authors of the impossible, of the self as one and not one? Who are our impossible authors of the divine double, past, present, and, most crucially, *future?* Might we be?

NOTES

ACKNOWLEDGMENTS

INDEX

Notes

Book Epigraphs

Acts of John 95:25, trans. Knut Schäferdiek, in W. Schneemelcher, ed., *New Testament Apocrypha*, vol. 2 (Louisville, KY: Westminster John Knox, 1992), 183.

Jacques Derrida, *The Beast and the Sovereign* (Chicago: University of Chicago Press, 2009), 334. The English translation, attempting to capture the ambiguity of "plus," reads: "More than a single single; no more a single single. That's where we are."

Introduction

Epigraph: I borrow here Shadi Bartsch's translation of this passage in *The Mirror of the Self: Sexuality, Self-Knowledge, and the Gaze in the Early Roman Empire* (Chicago: University of Chicago Press, 2006), 91.

1. Conon, *Narrations* 24. See Malcolm Brown, trans., *The Narratives of Konon* (Munich: Saur, 2002).
2. Pausanias, *Description of Greece*, IV.xxxi.6–9. See W. H. S. Jones, trans., *Pausanias: Description of Greece*, 5 vols. (Cambridge, MA: Harvard University Press, 1931–1955).
3. Ovid, *Metamorphoses*, 3.348 (68). Unless otherwise noted, citations are from Rolfe Humphries's translation (Bloomington: Indiana University Press, 1955).
4. Ibid., 3.405–407 (70).
5. Ibid., 3.423 (70).
6. Ibid., 3.463–464; here I have again borrowed Bartsch's translation in *Mirror of the Self*, 91.
7. Ibid., 3.492 (72).
8. See Bartsch, *Mirror of the Self*, 90–94.

9. I am acutely aware that these may not be the only late antique traditions in which one finds the divine double. I have not included discussions of the divine double in Judaism, Hermeticism, or Sethian Gnosticism.

10. Raymond Kuntzmann, *Le symbolisme des jumeaux au Proche-Orient ancien: Naissance, fonction et évolution d'un symbole* (Paris: Beauchesne, 1983). His scope stretches from the Hebrew Bible (Jacob and Esau), to Babylonian epic (Gilgamesh and Enkidu), to the New Testament and its apocrypha (Jesus and Judas Thomas). See also Véronique Dasen, *Jumeaux, jumelles dans l'antiquité Grecque et Romaine* (Kilchberg: Akanthus, 2005); Reinhard Rathmayr, *Zwillinge in der griechisch-römischen Antike* (Vienna: Böhlau Verlag, 2000).

11. Wendy Doniger, *Splitting the Difference: Gender and Myth in Ancient Greece and India* (Chicago: University of Chicago Press, 1999). See also Doniger, *The Woman Who Pretended to Be Who She Was* (Oxford: Oxford University Press, 2005).

12. Doniger, *Splitting the Difference*, 3.

13. Bartsch, *Mirror of the Self*, esp. the intro. and chaps. 1 and 2.

14. Henry Corbin, *L'homme de lumière dans le soufisme iranien* (Paris: Éditions Présence, 1971); English translation by Nancy Pearson, *The Man of Light in Iranian Sufism* (New Lebanon, NY: Omega, 1994).

15. Ibid., 4, 6, 7; see also Charles M. Stang, "A *Unus-ambo* Anthropology: The Divine Twin in the *Gospel of Thomas*, the *Cologne Mani Codex*, and Plotinus' Enneads," in *Gemini and the Sacred: Twins in Religion and Myth*, ed. Kimberley Patton (London: I. B. Tauris, forthcoming).

16. Ibid., 9.

17. See Kuntzmann, *Le symbolisme des jumeaux*, 217, where he too appeals to a simple mathematical formula, by contrast: "Le troisième acteur de cette symbolique illustre bien que le symbole ne repose pas sur une simple arithmétique (1+1), mais sur un processus mythique, un drame dont le movement ouvre un sens à la lecture."

18. I am borrowing the concept of the "dividual" from Simon Critchley, *The Faith of the Faithless: Experiments in Political Theology* (Brooklyn: Verso, 2012), 6–7, where it means something quite specific: "The self shapes itself in relation to the experience of an overwhelming, infinite demand that divides it from itself . . . The infinite ethical demand allows us to become the subjects of which we are capable by dividing us from ourselves, by forcing us to live in accordance with an asymmetrical and unfulfillable demand—say the demand to be Christlike—while knowing that we are all too human."

19. Charles M. Stang, *Apophasis and Pseudonymity in Dionysius the Areopagite: "No Longer I"* (Oxford: Oxford University Press, 2012); Stang, "Dionysius, Paul and the Significance of the Pseudonym," in *Rethinking Dionysius the Areopagite*, ed. Sarah Coakley and Charles M. Stang (Oxford: Wiley-Blackwell, 2009), 11–25; Stang, "'Neither Oneself nor Someone Else': The Apophatic Anthropology of Dionysius the Areopagite," in *Apophatic Bodies: Negative Theology, Incarnation, and Relationality*, ed. Catherine Keller and Christ Boesel (New York: Fordham University Press, 2009), 59–75.

20. Corbin, *The Man of Light*, 9.

21. Lloyd P. Gerson, *Knowing Persons: A Study in Plato* (Oxford: Oxford University Press, 2003). I have certain hesitations regarding the language of "achievement;" I will spell these out more clearly in Chapter 1.

22. See John Behr, trans., Athanasius, *On the Incarnation* (Yonkers, NY: St. Vladimir's Seminary Press, 2011). See also Norman Russell, *The Doctrine of Deification in the Greek Patristic Tradition* (Oxford: Oxford University Press, 2006).

23. Bernard McGinn, *The Foundations of Mysticism* (New York: Crossroad, 1991), 92.

24. Unless otherwise noted, all citations from Plato are from the translations collected in John M. Cooper, ed., *Plato: Complete Works* (Indianapolis: Hackett, 1997). For the Greek text, I have consulted J. Burnet, ed., *Platonis opera*, 5 vols. (Oxford: Clarendon Press, 1900–1907; reprint 1967).

25. See Pauliina Remes's very judicious discussion in *Plotinus on Self: The Philosophy of the 'We'* (Cambridge: Cambridge University Press, 2007), 3–4. See also Frederick M. Schroeder, "The Self in Ancient Religious Experience," in *Classical Mediterranean Spirituality: Egyptian, Greek, Roman*, ed. A. H. Armstrong (New York: Crossroad, 1986), 337–338.

26. Remes, *Plotinus on Self*, 4.

27. Sigmund Freud, "Three Essays on the Theory of Sexuality," "On Narcissism: An Introduction," and "Mourning and Melancholia," *The Standard Edition of Complete Psychological Works of Sigmund Freud*, ed. and trans. James Strachey (London: Hogarth Press, 1957), 7:130–243 (here, 145), 14:73–102, 14:237–258 (here, 249). Very closely related to Narcissus is the figure of the double or mirror image. See, for example: Freud's essay "The 'Uncanny,'" in *Art and Literature*, trans. James Strachey (London: Penguin, 1990); Otto Rank's *The Double* (Chapel Hill: University of North Carolina Press, 1971) and "The Double as Immortal Self," in *Beyond Psychology* (New York: Dover, 2011), 62–101; or Jacques Lacan's "The Mirror Stage as Formative of the *I* Function as Revealed in Psychoanalytic Experience," in *Ecrits: A Selection*, trans. Bruce Fink (New York: Norton, 2007), 75–81.

28. Freud, "The Uncanny," 210.

29. Ibid., 211.

30. Ibid., 212.

31. Ibid., 222.

32. Lynn Holden, "Reflections on the Double," in *The Book of the Mirror: An Interdisciplinary Collection Exploring the Cultural Story of the Mirror*, ed. Miranda Anderson (Newcastle, UK: Cambridge Scholars, 2007), 122.

33. Including Mark Pendergast, *Mirror Mirror: A History of the Human Love Affair with Reflection* (New York: Basic Books, 2004), 1–27; Andrew J. Webber, *The Doppelgänger: Double Visions in German Literature* (Oxford: Clarendon Press, 1996); Carl Francis Keppler, *The Literature of the Second Self* (Tucson: University of Arizona Press, 1972); Victor I. Stoichita, *A Short History of the Shadow* (London: Reaktion Books, 1997); Christoph Forderer, *Ich-Eklipsen: Doppelgänger in der Literatur seit 1800* (Stuttgart: J. B. Metzler, 1999); Robert Rogers, *The Double in Literature: A Psychoanalytic Study* (Detroit: Wayne State University Press, 1970); Dimitris Vardoulakis, *The Doppelgänger: Literature's Philosophy*

(New York: Fordham University Press, 2010); Marina Warner, *Fantastic Metamorphoses, Other Worlds: Ways of Telling the Self* (Oxford: Oxford University Press, 2002); Hillel Schwartz, *The Culture of the Copy: Striking Likenesses, Unreasonable Facsimiles* (New York: Zone Books, 1996). Articles and chapters include: J.-P. Vernant, "Figuration de l'invisible et catégorie psychologique du double," *Mythe et pensée chez les grécs*, vol. 2 (Paris, 1974), 65–78; J. S. Grotsein, "Autoscopy: The Experience of Oneself as a Double," *Hillside Journal of Clinical Psychiatry* 5, no. 2 (1983): 259–304; Albert J. Guerard, "Concepts of the Double" in *Stories of the Double*, ed. A. J. Guerard (Philadelphia: J. B. Lippincott, 1967) 1–14; Patrick McNamara, "Memory, Double, Shadow, and Evil," *Journal of Analytical Psychology* 39, no. 2 (1994): 233–251; Milica Zivkovic, "The Double as the 'Unseen' of Culture: Toward a Definition of Doppelgänger," *Facta Universitatis—Linguistics and Literature* 7, no. 2 (2000): 121–128.

1 Reading Plato's Many Doubles

1. Unless otherwise noted, all citations from Plato are from the translations collected in John M. Cooper, ed., *Plato: Complete Works* (Indianapolis: Hackett, 1997). For the Greek text, I have consulted J. Burnet, ed., *Platonis opera*, 5 vols. (Oxford: Clarendon Press, 1900–1907; reprint 1967).

2. See the discussion of *Alcibiades I* later in this chapter.

3. Lloyd P. Gerson, *Knowing Persons: A Study in Plato* (Oxford: Oxford University Press, 2003), 3 (my emphasis). Gerson readily admits that Plato does not have a distinct term for "person" or "self" apart from the ordinary Greek terms for human being, such as *anthropos*. Nevertheless, he argues, a case can be made for such a concept of the person that makes good sense of Plato's different discussions of anthropology and psychology.

4. Ibid., 3.
5. Ibid., 4.
6. Ibid., 9.
7. Ibid., 10.

8. I have changed Grube's translation slightly: he inserts "sign" into this passage. It appears later, but I will discuss the different language Socrates uses to describe his divine double.

9. Luc Brisson, "Socrates and the Divine Signal according to Plato's Testimony: Philosophical Practice as Rooted in Religious Tradition," in *Socrates' Divine Sign: Religion, Practice and Value in Socratic Philosophy*, ed. Pierre Destrée and Nicholas D. Smith, special issue, *Apeiron* 38, no. 2 (2005): 2: "There can therefore be no question of a revelation."

10. All this is consistent with the other accounts, but for the curious addition of a single detail: Socrates says that the voice forbade him "until I made atonement for some offense against the gods" (242b). Some have wondered whether this clause suggests that his *daimonion* is offering more than simply apotreptic guidance, whether it in fact informs him of the nature of his offense and allows him to make penance. See John M. Rist, "Plotinus and the *Daimonion* of Socrates," *Phoenix* 17, no. 1 (1963): 15: "The addition of the phrase *prin an aphosiōsomai* seems to attribute to the voice some kind of hortatory power of

the kind that the Platonic Socrates normally disdains. I do not think it likely that this passage from the *Phaedrus* should be taken to imply an account of the *daimonion* at variance with the other Platonic evidence, but I am not the first to believe that it may well have been a source from which the idea that the voice gave positive commands was derived."

11. Perhaps this is the moment to remember that Plato is not our only witness to Socrates. Plato's contemporary, the jack-of-all-trades Xenophon, also wrote a number of works about the Athenian gadfly *(Memorabilia, Oeconomicus, Symposium, Apology, Hiero)*. Two are of interest for our purposes: his own version of Socrates's defense speech, also entitled *Apology*, and another apologetic work in the form of a collection of Socratic dialogues, entitled *Memorabilia*. The differences between Plato's and Xenophon's portraits of Socrates are many, and very interesting, especially when it comes to the *daimonion*. See, for example, *Xénophon et Socrate: Actes du colloque d'Aix-en-Provence (6–9 novembre 2003)*, ed. Michel Narcy and Alonso Tordesillas (Paris: J. Vrin, 2008); Leo Strauss, *Xenophon's Socrates* (Ithaca, NY: Cornell University Press, 1972). The most striking difference in Xenophon's account is that Socrates's *daimonion* is explicitly protreptic, that is, it signals to Socrates not only what *not* to do (à la Plato), but also very much what *to do* (*Memorabilia* 4.8.1, 4.3.12). And the *daimonion*'s advice extends to Socrates's friends as well (*Memorabilia* 1.1.4). Thus, the subtle suggestion in Plato's *Phaedrus* is an outright assertion in Xenophon's account: the *daimonion* guide offers both negative *and* positive stimuli. What are we to make of this striking difference? Some scholars see Xenophon as an author decidedly not up to the task of representing Socrates's subtle philosophical stance—a task better suited to Plato. Thus Rist, "Plotinus and the *Daimonion* of Socrates," 17: "We can only regard [Xenophon's account] as a vulgarization of the whole concept of the sign." For our purposes, we need not decide so definitively. More important than adjudicating between Plato and Xenophon as reliable witnesses to the historical Socrates is the range of opinion on the *daimonion*, and what possibilities this range of opinion provides later traditions of the divine double.

12. Mark L. McPherran, "Introducing a New God: Socrates and His *Daimonion*," in Destrée and Smith, *Socrates' Divine Sign*, 16.

13. Rist, "Plotinus and the *Daimonion* of Socrates," 19, 20.

14. Brisson, "Socrates and the Divine Signal," 5: "[Socrates's *daimonion*] therefore has no theoretical dimension, nor does it, by itself, permit any considerations of a general nature."

15. John E. Rexine, "Daimon in Classical Greek Literature," *Greek Orthodox Theological Review* 30 (1985): 336.

16. Heraclitus's fragment CXIV, Charles Kahn, trans., *The Art and Thought of Heraclitus* (Cambridge: Cambridge University Press, 1979), 80.

17. Henry George Liddell and Robert Scott, *A Greek-English Lexicon*, 9th ed. with rev. supplement (Oxford: Clarendon Press, 1996), 366.

18. Plato, *Cratylus* 398b–c: "It is principally because daemons are wise and knowing *(daēmones)*, I think, that Hesiod says they are named 'daemons' *(daimones)*. In our older Attic dialect, we actually find the word '*daēmones*.' So, Hesiod and many other good poets speak well when they say that when a good

man *(tis agathos)* dies, he has a great destiny and a great honor and becomes a 'daemon,' which is a name given to him because it accords with wisdom. And I myself assert, indeed, that every good man, whether alive or dead, is daemonic *(daimonion)*, and is correctly called a 'daemon' *(daimon)*."

19. Destrée and Smith, *Socrates' Divine Sign*, viii.

20. Pierre Destrée, "The *Daimonion* and the Philosophical Mission: Should the Divine Sign Remain Unique to Socrates?," in Destrée and Smith, *Socrates' Divine Sign*, 79.

21. See Roslyn Weiss, "For Whom the *Daimonion* Tolls," in Destrée and Smith, *Socrates' Divine Sign*, 81–96; both Destrée's and Weiss's essays argue against Socrates being unique in having a *daimōn*.

22. Rist, "Plotinus and the *Daimonion* of Socrates," 14.

23. See chapter 5 on Plotinus's allusion to this passage in "On Beauty," *Ennead* 1.6.9.

24. See Shadi Bartsch, *The Mirror of the Self: Sexuality, Self-Knowledge, and the Gaze in the Early Roman Empire* (Chicago: University of Chicago Press, 2006), 41; Jean-François Pradeau, *Alcibiade* (Paris: Flammarion 1999), 24–29. Those who argue for the authenticity of *Alcibiades I* include Julia Annas, "Self-Knowledge in Early Plato," in *Platonic Investigations*, ed. Dominic J. O'Meara (Washington, DC: 1985), 111–138; Paul Friedländer, *Der grosse* Alcibiades: *Ein Weg zu Plato*, 2 vols. (Bonn: F. Cohen, 1921), 2:28–29; Owen Goldin, "Self, Same, and the Soul in *Alcibiades I* and the *Timaeus*," *Freiburger Zeitschrift für Philosophie und Theologie* 40 (1993): 5–19; and Pradeau as well.

25. Diogenes Laertius, *Lives of Eminent Philosophers*, 3.62. See Bartsch, *Mirror of the Self*, 41; Cooper, *Plato: Complete Works*, 557; on the reception of *Alcibiades I* in antiquity, see the introduction in A. Ph. Segond, ed. and trans., *Sur le premier Alcibiade de Platon / Proclus* (Paris: Belles Lettres, 1985–1986). For the latest scholarship on *Alcibiades I*, see Harold Tarrant and Marguerite Johnson, eds., *Alcibiades and the Socratic Lover-Educator* (Bristol: Bristol Classical Press, 2012).

26. I have benefited enormously from Shadi Bartsch's discussion of this dialogue in *Mirror of the Self*, esp. 41–56.

27. Bartsch, *Mirror of the Self*, 25. On *gnōthi seauton*, see Eliza Gregory Wilkins, *"Know Thyself" in Greek and Latin Literature* (Menasha, WI: George Banta, 1917); Pierre P. Courcelle, *Connais-toi toi-même: De Socrates à saint Bernard* (Paris: Études augustiniennes, 1974–1975).

28. It is worth noting, however, that it is not at all clear how best to understand the phrase *auto to auto* in 129b and later in 130c–d. The phrase does not appear elsewhere in the Platonic corpus. The current standard English translation by D. S. Hutchinson that I have cited renders it "the self itself." W. R. M. Lamb prefers "the same-in-itself" and explains that *auto to auto* "seems to be a sudden adumbration of the Platonic 'idea' or form which remains constant, and so 'the same'": W. R. M. Lamb, trans., *Alcibiades I* (Cambridge, MA: Harvard University Press, 1927; reprint 1955), 195, 194n1. Greek *autos* functions as a reflexive or intensive pronoun; Lamb has combined the two in his translation: the same (intensive) in itself (reflexive). Hutchinson has opted instead to hy-

postasize the pronoun as "the self," a concept for which Greek has no exact word. The two translations furnish two very different interpretive options: Is Socrates asking how we know an intelligible Form, and so somehow "what we ourselves are," or is he asking how we know something called the "self," whatever that might be? The phrase *auto to auto* has generated a fair amount of attention, most famously from Michel Foucault. See Foucault, *The Hermeneutics of the Subject: Lectures at the Collège de France, 1981–82* (New York: Palgrave Macmillan, 2005). See also Christopher Gill, *The Structured Self in Hellenistic and Roman Thought* (Oxford: Oxford University Press, 2006).

29. Some modern editors and translators have emended one word in this last quote: they prefer *thean*, "vision," to *theon*, "god." Without the emendation, Socrates would seem to say that in our double, our lover or beloved, we see god as our own soul, or our own soul as a god. But given that Socrates has just said that someone will see and grasp "everything divine" *(pan to theion gnous)*, to specify further the object of sight as *theon* seems redundant. These same scholars also omit the following lines (133c8–17), on the assumption that they are interpolation by a later Neoplatonist scribe, the same scribe who may have been responsible for changing *thean* to *theon* in the first place:

> *Socrates:* Just as mirrors are clearer, purer, and brighter than the reflecting surface of the eye, isn't God *(theos)* both purer and brighter than the best part of the soul?
> *Alcibiades:* I would certainly think so, Socrates.
> *Socrates:* So the way we can best see and know ourselves is to use the finest mirror available and look at God *(theon)* and, on the human level, at the virtue of the soul.
> *Alcibiades:* Yes.

I am inclined to agree and omit these lines, for they seem to depart from Socrates's logic. These lines suggest that we need not look at another's soul as a mirror, but that we can look directly into the very finest mirror, God, and see and know ourselves thus. I take Socrates's point to be that the only view of what is divine is precisely *through* the soul of another in which we see our own soul reflected, and thus that the vertical contemplation is by way of the horizontal.

30. Bartsch, *Mirror of the Self*, 2.
31. Ibid., 23.
32. Diogenes Laertius, *Lives of Eminent Philosophers*, 2.33.
33. Bartsch, *Mirror of the Self*, 55.
34. Ibid., 42.
35. See Charles M. Stang, "Doubting Thomas, Restaged: Between Athens and Jerusalem," *Harvard Divinity Bulletin* (Winter / Spring 2013): 41–50.
36. I am borrowing the concept of the "dividual" from Simon Critchley, *The Faith of the Faithless: Experiments in Political Theology* (Brooklyn: Verso, 2012), 6–7.
37. Mary Louise Gill, trans., *Plato: Parmenides* (Indianapolis: Hackett, 1996), 1. The scholarly bibliography on Plato's *Parmenides* is vast, and I have

benefited enormously from it. But space demands that I bracket much of that scholarship and attempt my own reading based on the text itself. I have, however, found Mary Louise Gill's introduction to the Hackett edition very helpful and exceedingly clear, especially in her outline of the various arguments in the second half of the dialogue.

38. Ibid., 17.

39. See Mary Louise Gill's sixfold taxonomy (ibid., 18): (1) Scope of Forms (130b–e), (2) Whole–Part Dilemma (130e–131e), (3) Largeness Regress (132a–b), (4) Forms Are Thoughts (132b–c), (5) Likeness Regress (132c–133a), and (6) Separation Argument (133a–134e).

40. Ibid., 49.

41. On the figure of Parmenides, see G. S. Kirk, J. E. Raven, and M. Schonfeld, eds., *The Presocratic Philosophers: A Critical History with a Selection of Texts*, 2nd ed. (Cambridge: Cambridge University Press, 1984), 239–262.

42. Gill, *Plato: Parmenides*, 58.

43. See ibid., 63, for citations of authors on both sides of this debate.

44. See E. R. Dodds, "The *Parmenides* of Plato and the Origins of the Neoplatonic One," *Classical Quarterly* 22 (1928): 129–142; and John M. Rist, "The Neoplatonic One and Plato's *Parmenides*," *Transactions and Proceedings of the American Philological Association* 93 (1962): 389–401.

45. Gill, *Plato: Parmenides*, xx.

46. Ibid., 85.

47. Is it possible that Plato has described precisely this instant in the famous ascension from the *Symposium*, where Socrates recalls Diotima's description of the lover's final vision of beauty: "You see, the man who has been thus far guided in matters of Love, who has beheld beautiful things in the right order and correctly, is coming now to the goal of loving: all of a sudden *(exaiphnēs)* he will catch sight of something wonderfully beautiful in its nature; that, Socrates, is the reason for all his earlier labors" (210e).

48. See Charles M. Stang, *Apophasis and Pseudonymity in Dionysius the Areopagite: "No Longer I"* (Oxford: Oxford University Press, 2012), 95–98.

49. *Ep.* 3 1069B; *Corpus Dionysiacum* II 159.7–10; John H. Parker, trans., *The Complete Works of Dionysius the Areopagite* (London: James Parker and Co., 1897–1899); for the Greek, see Günter Heil and Adolf Martin Ritter, eds. and trans., *Corpus Dionysiacum II* (Berlin: de Gruyter, 1991).

50. See Andrew Radde-Gallwitz, "Pseudo-Dionysius, the *Parmenides*, and the Problem of Contradiction," in *Plato's* Parmenides *and Its Reception in Platonic, Gnostic, and Christian Neoplatonic Texts*, ed. Kevin Corrigan and John D. Turner (Atlanta: Society of Biblical Literature, 2010), 243–254.

51. Gal 3:27–28: "For as many of you as were baptized into Christ have put on Christ. There is neither Jew nor Greek, there is neither slave nor free, there is neither male for female; for you are all one in Christ Jesus." See also Col 3:9–11: "Do not lie to one another, seeing that you have put off the old nature with its practices and have put on the new nature, which is being renewed in knowledge after the image of its creator. Here there cannot be Greek and Jew, circumsized and uncircumsized, barbarian, Scythian, slave, free man, but Christ is all, in all."

52. Aristotle, *Physics* 209b: "It is true, indeed, that the account he gives there [in *Timaeus*] of the participant is different from what he says in his so-called *unwritten teachings (agrapha dogmata)*."

53. John Dillon, *The Middle Platonists: A Study of Platonism, 80 BC to AD 220* (Ithaca, NY: Cornell University Press, 1977), 1–11; Charles H. Kahn, *Pythagoras and the Pythagoreans: A Brief History* (Indianapolis: Hackett, 2001), 39–62.

54. *Metaphysics* 987a–988a.

2 Thomas, Who Is Called "Twin"

1. Robert C. Gregg, trans., *Athanasius: The Life of Antony and Letter to Marcellinus* (Mahwah, NJ: Paulist Press, 1980), §12 (111). For the Greek text, see *Epistula ad Marcellinum de interpretatione Psalmorum*, in Migne, *Patrologia Graece* 27 (1887), cols. 11–46.

2. Ibid., §10 (108).

3. There is something odd, of course, in referring to Origen of Alexandria as "orthodox," given his eventual condemnation at the Second Council of Constantinople in 553. But certainly Origen was an enormous influence on the architects of conciliar orthodoxy in the fourth and fifth centuries.

4. All citations from Thomas Lambdin's translation of the *Gospel of Thomas* in *Nag Hammadi II, 2–7: Together with XIII, 2*, Brit. Lib. Or. 4926(1), and P. Oxy. 1, 654, 655: with Contributions by Many Scholars* ed. Bentley Layton, (Leiden: Brill, 1989), which includes a critical edition of the Coptic (§ refers to a single numbered saying, §§ to more than one). This also includes an appendix with the *Testimonia* to the *Gospel of Thomas* and the Greek Oxyrhynchus fragments, edited and translated by Harold Attridge. I have consulted the Coptic-English interlinear edition compiled by Michael Grondin (http://gospel-thomas.net/x_transl.htm). Other useful online resources, including extensive bibliography, can be found at http://agraphos.com/thomas/about/ and http://users.misericordia.edu//davies/thomas/Thomas.html.

5. H. J. W. Drijvers, trans., "The Acts of Thomas," in *New Testament Apocrypha*, vol. 2, ed. W. Schneemelcher, (Louisville, KY: Westminster John Knox, 1992), 325.

6. Bentley Layton, *The Gnostic Scriptures* (Garden City, NY: Doubleday, 1987), 359–360.

7. Risto Uro, "Is *Thomas* an Encratite Gospel?," in *Thomas at the Crossroads*, ed. Risto Uro (Edinburgh: T&T Clark, 1998), 147. See also Uro, *Thomas: Seeking the Historical Context of the Gospel of Thomas* (New York: T&T Clark, 2003).

8. Gregory J. Riley, "Didymos Judas Thomas, the Twin Brother of Jesus," in *Gemini and the Sacred: Twins in Religion and Myth*, ed. Kimberley Patton (London: I. B. Tauris, forthcoming).

9. See Charles M. Stang, "Doubting Thomas, Restaged: Between Athens and Berlin," *Harvard Divinity Bulletin* (Winter / Spring 2013): 41–50; Glenn Most, *Doubting Thomas* (Cambridge, MA: Harvard University Press, 2005).

10. Cf. Mark 6:3: "Is not this the carpenter, the son of Mary and brother of James and Joses and Judas and Simon, and are not his sisters here with us?"

11. Jesus's brother Judas must be distinguished from three other figures from the New Testament who share this very common proper name: (1) Judas Iscariot; (2) Judas, the son of James (Luke 6:16, Acts 1:13); and (3) Judas Barsabbas (Acts 15:22).

12. P. Oxy. 654.2–3; Attridge, appendix, 113 (126). P. Oxy. 654 has lacunae in lines 1–3. Strictly speaking, it reads: "These are the [secret] sayings which the living Jesus [spoke and which Judas, who is] also Thomas, [wrote down]" *(hotoi hoi [oi] logoi hoi [apokryphoi hous ela]lēsan Iē(sou)s ho k[ai egrapsen Iouda ho] kai thōma)*. The reconstruction is based in part on what we read in *NHC II (Nag Hammadi Codex II)*. But an alternative reconstruction of P. Oxy. 654 could yield a different reading: "[... and which Didymus, who is] also Thomas, [wrote down]" *(k[ai egrapsen didymos ho] kai thōma)*. At issue, then, is whether the earlier witness, P. Oxy. 654, equates Thomas with Judas (as happens in the *NHC II* and several other later witnesses) or not.

13. "The secret words that the savior spoke to Judas Thomas which I, even I Mathaias, wrote down, while I was walking, listening to them speak with one another."

14. *Acts of Thomas* §1; see H. J. W. Drijvers, "The Acts of Thomas," 339.

15. Eusebius, *Ecclesiastical History* 1.13.10: "After the ascension of Jesus, Judas, who was also called Thomas, sent to him Thaddeus, an apostle, one of the Seventy" (my translation). For the Greek, see Gustave Bardy, trans., *Eusèbe de Césarée: Histoire ecclésiastique*, SC 31, 41, 55 (Paris: Éditions du Cerf, 1952–1960).

16. A. F. J. Klijn, "John XIV:22 and the Name Judas Thomas," in *Studies in John Presented to Professor Dr. J. N. Sevenster on the Occasion of His Seventieth Birthday* (Leiden: Brill, 1970), 88–96; J. J. Gunther, "The Meaning and Origin of the Name 'Judas Thomas,'" *Le Muséon* 93 (1980): 113–148.

17. Riley, "Didymos Judas Thomas."

18. Ibid. Riley notes that the Latin Vulgate does not translate the Greek work *didymos* as *geminus* ("twin" in Latin) but reads: *Thomas qui dicitur Didymus*. Thus, "for readers of the Vulgate, for Christians in the Latin West, the whole idea that Thomas is a twin is lost. Latin Christians would just hear two foreign sounding names: Thomas Didymus."

19. Layton, *The Gnostic Scriptures*, 267.

20. Nicola Denzey Lewis, *Introduction to "Gnosticism": Ancient Voices, Christian Worlds* (New York: Oxford University Press, 2013), 104.

21. Uro, "Is *Thomas* an Encratite Gospel?," 24.

22. Gregory J. Riley, *Resurrection Reconsidered: Thomas and John in Controversy* (Minneapolis: Fortress Press, 1995), 2.

23. See, for example, Stephen J. Patterson, Hans-Gebhard Bethge, and James M. Robinson, *The Fifth Gospel: The Gospel of Thomas Comes of Age* (London: Trinity, 1998).

24. Elaine Pagels, *Beyond Belief: The Secret Gospel of Thomas* (New York: Random House, 2003).

25. I have benefited enormously from my conversations with my student J. Gregory Given regarding his doubts about the alleged Syrian provenance

of the *Gospel of Thomas* and the ideological reasons for that hypothesis's continuing hold in scholarship.

26. For the origin of the *Gospel of Thomas* in the Syrian encratite tradition, see D. A. Baker, "The '*Gospel of Thomas*' and the Syriac 'Liber Graduum,'" *New Testament Studies* (1965–1966): 49–55; A. F. J. Klijn, *Edessa, die Stadt des Apostels Thomas: Das älteste Christentum in Syrien*, Neukirchener Studienbücher 4 (Neukirchen-Vluyn: Neukirchener Verlag, 1965); L. W. Barnard, "The Origins and Emergence of the Church of Edessa during the First Two Centuries," *Vigiliae Christianae* 22 (1968): 161–175; P. Perkins, *The Gnostic Dialogue: The Early Church and the Crisis of Gnosticism* (New York: Paulist Press, 1980), 99–112; H. J. W. Drijvers, "Facts and Problems in Early Syriac-Speaking Christianity," *Second Century* 2, no. 3 (1982): 157–175.

27. B. P. Grenfell and A. S. Hunt, *Logia Iesou, Sayings of Our Lord* (Egypt Exploration Fund; London: Frowde, 1897).

28. B. P. Grenfell and A. S. Hunt, *New Sayings of Jesus and Fragment of a Lost Gospel from Oxyrhynchus* (London: Frowde, 1904).

29. AnneMarie Luijendijk, "Reading the Gospel of Thomas in the Third Century: Three Oxyrhynchus Papyri and Origen's Homilies," in *Reading New Testament Papyri in Context / Lire les papyrus du Nouveau Testament dans leur contexte*, ed. Claire Clivaz and Jean Zumstein (Leuven: Peeters, 2011), 241–267 (here, 257).

30. The variations on the story of the discovery of the cache all owe to James Robinson's different tellings; recently the story has been subject to suspicion and criticism: Mark Goodacre, "How Reliable Is the Story of the Nag Hammadi Discovery?," *Journal for the Study of the New Testament* 35, no. 4 (2013): 303–322; and Nicola Denzey Lewis, "Rethinking the Origins of the Nag Hammadi Codices," *Journal of Biblical Literature* 133, no. 2 (2014): 399–419.

31. The division of the *Gospel of Thomas* into a prologue and 114 sayings derives from the *editio princeps* of A. Guillaumont, H.-Ch. Puech, G. Quispel, W. C. Till, and Y. 'Abd Masih, [English edition] *The Gospel According to Thomas: Coptic Text Established and Translated* (Leiden: Brill; London: Collins; New York: Harper and Brothers, 1959). Most scholars have followed this numbering convention. But J. Leipoldt, "Ein neues Evangelium? Das koptische Thomasevangelium übersetzt und besprochen," *Theologischen Literaturzeitung* 83 (1958): 481–496, counted only 112 sayings in the text. R. Kasser, *L'Évangile selon Thomas: Présentation et commentaire théologique* (Bibliothèque théologique; Neuchâtel: Delachaux et Niestlé, 1961), argued that the *Gospel of Thomas* is a Gnostic hymn, and divided the text into 250 verses.

32. See, for example, Simon Gathercole, *The Composition of the Gospel of Thomas: Original Languages and Influences* (Cambridge: Cambridge University Press, 2012); and Mark Goodacre, *Thomas and the Gospels: The Case for Thomas's Familiarity with the Synoptics* (Grand Rapids, MI: Eerdmans, 2012).

33. Some have suspected that the *Gospel of Thomas* was originally written in Syriac, not Greek. The most recent representative of this view is Nicholas Perrin. See his *Thomas and Tatian: The Relationship between the Gospel of Thomas and the Diatessaron* (Atlanta: SBL, 2004) and "NHC II,2 and the Oxyrhynchus

Fragments (P. Oxy 1, 654, 655): Overlooked Evidence for Syriac '*Gospel of Thomas*,'" *Vigiliae Christianae* 58, no. 2 (2004): 138–151. For a critique of Perrin, see P. J. Williams, "Alleged Syriac Catchwords in the *Gospel of Thomas*," *Vigiliae Christianae* 63 (2009): 71–82.

34. See Bertil Gärtner, *The Theology of the Gospel of Thomas* (New York: Harper, 1961), 92.

35. See James Kugel, *In Potiphar's House: The Interpretive Life of Biblical Texts* (Cambridge, MA: Harvard University Press, 1994), 247–270.

36. Stanley Cavell, *Must We Mean What We Say? A Book of Essays* (Cambridge: Cambridge University Press, 2002), xxiii (my emphasis).

37. Stanley Cavell, *The Senses of Walden: An Expanded Edition* (Chicago: University of Chicago Press, 1992). Consider its opening: "What hope is there in a book about a book? My interest in this question of criticism, as I wrote my book about *Walden*, lay in determining why *Walden* is itself about a book, about its own writing and reading; and in entertaining certain experiments to determine how one philosophical text is prompted by another, why the history of philosophy is a history of such promptings, and what, accordingly, constitutes an original, or initiating, text" (xiii).

38. A. F. J. Klijn, *The* Acts of Thomas: *Introduction, Text, and Commentary* (Leiden: Brill, 2003), 7.

39. For example, Gärtner, *Theology of the Gospel of Thomas*, 98–111.

40. Including two other prominent texts "by" or about Judas Thomas: *The Book of Thomas the Contender* and the *Acts of Thomas*, both of which have Jesus as a character only *after* the resurrection.

41. Helmut Koester in his introduction to the *Gospel of Thomas:* "The proclamation of Jesus' suffering, death, the resurrection as well as the Christological titles Lord, Messiah / Christ, and Son of man . . . do not occur in the *GTh* (even in questions of the disciples and in self-designations of Jesus). In this, the *GTh* offers a sharp contrast to other writings from the Nag Hammadi library where Christological titles are frequently used and where the kerygma of cross and resurrection can at least be presupposed." (Layton, *Nag Hammadi II*, 2–7, 40).

42. Indeed §55 reads, "Jesus said, 'Whoever does not hate his father and his mother cannot be a disciple to me. And whoever does not hate his brothers and sisters and take up his cross in my way will not be worthy of me." This is the singular, oblique reference to the death of Jesus on the cross.

43. "He will become king (^{e}rro, §2)" and the "kingdom" ($m^{e}ntero$, §3) have the same root *(rro)*.

44. P. Oxy. 654.16–18 makes no mention of being known: "And, the [kingdom of God] is inside of you, [and it is outside of you. Whoever] knows [himself] will discover this."

45. This exchange is made fully reciprocal in P. Oxy. 654.26, which adds, "and the last will be first."

46. Uro, "Is *Thomas* an Encratite Gospel?," 150.

47. Ibid.

48. Gilles Quispel, "The *Gospel of Thomas*, Revisited," in *Colloque international sur les texts de Nag Hammadi*, ed. B. Bard, Bibliothèque copte de Nag

Hammadi, "Études" 1 (Quebec: University of Laval; Louvain: Peeters, 1981), 218–266 (here, 234). See also Gilles Quispel, *Makarius, das Thomasevangelium und das Lied von der Perle*, NovTSup 15 (Leiden: Brill, 1967); Quispel, "The Study of Encratism: A Historical Survey," in *La tradizione dell'enkrateia: Motivazioni ontologiche e protologiche; Atti de Colloquio Internazionale Milano, 20–23 aprile, 1982*, ed. U. Bianchi (Rome: Edizioni dell'ateneo), 35–81.

49. On primordial androgyny, see Wayne A. Meeks, "The Image of the Androgyne: Some Uses of a Symbol in Earliest Christianity," *History of Religions* 13 (1973–1974): 165–208; D. R. MacDonald, *There Is No Male and Female*, HDR 20 (Philadelphia: Fortress Press, 1987).

50. A. F. J. Klijn, "The 'Single One' in the *Gospel of Thomas*," *Journal of Biblical Literature* 81 (1962): 271–278 (here, 272). Klijn argues that the translator uses such Coptic terms as "one" *(oua)*, "single one" *(oua ouōt)*, and "solitary" *(monachos)* to translate the Greek word "one" *(heis)* or perhaps even the Syriac word "single one" *(īhīdāyā)*.

51. Ibid., 273–276.

52. Ibid., 276–278. See also R. A. Baer, *Philo's Use of the Categories Male and Female* (Leiden: Brill, 1970).

53. April DeConick, *Recovering the Original Gospel of Thomas* (London: T&T Clark, 2005), and the companion volume, DeConick, *The Original Gospel of Thomas in Translation* (London: T&T Clark, 2007). The first of these volumes is in fact dedicated to her *Großdoktorvater* Gilles Quispel. See also DeConick, "Mysticism and the *Gospel of Thomas*," in *Das Thomasevangelium: Entstehung, Rezeption, Theologie*, ed. Jörg Frey et al. (Berlin: De Gruyter, 2008), 206–221; DeConick, *Seek to See Him: Ascent and Vision Mysticism in the Gospel of Thomas* (Leiden: Brill, 1996); DeConick, *Voices of the Mystics* (New York: T&T Clark, 2001).

54. DeConick, *The Original Gospel of Thomas in Translation*, 9: "According to the contents of these accretions, they thought that their church was Paradise on earth. They were Adam and Eve before the Fall. Through encratic performance and visionary experience, they came to believe that they had achieved the eschatological promises of God in the present. The grandest of these promises was the complete transformation of their bodies into the original luminous Image of God."

55. See Clement, *Stromata* I.xv; VII.xvii; but also *Paedagogus* II.ii.33.

56. Klijn, "The 'Single One' in the *Gospel of Thomas*," 271.

57. DeConick, *The Original Gospel of Thomas in Translation*, 115–118.

58. The word *pōh* appears twice in §77 in two different senses. In the first case, *pōh* means "attain" or "reach," as in "unto me did the all extend *(pōh)*." The same sense of *pōh* appears in §97 as a verb: "When [a certain woman] reached *(entares-pōh)* her house." In the second case of §77, *pōh* means "split" or "divide" (hence in P. Oxy 1.29 it appears as *schizon*). The same sense of *pōh* appears in §21 ("Let there be among you a man of understanding. When the grain ripened [literally, split open *(pōh)*], he came quickly with his sickle in his hand and reaped it. Whoever has ears to hear, let him hear") and §47 ("An old patch is not sewn onto a new garment, because a tear [*pōh*] would result").

59. Uro, "Is *Thomas* an Encratite Gospel?," 157: "*Monachos*, although a Greek loan-word, has not been preserved in the Greek fragments of the gospel, and it has sometimes been suggested that it derives from a fourth-century Coptic editor and not from (the) earlier Greek author(s)."

60. E. A. Judge, "The Earliest Use of Monachos for 'Monk' (P. Coll. Youtie 77) and the Origins of Monasticism," *Jahrbuch für Antike und Christentum* 20 (1977): 72–89; F. E. Morard, "Monachos: Une importation sémitique en Égypte?," *Studia Patristica* 12 (1975): 242–246; Morard, "Encore quelques reflexions sur Monachos," *Vigiliae Christianae* 34 (1980): 395–401.

61. Sidney Griffith, "Asceticism in the Church of Syria: The Hermeneutics of Early Syrian Monasticism," in *Asceticism*, ed. Vincent L. Wimbush and Richard Valantasis (Oxford: Oxford University Press, 1998), 224–225.

62. Uro, "Is *Thomas* an Encratite Gospel?," 159.

63. See Chapter 1.

64. DeConick, *The Original Gospel of Thomas in Translation*, 119.

65. Richard Valantasis, *The Making of the Self: Ancient and Modern Asceticism* (Eugene, OR: Cascade, 2008), 191; originally published as "Is the *Gospel of Thomas* Ascetical? Revisiting an Old Problem with a New Theory," *JECS* 7, no. 1 (1999): 55–81. Much of Valantasis's book is devoted to redefining asceticism and applying that redefinition to other early Christian literature. See esp. chap. 5, "A Theory of Asceticism, Revised." See also his translation and commentary, *The Gospel of Thomas* (London: Routledge, 1997).

66. Ibid., 195.

67. Ibid., 204.

68. Ibid.

69. Denzey Lewis, *Introduction to "Gnosticism,"* 115.

70. Henry Corbin, *L'homme de lumière dans le soufisme iranien* (Paris: Éditions Présence, 1971): $1 \times 1 = 1$. But here if 1_1 is Jesus, and 1_2 is Thomas, then $1_1 = 1_2$ (although $1_2 \neq 1_1$), but $1_2 \leq 1_1$.

71. Denzey Lewis, *Introduction to "Gnosticism,"* 115. As she points out, the *Gospel of Thomas* never uses the term "Christ."

72. Uro, *Thomas*, 44. It is paired with an equally baffling saying: "Jesus said, 'The images are manifest to man, but the light in them remains concealed in the image of the light of the father. He will become manifest, but his image will remain concealed by his light'" (§83).

73. S. L. Davies, "The Christology and Protology of the *Gospel of Thomas*," *Journal of Biblical Literature* 11 (1992): 663–682; E. Pagels, "Exegesis of Genesis 1 in the Gospel of Thomas and John," *Journal of Biblical Literature* 118 (1999): 477–496.

74. DeConick, *Seek to See Him*, 148–172.

75. Ibid., 154; see also J. Fossum, *The Name of God and the Angel of the Lord: Samaritan and Jewish Concepts of Intermediation and the Origin of Gnosticism* (Tübingen: Mohr Siebeck, 1985).

76. III.20, IV.23. See Joseph Wilson Trigg, trans., *Origen* (New York: Routledge, 1998), 108, 109. For the Greek of the *Commentary on John*, see C. Blanc, ed. and trans., *Origène: Commentaire sur saint Jean*, 3 vols. SC 120, 157, 222 (Paris: Cerf, 1: 1966; 2: 1970; 3: 1975).

77. IV.2, in Trigg, *Origen*, 109.
78. IV.23, in Trigg, *Origen*, 109.
79. See Luigi S. M. Gambero, *Mary and the Fathers of the Church: The Blessed Virgin Mary in Patristic Thought* (San Francisco: Ignatius Press, 1999), 75–77.
80. *Homily* 1.2, in Origen, *Homilies on Luke*, trans. Joseph T. Leinhard (Washington, DC: Catholic University of America Press, 1996), 5–6.
81. For a discussion of the different views on the dating of the *Homilies*, see Leinhard's preface to *Homilies on Luke*, xxiv.
82. Luijendijk, "Reading the Gospel of Thomas," 261.
83. This phrase occurs in the first case, *Hom.Jer.* 27.3.7. In both cases he quotes a saying that corresponds to §82 in the *NHC II*: "Jesus said, 'Whoever is near me is near the fire, and whoever is far from me is far from the kingdom." In the second case, *Hom.Josh.* 4.3, he adds lines that are not part of *NHC II* §82: "If you are gold and silver and have drawn near to the fire, you will shine forth more splendid and glowing because of the fire." The first case occurs in Origen, *Hom.Jer.* 27.3.7: for an English translation, see J. C. Smith, trans., *Origen: Homilies on Jeremiah, Homily on 1 Kings 28* (Washington, DC: Catholic University of America Press, 1998), Homily 27 (50), 254–255; for the Latin translation, see P. Husson, ed. and trans., *Origène: Homélies sur Jérémie*, SC 238 (Paris: Cerf, 1977). The second case occurs in Origen, *Hom.Josh.* 4.3: for an English translation, see B. J. Bruce, trans., and C. White, ed., *Origen: Homilies on Joshua* (Washington, DC: Catholic University of America Press, 2002), Homily 4, 55–56; for the Latin translation, see Annie Jaubert, ed. and trans., *Origène: Homélies sur Josué* (Paris: Cerf, 1960), 154, 156.

3 Syzygies, Twins, and Mirrors

1. Two other ancient Christian texts are associated with the figure of Thomas: the *Infancy Gospel of Thomas* and the *Apocalypse of Thomas*, but neither is relevant for the tradition of the divine double. The *Infancy Gospel of Thomas* is attributed to Thomas, who is described as "the holy apostle" (Greek MS B) or "the Israelite philosopher" (Greek MS A). There is nothing to suggest that this text regards Thomas as the twin of Jesus, apart from the inference that Thomas might be the source for these stories about Jesus's childhood. In other words, there is no discernible theology of the twin, and the text does not seem to have any connection to the *Gospel of Thomas*, or any of the other texts that compose the Thomas "tradition." Similarly, in the *Apocalypse of Thomas* Jesus tells Thomas about the signs that will attend the end of the world, but neither the fact of Thomas's being the twin of Jesus nor any broader significance of that fact is explored in the revelation.

2. All quotations from Tatian's *Oratio* are from M. Whittaker, trans., *Tatian: Oratio ad Graecos and Fragments* (Oxford: Clarendon, 1982), who in turns draws on E. Schwartz, ed., *Oratio ad Graecos* (TU 4.1; Leipzig: J. C. Hinrichs, 1888). Here the quotation is from *Oratio* 43.10 (77), that is, Schwartz's page and line number (page number in Whittaker). For more on Tatian, see Naomi Koltun-Fromm, "Re-imagining Tatian: The Damaging Effects of Polemical Rhetoric," *Journal of Early Christian Studies* 16 (2008):

1–30; and Emily J. Hunt, *Christianity in the Second Century: The Case of Tatian* (London: Routledge, 2003).
3. *Oratio* 20.16 (36); Whittaker, ix.
4. Tatian never speaks of Christianity or, for that matter, Christ. On the antiquity of the barbarian philosophy, see *Oratio* 30.4 (55), 31.4–5 (55, 57).
5. Koltun-Fromm, "Re-imagining Tatian," 4.
6. *Oratio* 5.23 (10).
7. *Oratio* 6.9–11 (10).
8. H. J. W. Drijvers, "The Acts of Thomas," in *New Testament Apocrypha*, vol. 2, ed. W. Schneemelcher (Louisville, KY: Westminster John Knox, 1992), 335. See also H. J. W. Drijvers and G. J. Reinink, "Taufe und Licht: Tatian, Ebionäeevangelium und Thomasakten," in *Text and Testimony: Essays on New Testament and Apocryphal Literature in Honor of A. F. J. Klijn*, ed. T. Baarda et al. (Kampen: Kok, 1988), 91–110.
9. *Oratio* 7.30 (14).
10. *Oratio* 12.18–22 (22).
11. *Oratio* 14.21–15.7 (26–28).
12. See, for example, Plato's famous analogy of the soul as a charioteer with two horses. At *Phaedrus* 254a5 the obedient horse is described as the *syzygos* or "yokemate" of its violent, disobedient counterpart.
13. *Oratio* 23.3–5 (42).
14. *Oratio* 16.4–6 (28).
15. *Oratio* 27.19 (48); compare this with *Gospel of Thomas* 3: "Jesus said, 'If those who lead you say to you, 'See, the kingdom is in the sky,' then the birds of the sky will precede you. If they say, 'It is in the sea,' then the fish will precede you. Rather, the kingdom is inside you, and it is outside of you. When you come to know yourselves, then you will become known, and you will realize that it is you who are the sons of the living father. But if you do not know yourselves, you dwell in poverty and it is you who are that poverty."
16. The so-called "Great Account" in *Against Heresies* 1.1–8.
17. See Nicola Denzey Lewis, *Introduction to "Gnosticism": Ancient Voices, Christian Worlds* (New York: Oxford University Press, 2013), 64–66. For another introduction to Valentinus and Valentinianism, see Ismo Dunderberg, "The School of Valentinus," in *A Companion to Second-Century Heretics*, ed. Antti Marjanen and Ptri Luomanen (Leiden: Brill, 2005). For a study that is especially attentive to the differences between Valentinus and his successors, see Christoph Markschies, *Valentinus Gnosticus? Untersuchungen zur valentinianischen Gnosis mit einem Kommentar zu den Fragmentum Valentins* (Tübingen: J. C. B. Mohr, 1992); see also Markschies, "Valentinian Gnosticism: Toward the Anatomy of a School," in *The Nag Hammadi Library after Fifty Years: Proceedings of the 1995 Society of Biblical Literature Commemoration*, ed. John D. Turner and Anne McGuire (Leiden: Brill, 1997).
18. All citations of the *Gospel of Philip* are from Wesley W. Isenberg's translation in Bentley Layton, ed., *The Coptic Gnostic Library: A Complete Edition of the Nag Hammadi Codices*, vol. 2 (Leiden: Brill, 2000). See also Hans-Martin Schenke's commentary, *Das Philippus-Evangelium* (Berlin: Akademie Verlag, 1997).

19. Isenberg's introduction in James R. Robinson, ed. *The Nag Hammadi Library in English* (San Francisco: Harper and Row, 1981), 139.

20. *Gospel of Philip* 67,27–30: "The lord did everything in a mystery, a baptism, and a chrism and a eucharist and a redemption and a bridal chamber."

21. Isenberg's introduction in Robinson, *The Nag Hammadi Library in English*, 140. I will discuss 58,10–14 in what follows. The other passages Isenberg cites in support of this summary are these: "When Eve was still in Adam death did not exist. When she was separated from him death came into being. If he enters again and attains his former self, death will be no more" (68,22–26); "If the woman had not separated from the man, she should not die with the man. His separation became the beginning of death. Because of this Christ came to repair the separation which was from the beginning and unite the two, and to give life to those who died as a result of the separation and unite them. But the woman is united to her husband in the bridal chamber. Indeed those who have united in the bridal chamber will no longer be separated. Thus Eve separated from Adam because it was not in the bridal chamber that she united with him" (70,10–22).

22. April DeConick, *Seek to See Him: Ascent and Vision Mysticism in the Gospel of Thomas* (Leiden: Brill, 1996), 149.

23. On the ambiguity of "bridal chamber," see Denzey Lewis, *Introduction to "Gnosticism,"* 97: "Equally mysterious to the Redemption is the Valentinian rite known as the Bridal Chamber. People have spent a lot of time trying to decide if the Valentinians celebrated an actual earthly marriage of a man and a woman, or whether the Bridal Chamber was a sort of ritual of sexual intercourse between husband and wife, or whether the rite refers not to social or sexual practices on earth but was actually some kind of 'spiritual marriage' performed in the higher realms between a soul and its spiritual counterpart."

24. For the standard Greek-English version of the *Excerpta ex Theodoto*, see Robert Pierce Casey, *The Excerpta ex Theodoto of Clement of Alexandria* (London: Christophers, 1934). Translations are my own.

25. DeConick, *Seek to See Him*, 149–150.

26. Einar Thomassen, *The Spiritual Seed: The Church of the "Valentinians"* (Leiden: Brill, 2006), 380.

27. Here I have followed Thomassen's own translation in ibid., 381.

28. Ibid., 382. Thomassen continues, "In any case baptism seems to have brought about a personal and intimate relationship between the individual initiate and his or her angel, a relationship where the angel acts as a helper and a paraclete for the individual vis-à-vis the Pleroma—a moral support in this world, no doubt, but above all a reliable companion on the journey to the beyond."

29. Ibid., 383.

30. All citations from the *Book of Thomas* are from John D. Turner's English translation and the critical edition of the Coptic text in Bentley Layton, ed., *Nag Hammadi Codex II, 2–7* (Leiden: Brill, 1989), 173–205.

31. Unlike the *Gospel of Thomas*, however, which has produced its own scholarly cottage industry, the *Book of Thomas* has been studied almost exclusively

by a single scholar, John D. Turner. See John D. Turner, "A New Link in the Syrian Judas Thomas Tradition," in *Essays on the Nag Hammadi Texts in Honor of Alexander Böhlig*, ed. Martin Krause, Nag Hammadi Studies 3 (Leiden: Brill, 1972), 109–119; Turner, *The Book of Thomas the Contender: Coptic Text with Translation, Introduction, and Commentary*, Society of Biblical Literature Dissertation Series 23 (Missoula, MT: Scholars Press, 1985); see also D. Kirchner et al., "Das Buch des Thomas," *Theologische Literaturzeitung* 102 (1977): 793–804. Turner regards the *Book of Thomas* as rather artlessly stitched together from two different sources. The first half, §A, was originally a "revelation dialogue" between Jesus and Thomas set after Jesus's death and resurrection, on the eve of his ascension. But this dialogue is anything but Platonic: rather than a rigorous dialectic by which Socrates helps birth the truth in and for his interlocutor, this text stages a series of "questions and answers" *(erotapokriseis)*, in which Thomas's queries prompt Jesus to give short teachings. On the question of the relationship of *Book of Thomas* to Plato, see John D. Turner, "The Book of Thomas and the Platonic Jesus," in *Colloque international "L'évangile selon Thomas et les textes de Nag Hammadi*," ed. Louis Painchaud and Paul-Hubert Poirier (Quebec: Presses de l'Université Laval, 2007), 599–633; on the question of the genre of *Book of Thomas*, see H. Dörries, "Erotapokriseis," *Reallexikon für Antike und Christentum* 6 (Stuttgart: Hiersemann, 1966): 342–370. The second half, §B, is a long monologue by Jesus, without interruption or prompt, as recorded by a disciple Mathaias. According to Turner, §B was originally a collection of sayings by Jesus: but in this case, an original sayings collection (such as one finds in the *Gospel of Thomas*) has been filled in (like cracks with mortar) with all manner of secondary interpretation—thus the sayings now resemble a didactic monologue. On the genre of "sayings collections," see J. M. Robinson, "Logoi Sophon: On the Gattung of Q," in J. M. Robinson and H. Koester, *Trajectories through Early Christianity* (Philadelphia: Westminster, 1971), 71–113. §A and §B were stitched together, and the didactic monologue became Jesus's parting speech, his last will and testament before ascending.

32. Coptic *pa-soeiš*, "my twin," translating *didymos*, and *pašbⁿrⁿmmāe*, "my true companion," translating *syzygos*. Gregory J. Riley, "Didymos Judas Thomas, the Twin Brother of Jesus," in *Gemini and the Sacred: Twins in Religion and Myth*, ed. Kimberley Patton (London: I. B. Tauris, forthcoming).

33. As Bentley Layton does in his translation of *The Book of Thomas* in his collection, *The Gnostic Scriptures* (Garden City, NY: Doubleday, 1987), 400–412.

34. The author(s) of the *Book of Thomas* almost certainly knew the *Gospel of Thomas*, as the allusions above (and others) suggest: *Book of Thomas* 181:1f is an allusion to the prologue to the *Gospel of Thomas*; *Book of Thomas* 140.41–141.4 is an allusion to *Gospel of Thomas* §2. Turner further speculates that the *Gospel of Thomas*, the *Book of Thomas*, and the *Acts of Thomas* were all written in Edessa (see Turner, "A New Link in the Syrian Judas Thomas Tradition"). As I suggested in Chapter 2, I am somewhat wary of scholars' attempts to fix the provenance of these texts, as they often serve to overdetermine our interpretation of them. Turner, for example, proposes that the *Book of Thomas* is a "new link"

in our understanding of the Thomas tradition. He maps the chronological sequence of these three Thomas texts on a progression in terms of their (a) genre, (b) the prominence of Judas Thomas, and (c) their views of asceticism. With respect to genre: (1) The *Gospel of Thomas* preserves the early Christian genre of "sayings collection"; (2) the *Book of Thomas* is a decadent form of this early genre, in which sayings are ossified and set into a staged dialogue, which functions more as a revelatory and didactic monologue; (3) finally, the *Acts of Thomas* recasts the drama as a romance or ancient novel. Corresponding to the shift in genre is the shift in the prominence of Thomas: (1) Thomas is relatively marginal to the *Gospel of Thomas* (according to Turner, at least), appearing only in the prologue and §13; (2) Thomas becomes more prominent in the *Book of Thomas*, where he is Jesus's dialogue partner and the recipient of his private revelations; (3) Thomas becomes the main character in the *Acts of Thomas*, displacing Jesus almost entirely. Finally, Turner sees both of these shifts reflected in the mounting asceticism of the Thomas tradition: "All three texts have a dualistic view of man. In the *Gospel* the motif of sexual abstinence is merely present, being neither dominant nor explicit (sayings 22, 79, 101, 105, 114). While in [the *Book of Thomas*] and the *Acts of Thomas* asceticism is more developed, and Thomas's apostolic mission is to exhort mankind to abandon sexual passion" (ibid., 117).

On the one hand, I commend Turner for acknowledging that the *Gospel of Thomas* does *not* forward an ethic of sexual renunciation. This comports nicely with my own anti-encratic interpretation of the gospel, especially its meditation on the one and the two, the solitary and the single one (see Chapter 2). Furthermore, Turner is certainly right that the *Book of Thomas* and the *Acts of Thomas* do forward an ethic of sexual renunciation. On the other hand, by putting the three texts on some neat scheme of progression, he suggests that the encratic asceticism of the later texts was already present in the gospel *in potentia*. The same goes for the other progressions he maps: they are simply disparate points on a grid that do not form a single line or a neat scheme of progression. Different genres (sayings, dialogues, romances), for instance, need not be mapped diachronically: they can serve different purposes at different times. So too with character: the prominence of Thomas largely correlates to the genre. Thomas becomes prominent in a dialogue because a dialogue has two speaking roles. Thomas displaces Jesus in the *Acts of Thomas* precisely because it is a book of "Acts" narrating the missionary activity of the apostles rather than the life and ministry of the savior. Turner's tripartite progression indulges in arranging sparse ancient witnesses into overdetermined narratives.

35. Lautaro Roig Lanzillotta has recently argued, against the consensus, that the *Acts of Thomas* were originally composed in Greek, and much earlier (second century) than usually thought. He also argues that the "Hymn of the Pearl" is original to the *Acts*, and not a later insertion. See "A Syriac Original for the *Acts of Thomas*?: The Hypothesis of Syriac Priority Revisited," in *Early Christian and Jewish Narrative: The Role of Religion in Shaping Narrative Forms*, ed. Ilaria Ramelli and Judith Perkins (Tübingen: Mohr Siebeck, 2015), 105–133.

36. Drijvers, "The Acts of Thomas," 23.

37. Ibid., 325, 327.
38. Ibid., 327.
39. All citations are based on Drijvers's English translation, which largely follows M. Bonnet's Greek text in *Acta apostolorum apocrypha*, vol. 2.2 (Leipzig: Mendelssohn, 1903; reprint 1972). I have taken the liberty of changing his thee / thou / thy to "you" and "your." Citations of the Greek *Acts of Thomas* provide number of the act, the section in Bonnet's edition, and the page number in Drijver's translation in parentheses: e.g., *ATh* x.x (xxx). For the Syriac text and English translation, see W. Wright, *Apocryphal Acts of the Apostles* (London: Williams and Norgate, 1871; reprint Hildesheim: G. Olms, 1990), 1:171ff (Syriac), 2:146ff (English). See also A. F. J. Klijn, *The Acts of Thomas: Introduction, Text, and Commentary* (Leiden: Brill, 2003). Citations of the Syriac *Acts* provide the number of the act, the section in Wright's edition, and the page number in Klijn (which reprints Wright's translation, along with commentary). See also Harold Attridge's recent English translation, *The Acts of Thomas* (Salem, OR: Polebridge, 2010); see also the recent edition of A. Piñera and G. del Cerro, eds., *Hechos apócrifos de los* apostolos, vol. 2 (Madrid: Biblioteca de Autores Cristianos, 2004–2005). For a recent collection of essays and a very helpful bibliography, see Jan N. Bremmer, ed., *The Apocryphal Acts of Thomas* (Leuven: Peeters, 2001).
40. Drijvers, "The Acts of Thomas," 327.
41. See J. Michael LaFargue, *Language and Gnosis: The Opening Scenes of the* Acts of Thomas (Philadelphia: Fortress Press, 1985).
42. *ATh* 1.1 (339).
43. Ibid.
44. *ATh* 1.2 (340).
45. *ATh* 1.6–7 (341–342).
46. *ATh* 1.8 (342).
47. *ATh* 1.9 (343).
48. *ATh* 1.10 (343).
49. Syriac *ATh* 1.10 (42).
50. On the titles "companion" and "fellow traveler," see Klijn, *The* Acts of Thomas, 43–44.
51. *ATh* 1.11 (343).
52. *ATh* 1.11 (344).
53. *ATh* 1.12 (344).
54. Ibid.
55. *ATh* 1.14 (344).
56. For a very insightful comparison of the bride and bridegroom's confessions, see Richard Valantasis, "The Nuptial Chamber Revisited: The *Acts of Thomas* and Cultural Intertextuality," in *Semeia* 80 (1997): 261–276. For more on intertextuality, see Harold A. Attridge, "Intertextuality in the *Acts of Thomas*," *Semeia* 80 (1997): 87–124. On further issues of gender in the *Acts of Thomas*, see also Paul Germond, "A Rhetoric of Gender in Early Christianity: Sex and Salvation in the *Acts of Thomas*," in *Rhetoric, Scripture, and Theology: Essays from the 1994 Pretoria Conference*, ed. Stanley E. Porter and Thomas H. Olbricht (Sheffield: Sheffield Academic Press, 1996), 350–368;

Harold W. Attridge, "'Masculine Fellowship' in the *Acts of Thomas*," in *The Future of Early Christianity*, ed. Birger Pearson (Minneapolis: Augsburg-Fortress, 1991), 406–413.

57. *ATh* 1.15 (345).

58. See Klijn, *The* Acts of Thomas, 38–39. Klijn suggests that the original wedding hymn was a celebration of a heavenly female being, a divine Mother to match God the Father. While I do think that there is evidence of such a view of a divine Father and Mother in the *Acts*, I am not convinced that the daughter of light was originally such a divine Mother. On the contrary, I think the daughter of light was originally the individual soul betrothed to Christ the bridegroom, which is more or less preserved in the Greek.

59. *ATh* 1.7 (342).

60. Syriac *ATh* 1.7 (29).

61. See Susan E. Myers, "The Spirit as Mother in Early Syriac-Speaking Christianity," in *Women and Gender in Ancient Religions: Interdisciplinary Approaches*, ed. Stephen P. Ahearne-Kroll et al. (Tübingen: Mohr Siebeck, 2010), 427–462, esp. 442–455.

62. *ATh* 2.27 (349–350).

63. *ATh* 5.50 (360).

64. As cited in Susan E. Myers, "The Spirit as Mother," 449n96.

65. Drijvers, "The Acts of Thomas," 333–334; Caroline Johnson follows Drijvers's interpretation in "Ritual Epicleses in the Greek *Acts of Thomas*," in *The Apocryphal Acts of the Apostles: Harvard Divinity School Studies*, ed. François Bovon, Ann Graham Brock, and Christopher R. Matthews (Cambridge, MA: Harvard University Press, 1999), 203.

66. *ATh* 3.31 (352).

67. *ATh* 3.32 (352).

68. Forming a diptych with the serpent is another fantastic animal, the ass's colt from the fourth act, who upon seeing Thomas addresses him, "Twin of Christ, apostle of the Most High and fellow-initiate into the hidden word of Christ, who did receive his secret saying, fellow-worker of the Son of God, who being free did become a slave and being sold did lead many to freedom" (*ATh* 4.39 [355]).

69. *ATh* 3.34 (353). The only other character said to have two forms is a demon who has afflicted a woman for years: he once appeared simultaneously as a young man and an old man to her and her handmaiden: see *ATh* 4.43 (357). But this is different from Thomas's own dyomorphy, which straddles the present world and the afterlife.

70. *ATh* 3.34 (353).

71. Ibid.

72. *ATh* 3.34 (353–354).

73. *ATh* 6.54 (362).

74. *ATh* 6.57 (363).

75. *ATh* 6.61 (364).

76. *ATh* 3.34 (353), 4.39 (355).

77. *ATh* 9.86 (373).

78. *ATh* 13.153 (399).

79. On the theme of polymorphic Christology in the *ATh* and other apocryphal acts, see David R. Cartlidge, "Transfigurations of Metamorphosis Traditions in the Acts of John, Thomas, and Peter," *Semeia* 38 (1986): 53–66; and Paul Foster, "Polymorphic Christology: Its Origins and Development in Early Christianity," *Journal of Theological Studies* 58, no. 1 (2007): 66–99.

80. The Greek manuscript is held in the British Library (BM Add. 14645, folios 30^v to 32^r); the Syriac manuscript is held in the Biblioteca Vallicelliana in Rome (B35, folios 124^r to 125^v).

81. *HP* Incipit (38). Citations of the "Hymn of the Pearl" are from Johan Ferreira, trans., *The Hymn of the Pearl: The Syriac and Greek Texts with Introduction, Translations, and Notes* (Sydney: St. Paul's, 2002). Citations will be: *HP* line number (and page number in Ferreira's edition).

82. Gerard P. Luttikhuizen, "The Hymn of Jude Thomas, the Apostle, in the Country of the Indians," in Bremmer, *The Apocryphal Acts of Thomas*, 103.

83. Bentley Layton, *The Gnostic Scriptures*, 366; contested by Luttikhuizen, "The Hymn of Jude Thomas," 112–113.

84. Luttikhuizen, "The Hymn of Jude Thomas," 104–105.

85. *HP* 15 (182).

86. *HP* 48 (48); on the notion of the brother as "viceroy," see Paul-Hubert Poirier, *L'Hymne de la Perle des Actes de Thomas: Introduction, Texte, Traduction, Commentaire* (Louvain: P. Pierier, 1981), 212–223; on the notion of the brother as a "second in command" or "double," see ibid., 223–227. The word *trayānā* appears in two other verses in the Syriac (§§42, 60).

87. *ATh* 5.50 (360).

88. *HP* 15 (42).

89. See also Gal 3:29; Eph 5:5; Col 3:24; Heb 6:17, 11:19; Jas 2:5.

90. *HP* 16, 20 (42).

91. *HP* 23 (44).

92. *HP* 25 (44).

93. *HP* 26–27 (44).

94. *HP* 43, 44–46 (48).

95. *HP* 46, 48 (48).

96. *HP* 55 (50).

97. The Greek reads, "and what had been written there / [was according to] what was engraved in my heart" (55 [90]).

98. *HP* 65 (52).

99. *HP* 66 (52); 72, 67, 67, 68 (54).

100. *HP* 75–80 (56), 88 (58).

101. Hans Jonas, *The Gnostic Religion* (Boston: Beacon Press, 2001), 122: "In our narrative the garment has become this figure itself and acts like a person. It symbolizes the heavenly or eternal self of the person, his original idea, a kind of double or *alter ego* preserved in the upper world while he labors down below: as a Mandaean text puts it, 'his image is kept safe in its place' (G 90). It grows with his deeds and its form is perfected by his toils. It fullness marks the fulfillment of his task and therefore his release from exile in the world."

102. *HP* 80 (56).

103. *HP* 99 (62).
104. *HP* 105 (64).

4 Mani and His Twin-Companion

1. See Albert Henrichs, "Mani and the Babylonian Baptists: A Historical Confrontation," *Harvard Studies in Classical Philology* 77 (1973): 23–59. Henrichs opens his brilliant essay with this same episode. This and the other quotations are Henrichs's somewhat free adaptations of the surviving Coptic translation of the *Kephalaia of the Teacher*. Iain Gardner's more literal translation reads, "Please, / our master [Manich]aios, give us two Manis *(nen manichaios sneu)* resembling you; / [pass]ing for you! Good, peaceful, and compassionate [. . .] disciples in righteousness [like] you / [. . .] one Mani will remain with us as you; / [and the other will go to] King [Sha]pur, his [mind] at ease, / [and proclaiming it] to him" (*Keph.* 183,27–33). All subsequent citations are from Iain Gardner's English translation, *The Kephalaia of the Teacher: The Edited Coptic Manichaean Texts in Translation with Commentary* (Leiden: Brill, 1995). Citations of the Coptic are from H. J. Polotsky and A. Böhlig, eds. and trans., *Kephalaia I*, 1, Hälfte (Lieferung 1–10) (Stuttgart: W. Kohlhammer, 1940). Citations are of page and line numbers in Polotsky and Böhlig's edition, which Gardner also follows.
2. "And thus, if tw[o] Manis had [come] to the world, what place would be able to tolerate them, or [what land] would / [be able] to accept them?" (*Keph.* 188,4–6).
3. "I, a single Mani *(anak ou-manichaios en-ouōt)*" (*Keph.* 184,3).
4. Ludwig Koenen, "Augustine and Manichaeism in Light of the Cologne Mani Codex," *Illinois Classical Studies* 3 (1978): 173: "The *Nous* (mind) of Mani and his Twin are the two complementary aspects of Mani's identity. The first represents him as incorporated in the body; the second represents his being as it is outside the body. Together they are the one complete Mani."
5. Henrichs, "Mani and the Babylonian Baptists," 26.
6. *Keph.* 15,19.
7. This section owes much to the work of Jason David BeDuhn, Nicholas Baker-Brian, Albert Henrichs, Hans-Joachim Klimkeit, Iain Gardner, and Samuel N. C. Lieu.
8. Jason David BeDuhn, *The Manichaean Body: In Discipline and Ritual* (Baltimore: Johns Hopkins University Press, 2000), ix.
9. Ibid., 5.
10. Much of what follows depends on the excellent introduction by Iain Gardner and Samuel N. C. Lieu to their compilation, *Manichaean Texts from the Roman Empire* (Cambridge: Cambridge University Press, 2004), 1–25.
11. Mani's canon consisted of seven works: (1) *The Living* (or *Great*) *Gospel*; (2) *The Treasure of Life*; (3) *The Pragmateia* (or *Treatise* or *Essay*); (4) *The Book of Mysteries*; (5) *The Book of the Giants*; (6) *Letters*; (7) *Psalms* and *Prayers*.
12. The structure of the church is in fact more elaborate than this. The church was headed by Mani and after him his deputy (*archēgos* or *princeps*). Below the deputy were 12 apostles, followed by 72 bishops, and 360 presbyters. Below

this ecclesiastical hierarchy were the ranks of the elect and the catechumens (*auditores*).

13. Gardner and Lieu, *Manichaean Texts*, 9–10.
14. Ibid., 8.
15. See John C. Reeves's recent book, *Prolegomena to a History of Islamicate Manichaeism* (Oakville, CT: Equinox Press, 2011).
16. See C. Eduard Sachau, ed., *Albērūnī, Chronologie orientalischer Völker* (Leipzig: Brockhaus, 1878); English translation also by Sachau, *Al-Bīrūnī, the Chronology of All Nations* (Frankfurt: Minerva-Verl., 1969). Citations include the page number from Sachau's Arabic text, followed by the page number from his translation (e.g., 207, 190).
17. Nicholas Baker-Brian, *Manichaeism: An Ancient Faith Rediscovered* (New York: T&T Clark, 2011), 26–28.
18. On this and other sources for al-Bīrūnī, see Michael H. Browder, "Al-Bīrūnī's Manichaean Sources," in *Manichaean Studies: Proceedings of the First International Conference on Manichaeism*, ed. Peter Bryder (Lund: Plus Ultra, 1998), 19–28.
19. *Chronology* 207, 190.
20. *Chronology* 208, 190.
21. *Chronology* 208, 191.
22. Baker-Brian, *Manichaeism*, 43.
23. Bayard Dodge, ed. and trans., *The Fihrist of al-Nadīm: A Tenth-Century Survey of Muslim Culture* (New York: Columbia University Press, 1970), 774. I have taken the liberty of updating Dodge's language, changing thee / thou to you / your, etc.
24. This is the standard Arabic word for twin (*at-taw'am*) with the *hamzah* having been omitted, as is common in old manuscripts.
25. François de Blois, "Manes' 'Twin' in Iranian and non-Iranian Texts," in *Religious Themes and Texts of Pre-Islamic Iran and Central Asia*, ed. C. G. Cereti, M. Maggi, and E. Provasi (Wiesbaden: Reichert, 2003), 12–13.
26. Ibid., 14.
27. Dodge, *The Fihrist of al-Nadīm*, 775.
28. Ibid., 776.
29. *Ecclesiastical History* 7.31. This and subsequent citations are from Paul L. Maier, trans., *Eusebius: The Church History* (Grand Rapids, MI: Kregel, 1999).
30. Frederick W. Danker, *A Greek-English Lexicon of the New Testament and Other Early Christian Literature* (Chicago: University of Chicago Press, 2000), 764–765.
31. Ibid., 766.
32. See Christine Trevett, *Montanism: Gender, Authority and the New Prophecy* (Cambridge: Cambridge University Press, 1996); Laura Nasrallah, *An Ecstasy of Folly: Rhetorical Strategies in Early Christian Debates over Prophecy* (Cambridge, MA: Harvard Theological Studies, 2003).
33. *Ecclesiastical History* 5.14.1.
34. *Ecclesiastical History* 7.31.
35. *Chronology* 207, 190; Dodge, *The Fihrist of al-Nadīm*, 776.
36. Gardner and Lieu, *Manichaean Texts*, 38.

37. G. Widengren, "Alexander of Lycopolis," *Encyclopaedia Iranica*, I / 8, p. 830; available online at http://www.iranicaonline.org/articles/alexander-of-lycopolis.

38. Gardner, *Kephalaia of the Teacher*, xxi.

39. Mani is the "Paraclete and leader of the apostleship in this generation" (17,4–7); Mani wrote about his revelations so that no one might doubt "this apostleship of the Spirit, the Paraclete" (46,1–3); Mani is "the Paraclete of Truth" (63,21–23); finally, the editor writes, "Now very many other extraordinary things like these are in the books of our father, which demonstrate both his revelation and the rapture of his apostleship. For very great is the abundance of his coming which, through *(dia)* the Paraclete, the Spirit of Truth, is coming to us" (70,10–23).

40. Johannes van Oort, "The Paraclete of Mani as the Apostle of Jesus Christ and the Origins of a New Church," in *The Apostolic Age in Patristic Thought*, ed. A. Hilhorst (Leiden: Brill, 2004), 155–156.

41. Henrichs, "Mani and the Babylonian Baptists," 40.

42. Werner Sundermann, "Cologne Mani Codex," *Encyclopaedia Iranica*, VI / 1, pp. 43–46; available online at http://www.iranicaonline.org/articles/cologne-mani-codex-parchment.

43. Albert Henrichs, "The Cologne Mani Codex Reconsidered," *Harvard Studies in Classical Philology* 83 (1979), 342.

44. The abbreviation *CMC* can stand equally for the Latin title, *Codex Manichaicus Coloniensis*, or the English translation, *Cologne Mani Codex*. Citations of pp. 1–99 are from Ron Cameron and Arthur J. Dewey, trans., *The Cologne Mani Codex (P. Colon. inv. no. 4780), "Concerning the Origin of His Body"* (Missoula, MT: Scholars Press, 1979). Citations from pp. 99ff are from Gardner and Lieu, *Manichaean Texts*; for the critical edition of the Greek text, see A. Henrichs, L. Koenen, and C. Römer, eds. and trans., *Der Kölner Mani-Codex: Über das Werden seines Leibes* (Opladen: Westdeutscher Verlag, 1988).

45. L. Koenen forwarded this second interpretation in "Augustine and Manichaeism in Light of the Cologne Mani Codex," *Illinois Classical Studies* 3 (1978): 164–66, but has since retracted it: Henrichs, Koenen, and Römer, *Der Kölner Mani-Codex*, xv, n. 2, 51, n. 2. See Sundermann, "Cologne Mani Codex."

46. The disciples include: Salmaios the Ascetic, Baraies the Teacher, Timotheos, Abiesus the Teacher, Innaios the brother of Zabed, a certain Za[cheas?], Koustaios the Son of the Treasure of Life, and Ana the brother of Zabed the Disciple.

47. Dodge, *The Fihrist of al-Nadīm*, 774.

48. Ibid., 811.

49. J. P. Asmussen, "Alchasai," *Encyclopaedia Iranica*, I / 8, pp. 824–825; an updated version is available online at http://www.iranicaonline.org/articles/alchasai-a-sectarian-in-the-early-christian-church-1st-2nd-centuries-a; see also W. Brandt, *Elchasai ein Religionsstifter und sein Werk* (Leipzig: J. C. Hinrichs, 1912); and more recently, F. Stanley Jones, *Pseudoclementina Elchasaiticaque inter judaeochristiana: Collected Studies* (Leuven: Uitgeverij Peeters en Departement Oosterse Studies, 2012).

50. Henrichs, "Mani and the Babylonian Baptists," 47–56.

51. Baker-Brian, *Manichaeism*, 22-23.

52. Guy Stroumsa, "The Manichaean Challenge to Egyptian Christianity," in *The Roots of Egyptian Christianity*, ed. B. A. Pearson and J. E. Goehring (Philadelphia: Fortress, 1986), 308; as cited in Jason David BeDuhn, *Augustine's Manichaean Dilemma*, I: *Conversion and Apostasy 373-388 C.E.* (Philadelphia: University of Pennsylvania Press, 2010), 26.

53. Baker-Brian, *Manichaeism*, 23.

54. This story also bears comparison with what the *CMC* says about Alchasai, namely that he was twice about to bathe when "an image of a man" appeared to him in the waters, and told him not to bathe (94,1–96,16). The image is not of Alchasai himself, and thus raises the question of whether this image too is the *syzygos*, the divine companion to the Apostle of Light, who is here visiting not one of the apostles proper (e.g., Buddha, Zoroaster, Jesus), but instead visiting and guiding a figure, Alchasai, who will establish the law of the baptists in whose midst Mani will be raised.

55. Amin Maalouf, *The Gardens of Light* (London: Quartet, 1996), 47.

56. The voice Mani hears, on the other hand, is much more like Xenophon's rendition of Socrates's *daimonion*.

57. Here [. . .] marks my ellipsis, not the *CMC*'s.

58. H. W. Smyth, *Greek Grammar*, rev. Gordon M. Messing (Cambridge, MA: Harvard University Press, 1984): §1257 notes how the demonstrative *ekeinos* refers back to something previously mentioned, and only rarely forward in anticipation of something about to be mentioned.

59. Hans Dieter Betz, "Paul in the Mani Biography (Codex Manichaicus Coloniensis)," in *Codex Manichaicus Coloniensis: Atti de simposio internazionale (Rende-Amantea 3-7 settembre 1984)*, ed. L. Cirillo and A. Roselli (Consenza: Marra, 1986), 223.

60. Consider also Rom 8:29: "For those whom he foreknew he also predestined to be conformed to the image of his Son, in order that he might be the first-born among many brethren"; 1 Cor 15:49: "Just as we have borne the image of the man of dust, we shall also bear the image of the man of heaven"; 2 Cor 4:4: "In their case the god of this world has blinded the minds of the unbelievers, to keep them from seeing the light of the gospel of the glory of Christ, who is the likeness *(eikōn)* of God"; Col 1:15: "[The Son] is the image *(eikōn)* of the invisible God, the first-born of all creation"; Col 3:9-10: "Do not lie to one another, seeing that you have put off the old nature with its practices and have put on the new nature, which is being renewed in knowledge after the image *(eikona)* of its creator."

61. De Blois, "Manes' 'Twin,'" 12-13.

62. Danker, *A Greek-English Lexicon*, 954.

63. The fact that the only New Testament citation of *syzygos* comes from Paul's letter to the Philippians raises the more general question of the relationship between Mani and the apostle Paul in the *CMC*, on which see again Betz, "Paul in the Mani Biography." Paul is explicitly invoked in the third section (pp. 45-72) as the immediate forerunner to Mani. But even before that section, Betz argues, the *CMC* (especially those sections attributed to Baraies the Teacher) is steeped in Pauline theology. Mani's (or Baraies's) understanding of

Paul is based primarily on the apostle's letters to the Galatians and Corinthians, as interpreted through the letter to the Ephesians (not Philippians, where we find the single citation of *syzygos*). Betz notes that "Mani's preference for Galatians and Corinthians may be due to the influence of Marcion's canon which began with these letters" (221–222). Mani's title, "Apostle of Jesus Christ through the will of God, the Father of Truth," is a variation on Paul's, "called by the will of God to be an apostle of Christ Jesus" (1 Cor 1:10)—both titles, of course, self-awarded (217). For other Pauline parallels, see 2 Cor 1:1, Col 1:1, Eph 1:1, 2 Tim 1:10. Mani's description of his *syzygos* uses "the same soteriological language Paul uses in his Christology": just as Christ "redeemed us from the curse of the (Mosaic) law" (Gal 3:13, 4:5), so Mani's *syzygos* was sent "so that he might redeem and ransom me [from] the error of those followers of <that> Law (i.e., the baptists)" (69,17–20). Mani's *syzygos* explicitly "elects" (*exelexato*) him (70,5). And whereas Paul himself speaks not of his own election, but that of Christians, Acts 9:15 gives to him the title "chosen vessel" or "elected instrument" (*skeuos eklogēs*). The revelation of Mani's *syzygos* is described with a verb (*ōphthē*) that recalls 1 Cor 15:5–8: "[The risen Christ] appeared (*ōphthē*) to Cephas, then to the twelve. Then he appeared (*ōphthē*) to more than five hundred brethren at one time, most of whom who are still alive, though some have fallen asleep. Then he appeared (*ōphthē*) to James, then to all the apostles. Last of all, as to one untimely born, he appeared (*ōphthē*) also to me." Mani's allusion to this list of the risen Christ's appearances situates the revelation of his own *syzygos* squarely in that legacy. It is curious, however, that amid his enthusiasm for Paul, Mani shows no interest in the appearance of the luminous, risen Christ to Paul on the road to Damascus (Acts 9:3–9; 22:6–11; 26:13–18)—this despite his *syzygos* appearing "immediately" (*parachrēma*), similar to Christ's "sudden" (*exaiphnēs*) appearance to Paul. And if Betz is right that Mani's first-person declaration—"I, Mani" (66,4)—mimics Paul's—"I, Paul" (Eph 3:1); and if Mani's "I" is understood as already doubled (as the joke from the *Kephalaia* with which this chapter began makes abundantly clear); and if Mani's Pauline preferences include his letter to the Galatians, then it is all the more curious that in the *CMC* Mani does not avail himself of Paul's confession from Gal 2:20, "it is no longer I who live, but Christ who lives in me." This would seem the perfect verse to describe his own doubled selfhood (as Apostle of Light conjoined to his twin-companion) on the model of Christ's indwelling in Paul. Evidently there are limits to Mani's persistent *imitatio Pauli*.

64. And here may be the clue as to Mani's silence on Gal 2:20. Perhaps Mani was wary of saying, as Paul does, "*no longer* I, but Christ who lives in me," wary of the suggestion that his "I" might be replaced by the *syzygos*. Paul himself hedges against the extinction of his "I" with the addition of *in me*, thus preserving an "I" in whom Christ may dwell. But Mani's self-conception seems to be clearly centered on his "I" as doubled: I, Mani, am only I myself (*egō autos*) when I am also that one (*ekeinos*) from whom I was once but am no longer separated.

65. Henrichs, "Mani and the Babylonian Baptists," 24.

66. See, for example, Michael Williams, *Rethinking "Gnosticism": An Argument for Dismantling a Dubious Category* (Princeton, NJ: Princeton University

Press, 1996); Karen L. King, *What Is Gnosticism?* (Cambridge, MA: Harvard University Press, 2003); for a judicious rehabilitation of the category, see David Brakke, *The Gnostics: Myth, Ritual, and Diversity in Early Christianity* (Cambridge, MA: Harvard University Press, 2010).

67. Henrichs, "Mani and the Babylonian Baptists," 39.

68. Cyril, *Catechesis* 6.31 (PG col. 593A); cited in J. Kevin Coyle, "The *Gospel of Thomas* in Manichaeism?," in *Colloque international "L'évangile selon Thomas et les texts de Nag Hammadi*," ed. Louis Painchaud and Paul-Hubert Poirier (Quebec: Presses de l'Université Laval, 2007), 80n34.

69. Henrichs, "Mani and the Babylonian Baptists," 38. He cites some of the relevant, earlier bibliography on the question.

70. W.-P. Funk, "'Einer aus tausend, zwei aus zehntausend': Zitate aus dem Thomas-Evangelium in den koptischen Manichaica," in *For the Children, Perfect Instruction: Studies in Honor of Hans-Martin Schenke on the Occasion of the Berliner Arbeitskreis für kotisch-gnostische Schriften's Thirtieth Year*, ed. H.-G. Bethge, Nag Hammadi and Manichaean Studies 54 (Leiden: Brill, 2002), 67–94.

71. Coyle remains skeptical: "Thus there is no doubt about the expression's popularity among Manichaeans. That it also circulated beyond Manichaeism precludes a definite conclusion as to its influence upon or by the Gos. Thom" ("The *Gospel of Thomas* in Manichaeism?," 85).

72. Ibid., 91.

73. Leo Sweeney, "Mani's Twin and Plotinus: Questions of 'Self,'" in *Neoplatonism and Gnosticism*, ed. Richard T. Wallis (Albany: SUNY Press, 1992), 381–424. Sweeney is wary of using the term "self" when speaking about Mani's and Plotinus's accounts of the "couple" that is made from the "higher" and "lower" man, on the grounds that the term "self" carries with it a confused and confusing set of meanings in its modern usage. Furthermore, there is no word in Mani's or Plotinus's Greek that can be translated as "self." I appreciate Sweeney's concern regarding the term, but I employ it nevertheless out of the conviction that the confused and confusing meanings associated with the concept, if not the term, are no less present in antiquity than in modernity.

74. *Enneads* IV, 4 (22), 14, as quoted in Sweeney, "Mani's Twin and Plotinus," 394.

75. On the fact that the five apocalypses are unattested, see David Frankfurter, "Apocalypses Real and Alleged in the Mani Codex," *Numen* 44 (1997): 60–73.

76. Van Oort, "The Paraclete of Mani," 153.

77. Manshour Shaki, "Dēn," VII / 3, pp. 279–281; available online at http://www.iranicaonline.org/articles/den.

78. I would like to acknowledge and thank Jason David BeDuhn for bringing this other dimension of the Light Form to my attention.

79. Two earlier passages, in a much more fragmentary state, seem to discuss this same issue: "[the apostles] choose a selection of the [. . . t]hey make [. . .] the elect and the catechumens [. . .] their forms, and they make them

[free]" (1,10.13–15); "[a]s I have t[ol]d you, that when they [. . .] before everything he shall [. . .] free above first" (1,10.32–34).

5 Plotinus and the Doubled Intellect

1. *Vita Plotini* 3.16–17, trans. A. H. Armstrong, *Plotinus: Enneads*, 7 vols. (Cambridge, MA: Harvard University Press, 1966–1988), vol. 1.

2. Ibid., 2.25–27. On the last words of Plotinus, see P. Henry, "La dernière parole de Plotin," *Studi classici e orientali* 11 (Pisa, 1953): 113–120; and more recently Glenn W. Most, "Plotinus' Last Words," *Classical Quarterly* 53, no. 2 (2003): 576–587.

3. Armstrong, *Plotinus*, 1:xv. Unless otherwise noted, all citations are from Armstrong's English translation in *Plotinus: Enneads*. All Greek citations are from the *en face* Greek of this same edition, which is in turn based on Paul Henry and Hans-Rudolf Schwyzer, eds., *Plotini Opera*, 3 vols. (Oxonii: E Typographeo Clarendoniano, 1964–1982). I cite the *Enneads* by individual *Ennead* (1–6), chapter, and lines (x.xx.xxx).

4. See also Leo Sweeney, "Mani's Twin and Plotinus: Questions on 'Self,' " in *Neoplatonism and Gnosticism*, ed. Richard T. Wallis (Albany: SUNY Press, 1992), 381–424; Henry Blumenthal, *Plotinus' Psychology: His Doctrine of the Embodied Soul* (The Hague: Martinus Nijhoff, 1971); Gerard O'Daly, *Plotinus' Philosophy of the Self* (Shannon: Irish University Press, 1973) (engages earlier scholarship, including Emile Bréhier, E. R. Dodds, Pierre Hadot, W. Himmerich, Willy Theiler, and Jean Trouillard); Carlos Steel, *The Changing Self: A Study on the Soul in Later Neoplatonism: Iamblichus, Damascius and Priscianus* (Brussels Paleis der Academiën, 1978); Robert Bolton, *Person, Soul, and Identity: A Neoplatonic Account of the Principle of Personality* (London: Minerva, 1994); Gary Gurtler, *Plotinus: The Experience of Unity* (New York: Peter Lang, 1984); Lloyd Gerson, *Plotinus* (London: Routledge, 1994); Manfred Krüger, *Ichgeburt: Origenes und die Entstehung der christlichen Idee der Wiederverkörperung in der Denkbewegung von Pythagoras bis Lessing* (Hildesheim: Olms, 1996); Werner Beierwaltes, *Das wahre Selbst: Studien zu Plotins Begriff des Geistes und das Einen* (Frankfurt am Main: Vittorio Klostermann, 2001); Pauliina Remes, *Plotinus on Self: The Philosophy of the 'We'* (Cambridge: Cambridge University Press, 2007).

5. See A. H. Armstrong, "The One and Intellect," in *The Cambridge History of Later Greek and Early Medieval Philosophy*, ed. A. H. Armstrong (Cambridge: Cambridge University Press, 1980), 236–249, esp. 241; see also Armstrong, "'Emanation' in Plotinus," *Mind* 46, no. 181 (1937): 61–66.

6. Maria Luisa Gatti appeals to Plotinus's own distinction between activities *of* and *from* in "The Platonic Tradition and the Foundation of Neoplatonism," in *The Cambridge Companion to Plotinus*, ed. Lloyd Gerson (Cambridge: Cambridge University Press, 1996), 30: (a) the activity *of* being, which "coincides with that which the thing is," and (b) the activity *from* being, "follow[ing] necessarily from [the being] and is distinct from it"; see also Armstrong, "The One and Intellect," 242.

7. Gatti, "The Platonic Tradition and the Foundation of Neoplatonism," 31–32. Although this third moment is the explicitly contemplative one, she argues that the entire triadic rhythm is the very structure of contemplation, and thus that we should understand Plotinian procession as "contemplative procession." For a fuller version of her argument, see Maria Luisa Gatti, *Plotino e la metafisica della contemplazione* (Milano: Vita e pensiero, 1996).

8. See 2.4, "On the Two Kinds of Matter," and 1.8, "On the Nature of Evils." I intend to wade into these waters in a forthcoming book (see Chapter 6).

9. See below on the numerical (as opposed to qualitative) difference that establishes the individuality of intellect-Forms.

10. Plotinus, *Enneads*, vol. 5, p. 34 n 1. Armstrong acknowledges that the editors of the critical edition, Henry and Schwyzer, accept that the subject is the same, and thus that it is the One who is said to return to and see itself. Armstrong follows other scholars (Cilento, Igal, et al.) who propose an abrupt change in subject.

11. Armstrong, "The One and Intellect," 242: "What happens, according to Plotinus, in Intellect's normal contemplation of the One is that, though it directs itself towards the absolute unity of its source, it cannot receive it as it is, but 'breaks it up' or 'makes it many', and so, by the power of the One, constitutes itself as a unity-in-multiplicity, the World of Forms which, though it is as unified as anything except the One can be, is many as well as one, a rich and complex whole of parts."

12. Henry George Liddell and Robert Scott, *A Greek-English Lexicon*, 9th ed. with rev. supplement (Oxford: Clarendon Press, 1996), 306.

13. Lloyd Gerson objects to Armstrong's translation and the notion that the individual intellect is identical to a Form. He takes *hekaston de eidos nous hekaston* to mean "and each Form is each intellect": "This text thus rendered only affirms the cognitive identity of each intellect with all Forms. It does not obliterate the distinction between intellect and Forms or that between the activity of intellection and its intentional objects" (*Plotinus*, 55).

14. Henry J. Blumenthal, "On Soul and Intellect," in Gerson, *Cambridge Companion to Plotinus*, 93: "These Forms . . . are not simply self-subsistent universals but beings which think: that follows from the identifications of Intellect with the Forms (V.1.4.26–29) and of individual Forms with individual intellects (V.9.8.3–7). Thus each Form is capable of thinking and of being the object of thought, realizing that identity of thought and its objects which Aristotle presented as a feature of pure thought in the *De anima* (431a1) . . . [and] also correspond to the divine intellect of *Metaphysics* L 9."

15. Gerson, *Plotinus*, 44.

16. *Hymn of the Pearl* 55 (50), 76–77 (56).

17. Remes, *Plotinus on Self*, 108.

18. Ibid., 51.

19. Jean Trouillard, "The Logic of Attribution in Plotinus," *International Philosophical Quarterly* 1 (1961): 137; Armstrong, "Plotinus," in *Cambridge History of Later Greek and Medieval Philosophy*, 245; both as cited in Gerson, *Plotinus*, note 55, pp. 249–250. Gerson backs away from this suggestion somewhat: "It would seem, then, that inter-awareness of this choir of angels or community

of spirits must consist in each knowing the other as Form or intelligible object, not in some more intimate penetration of the subjective" (Gerson, *Plotinus*, 56).

20. Frederic M. Schroeder, "Plotinus and Language," in Gerson, *Cambridge Companion to Plotinus*, 345–346.

21. Gerson, *Plotinus*, 59.

22. Ibid., 60.

23. Ibid., 59–60.

24. Ibid., 136.

25. Stephen R. L. Clark, "Plotinus: Body and Soul," in Gerson, *Cambridge Companion to Plotinus*, 276.

26. Remes, *Plotinus on Self*, 12.

27. Hans J. Blumenthal, "Did Plotinus Believe in Ideas of Individuals?," *Phronesis* 11, no. 1 (1966): 61.

28. Remes, *Plotinus on Self*, 5.

29. John M. Dillon, "An Ethic for the Late Antique Sage," in Gerson, *Cambridge Companion to Plotinus*, 327.

30. Blumenthal, "Did Plotinus Believe in Ideas of Individuals?," 61.

31. On the concept of the "dividual," see Simon Critchley, *The Faith of the Faithless: Experiments in Political Theology* (Brooklyn: Verso, 2012), 6–7.

32. Sweeney, "Mani's Twin and Plotinus," 398.

33. See John M. Rist, "Plotinus and the *Daimonion* of Socrates," *Phoenix* 17, no. 1 (1963): 16: "[Socrates's *daimonion*] may however be a superior version of [the *daimōn*], possessed by very few specially fortunate morals. In other words, the Socratic *daimonion* may have some kinship with the highest kind of *daimōn* that can guide a human life, perhaps with the only kind that can give a first impulse to philosophy . . . if the *daimonion* bears some resemblance to the *daimōn* of the myth of Er, it is a superior version of it."

34. Ibid., 17ff.

35. In "Theurgy and Its Relationship to Neoplatonism," *Journal of Roman Studies* 37 (1947): 55–69, E. R. Dodds claimed that Plotinus was neither a magician nor a theurgist. Philip Merlan took issue with Dodds in "Plotinus and Magic," *Isis* 44 (1953): 341–348. A. H. Armstrong, however, supported Dodds in "Was Plotinus a Magician?," *Phronesis* 1 (1955): 73–79. J. M. Rist and G. Luck side with Armstrong and consider the debate "closed"—see Luck, "Theurgy and Forms of Worship in Neoplatonism," in *Religion, Science, and Magic: In Concert and in Conflict*, ed. J. Neusner, E. S. Frerichs, and P. V. McCracken (New York: Oxford University Press, 1989), 185–225 (here, 205). And yet there is evidence that the debate is still open. See the recent work of Zeke Mazur, "Unio Magica , Part 1: On the Magical Origins of Plotinus' Mysticism," *Dionysius* 21 (2003): 23–52, and "Unio Magica , Part 2: Plotinus, Theurgy and the Question of Ritual," *Dionysius* 22 (2004): 29–56. See also Charles M. Stang, "From the *Chaldean Oracles* to the *Corpus Dionysiacum:* Theurgy between the 3rd and 6th Centuries," *Journal of Late Antique Religion and Culture* 5 (2011): 1–13.

36. *Republic* X, 617e1.

37. A. H. Armstrong, "Was Plotinus a Magician?," 76, summarizes 3.4, "On Our Allotted Guardian Spirit," thus: "What it does is to give a rational interpretation in terms of Plotinus's own philosophy of this difference [in rank

of tutelary spirit] which shows that it is, in the last resort, our own decision whether to live by the higher or the lower in us (a decision of course whose effects extend over more than one bodily life) which determines the rank of our tutelary spirit, which is according to Plotinus the next highest level in the hierarchy of being above that which our personality at its highest reaches."

38. See Rist, "Plotinus and the *Daimonion* of Socrates," 13: "The God who is the philosopher's *daimon* in 3.4.6 is the One"; see also ibid., 15, 23; Rist relies on A. H. Armstrong, "Was Plotinus a Magician?"

39. Rist, "Plotinus and the *Daimonion* of Socrates," 23.

40. John M. Rist, "Forms of Individuals in Plotinus," *Classical Quarterly* 13:2 (1963): 223.

41. In his handbook, Albinus remarks that "most Platonists do not accept that there are Forms . . . of individuals, like Socrates and Plato"; quoted in Paul Kalligas, "Forms of Individuals in Plotinus: A Re-examination," *Phronesis* 42 (1997): 207.

42. For a reassessment of Aristotle's own view of Forms of individuals, see Kalligas, "Forms of Individuals in Plotinus," 207–208.

43. For what Remes calls the first "wave," see A. H. Armstrong, "Form, Individual, and Person in Plotinus," *Dionysius* 1 (1977): 49–68; Blumenthal, "Did Plotinus Believe in Ideas of Individuals?," 61–80; P. S. Mamo, "Forms of Individuals in the *Enneads*," *Phronesis* 14 (1969): 77–96; John M. Rist, "Forms of Individuals in Plotinus," *Classical Quarterly* 23 (1963): 223–231. For the second "wave," see F. Ferrari, "Esistono forme di *kath'hekasta?* Il problema dell'individualità in Plotino e nella tradizione platonica antica," *Atti della Accademia delle Scienze di Torino* 131 (1997): 23–63; Gerson, *Plotinus*; P. Kalligas, "Forms of Individuals in Plotinus"; D. J. O'Meara, "Forms of Individuals in Plotinus: A Preface to the Question," in *Traditions of Platonism: Essays in Honour of John Dillon*, ed. J. J. Cleary (Alsershot; UK: Ashgate, 1999), 265–269. Remes, *Plotinus on Self*, 59n92: "The participants of the second wave of the debate all posit forms of individuals for Plotinus, some more hesitatingly than others."

44. For example, Rist, "Forms of Individuals in Plotinus," 227: "We seem to have a clear development in Plotinus' thought in the period between 5.9 and 5.7."

45. Blumenthal, "Did Plotinus Believe in Ideas of Individuals?," 76.

46. Ibid., 79–80.

47. Perhaps the best spokesman of this second wave is Paul Kalligas, whose view has influenced my own. More recently, Remes has parted ways with this consensus, suggesting instead that individuation is not the domain of the Forms per se, but a lower level of mediating intelligible emanation, the *logoi* or "formative principles." See Remes, *Plotinus on Self*, 68–91.

48. Rist, "Forms of Individuals in Plotinus," 223.

49. Kalligas, "Forms of Individuals in Plotinus," 212.

50. See also John Bussanich, "Rebirth Eschatology in Plato and Plotinus," in *Philosophy and Salvation in Greek Religion*, ed. Vishwa Adluri (Berlin: De Gruyter, 2013), 243–288.

51. Kalligas, "Forms of Individuals in Plotinus," 216.

52. *Theaetetus* 176b: "That is why a man should make all haste to escape from earth to heaven; and escape means becoming as like God as possible; and a man becomes like God when he becomes just and pure, with understanding." Rist offers three places where Plotinus drops *kata to dynaton* (1.2.1.4, 1.2.3.5–6, 1.6.6.19–20), and once where he retains it (2.9.9.50–51).

53. Rist, "Forms of Individuals in Plotinus," 231. Rist here cites R. Arnou, whose phrase "a certain duality" I have supplied. The full citation is as follows: "Ces mots composés de *syn*, *para*, que Plotin emploie d'ordinaire, suggèrent qu'une certaine dualité demeure dans l'unité" (*Le Désir de Dieu dans la philosophie de Plotin* [Paris, 1921], 246).

54. Ibid., 231.

55. In his introduction to Pierre Hadot, *Plotinus, or the Simplicity of Vision* (Chicago: University of Chicago Press, 1998), Arnold I. Davidson remarks that "Plotinus' texts do sometimes seem to displace the Platonic dialogue between master and disciple by an erotic monologue directed toward the self" (11). If it is a displacement of that erotic and dialogical tension, it is an *internalization* of it.

56. Hadot, *Plotinus, or the Simplicity of Vision*, 21: "When, however, sculptor and statue are one—when they are both one and the same soul—soon the statue is nothing other than vision itself, and beauty is nothing more than a state of complete simplicity and pure light"; Emerson, *Nature*: "Standing on the bare ground,—my head bathed by the blithe air, and uplifted into infinite spaces,—all mean egotism vanishes. I become a transparent eye-ball; I am nothing; I see all; the currents of the Universal Being circulate through me; I am part or particle of God"; on the connection between Emerson and Plotinus, see Stanley Brodwin, "Emerson's Version of Plotinus: The Flight to Beauty," *Journal of the History of Ideas* 35 (1974): 465–483.

57. Davidson, introduction to Hadot, *Plotinus*, 10.

58. Richard Harder, *Plotinus Schriften* (Hamburg: Meiner, 1956–1971), 1:381; cited in Davidson, introduction to Hadot, *Plotinus*, 11n14.

59. Davidson, introduction to Hadot, *Plotinus*, 11.

60. Julia Kristeva, *Tales of Love* (New York: Columbia University Press, 1987), 107.

61. Ovid, *Metamorphoses*, 3.463–464. Rolfe Humphries, trans., *Ovid's Metamorphoses* (Bloomington: Indiana University Press, 1955).

62. Kristeva, *Tales of Love*, 108.

63. Pierre Hadot, "Le mythe de Narcisse et son interprétation par Plotin," *Nouvelle revue de psychoanalyse* 13 (1970): 106; cited in Davidson, introduction to Hadot, *Plotinus*, 13.

64. Kristeva cites a passage from *Ennead* 6.8.15, where Plotinus speaks of the One as the "father of reason and cause and causative substance" (6.8.14.37–38) and says that he "is lovable and love and love of himself, in that he is beautiful only from himself and in himself" (6.8.15.1–2). She combines these two accounts to form a composite picture in the service of a grand narrative—much grander than Harder's—about the "western consciousness of self": "That *autos eros* that I see as sublime hypostasis of narcissistic love was to constitute the decisive step in the assumption of inner space, the introspective space of the western psyche. God is Narcissus, and if the *narcissistic* illusion is for Myself a

sin, my ideal is nonetheless *Narcissan*" (*Tales of Love*, 111). Elsewhere it is clear that her real target is the interiority or "internality" of self and God, which she takes to be the hallmarks of "the West." Plotinus's conflicted appropriation of Narcissus is, for Kristeva, a hinge moment in the development of that internality.

65. 6.9.5.30–42: "this marvel of the One, which is not existent, so that 'one' may not here also have to be predicated of something else, which in truth has no fitting name, but if we must give it a name, 'one' would be an appropriate ordinary way of speaking of it . . . its nature is of such a kind that it is the source of the best and the power which generates the real beings, abiding in itself and not being diminished and not being one of the things which it brought into being. Whatever is even before these, we give the name of 'one' to by necessity, to indicate its nature to one another, bringing ourselves by the name to an indivisible idea and wanting to unify our souls."

66. Mazur has published a number of relevant studies on Plotinus, but the most relevant, and the one that I will be citing, is an unpublished paper, "Mystical Self-Reversion in Sethian Gnosticism and Plotinus," presented at a colloquium entitled "La mystique dans la gnose et chez Plotin," at L'Université Laval, Quebec, March 2009. I would like to thank him for allowing me to access this and other unpublished papers, which have influenced my interpretation of Plotinus.

67. Mazur, "Mystical Self-Reversion." See 6.9.3.36–45, 6.7.32–34.
68. Ibid.
69. Hadot, *Plotinus*, 49.
70. Ibid., 51.
71. Ibid.
72. Ibid., 50.
73. Ibid., 56.
74. Kristeva, *Tales of Love*, 111.
75. See Plotinus's discussion of substance and activity in 6.8.20.
76. Hadot, *Plotinus*, 59.
77. Mazur, "Mystical Self-Reversion."
78. My translation. Armstrong has: "But the soul sees by a kind of confusing and annulling the intellect which abides within it."

6 Whither the Divine Double?

1. See Hans-Joachim Klimkeit, *Gnosis on the Silk Road: Gnostic Texts from Central Asia* (San Francisco: HarperSanFrancisco, 1993), 84, 124, 137, 216.

2. The dispute between Porphyry and Iamblichus took place through two texts. See Porphyry's *Letter to Anebo*, which survives only in fragments: Angelo R. Sodano, ed. and trans., *Porfirio: Letter ad Anebo* (Naples: L'Arte pografica, 1958), and more recently, H. D. Saffrey and A.-P. Segonds, eds. and trans., *Lettre à Anébon l'Égyptian* (Paris: Les Belles Lettres, 2012); Iamblichus wrote a pseudonymous reply, *On the Mysteries: Iamblichus: De mysteriis*, trans. E. Clark, J. Dillon, and J. P. Hershbell (Leiden: Brill, 2004).

3. The first quotation regarding the *hetera archē* is from *De Mysteriis* 270.6–7, as cited by Gregory Shaw, "The Soul's Innate Gnosis of the Gods: Rev-

elation in Iamblichean Theurgy," in *Revelation, Literature, and Community in Late Antiquity*, ed. P. Townsend and M. Vidas (Tübingen: Mohr Siebeck, 2011), 119. Shaw's citations of Iamblichus are from the 2004 edition and translation by E. Clark, J. Dillon, and J. P. Hershbell, following the Parthey numbering they employ. The second quotation regarding *to hen tēs psychēs* is from J. Dillon, ed., *Iamblichi Chalcidensis: In Platonis Dialogos Commentariorum Fragmenta* (Leiden: Brill, 1973), 96–97.

4. As reported by Simplicius: see M. Hayduck, ed., *De Anima* (Berlin: B. Reimeri, 1882), 223.26, as cited by Shaw, "The Soul's Innate Gnosis," 126.

5. Shaw, "The Soul's Innate Gnosis," 117ff. Much of my discussion on Iamblichus, here as elsewhere, owes to Shaw's work. For more, see Shaw, *Theurgy and the Soul: The Neoplatonism of Iamblichus* (University Park: Pennsylvania State University, 1995).

6. Porphyry, *Vita Plotini* 10, trans. A. H. Armstrong, *Plotinus: Enneads*, 7 vols. (Cambridge, MA: Harvard University Press, 1966–1988), vol. 1.

7. *De mysteriis* 204.14, as cited by Shaw, "The Soul's Innate Gnosis," 125.

8. *De mysteriis* 144.10–11, as cited by Shaw, "The Soul's Innate Gnosis," 125.

9. *De mysteriis* 47.13–48.4, as cited by Shaw, "The Soul's Innate Gnosis," 125.

10. On the ambiguity in the term "theurgy" and how that ambiguity plays out for its advocates and critics, see Charles M. Stang, "From the *Chaldean Oracles* to the *Corpus Dionysiacum:* Theurgy between the 3rd and 6th Centuries," *Journal of Late Antique Religion and Culture* 5 (2011): 1–13, which in turn leans on Gregory Shaw, "Neoplatonic Theurgy and Dionysius the Areopagite," *Journal of Early Christian Studies* 7, no. 4 (1999): 573–599.

11. For one such effort, see H. Feichtinger, "*Oudeneia* and *Humilitas:* Nature and Function of Humility in Iamblichus and Augustine," *Dionysius* 21 (2003): 123–160.

12. Of course the development of the Christian doctrine of deification is much more complicated than this single lineage suggests. For a fine-grained treatment of the subject, see Norman Russell, *The Doctrine of Deification in the Greek Patristic Tradition* (Oxford: Oxford University Press, 2006).

13. Clement, *Protrepticus* 1.8.4.7–9: [H]*o logos ho tou theou anthrôpos genomenos, hina dê kai su para anthrôpu mathês, têi pote ara anthrôpos genêtai theous;* Athanasius, *De Incarnatione* 54: *autos gar enênthrôpêsen, hina hêmeis theopoiêthômen.*

14. See John Behr, trans., Athanasius, *On the Incarnation* (Yonkers, NY: St. Vladimir's Seminary Press, 2011), §9.

15. See Harold Attridge's appendix to the *Gospel of Thomas* in Bentley Layton, ed., *Nag Hammadi II, 2–7: Together with XIII, 2*, Brit. Lib. Or. 4926(1), and P.Oxy. 1, 654, 655: with Contributions by Many Scholars* (Leiden: Brill, 1989), which includes all the ancient *testimonia* to the *Gospel of Thomas*.

16. Eusebius of Caesarea, *Ecclesiastical History* 3.25.6, as cited in Attridge's appendix, 105.

17. Cyril, *Catechesis* 6.31 (PG 33.593), dated ca. 348, as cited in Attridge's appendix, 105–106: "This one (Mani) had three disciples, Thomas, Baddas, and

Hermas. Let no one read the *Gospel According to Thomas*. For he is not one of the twelve apostles, but one of the three wicked disciples of Mani."

18. J.-D. Kaestli, "L'utilisation des actes apocryphes des apôtres dans le manichéisme," in *Gnosis and Gnosticism*, ed. M. Krause (Leiden: Brill, 1977), 107–116; H. J. W. Drijvers, "*Odes of Solomon* and *Psalms of Mani:* Christians and Manichaeans in Third-Century Syria," in *Studies in Gnosticism and Hellenistic Religions: Presented to Gilles Quispel*, ed. R. van den Broek and M. J. Vermaseren (Leiden: Brill, 1981), 117–130; Paul-Hubert Poirier, "L'*Hymne de la Perle* et le manichéisme à la lumière du *Codex manichéen de Cologne*," in *Codex Manichaicus Coloniensis: Atti de simposio internazionale (Rende-Amantea 3–7 settembre 1984)*, ed. L Cirillo and A. Roselli (Consenza: Marra, 1986), 235–248; for a recent and sober assessment, see J. Kevin Coyle, "The Gospel of Thomas in Manichaeism?," in *Manichaeism and Its Legacy*, ed. J. Kevin Coyle (Leiden: Brill, 2009), 76–91.

19. Perhaps this doctrine of deification and model of selfhood did not fade so thoroughly from the scene, as the case of Pseudo-Macarius shows. The famous Egyptian monk Macarius the Great died in the late fourth century, but within a few generations a body of writings was attributed to him, including fifty homilies and a so-called *Great Letter:* see the translation by George A. Maloney, *Pseudo-Macarius: The Fifty Spiritual Homilies and* Great Letter (New York: Paulist Press, 1992); see also H. Dörries, E. Klostermann, and M. Kroeger, *Die 50 Geistlichen Homilien des Makarios* (Berlin: De Gruyter, 1964). In *Seek to See Him: Ascent and Vision Mysticism in the Gospel of Thomas* (Leiden: Brill, 1996), 163–164, April DeConick argues that the Macarian tradition carries forward earlier themes and threads of the divine double: the soul, stripped of the spirit, longs for "the spiritual garment" (*Hom* 20.1); is thereby "joined and united with the Lord" (*Great Letter*, p. 269 in Maloney's translation); "lives in the fellowship of only the divine Spouse, is totally simple in his single-mindedness" (*GL* 257); and, most tantalizingly, this union with the divine renders us doubled or twofold (*diplous;* see Dörries et al., *Makarios*, 140). This may also have something to do with the concept of the "two souls" also associated with the Macarian legacy: see Marcus Plested, *The Macarian Legacy: The Place of Macarius-Symeon in the Eastern Christian Tradition* (Oxford: Oxford University Press, 2004), 25, 30, 225–226. The continuity of the divine double in the Pseudo-Macarian legacy, and more broadly in the ascetic and mystical traditions of Syriac Christianity, is certainly an avenue worthy of further research.

20. A third discourse from late antiquity is angelology, especially the emergence of the notion of guardian angels. On the "companion angel" tradition, see chapters 3 and 4 in Ellen Muehlberger, *Angels in Late Antique Christianity* (Oxford: Oxford University Press, 2013).

21. Gottfried Leibniz coined the term in his 1710 work *Théodicée*.

22. See Jon D. Levenson, *Creation and the Persistence of Evil: The Jewish Drama of Divine Omnipotence* (Princeton, NJ: Princeton University Press, 1994).

23. The bibliography on Plotinus's views on evil and matter is quite vast. I have found the following helpful: Kevin Corrigan, *Plotinus' Theory of Matter-Evil and the Question of Substance: Plato, Aristotle, and Alexander of Aphrodisias* (Leuven: Peeters, 1996); Edward B. Costello, "Is Plotinus Consistent on the

Nature of Evil?," *International Philosophical Quarterly* 7 (1967): 483–497; Zeke Mazur, "Plotinus' Philosophical Opposition to Gnosticism and the Implicit Axiom of Continuous Hierarchy," in *History of Platonism: Plato Redivivus*, ed. John F. Finamore and Robert M. Berchman (New Orleans: University Press of the South, 2005), 95–112; Denis O'Brien, "Plotinus on Matter and Evil," in *The Cambridge Companion to Plotinus*, ed. Lloyd P. Gerson (Cambridge: Cambridge University Press, 1996), 171–195; Eric Perl, *Theophany: The Neoplatonic Philosophy of Dionysius the Areopagite* (Albany: SUNY Press, 2008), 53–64; John Rist, "Plotinus on Matter and Evil," *Phronesis* 6, no. 2 (1961): 154–166; Christian Schäfer, "Matter in Plotinus' Normative Ontology," *Phronesis* 49, no. 3 (2004): 266–294; Gerd Van Riel, "Horizontalism or Verticalism? Proclus vs. Plotinus on the Procession of Matter," *Phronesis* 46, no. 2 (2001): 129–153.

24. I am for the moment setting aside the question of "intelligible matter" in Plotinus, and its relationship to base matter at the extremity of procession. See John Rist, "The Indefinite Dyad and Intelligible Matter in Plotinus," *Classical Quarterly* 12, no. 1 (1962): 99–107.

25. (a) Here I am skipping over any discussion of how the soul's failed "self-reversion" gives rise to the procession of matter, a procession that is different from the "previous" processions of One > Mind and Mind > Soul. (b) Strictly speaking, souls can be evil by virtue of their care for matter; their assent is a necessary condition for evil. (c) There seems to be some tension between how Plotinus discusses forms and matter: here in 1.8.8, the forms are working from within, informing so to speak; but in those passages Denis O'Brien highlights, which have to do with the relationship of the soul to matter, the soul covers over matter with forms, but in a strictly external, almost cosmetic way.

26. See Jan Opsomer and Carlos Steel, trans., *Proclus: On the Existence of Evils* (Ithaca, NY: Cornell University Press, 2003). Much of my discussion of Proclus has been influenced by their very helpful introduction to this translation.

27. I would like to propose, then, a sequel to *Our Divine Double*, another installment in this series exploring Paul's phrase "no longer I." This book, entitled *Beyond God and Evil*, will closely and carefully move through the proponents of this tradition, Christians and Neoplatonists, attending to the nuances of their arguments, the manner in which evil comes to resemble God or the One, and their anxious efforts to keep them distinct. Why is it that these thinkers leave us with the distinct impression that evil is very much like the ineffable One or the God beyond being, that evil is somehow transcendent and divine? Let me be clear that none of them say as much. But what they do say suggests as much. I will spend considerable effort showing how each thinker attempts to obscure the disturbing implications of this convergence of (the One) God and evil, or to dull its edge through various means, both scholastic and rhetorical. I aim to draw attention precisely to this convergence, and to press, rather than suppress, its implications. I do not believe I am alone in having noticed this convergence. See, for example, Michel Foucault, "The Prose Actaeon," in *Michel Foucault: Aesthetics, Method, and Epistemology*, ed. James D. Faubion (London: Penguin, 2000), 123: "Pierre Klossowski reconnects with a long-lost experience. Today only a few vestiges of that experience are left to evoke it; and

they would be enigmatic no doubt if they had not been reanimated and made manifest in this language. And if they had not begun to speak once more, saying that the Demon is not the Other, the pole far removed from God, the Antithesis without remedy (or almost), evil matter, but something strange, bewildering which leaves one speechless and immobile—the Same, the exact Likeness"; and Jacques Derrida, "How to Avoid Speaking: Denials," in *Derrida and Negative Theology*, ed. Toby Foshay (Albany: SUNY Press, 1992), 110: "Evil is even more without essence than the Good. If possible, one should draw the full consequences of this singular axiomatics."

28. Much of what follows expands on my longer review essay, "The Two 'I's of Christ: Revisiting the Christological Controversy," *Anglican Theological Review* 94, no. 3 (2012): 529–547.

29. "The First Letter of Nestorius to Celestine," in *Christology of the Later Fathers*, ed. Edward R. Hardy (Philadelphia: Westminster Press, 1954), 348.

30. John McGuckin, *Saint Cyril and the Christological Controversy* (Crestwood, NY: St. Vladimir's Seminary Press, 2004).

31. Ibid., 156.

32. Ibid., 157.

33. Ibid., 144, 163.

34. In a short article buried in a *festschrift*, H. J. W. Drijvers argues that the Christological dualism of the Antiochene tradition can be traced to early texts and traditions in Antioch's vicinity, namely the *Odes of Solomon* and the *Acts of Thomas*: H. J. W. Drijvers, "Early Forms of Antiochene Christology," in *After Chalcedon: Studies in Theology and Church History Offered to Professor Albert Van Roey for His Seventieth Birthday*, eds. C. Laga, J. A. Munitz, and L. Van Rompay (Leuven: Dept. Oriëntalistiek, Uitgeverij, 1985), 99–113. If Drijvers is right, then there is a direct influence of the earlier tradition of the divine double on the later tradition. Of that I am not at all certain. But it is an intriguing lead, which I intend to pursue, along with a much more sustained investigation into (1) the origins and proponents of the Antiochene tradition and its afterlife in the East Syrian (Nestorian) tradition in Syriac; (2) the Alexandrian tradition, especially Cyril, but also his subsequent miaphysite proponents; (3) the Christological Definition of the Council of Chalcedon in 451, which seems to strike a balance between Cyril and Nestorius, Alexandria and Antioch; and (4) Chalcedon's interpreters, especially Maximus the Confessor's strongly dyophysite stance. Such a study would also gain by continuing to look at how modern scholars and theologians have framed this controversy, and how their frameworks for understanding Christology bear on their own (often implicit) understandings of selfhood. This is, like *Beyond God and Evil*, a provisional project, another installment in the "no longer I" series.

Conclusion

Epigraph: Ralph Manheim, trans., *Lectures on the Essence of Religion* (New York: Harper and Row, 1967), 311, as cited in Jeffrey J. Kripal, *The Serpent's Gift: Gnostic Reflections on the Study of Religion* (Chicago: University of Chicago Press, 2007), 162.

1. Auden, "In Memory of Ernst Toller," in *Another Time* (London: Faber and Faber, 1940).
2. Robert Lamberton, trans., in *The Station Hill Blanchot Reader* (Barrytown, NY: Station Hill Press, 1999), 66.
3. Nancy Pearson, trans., *The Man of Light in Iranian Sufism* (New Lebanon, NY: Omega, 1994), 9.
4. Jeffrey J. Kripal, *The Serpent's Gift: Gnostic Reflections on the Study of Religion* (Chicago: University of Chicago, 2007), quoting from Harold Bloom, *Omens of Millennium: The Gnosis of Angels, Dreams and Resurrection* (New York: Riverhead Books, 1996).
5. Bloom, *Omens of Millennium*, 15, 16; as cited in Kripal, *The Serpent's Gift*, 176.
6. Bloom, *Omens of Millennium*, 23, 184; as cited in Kripal, *The Serpent's Gift*, 176.
7. Jeffrey J. Kripal, *Authors of the Impossible: The Paranormal and the Sacred* (Chicago: University of Chicago Press, 2010), 269–270.
8. Ibid., 270.
9. Charles M. Stang, "'Neither Oneself nor Someone Else': The Apophatic Anthropology of Dionysius the Areopagite," in *Apophatic Bodies: Negative Theology, Incarnation, and Relationality*, ed. Catherine Keller and Christ Boesel (New York: Fordham University Press, 2009), 59–75; Stang, *Apophasis and Pseudonymity in Dionysius the Areopagite: "No Longer I"* (Oxford: Oxford University Press, 2012), esp. 197–205; Stang, "Writing," in *The Cambridge Companion to Christian Mysticism*, ed. Amy Hollywood and Patricia Z. Beckman (Cambridge: Cambridge University Press, 2012), 252–263.
10. *Mystical Theology* 1.3 1001A; *Corpus Dionysiacum* II 144.13; John H. Parker, trans., *The Complete Works of Dionysius the Areopagite* (London: James Parker and Co., 1897–1899); for the Greek, see Günter Heil and Adolf Martin Ritter, eds. and trans., *Corpus Dionysiacum II* (Berlin: de Gruyter, 1991).
11. Stang, "'Neither Oneself nor Someone Else,'" 70.
12. Kripal, *Authors of the Impossible*, 270: "We might at least begin to take back the book of our lives from those who wrote us long ago, for their own good reasons, no doubt, and begin writing ourselves anew, for our own good reasons now."

Acknowledgments

I HAVE BEEN thinking about writing this book for well over ten years, and have been actively writing it for about three. That is a long stretch of time in which to incur debts, and I have many. First and foremost, I should thank Harvard Divinity School, and its two successive deans, William Graham and David Hempton, who each generously granted me a research leave.

I spent my first research leave as an affiliate of the Department of Comparative Religion at the Hebrew University of Jerusalem in Israel, thanks to a Golda Meir Postdoctoral Fellowship. I would like to thank my host and sponsor, Brouria Bitton-Ashkelony, for her hospitality and friendship, then and now. I would especially like to thank her for the invitation to deliver the 2011 Sternberg Lecture in the Study of Religion at HUJI, which gave me an opportunity to work out my thoughts on the figure of Judas Thomas the Twin and Aristophanes's tragic myth from Plato's *Symposium*. In addition to HUJI, the Shalom Hartman Institute and the Van Leer Jerusalem Institute became second homes for me during that year away. Moving among the three places I found a number of conversation partners, including Adam Afterman, Michael Fagenblat, Merav Mack, Sinai Rusinek, David Satran, and Guy Stroumsa. While in Israel, two other dear friends, unaffiliated with any of these centers or institutes, continued to fire my mind for this topic: Stephanie Saldaña and Benjamin Balint. The fire was often fueled by very strong coffee, and sheltered by the wide expanse of a desert sky.

I am fortunate at HDS to have incredible students and colleagues, from whom I continue to learn a great deal. Two seminars I have taught in recent years have deeply influenced this book. The first, taught together with my friend and colleague Giovanni Bazzana, was on the ancient sources associated with the apostle Thomas. The second was on Plotinus's *Enneads*. Students in both seminars are to be especially commended for their patience as I tried to forward my own peculiar readings of these texts, often before I had clearly articulated them to myself. At least one poor soul, J. Gregory Given, was in both seminars, for which he deserves not only special commendation but also consolation. His participation in both was of enormous help, as was his gathering for me many of the relevant ancient sources before I left for a year in Jerusalem.

Once I finished a full manuscript of this book, the Weatherhead Center for International Affairs at Harvard University kindly hosted a workshop on it in November 2014. Colleagues from HDS and elsewhere offered incisive and insightful criticism on the draft, which I have tried mightily to incorporate. From HDS I would like to thank my colleagues Amy Hollywood, Mark Jordan, and Karen King for their participation. Even greater appreciation is due to those four who had to travel to attend this event: Virginia Burrus, Patricia Cox Miller, Ellen Muelhberger, and Gregory Shaw. If any of them find within themselves the patience to read this book a second time, I hope they will recognize the many improvements made at their suggestion, and forgive the remaining (and in some cases new) infelicities. Special thanks go to Amy Hollywood, who helped me interpret and correlate that feedback, and to David Brakke, who at a crucial moment late in the revisions, when I was flagging, uttered something to effect of "just do it." And so I did.

Speaking of feedback on the manuscript, I am deeply grateful to the two anonymous readers from Harvard University Press, whose comments, like those of the participants in the day-long workshop, have made this book much better than it would otherwise have been. At HUP, I am also deeply grateful to my editor, Sharmila Sen, and to Heather Hughes, who have made the publishing process as painless as possible (apart from the writing, of course, which always has a measure of pain).

ACKNOWLEDGMENTS

Some of what follows I have shared in other venues. I presented a paper "The 'Twin' in the Literature of Thomas, Mani, and Plotinus" at the 2010 Annual Meeting of the Society of Biblical Literature, in the "Nag Hammadi and Gnosticism" unit. I would thank to thank Jared Cramer and Bill Carroll for inviting me to share some of my early research on the *Gospel of Thomas* at the Fourth Annual Conference of the Society of Catholic Priests in October 2011. More recently, in April 2015, I shared a draft of Chapter 4 with the Boston Patristics Group and received rich feedback. Around that same time I spent a week at the Esalen Institute in Big Sur, California, for a conference titled "Esoteric Anatomies and the Dual Aspect of the Soul" hosted by the Center for Theory and Research. I would like to thank Michael Murphy and Gregory Shaw for the opportunity to present a preview of my book at that gathering. The connections made during that week were amazing, and I would like to thank the other participants for their enthusiasm about this project and their encouragement to finish it. The discovery of shared interests with Jeffrey K. Kripal has already touched this book, as will be evident from the Conclusion.

Other dear friends and colleagues who have offered encouragement throughout and in some cases crucial contributions over these many years include Giovanni Bazzana, Ryan Coyne, Benjamin Dunning, Brett Grainger, Sarah Hammerschlag, Zeke Mazur, Kimberley Patton, P. Oktor Skjaervo, and Rachel Smith. Nicola Denzey Lewis swooped in the eleventh hour as an angelic guide through the Valentinian sources. Finally, to Sarabinh, my *syzygos* and best interlocutor, I owe too much to put in words: my life, and more so the lives of our dear daughters, Vivian and Saskia.

Index

abstinence. *See* celibacy
acheived self, 25–26
Acts of the Apostles, 59–60
Acts of Thomas: bridal chamber theology, 15, 91, 114–115, 124, 126–128, 133, 251; in chronology of Thomas texts, 65, 276n34, 277n35; Drijvers on, 67, 109, 123, 129, 138, 296n34; Klijn on, 78, 279n58; Act 1, 124–129; Acts 2–6, 129–132, 279nn68–69; Acts 7–13, 132–134. *See also* "Hymn of the Pearl"; Judas Thomas
Acts of Thomas (Drijvers), 67. *See also* Drijvers, H. J. W.
Adam, 114–116, 179–180, 275n21
Address to the Greeks (Tatian). See *Oratio ad Graecos* (Tatian)
Against Heresies (Irenaeus), 113–114
"Against the Gnostics" (Plotinus), 199
Alchasai/Elchasai, 165–166, 284n54
Alcibiades I (Plato): on lover and beloved, 3, 21, 40, 42–46, 171; on Socrates's *daimonion*, 30–31; on essence of the soul, 210, 216
androgyny. *See* gender differentiation
angelic emanation, 115–118, 275n28
angelic revelations of Mani, 179–180
annihilation, 228–229
anthrōpos, 10, 262n3
Antiochene Christology, 134, 245–246, 248, 296n34
aphanizō, 228–229
Apollo, 26, 27, 31, 41, 47
Apology (Plato), 26–30, 262n10

Apology (Xenophon), 263n11
apophatic anthropology, 7–8
Apostle of Light. *See* Mani and Manichaeism
archē, 192–193, 196
Aristarchus, 77
Aristophanes, 13, 21–22, 46–50
Aristotle, 7, 196
Armstrong, A. H., 186, 195, 229, 288nn10–11, 289n37
Arnou, R., 212, 229, 230
asceticism, 95, 277n34
Athanasius of Alexandria: doctrine of deification by, 8–9, 18, 234–235; divine double by, 64, 245; on Psalter, 101, 253–254
Auden, W. H., 250
autoeroticism, 216–218, 291n55. *See also* Narcissus
auto-interpretation, textual, 76–78. *See also* reading and interpretation, textual
autophany, 221, 223–224. *See also* autoscopy
autos/auto tauto, 10, 41–44, 264n28
autoscopy: defined, 5, 6–7; Plato's use of, 13, 41–44, 171, 264n28; Plotinus's use of, 16–17, 187, 191, 215–219, 221, 225; in *Acts of Thomas*, 140–141; Ovid's use of, 183. *See also* self-knowledge theology

Baker-Brian, Nicholas, 167
Balsamos, 179
Baraies the Teacher, 170
Bartsch, Shadi, 5, 44–45

303

BeDuhn, Jason David, 148, 152
Betz, Hans Dieter, 172, 284n63
al-Bīrūnī, 152–154
bi-unity. *See* unity-in-duality
Blanchot, Maurice, 254
Bloom, Harold, 255
Blumenthal, H. J., 200, 208
Book of Thomas the Contender Writing to the Perfect, The, 65, 69, 111, 119–123, 275n31, 276n34. *See also* Judas Thomas
bridal chamber theology: in *Acts of Thomas*, 15, 91, 114–115, 124, 126–128, 133, 251; in *Gospel of Philip*, 114–116, 275n21; in *Excerpta ex Theodoto*, 116; ambiguity of, 275n23. *See also* celibacy
Brisson, Luc, 27

Cavell, Stanley, 77, 270n37
celestial parade, 37
celibacy: in Syria, 72; *Gospel of Thomas* and, 85, 87, 91–93, 95, 277n34; in *Book of Thomas*, 119–120, 277n34; in *Acts of Thomas*, 131, 277n34; Alchasai on, 166. *See also* bridal chamber theology
Christianity: defined, 4, 79; divisions of orthodoxy and heterodoxy in, 67–68, 166–167; Syriac Christianity, 72–73, 91–92, 294n19; Mani's early influence of, 165–166, 183; evil and, 237–239, 244, 295n27. *See also* deification; Jesus Christ
Christology, 18, 65, 134, 244–248, 296n34. *See also* Jesus Christ
Chronology of All Nations, The (al-Bīrūnī), 152–153
Clement of Alexandria, 9, 86, 116, 173, 234
Cologne Mani Codex (CMC): background of, 16, 147, 164–165, 231; mirrored doubling in, 162–163, 168–171, 174; on Alchasai, 165–166, 284n54; Paul in, 170–172, 284n63, 285n64; first person declarations in, 174–175, 177–178; revelations on selfhood, 178–179. *See also* Mani and Manichaeism; *syzygia/syzygos*
comedy of the divine double, 13, 21–22, 49–50
Commentary on John (Origen), 105
conjunction of Christ, 245–248

Conon, 1
Corbin, Henry, 6–8, 255
Council of Constantinople, 18, 234
Council of Nicaea, 18
Cratylus (Plato), 32, 33
criticism, textual. *See* reading and interpretation, textual
Cyril of Jerusalem, 176, 235, 245, 246, 247

daēmones, 32, 263n18, 279n69
daēnā, 181, 182, 184
daimōn: *daimonion* of Socrates, 13, 20–21, 27–31, 263nn10–11; vs. *daimonion*, 31–36, 202, 263n18, 289n33; Plotinus on, 202–207, 289n37
Davidson, Arnold I., 216, 218–219, 291n55
De Blois, François, 155–156, 173
DeConick, April, 86, 87, 91, 100, 271n54, 294n19
deification: Athanasius on, 8–9, 18, 234–235; Plato on, 9, 59–60, 238–239, 266n51; in orthodox Christianity, 235–236, 294n19. *See also* Christianity
Denzey Lewis, Nicola, 71, 98, 99–100
Destrée, Pierre, 32–34
dialogues of Plato. *See specific dialogues*
didymos/didymus, 66, 69, 120–121, 268n18
Didymus Judas Thomas. *See* Judas Thomas
Dillon, John, 200
Diodore of Tarsus, 246
Dionysius the Areopagite, "Pseudo," 8, 198, 256
"dividual," 7, 47–48, 63, 260n18
divine likeness, 39, 100–102, 110
divine Mother, 128–129, 279n58. *See also* Mary
divine sign of Socrates's *daimonion*, 27–30, 35, 36, 262n10, 263n11
divinization. *See* deification
division of sensible worlds, 5, 20–26, 38, 46–50, 199. *See also* Forms, theory of
Doniger, Wendy, 5
doppelgänger, 12, 36, 133. *See also* twinning theology
Drijvers, H. J. W., 67, 109, 123, 129, 138, 296n34
duality. *See* unity-in-duality

dyad, indefinite, 60, 62–63, 189–190, 201, 229–230. *See also* primordial otherness of intellect
dyomorphy, 133–134, 279n69

Ecclesiastical History (Eusebius), 69
eidōlon, 216
eikōn, 20, 23–24. See also *ikōn*
eine, 100–102, 141
Elchasaite baptist history, 165–166, 284n54
Emerson, Ralph Waldo, 215, 291n56
encratic intepretation: defined, 15, 85, 120; Syria and, 72–73; of *Gospel of Thomas*, 85–88, 95, 271n54. *See also* reading and interpretation, textual; *specific texts*
endowment, human, 8, 10
Enoch, 179–180
Enosh, 179–180
epistēmē, 24
erotic love, 37–38, 215. *See also* auto-eroticism
Eryximachus, 49–50
esoptron, 171
Eusebius of Caesarea, 69, 158, 235
Euthydemus (Plato), 30
Euthyphro (Plato), 30
Eve, 114–116, 275n21
evil, 237–244, 295n25, 295n27
exaiphnēs, 59–60, 93, 141, 266n47, 266n51
Excerpta ex Theodoto, 116–119, 183

Fackelmann, Anton, 164
Feuerbach, Ludwig, 249
Fihrist. See *Kitab al-Fihrist* (al-Nadīm)
fire, 90, 273n83
Forms, theory of: introduction to, 13–14; division of sensible worlds, 20–26, 38, 46–50, 199; Plotinus on, 189, 193–195, 207–213, 288n14; Gerson on, 193, 194, 228n13, 288n13, 288n19. See also *Republic, The* (Plato); soul
Foundations of Mysticism, The (McGinn), 9
Freud, Sigmund, 11–12
Funk, W.-P., 176–177

Gardens of Light, The (Maalouf), 168–169
garment, royal, 136–142, 194, 280n101
Gärtner, Bertil, 76

gender differentiation, 46, 87, 92–93, 114–116
Gerson, Lloyd: on human endowment vs. achievement, 8, 10, 41; on person (concept), 25–26, 262n3; on theory of Forms, 193, 194, 228n13, 288n19
Gill, Mary Louise, 52, 55–56, 265n37
gnostic category, defined, 79
Gnostic Scriptures (Layton), 67
gnōthi seauton, 40–41, 44–45
God: divine sign of Socrates's *daimonion*, 27–30, 35, 36, 262n10, 263n11; divine likeness, 39, 100–102, 110; evil and, 237–239, 244, 295n27. *See also* Christianity; deification
Gordian III, 185
Gospel of John, 15, 68, 102–106, 157, 183
Gospel of Philip, 114–118
Gospel of Thomas: description of, 14–15, 62; background of, 64–65, 73–76, 102, 235, 293n17; school hypothesis and, 70–72; textual reading approach for, 76–78, 276n34; prologue of, 78–79; sayings 1–4 as interpretive key for, 80–83; Plato's dialogues and, 83, 93; unity-in-duality in, 83, 88–97; sayings on oneness in, 84–85, 97; encratic interpretations of, 85–88, 95, 271n50, 271n54; twinning theology of, 97–100; Mani and, 147, 176–178, 183. *See also* Judas Thomas
grace, 226
Great Gospel, The (Mani), 153
Grenfell, B. P., 73
Griffith, Sidney, 91
guardian spirit. See *daimōn*

Hadot, Pierre, 17, 215, 217–219, 226, 291n56
Harder, Richard, 217
heimisch, 11–12
heis/heis monos, 83, 84
Henrichs, Albert, 146, 163–164, 175, 176
Hephaestus, 49
hetera archē, 232
Hippolytus, 165, 235
Hoffman, E. T. A., 12
Homilies on Luke (Origen), 104–105
L'homme de lumière dans le soufisme iranien (Corbin), 6
homoiōma, 38, 39, 224

horizontal doubling: Plato on, 3, 21, 38–40, 45–46, 214–215; defined, 12, 13, 25–26; in *Acts of Thomas*, 133–134. *See also* mirrored doubling; vertical doubling
Hunt, A. S., 73
Hutchinson, D. S., 264n28
"Hymn of the Pearl," 65, 71, 135–143, 280n80, 280n101. *See also Acts of Thomas*; Judas Thomas

Iamblichus of Chalcis, 17–18, 232–233
īhīdāyā, 91–92, 271n50
ikōn, 100–102, 141. *See also eikōn*
image, divine, 20, 23–24, 100–102. *See also specific terms for*
intelligible reality. *See* Forms, theory of
interpretation. *See* reading and interpretation, textual
Irenaeus of Lyons, 9, 113, 114, 234

Jesus Christ: resurrection of, 59–60, 68–69; apostles of, 68; brothers of, 69, 121–122, 267n10; interpretation of, as "living," 79–81; in *Kephalaia of the Teacher*, 159–161; conjunction of, 245–246. *See also* Christianity; *Gospel of Thomas*; Judas Thomas; twinning theology
Jesus the Splendor, 167–168. *See also* Light Mind
Jewish tradition: -Christian category, 100–101, 166–167; on evil, 237
John the Apostle, 102–103. *See also Gospel of John*
Judas Thomas: evidence of, as Jesus's twin, 3, 8, 14; origin of name, 14, 65–66, 68; vs. related figures in early texts, 70, 268n11, 273n1; as Jesus's brother (title), 121–122. *See also* Jesus Christ; twinning theology; *specific texts on*

Kahn, Charles, 32
Kalligas, Paul, 209–210, 290n47
katoptron, 39–40, 43, 171–172. *See also* mirrored doubling
Kephalaia of the Teacher: introduction to, 16, 146–147, 158–159, 231; on Light Mind, 159–160, 168, 174–175, 179–180; on Apostle of Light, 160–161, 181–182; on Paraclete, 161–164; first-person declarations in, 176–177, 183; on Light Form, 180–181; translations of, 281n1. *See also* Mani and Manichaeism
Kitab al-Fihrist (al-Nadīm), 154–155, 165
Klijn, A. F. J.: on *Acts of Thomas*, 78, 279n58; on *Gospel of Thomas*, 85–87, 92, 95, 271n50
Knowing Persons (Gerson), 25–26
"Know thyself," 40–43
Koenen, Ludwig, 164
Kripal, Jeffrey J., 255–256, 297n12
Kristeva, Julia, 16, 217–219, 227, 291n64
Kuntzmann, Raymond, 5
kyriōteron, 42, 45

Lamb, W. R. M., 264n28
Lambdin, Thomas, 91
Lanzillotta, Lautaro Roig, 277n35
Layton, Bentley, 67, 70–71, 72
Life of Plotinus (Porphyry), 186, 200
light, divine, 88–90, 96, 150–151
Light Form, 160, 180–181, 232
Light Mind, 151–152, 159–160, 168, 179–180. *See also* Jesus the Splendor
lightning revelation, 167
Light Soul, 152
Liriope, 2
"living" Jesus interpretation, 79–81
logos, 27–28, 109, 112–113, 183, 290n47
lover and beloved: Plato on, 3, 21, 37–39, 42, 171, 214–215; Plotinus on, 226–228. *See also* Narcissus
Luttikhuizen, Gerard P., 136

Maalouf, Amin, 168–169
Macarius the Great, 294n19
Mani and Manichaeism: introduction to, 4, 16, 148–152, 165, 231–232; background of dualism in, 145–148, 150, 166, 183, 281n4; *Gospel of Thomas* and, 147, 176–178; canon of scriptures by, 149, 281n11; structure of church, 149, 281n12; al-Bīrūnī on, 152–154; Paraclete and, 153, 157–158, 160–164, 283n39; al-Nadīm on, 154–156, 165, 170; *CMC* on relationships with baptists, 165–166, 173–174; on doubled selfhood, 174–175, 178–183, 286n73; on good and evil, 237; disciples of,

283n46, 293n17; titles of, 285n63; twin-companion of (see *syzygos* of Mani). See also *Cologne Mani Codex*; *Kephalaia of the Teacher*
Manichean Body, The (BeDuhn), 148
Mary, 102–104, 245, 246
Mazur, Zeke, 195, 221, 223, 229, 292n66
McGinn, Bernard, 9
McGuckin, John, 246–248
Memorabilia (Xenophon), 263n11
Metamorphoses (Ovid), 3, 217–218
Metaphysics (Aristotle), 60
metempsychosis, 34
Meteorology (Aristotle), 7
mimēsis, 20
mirrored doubling: Narcissus and, 1–4; Plato on, 3, 21, 38–40, 43–45, 171, 195; through readings, 61–62, 253–254; in *Gospel of Thomas*, 100–102; in "Hymn of the Pearl," 140–141; in *Cologne Mani Codex*, 162–163, 168–171, 174; *katoptron*, 171–172. See also horizontal doubling; twinning theology
Mirror of the Self, The (Bartsch), 5, 44–45
monachos, 84–85, 91, 94, 272n59
Montanus, 158
morphē, 181–182

Nabataean, 155
al-Nadīm, Ibn, 154–156, 165, 170
Nag Hammadi Codex II (NHC II), 74, 114, 119
Nag Hammadi library, 65, 69, 79, 119. See also specific titles from
narcissism, 11, 291n64
Narcissus: Conon on, 1; Pausanias on, 2, 3; Ovid on, 2–4; Freud on, 11–12; Kristeva on, 16, 217–219, 221, 227, 291n64; Mani and, 169; Plotinus on, 190, 213–220, 222, 291n55, 291n64. See also lover and beloved
Nature (Emerson), 215, 291n56
"'Neither Oneself nor Someone Else'" (Stang), 256
Nemesis, 1, 2
Neoplatonism, 4, 232–234. See also Plato and Platonism; Plotinus; Proclus
Nestorius, 245–247
New Criticism, 76–77
New Testament, 69–70, 173, 268n11. See also specific books in

Nicene Creed, 8–9, 18, 234–235
noēsis, 193, 197
noēton, 193
nothingness, 229, 233
not-one, 60, 62–63, 249–253. See also oneness
nous, 3, 24, 34–35, 161, 193. See also soul

"On Beauty" (Plotinus), 190, 213–220, 222, 291n55, 291n64
oneness, 55–60, 84–88, 114–118, 222, 249–253. See also unity-in-duality; specific terms for
"On Our Allotted Guardian Spirit" (Plotinus), 202–207
Oratio ad Graecos (Tatian), 65, 108–113
Origen of Alexandria: on *Gospel of Thomas*, 14–15, 65, 105, 235; *Gospel of John*, 102–104, 183; *Homilies on Luke*, 104–105; *Commentary on John*, 105; conciliar orthodoxy and, 235, 267n3
oua/oua ouōt, 83, 84–85, 93, 146, 163, 176–177
oudaneia, 233
overflow, 188
Ovid, 2–4, 16, 217–218. See also Narcissus

Pagels, Elaine, 72
Paraclete, 153, 157–158, 160–164, 283n39. See also Mani and Manichaeism
paraklētos, 156
parhypostasis, 242–243
Parmenides (Plato): on theory of Forms, 13–14, 21–22, 51–55, 199; on oneness, 55–60, 222; *exaiphnēs* in, 59–60, 93, 141, 266n47
Paul the Apostle, 8, 141, 170–172, 180, 284n63, 285n64
Pausanias, 2, 3
pearl, 136–137, 142. See also "Hymn of the Pearl"
person (concept), 25–26, 262n3
Phaedo (Plato), 204, 205
Phaedrus (Plato): on lover and beloved, 3, 21, 37–39, 42, 171; on Socrates's *daimonion*, 30, 262n10; on beauty, 214–215
Philo, 86
phonic elements to divine double, 169
Physics (Aristotle), 60

Plato and Platonism: introduction to, 13, 20–25, 207, 249–250; on mirrored doubling, 21, 37–40, 42–45, 171, 195; on division of sensible worlds, 22–26, 38, 46, 199; on Socrates's *daimonion*, 27–32, 262n10, 263n11; on evil, 237–239. *See also* Neoplatonism; Socrates; *specific concepts*; *specific texts*
Plotinus: background of, 4, 185–186, 232; autoscopy and, 16–17, 187, 191, 215–219, 221, 225; return itinerary, 17, 213, 220–222; introduction to dynamic model of selfhood by, 22, 178, 186–187, 252–253, 286n73; *Life of Plotinus* (Porphyry), 186, 200; on the procession of Intellect from the One, 188–192; on primordial otherness of Intellect, 188–192, 222–225, 288n7; on theory of Forms, 189, 193–195, 207–213, 288nn13–14; "On Beauty," 190, 213–220, 222, 291n55, 291n64; on inner life of intellect, 192–196, 232–233, 288nn10–11; on *syzygos*, 193; on dualism of soul, 196–202; "Against the Gnostics," 199; "On Our Allotted Guardian Spirit," 202–207, 289n37; on lover and beloved, 226–228; on evil, 239–241. *See also* Porphyry of Tyre; Proclus; *specific scholars on*
Plotinus, or The Simplicity of Vision (Hadot), 215, 291n56
Porphyry of Tyre, 17–18, 185, 186, 232
primordial otherness of intellect, 188–192, 222–225, 288n7. *See also* dyad
Proclus, 18, 60, 209, 241–244
prosopon/prosopa of Christ, 246–247
Psalter, Athanasius on, 101, 253–254
psychē, 10

Quispel, Gilles, 85, 100

reading and interpretation, textual: reflective selfhood in, 61–62, 66, 254–255; Cavell on, 77–78, 270n37; description of, 80; of Thomas tradition, 276n34. *See also* encratic intepretation; writing as mystical practice; *specific texts*
received self, 25
reflective self. *See* mirrored doubling
Remes, Pauliina, 194, 199–200, 290n47
renunciation. *See* celibacy
Republic, The (Plato): on divided line, 23; on Socrates's *daimonion*, 33, 34, 204, 205; ignorance and illusion, 61–62; on Form Good, 224. *See also* Forms, theory of
resurrection of Christ, 59–60, 68–69
Richter, Jean Paul, 12
Riley, Gregory J., 71–72, 120
Rist, John, 36, 203, 207, 212, 229, 289n33, 291nn52–53

$šb^er$, 120, 121
sculptural theology, 38–39, 214–215, 217, 240, 291n56
Seek to See Him (DeConick), 100
Selbstfindung, 175
self-annihilation, 228–229
self-knowledge theology, 25, 42–44, 121–123, 128, 171, 175. *See also* autoscopy
self-reversion, 223–224
self-seeing. *See* autoscopy
self-unification, 223–224, 228–229
sensible reality. *See* division of sensible worlds; Forms, theory of
serpent, 136–137, 279n68
Sethel, 179–180
Shabuhragan (Mani), 153, 159
Shaw, Gregory, 232, 233
Shem, 179–180
sloughing, 5, 6
snau/snau oua, 84–85, 92, 93
Socrates: on deification, 9; *daimonion* of, 13, 20–21, 27–31, 263nn10–11; theory of Forms, 13–14, 21–22, 51–55; real vs. literary character of, 20; on divided line, 23; *apologia* by, 26–27; on *daimōn* vs. *daimonion*, 32; ignorance and illusion, 61–62. *See also* Plato and Platonism; *specific concepts*
soeiš, 120, 121, 276n32
soul: translations of, 10, 11; Gerson on, 25; essence of, 34–35, 110–111, 210, 216; Plotinus on dualism of, 196–202; evil and, 237–244, 295n25, 295n27. *See also* Forms, theory of; *nous*
Speussippus, 62–63
spirit, 110–111
Splitting the Difference (Doniger), 5
statue as beauty. *See* sculptural theology

INDEX

stoning, 98
Stroumsa, Guy, 166
sudden/suddenly. See *exaiphnēs*
Sweeney, Leo, 178–180, 201, 286n73
Le symbolisme des jumeaux au Proche-Orient ancien (Kuntzmann), 5
symbolon, 47–48
Symposium (Plato), 13, 40, 59–60, 266n47
synampho, 201
synchōreō, 204
Syriac Christianity, 72–73, 91–92, 294n19
syzygia/syzygos, 111–115, 193. See also twinning theology
syzygos of Mani: translation of term, 16, 122–123, 173; relationship of, 147, 174–175; Paraclete and, 153, 157–158, 160–161, 283n39; in early life, 167–170; revelations by, 170–171, 179; Paul on, 170–173, 284n63; apostles and, 179–182; revelations by, 285n63. See also *Cologne Mani Codex (CMC)*; Mani and Manichaeism
syzygy. See *syzygia/syzygos*

Tales of Love (Kristeva), 217–218
Tatian the Assyrian, 15, 65, 107, 108–113, 183
al-tawm, 155, 282n24
tāwmā, 68, 70, 97, 99, 120
textual interpretation. See reading and interpretation, textual
Theaetetus (Plato), 9, 30, 238–239, 290n52
Theages (Plato), 31
thean vs. *theon*, 265n29
theodicy, 18, 237
Theodore of Mopsuestia, 245, 246–247
theōsis, 234, 251
Theotokos, Christ as, 245–246
theurgy, 233–234
Thomassen, Einar, 117–118, 275n28
Thomas the Apostle. See Judas Thomas
Thomas the Obscure (Blanchot), 254
Thomas tradition in early texts, 273n1, 276n34, 277n35
Timaeus (Plato), 34–36, 45, 205–206, 243

tragedy of the divine double, 13
transmigration of souls, 34
trayānā, 137
Trouillard, Jean, 194–195
Turner, John D., 275n31, 276n34
twinning theology: Narcissus and, 1–2; in *Gospel of Thomas*, 3, 97–100; on the origin of, 3–4, 8, 14, 69–70, 273n1; doppelgänger, 12, 36, 133; defined, 65–68; in *Book of Thomas*, 119–123; in *Acts of Thomas*, 133–134; translation of, 268n18, 282n24. See also mirrored doubling; *syzygia/syzygos*; unity-in-duality
twoness, 60, 62–63, 87

"The Uncanny" (Freud), 11
unheimlich, 11–12
unity-in-duality: defined, 6–8, 14, 236; in *Gospel of Thomas*, 83, 88–97; conjunction of Christ as, 245–248. See also oneness; *syzygia/syzygos*
unus-ambo, 6–8
Uro, Risto, 67, 71, 92

Valantasis, Richard, 11, 95–96, 272n65
Valentinus, 107, 113–119
Van Oort, Johannes, 161–162, 180
vertical doubling: defined, 5, 12–13, 21, 25–26; in *Parmenides*, 52–53; in *Oratio ad Graecos*, 110–112; in *Acts of Thomas*, 133–134. See also horizontal doubling
virgin brides. See bridal chamber theology
vision mysticism, 100–101

writing as mystical practice, 256, 297n12. See also reading and interpretation, textual

Xenocrates, 63
Xenophon, 203, 263n11

zawgā, 155
Zeus, 38–39, 46–48
Zoroastrianism, 237. See also *daēnā*